Ford Aerostar Mini-van Owners Workshop Manual

by Larry Warren
and John H Haynes

Member of the Guild of Motoring Writers

Models covered:
All Ford Aerostar mini-vans
1986 through 1988

ABCDE
FGHIJ
KLMNO
PQR

Haynes Publishing Group
Sparkford Nr Yeovil
Somerset BA22 7JJ England

Haynes Publications, Inc
861 Lawrence Drive
Newbury Park
California 91320 USA

Acknowledgements

We are grateful for the help and cooperation of the Ford Motor Company for assistance with technical information, certain illustrations and vehicle photos, and the Champion Spark Plug Company who supplied the illustrations of various spark plug conditions.

© **Haynes Publishing Group 1988**

A book in the **Haynes Owners Workshop Manual Series**

Printed by J.H. Haynes & Co., Ltd. Sparkford Nr. Yeovil, Somerset BA22 7JJ, England

ISBN 1 85010 476 X

Library of Congress Catalog Card Number 88-081055

Contents

Ford Aerostar mini-van

About this manual

Its purpose

The purpose of this manual is to help you get the best value from your vehicle. It can do so in several ways. It can help you decide what work must be done, even if you choose to have it done by a dealer service department or a repair shop; it provides information and procedures for routine maintenance and servicing; and it offers diagnostic and repair procedures to follow when trouble occurs.

It is hoped that you will use the manual to tackle the work yourself. For many simpler jobs, doing it yourself may be quicker than arranging an appointment to get the vehicle into a shop and making the trips to leave it and pick it up. More importantly, a lot of money can be saved by avoiding the expense the shop must pass on to you to cover its labor and overhead costs. An added benefit is the sense of satisfaction and accomplishment that you feel after having done the job yourself.

Using the manual

The manual is divided into Chapters. Each Chapter is divided into numbered Sections, which are headed in bold type between horizontal lines. Each Section consists of consecutively numbered paragraphs.

At the beginning of each numbered section you will be referred to any illustrations which apply to the procedures in that section. The reference numbers used in illustration captions pinpoint the pertinent Section and the Step within that section. That is, illustration 3.2 means the illustration refers to Section 3 and Step (or paragraph) 2 within that Section.

Procedures, once described in the text, are not normally repeated. When it is necessary to refer to another Chapter, the reference will be given as Chapter and Section number i.e. Chapter 1/16). Cross references given without use of the word ''Chapter'' apply to Sections and/or paragraphs in the same Chapter. For example, ''see Section 8'' means in the same Chapter.

Reference to the left or right side of the vehicle is based on the assumption that one is sitting in the driver's seat, facing forward.

Even though extreme care has been taken during the preparation of this manual, neither the publisher nor the author can accept responsibility for any errors in, or omissions from, the information given.

NOTE

A **Note** provides information necessary to properly complete a procedure or information which will make the steps to be followed easier to understand.

CAUTION

A **Caution** indicates a special procedure or special steps which must be taken in the course of completing the procedure in which the **Caution** is found which are necessary to avoid damage to the assembly being worked on.

WARNING

A **Warning** indicates a special procedure or special steps which must be taken in the course of completing the procedure in which the **Warning** is found which are necessary to avoid injury to the person performing the procedure.

Introduction to the Ford Aerostar

The Ford Aerostar mini-van is a conventional front engine, rear drive vehicle available in passenger and cargo van configurations. The standard engine is a 2.3 liter overhead cam inline four-cylinder. Optional engines include a 2.8 liter V6 (available in 1986 only) and a 3.0 liter V6. All models other than those with the 2.8 liter V6 are equipped with port-type electronic fuel injection.

Transmissions installed in the Aerostar include a 5-speed manual overdrive and a 4-speed automatic overdrive. The 4-speed automatic transmission is equipped with a torque converter clutch, which eliminates torque converter slippage at high speeds and results in greater fuel economy.

The front suspension consists of upper and lower control arms (A-arms) and coil springs. A shock absorber is mounted inside each coil spring. The rear suspension is composed of longitudinally mounted control arms and coil springs attached to the outer ends of the solid rear axle.

The brakes are power assisted disc-type at the front and drum at the rear.

Vehicle identification numbers

Modifications are a continuing and unpublicized part of automotive manufacturing. Since spare parts manuals and lists are compiled on a numerical basis, individual vehicle numbers are essential to correctly identify new parts that may be needed.

Vehicle Identification Number (VIN)

A seventeen digit combination of numbers and letters forms the VIN. It's stamped on a metal plate attached to the dashboard near the windshield on the driver's side (see illustration). The VIN also appears on the Vehicle Certificate of Title and Registration and the Safety Compliance Certification label. It contains valuable information such as vehicle make and type, GVWR, brake system installed, model, body type, engine installed, etc. (see illustration).

Safety Compliance Certification label

The English Safety Compliance Certification label is attached to the door latch edge on the driver's side door. The French (Quebec) label is attached in the same location on the passenger's side door. The label contains the month and year of production, the certification statement and the VIN. It also includes GVWR, wheel and tire information and codes for additional vehicle data (see illustration).

Build date stamp

The build date is stamped on the front surface of the radiator support on the passenger side of the vehicle.

The VIN number is attached to the dash on the driver's side of the vehicle

Engine identification number

The number eight digit in the VIN denotes the type engine originally installed in the vehicle (see illustration). The engine identification number (serial number) is located on a tag, which is usually attached to the rocker arm cover (see illustration).

Vehicle Emissions Control Information label

The Vehicle Emissions Control Information label is attached to the underside of the hood (see Chapter 6 for an illustration).

SAMPLE VIN NUMBER

1 F T D A 1 4 A 5 G Z A 0 0 0 0 1

  ① ② ③ ④ ⑤ ⑥⑦⑧ ⑨

① Position 1, 2, and 3 — Manufacturer, Make and Type (World Manufacturer Identifier)

② Position 4 — Brake System/GVWR

③ Position 5, 6, and 7 — Model or Line, Series, Chassis, Cab Type

④ Position 8 — Engine Type

⑤ Position 9 — Check Digit

⑥ Position 10 — Model Year

⑦ Position 11 — Assembly Plant

⑧ Position 12 — Constant "A" until sequence number of 99,999 is reached, then changes to a constant "B" and so on

⑨ Position 13 through 17 — Sequence number — begins at 00001

Sample Vehicle Identification Number

SAFETY STANDARD COMPLIANCE LABEL VEHICLE DATA CODES
SUSPENSION — SPRING IDENTIFICATION CODES — AEROSTAR

Sample Safety Compliance Certification label

① Name and Location of Manufacturer
② Date of Manufacture
③ Front Gross Axle Weight Ratings in Pounds (LB) and Kilograms (KG)
④ Front Tire Size
⑤ Rim Size
⑥ Front Tire Cold PSI
⑦ Gross Vehicle Weight Rating in Pounds (LB) and Kilograms (KG)
⑧ Rear Gross Axle Weight Rating in Pounds (LB) and Kilograms (KG)
⑨ Rear Tire Size
⑩ Rim Size
⑪ Rear Tire Cold PSI
⑫ Vehicle Identification Number
 (a) World Manufacturer Identifier
 (b) Brake System and Gross Vehicle Weight Rating (GVWR) Class for Trucks and MPV's — Brake System (Only) for Incomplete Vehicles.
 (c) Model or Line, Series, Chassis and Cab Type
 (d) Engine Type
 (e) Check Digit
 (f) Model Year — (Ford-Complete Trucks and MPV's)
 (g) Assembly Plant Code
 (h) Sequential Serial and Model Year

⑬ Type Vehicle
⑭ Exterior Paint Codes (two sets of figures designates a two-tone)
⑮ Wheelbase in Inches
⑯ Model Code and GVW
⑰ Seat Type, Interior Color and Seating Codes
⑱ Transmission Code
⑲ Rear Axle Code

⑳ Tutone Accent Tape and Pinstriping Codes
㉑ Suspension Identification Codes
 (a) Aux/Opt Front Spring Code
 (b) Front Spring Code
 (c) Rear Spring Code
㉒ District/Special Order Codes
㉓ Front Axle Accessory Reserve Capacity in Pounds
㉔ Total Accessory Reserve Capacity in Pounds

ENGINE TYPE, DISPLACEMENT, CYLINDERS, FUEL TYPE, AND MANUFACTURER (VIN POSITION 8)

1FTDA14 [A] 5GZA00001

VIN Code	Displacement		Cylinders	Fuel	Manufacturer
	Liter	CID			
A	2.3 (EFI)	140	I-4	Gasoline	Ford
S	2.8	171	V-6	Gasoline	Ford
U	3.0	183	V-6	Gasoline	Ford

The number eight digit in the VIN denotes the engine type

LOCATIONS:
FRONT OF R.H. ROCKER COVER
TRUCK — R.H. ROCKER COVER

The engine serial number is located on a tag that's attached to the rocker arm cover (right hand cover on V6 engines — shown)

Buying parts

Replacement parts are available from many sources, which generally fall into one of two categories — authorized dealer parts departments and independent retail auto parts stores. Our advice concerning these parts is as follows:

Authorized dealer parts department: This is the best source for parts which are unique to your vehicle and not generally available elsewhere such as major engine parts, transaxle parts, trim pieces, etc. *Warranty information:* If your vehicle is still covered under warranty, be sure that any replacement parts you purchase — regardless of the source — do not invalidate your warranty! To be sure of obtaining the correct parts, have your engine and chassis numbers available and, if possible, take the old parts along for positive identification.

Retail auto parts stores: Good auto parts stores will stock frequently needed components which wear out relatively fast such as clutch components, exhaust systems, brake parts, tune-up parts, etc. These stores often supply new or reconditioned parts on an exchange basis, which can save a considerable amount of money. Discount auto parts stores are often very good places to buy materials and parts needed for general vehicle maintenance such as oil, grease, filters, spark plugs, belts, touch up paint, bulbs, etc. They also usually sell tools and general accessories, have convenient hours, charge lower prices, and can often be found not far from your home.

Maintenance techniques, tools and working facilities

Maintenance techniques

There are a number of techniques involved in maintenance and repair that will be referred to throughout this manual. Application of these techniques will enable the home mechanic to be more efficient, better organized and capable of performing the various tasks properly, which will ensure that the repair job is thorough and complete.

Fasteners

Fasteners are nuts, bolts, studs and screws used to hold two or more parts together. There are a few things to keep in mind when working with fasteners. Almost all of them use a locking device of some type, either a lockwasher, locknut, locking tab or thread adhesive. All threaded fasteners should be clean and straight, with undamaged threads and undamaged corners on the hex head where the wrench fits. Develop the habit of replacing all damaged nuts and bolts with new ones. Special locknuts with nylon or fiber inserts can only be used once. If they are removed, they lose their locking ability and must be replaced with new ones.

Rusted nuts and bolts should be treated with a penetrating fluid to ease removal and prevent breakage. Some mechanics use turpentine in a spout-type oil can, which works quite well. After applying the rust penetrant, let it work for a few minutes before trying to loosen the nut or bolt. Badly rusted fasteners may have to be chiseled or sawed off or removed with a special nut breaker, available at tool stores.

If a bolt or stud breaks off in an assembly, it can be drilled and removed with a special tool commonly available for this purpose. Most automotive machine shops can perform this task, as well as other repair procedures, such as the repair of threaded holes that have been stripped out.

Flat washers and lockwashers, when removed from an assembly, should always be replaced exactly as removed. Replace any damaged washers with new ones. Never use a lockwasher on any soft metal surface (such as aluminum), thin sheet metal or plastic.

Fastener sizes

For a number of reasons, automobile manufacturers are making wider and wider use of metric fasteners. Therefore, it is important to be able to tell the difference between standard (sometimes called U.S. or SAE) and metric hardware, since they cannot be interchanged.

All bolts, whether standard or metric, are sized according to diameter, thread pitch and length. For example, a standard 1/2 — 13 x 1 bolt is 1/2 inch in diameter, has 13 threads per inch and is 1 inch long. An M12 — 1.75 x 25 metric bolt is 12 mm in diameter, has a thread pitch of 1.75 mm (the distance between threads) and is 25 mm long. The two bolts are nearly identical, and easily confused, but they are not interchangeable.

In addition to the differences in diameter, thread pitch and length, metric and standard bolts can also be distinguished by examining the bolt heads. To begin with, the distance across the flats on a standard bolt head is measured in inches, while the same dimension on a metric bolt is sized in millimeters (the same is true for nuts). As a result, a standard wrench should not be used on a metric bolt and a metric wrench should not be used on a standard bolt. Also, most standard bolts have slashes radiating out from the center of the head to denote the grade or strength of the bolt, which is an indication of the amount of torque that can be applied to it. The greater the number of slashes, the greater the strength of the bolt. Grades 0 through 5 are commonly used on automobiles. Metric bolts have a property class (grade) number, rather than a slash, molded into their heads to indicate bolt strength. In this case, the higher the number, the stronger the bolt. Property class numbers 8.8, 9.8 and 10.9 are commonly used on automobiles.

Strength markings can also be used to distinguish standard hex nuts from metric hex nuts. Many standard nuts have dots stamped into one side, while metric nuts are marked with a number. The greater the number of dots, or the higher the number, the greater the strength of the nut.

Metric studs are also marked on their ends according to property class (grade). Larger studs are numbered (the same as metric bolts),

Bolt strength markings (top — standard/SAE/USS; bottom — metric)

Grade	Identification	Class	Identification	
Hex Nut Grade 5	3 Dots	Hex Nut Property Class 9	Arabic 9	CLASS 10.9
Hex Nut Grade 8	6 Dots	Hex Nut Property Class 10	Arabic 10	CLASS 9.8
				CLASS 8.8
Standard hex nut strength markings		Metric hex nut strength markings		Metric stud strength markings

while smaller studs carry a geometric code to denote grade.

It should be noted that many fasteners, especially Grades 0 through 2, have no distinguishing marks on them. When such is the case, the only way to determine whether it is standard or metric is to measure the thread pitch or compare it to a known fastener of the same size.

Standard fasteners are often referred to as SAE, as opposed to metric. However, it should be noted that SAE technically refers to a non-metric *fine thread* fastener only. Coarse thread non-metric fasteners are referred to as USS sizes.

Since fasteners of the same size (both standard and metric) may have different strength ratings, be sure to reinstall any bolts, studs or nuts removed from your vehicle in their original locations. Also, when replacing a fastener with a new one, make sure that the new one has a strength rating equal to or greater than the original.

Tightening sequences and procedures

Most threaded fasteners should be tightened to a specific torque value (torque is the twisting force applied to a threaded component such as a nut or bolt). Overtightening the fastener can weaken it and cause it to break, while undertightening can cause it to eventually come loose. Bolts, screws and studs, depending on the material they are made of and their thread diameters, have specific torque values, many of which are noted in the Specifications at the beginning of each Chapter. Be sure to follow the torque recommendations closely. For fasteners not assigned a specific torque, a general torque value chart is presented here as a guide. These torque values are for dry (unlubricated) fasteners threaded into steel or cast iron (not aluminum). As was previously mentioned, the size and grade of a fastener determine the amount of torque that can safely be applied to it. The figures listed here are approximate

Metric thread sizes	Ft-lb	Nm/m
M-6	6 to 9	9 to 12
M-8	14 to 21	19 to 28
M-10	28 to 40	38 to 54
M-12	50 to 71	68 to 96
M-14	80 to 140	109 to 154
Pipe thread sizes		
1/8	5 to 8	7 to 10
1/4	12 to 18	17 to 24
3/8	22 to 33	30 to 44
1/2	25 to 35	34 to 47
U.S. thread sizes		
1/4 — 20	6 to 9	9 to 12
5/16 — 18	12 to 18	17 to 24
5/16 — 24	14 to 20	19 to 27
3/8 — 16	22 to 32	30 to 43
3/8 — 24	27 to 38	37 to 51
7/16 — 14	40 to 55	55 to 74
7/16 — 20	40 to 60	55 to 81
1/2 — 13	55 to 80	75 to 108

Standard (SAE and USS) bolt dimensions/grade marks

G Grade marks (bolt strength)
L Length (in inches)
T Thread pitch (number of threads per inch)
D Nominal diameter (in inches)

Metric bolt dimensions/grade marks

P Property class (bolt strength)
L Length (in millimeters)
T Thread pitch (distance between threads in millimeters)
D Diameter

for Grade 2 and Grade 3 fasteners. Higher grades can tolerate higher torque values.

Fasteners laid out in a pattern, such as cylinder head bolts, oil pan bolts, differential cover bolts, etc., must be loosened or tightened in sequence to avoid warping the component. This sequence will normally be shown in the appropriate Chapter. If a specific pattern is not given, the following procedures can be used to prevent warping.

Initially, the bolts or nuts should be assembled finger-tight only. Next, they should be tightened one full turn each, in a criss-cross or diagonal pattern. After each one has been tightened one full turn, return to the first one and tighten them all one-half turn, following the same pattern. Finally, tighten each of them one-quarter turn at a time until each fastener has been tightened to the proper torque. To loosen and remove the fasteners, the procedure would be reversed.

Component disassembly

Component disassembly should be done with care and purpose to help ensure that the parts go back together properly. Always keep track of the sequence in which parts are removed. Make note of special characteristics or marks on parts that can be installed more than one way, such as a grooved thrust washer on a shaft. It is a good idea to lay the disassembled parts out on a clean surface in the order that they were removed. It may also be helpful to make sketches or take instant photos of components before removal.

When removing fasteners from a component, keep track of their locations. Sometimes threading a bolt back in a part, or putting the washers and nut back on a stud, can prevent mix-ups later. If nuts and bolts cannot be returned to their original locations, they should be kept in a compartmented box or a series of small boxes. A cupcake or muffin tin is ideal for this purpose, since each cavity can hold the bolts and nuts from a particular area (i.e. oil pan bolts, valve cover bolts, engine mount bolts, etc.). A pan of this type is especially helpful when working on assemblies with very small parts, such as the carburetor, alternator, valve train or interior dash and trim pieces. The cavities can be marked with paint or tape to identify the contents.

Whenever wiring looms, harnesses or connectors are separated, it is a good idea to identify the two halves with numbered pieces of masking tape so they can be easily reconnected.

Gasket sealing surfaces

Throughout any vehicle, gaskets are used to seal the mating surfaces between two parts and keep lubricants, fluids, vacuum or pressure contained in an assembly.

Many times these gaskets are coated with a liquid or paste-type gasket sealing compound before assembly. Age, heat and pressure can sometimes cause the two parts to stick together so tightly that they are very difficult to separate. Often, the assembly can be loosened by striking it with a soft-face hammer near the mating surfaces. A regular hammer can be used if a block of wood is placed between the hammer and the part. Do not hammer on cast parts or parts that could be easily damaged. With any particularly stubborn part, always recheck to make sure that every fastener has been removed.

Avoid using a screwdriver or bar to pry apart an assembly, as they can easily mar the gasket sealing surfaces of the parts, which must remain smooth. If prying is absolutely necessary, use an old broom handle, but keep in mind that extra clean up will be necessary if the wood splinters.

After the parts are separated, the old gasket must be carefully scraped off and the gasket surfaces cleaned. Stubborn gasket material can be soaked with rust penetrant or treated with a special chemical to soften it so it can be easily scraped off. A scraper can be fashioned from a piece of copper tubing by flattening and sharpening one end. Copper is recommended because it is usually softer than the surfaces to be scraped, which reduces the chance of gouging the part. Some gaskets can be removed with a wire brush, but regardless of the method used, the mating surfaces must be left clean and smooth. If for some reason the gasket surface is gouged, then a gasket sealer thick enough to fill scratches will have to be used during reassembly of the components. For most applications, a non-drying (or semi-drying) gasket sealer should be used.

Hose removal tips

Warning: *If the vehicle is equipped with air conditioning, do not disconnect any of the A/C hoses without first having the system depressurized by a dealer service department or an air conditioning specialist.*

Hose removal precautions closely parallel gasket removal precautions. Avoid scratching or gouging the surface that the hose mates against or the connection may leak. This is especially true for radiator hoses. Because of various chemical reactions, the rubber in hoses can bond itself to the metal spigot that the hose fits over. To remove a hose, first loosen the hose clamps that secure it to the spigot. Then, with slip-joint pliers, grab the hose at the clamp and rotate it around the spigot. Work it back and forth until it is completely free, then pull it off. Silicone or other lubricants will ease removal if they can be applied between the hose and the outside of the spigot. Apply the same lubricant to the inside of the hose and the outside of the spigot to simplify installation.

As a last resort (and if the hose is to be replaced with a new one anyway), the rubber can be slit with a knife and the hose peeled from the spigot. If this must be done, be careful that the metal connection is not damaged.

If a hose clamp is broken or damaged, do not reuse it. Wire-type clamps usually weaken with age, so it is a good idea to replace them with screw-type clamps whenever a hose is removed.

Tools

A selection of good tools is a basic requirement for anyone who plans to maintain and repair his or her own vehicle. For the owner who has few tools, the initial investment might seem high, but when compared to the spiraling costs of professional auto maintenance and repair, it is a wise one.

Micrometer set

Dial indicator set

Dial caliper

Hand-operated vacuum pump

Timing light

Compression gauge with spark plug
hole adapter

Damper/steering wheel puller

General purpose puller

Hydraulic lifter removal tool

Valve spring compressor

Valve spring compressor

Ridge reamer

Piston ring groove cleaning tool

Ring removal/installation tool

Ring compressor

Cylinder hone

Brake hold-down spring tool

Brake cylinder hone

Clutch plate alignment tool

Tap and die set

To help the owner decide which tools are needed to perform the tasks detailed in this manual, the following tool lists are offered: *Maintenance and minor repair, Repair/overhaul* and *Special*.

The newcomer to practical mechanics should start off with the maintenance and minor repair tool kit, which is adequate for the simpler jobs performed on a vehicle. Then, as confidence and experience grow, the owner can tackle more difficult tasks, buying additional tools as they are needed. Eventually the basic kit will be expanded into the repair and overhaul tool set. Over a period of time, the experienced do-it-yourselfer will assemble a tool set complete enough for most repair and overhaul procedures and will add tools from the special category when it is felt that the expense is justified by the frequency of use.

Maintenance and minor repair tool kit

The tools in this list should be considered the minimum required for performance of routine maintenance, servicing and minor repair work. We recommend the purchase of combination wrenches (box-end and open-end combined in one wrench). While more expensive than open end wrenches, they offer the advantages of both types of wrench.

Combination wrench set (1/4-inch to 1 inch or 6 mm to 19 mm)
Adjustable wrench, 8 inch
Spark plug wrench with rubber insert
Spark plug gap adjusting tool
Feeler gauge set
Brake bleeder wrench
Standard screwdriver (5/16-inch x 6 inch)
Phillips screwdriver (No. 2 x 6 inch)
Combination pliers — 6 inch
Hacksaw and assortment of blades
Tire pressure gauge
Grease gun
Oil can
Fine emery cloth
Wire brush

Battery post and cable cleaning tool
Oil filter wrench
Funnel (medium size)
Safety goggles
Jackstands (2)
Drain pan

Note: *If basic tune-ups are going to be part of routine maintenance, it will be necessary to purchase a good quality stroboscopic timing light and combination tachometer/dwell meter. Although they are included in the list of special tools, it is mentioned here because they are absolutely necessary for tuning most vehicles properly.*

Repair and overhaul tool set

These tools are essential for anyone who plans to perform major repairs and are in addition to those in the maintenance and minor repair tool kit. Included is a comprehensive set of sockets which, though expensive, are invaluable because of their versatility, especially when various extensions and drives are available. We recommend the 1/2-inch drive over the 3/8-inch drive. Although the larger drive is bulky and more expensive, it has the capacity of accepting a very wide range of large sockets. Ideally, however, the mechanic should have a 3/8-inch drive set and a 1/2-inch drive set.

Socket set(s)
Reversible ratchet
Extension — 10 inch
Universal joint
Torque wrench (same size drive as sockets)
Ball peen hammer — 8 ounce
Soft-face hammer (plastic/rubber)
Standard screwdriver (1/4-inch x 6 inch)
Standard screwdriver (stubby — 5/16-inch)
Phillips screwdriver (No. 3 x 8 inch)
Phillips screwdriver (stubby — No. 2)

Pliers — vise grip
Pliers — lineman's
Pliers — needle nose
Pliers — snap-ring (internal and external)
Cold chisel — 1/2-inch
Scribe
Scraper (made from flattened copper tubing)
Centerpunch
Pin punches (1/16, 1/8, 3/16-inch)
Steel rule/straightedge — 12 inch
Allen wrench set (1/8 to 3/8-inch or 4 mm to 10 mm)
A selection of files
Wire brush (large)
Jackstands (second set)
Jack (scissor or hydraulic type)

Note: *Another tool which is often useful is an electric drill motor with a chuck capacity of 3/8-inch and a set of good quality drill bits.*

Special tools

The tools in this list include those which are not used regularly, are expensive to buy, or which need to be used in accordance with their manufacturer's instructions. Unless these tools will be used frequently, it is not very economical to purchase many of them. A consideration would be to split the cost and use between yourself and a friend or friends. In addition, most of these tools can be obtained from a tool rental shop on a temporary basis.

This list primarily contains only those tools and instruments widely available to the public, and not those special tools produced by the vehicle manufacturer for distribution to dealer service departments. Occasionally, references to the manufacturer's special tools are inluded in the text of this manual. Generally, an alternative method of doing the job without the special tool is offered. However, sometimes there is no alternative to their use. Where this is the case, and the tool cannot be purchased or borrowed, the work should be turned over to the dealer service department or an automotive repair shop.

Valve spring compressor
Piston ring groove cleaning tool
Piston ring compressor
Piston ring installation tool
Cylinder compression gauge
Cylinder ridge reamer
Cylinder surfacing hone
Cylinder bore gauge
Micrometers and/or dial calipers
Hydraulic lifter removal tool
Balljoint separator
Universal-type puller
Impact screwdriver
Dial indicator set
Stroboscopic timing light (inductive pick-up)
Hand operated vacuum/pressure pump
Tachometer/dwell meter
Universal electrical multimeter
Cable hoist
Brake spring removal and installation tools
Floor jack

Buying tools

For the do-it-yourselfer who is just starting to get involved in vehicle maintenance and repair, there are a number of options available when purchasing tools. If maintenance and minor repair is the extent of the work to be done, the purchase of individual tools is satisfactory. If,

on the other hand, extensive work is planned, it would be a good idea to purchase a modest tool set from one of the large retail chain stores. A set can usually be bought at a substantial savings over the individual tool prices, and they often come with a tool box. As additional tools are needed, add-on sets, individual tools and a larger tool box can be purchased to expand the tool selection. Building a tool set gradually allows the cost of the tools to be spread over a longer period of time and gives the mechanic the freedom to choose only those tools that will actually be used.

Tool stores will often be the only source of some of the special tools that are needed, but regardless of where tools are bought, try to avoid cheap ones, especially when buying screwdrivers and sockets, because they won't last very long. The expense involved in replacing cheap tools will eventually be greater than the initial cost of quality tools.

Care and maintenance of tools

Good tools are expensive, so it makes sense to treat them with respect. Keep them clean and in usable condition and store them properly when not in use. Always wipe off any dirt, grease or metal chips before putting them away. Never leave tools lying around in the work area. Upon completion of a job, always check closely under the hood for tools that may have been left there so they won't get lost during a test drive.

Some tools, such as screwdrivers, pliers, wrenches and sockets, can be hung on a panel mounted on the garage or workshop wall, while others should be kept in a tool box or tray. Measuring instruments, gauges, meters, etc. must be carefully stored where they cannot be damaged by weather or impact from other tools.

When tools are used with care and stored properly, they will last a very long time. Even with the best of care, though, tools will wear out if used frequently. When a tool is damaged or worn out, replace it. Subsequent jobs will be safer and more enjoyable if you do.

Working facilities

Not to be overlooked when discussing tools is the workshop. If anything more than routine maintenance is to be carried out, some sort of suitable work area is essential.

It is understood, and appreciated, that many home mechanics do not have a good workshop or garage available, and end up removing an engine or doing major repairs outside. It is recommended, however, that the overhaul or repair be completed under the cover of a roof.

A clean, flat workbench or table of comfortable working height is an absolute necessity. The workbench should be equipped with a vise that has a jaw opening of at least four inches.

As mentioned previously, some clean, dry storage space is also required for tools, as well as the lubricants, fluids, cleaning solvents, etc. which will soon become necessary.

Sometimes waste oil and fluids, drained from the engine or cooling system during normal maintenance or repairs, present a disposal problem. To avoid pouring them on the ground or into a sewage system, pour the used fluids into large containers, seal them with caps and take them to an authorized disposal site or recycling center. Plastic jugs, such as old antifreeze containers, are ideal for this purpose.

Always keep a supply of old newspapers and clean rags available. Old towels are excellent for mopping up spills. Many mechanics use rolls of paper towels for most work because they are readily available and disposable. To help keep the area under the vehicle clean, a large cardboard box can be cut open and flattened to protect the garage or shop floor.

Whenever working over a painted surface, such as when leaning over a fender to service something under the hood, always cover it with an old blanket or bedspread to protect the finish. Vinyl covered pads, made especially for this purpose, are available at auto parts stores.

Booster battery (jump) starting

Certain precautions must be observed when using a booster battery to start a vehicle.

a) Before connecting the booster battery, make sure the ignition switch is in the Off position.

b) Turn off the lights, heater and other electrical loads.

c) Your eyes should be shielded. Safety goggles are a good idea.

d) Make sure the booster battery is the same voltage as the dead one in the vehicle.

e) The two vehicles MUST NOT TOUCH each other!

f) Make sure the transmission is in Neutral (manual) or Park (automatic).

g) If the booster battery is not a maintenance-free type, remove the vent caps and lay a cloth over the vent holes.

Connect the red jumper cable to the *positive* (+) terminals of each battery.

Connect one end of the black jumper cable to the *negative* (−) terminal of the booster battery. The other end of this cable should be connected to a good ground on the vehicle to be started, such as a bolt or bracket on the engine block **(see illustration)**. Use caution to ensure that the cable will not come into contact with the fan, drivebelts or other moving parts of the engine.

Start the engine using the booster battery, then, with the engine running at idle speed, disconnect the jumper cables in the reverse order of connection.

Make the booster battery cable connections in the numerical order shown (note that the negative cable of the booster battery is NOT attached to the negative terminal of the dead battery)

Jacking and towing

Jacking

The jack supplied with the vehicle should only be used for changing a tire or placing jackstands under the frame. **Warning:** *Never work under the vehicle or start the engine while this jack is being used as the only means of support!* If a hoist is available, be sure to raise the vehicle only at the points shown in the accompanying illustrations.

The vehicle should be on level ground with the wheels blocked and the transmission in Park (automatic) or Reverse (manual). If a tire must be changed, remove the hub cap or wheel cover (if equipped). Loosen the lug nuts one-half turn and leave them in place until the wheel is raised off the ground. **Caution:** *On vehicles equipped with an under chassis mounted spare tire, remove the spare before raising the vehicle.*

FRONT LIFT POINTS

REAR LIFT POINTS

Hoist lift points (twin post)

REAR LIFT POINTS

FRONT LIFT POINTS

WOOD BLOCK

HOIST ADAPTER

CAUTION: ALWAYS PLACE A WOOD BLOCK BETWEEN FRAME LIFT POINT AND HOIST ADAPTER TO PREVENT LOWER BODY DAMAGE

Hoist lift points — single post

FRONT JACKING POINTS

JACKING FRONT OF VEHICLE

JACKING POINTS

REAR JACKING POINTS

JACKING REAR OF VEHICLE

JACKING POINTS

Jacking points

Once it's in the air, removal of the spare may cause the vehicle to shift and fall.

Position the jack as shown in the accompanying illustrations.

When using a floor jack, position it under the axles or under the frame lift points, as close to the wheels as possible. Refer to the jacking decal and the vehicle's owner's guide if necessary.

Operate the jack with a slow, smooth motion until the wheel is raised off the ground. Remove the tire and install the spare.

Tighten the lug nuts until they're snug, but wait until the vehicle is lowered to use the wrench.

Lower the vehicle, remove the jack and tighten the lug nuts (if loosened or removed) in a criss-cross pattern.

Towing

As a general rule, the vehicle should be towed with the rear (drive) wheels off the ground. If they can't be raised, either place them on a dolly or disconnect the driveshaft from the differential. When a vehicle is towed with the rear wheels raised, the steering wheel must be clamped in the straight ahead position with a special device designed for use during towing. **Caution:** *Don't use the steering column lock to keep the front wheels pointed straight ahead.*

Vehicles can be towed with all four wheels on the ground, provided that speeds don't exceed 35 mph and the distance is not over 50 miles. When the rear wheels are off the ground there's no distance limitation, but don't exceed 50 mph.

Equipment specifically designed for towing should be used. It should be attached to the main structural members of the vehicle, not the bumpers or brackets.

Safety is a major consideration when towing and all applicable state and local laws must be obeyed. A safety chain system must be used at all times.

While towing, the parking brake should be released and the transmission must be in Neutral. The steering must be unlocked (ignition switch in the Off position). Remember that power steering and power brakes will not work with the engine off.

Automotive chemicals and lubricants

A number of automotive chemicals and lubricants are available for use during vehicle maintenance and repair. They include a wide variety of products ranging from cleaning solvents and degreasers to lubricants and protective sprays for rubber, plastic and vinyl.

Cleaners

Carburetor cleaner and choke cleaner is a strong solvent for gum, varnish and carbon. Most carburetor cleaners leave a dry-type lubricant film which will not harden or gum up. Because of this film it is not recommended for use on electrical components.

Brake system cleaner is used to remove grease and brake fluid from the brake system where clean surfaces are absolutely necessary. It leaves no residue and often eliminates brake squeal caused by contaminants.

Electrical cleaner removes oxidation, corrosion and carbon deposits from electrical contacts, restoring full current flow. It can also be used to clean spark plugs, carburetor jets, voltage regulators and other parts where an oil-free surface is desired.

Demoisturants remove water and moisture from electrical components such as alternators, voltage regulators, electrical connectors and fuse blocks. It is non-conductive, non-corrosive and non-flammable.

Degreasers are heavy-duty solvents used to remove grease from the outside of the engine and from chassis components. They can be sprayed or brushed on, and, depending on the type, are rinsed off either with water or solvent.

Lubricants

Motor oil is the lubricant formulated for use in engines. It normally contains a wide variety of additives to prevent corrosion and reduce foaming and wear. Motor oil comes in various weights (viscosity ratings) from 5 to 80. The recommended weight of the oil depends on the season, temperature and the demands on the engine. Light oil is used in cold climates and under light load conditions. Heavy oil is used in hot climates and where high loads are encountered. Multi-viscosity oils are designed to have characteristics of both light and heavy oils and are available in a number of weights from 5W-20 to 20W-50.

Gear oil is designed to be used in differentials, manual transaxles and other areas where high-temperature lubrication is required.

Chassis and wheel bearing grease is a heavy grease used where increased loads and friction are encountered, such as for wheel bearings, balljoints, tie rod ends and universal joints.

High temperature wheel bearing grease is designed to withstand the extreme temperatures encountered by wheel bearings in disc brake equipped vehicles. It usually contains molybdenun disulfide (moly), which is a dry-type lubricant.

White grease is a heavy grease for metal to metal applications where water is a problem. White grease stays soft under both low and high temperatures (usually from −100°F to +190°F), and will not wash off or dilute in the presence of water.

Assembly lube is a special extreme pressure lubricant, usually containing moly, used to lubricate high-load parts such as main and rod bearings and cam lobes for initial start-up of a new engine. The assembly lube lubricates the parts without being squeezed out or washed away until the engine oiling system begins to function.

Silicone lubricants are used to protect rubber, plastic, vinyl and nylon parts.

Graphite lubricants are used where oils cannot be used due to contamination problems, such as in locks. The dry graphite will lubricate metal parts while remaining uncontaminated by dirt, water, oil or acids. It is electrically conductive and will not foul electrical contacts in locks such as the ignition switch.

Moly penetrants loosen and lubricate frozen, rusted and corroded fasteners and prevent future rusting or freezing.

Heat-sink grease is a special electrically non-conductive grease that is used for mounting HEI ignition modules where it is essential that heat be transferred away from the module.

Sealants

RTV sealant is one of the most widely used gasket compounds. Made from silicone, RTV is air curing, it seals, bonds, waterproofs, fills surface irregularities, remains flexible, doesn't shrink, is relatively easy to remove, and is used as a supplementary sealer with almost all low and medium temperature gaskets.

Anaerobic sealant is much like RTV in that it can be used either to seal gaskets or to form gaskets by itself. It remains flexible, is solvent resistant and fills surface imperfections. The difference between an anaerobic sealant and an RTV-type sealant is in the curing. RTV cures when exposed to air, while an anaerobic sealant cures only in the absence of air. This means that an anaerobic sealant cures only after the assembly of parts, sealing them together.

Thread and pipe sealant is used for sealing hydraulic and pneumatic fittings and vacuum lines. It is usually made from a teflon compound, and comes in a spray, a paint-on liquid and as a wrap-around tape.

Chemicals

Anti-seize compound prevents seizing, galling, cold welding, rust and corrosion in fasteners. High temperature anti-seize, usually made with copper and graphite lubricants, is used for exhaust system and manifold bolts.

Anaerobic locking compounds are used to keep fasteners from vibrating or working loose, and cure only after installation, in the absence of air. Medium strength locking compound is used for small nuts, bolts and screws that you expect to be removing later. High strength locking compound is for large nuts, bolts and studs which you don't intend to be removing on a regular basis.

Oil additives range from viscosity index improvers to chemical treatments that claim to reduce internal engine friction. It should be noted that most oil manufacturers caution against using additives with their oils.

Gas additives perform several functions, depending on their chemical makeup. They usually contain solvents that help dissolve gum and varnish that build up on carburetor and intake parts. They also serve to break down carbon deposits that form on the inside surfaces of the combustion chambers. Some additives contain upper cylinder lubricants for valves and piston rings, and others chemicals to remove condensation from the gas tank.

Miscellaneous

Brake fluid is specially formulated hydraulic fluid that can withstand the heat and pressure encountered in brake systems. Care must be taken that this fluid does not come in contact with painted surfaces or plastics. An opened container should always be resealed to prevent contamination by water or dirt.

Weatherstrip adhesive is used to bond weatherstripping around doors, windows and trunk lids. It is sometimes used to attach trim pieces.

Undercoating is a petroleum-based tar-like substance that is designed to protect metal surfaces on the underside of the vehicle from corrosion. It also acts as a sound-deadening agent by insulating the bottom of the vehicle.

Waxes and polishes are used to help protect painted and plated surfaces from the weather. Different types of paint may require the use of different types of wax and polish. Some polishes utilize a chemical or abrasive cleaner to help remove the top layer of oxidized (dull) paint on older vehicles. In recent years many non-wax polishes that contain a wide variety of chemicals such as polymers and silicones have been introduced. These non-wax polishes are usually easier to apply and last longer than conventional waxes and polishes.

Safety first!

Regardless of how enthusiastic you may be about getting on with the job at hand, take the time to ensure that your safety is not jeopardized. A moment's lack of attention can result in an accident, as can failure to observe certain simple safety precautions. The possibility of an accident will always exist, and the following points should not be considered a comprehensive list of all dangers. Rather, they are intended to make you aware of the risks and to encourage a safety conscious approach to all work you carry out on your vehicle.

Essential DOs and DON'Ts

DON'T rely on a jack when working under the vehicle. Always use approved jackstands to support the weight of the vehicle and place them under the recommended lift or support points.

DON'T attempt to loosen extremely tight fasteners (i.e. wheel lug nuts) while the vehicle is on a jack — it may fall.

DON'T start the engine without first making sure that the transmission is in Neutral (or Park where applicable) and the parking brake is set.

DON'T remove the radiator cap from a hot cooling system — let it cool or cover it with a cloth and release the pressure gradually.

DON'T attempt to drain the engine oil until you are sure it has cooled to the point that it will not burn you.

DON'T touch any part of the engine or exhaust system until it has cooled sufficiently to avoid burns.

DON'T siphon toxic liquids such as gasoline, antifreeze and brake fluid by mouth, or allow them to remain on your skin.

DON'T inhale brake lining dust — it is potentially hazardous (see *Asbestos* below)

DON'T allow spilled oil or grease to remain on the floor — wipe it up before someone slips on it.

DON'T use loose fitting wrenches or other tools which may slip and cause injury.

DON'T push on wrenches when loosening or tightening nuts or bolts. Always try to pull the wrench toward you. If the situation calls for pushing the wrench away, push with an open hand to avoid scraped knuckles if the wrench should slip.

DON'T attempt to lift a heavy component alone — get someone to help you.

DON'T rush or take unsafe shortcuts to finish a job.

DON'T allow children or animals in or around the vehicle while you are working on it.

DO wear eye protection when using power tools such as a drill, sander, bench grinder, etc. and when working under a vehicle.

DO keep loose clothing and long hair well out of the way of moving parts.

DO make sure that any hoist used has a safe working load rating adequate for the job.

DO get someone to check on you periodically when working alone on a vehicle.

DO carry out work in a logical sequence and make sure that everything is correctly assembled and tightened.

DO keep chemicals and fluids tightly capped and out of the reach of children and pets.

DO remember that your vehicle's safety affects that of yourself and others. If in doubt on any point, get professional advice.

Asbestos

Certain friction, insulating, sealing, and other products — such as brake linings, brake bands, clutch linings, torque converters, gaskets, etc. — contain asbestos. *Extreme care must be taken to avoid inhalation of dust from such products since it is hazardous to health.* If in doubt, assume that they *do* contain asbestos.

Fire

Remember at all times that gasoline is highly flammable. Never smoke or have any kind of open flame around when working on a vehicle. But the risk does not end there. A spark caused by an electrical short circuit, by two metal surfaces contacting each other, or even by static electricity built up in your body under certain conditions, can ignite gasoline vapors, which in a confined space are highly explosive. Do not, under any circumstances, use gasoline for cleaning parts. Use an approved safety solvent.

Always disconnect the battery ground (–) cable *at the battery* before working on any part of the fuel system or electrical system. Never risk spilling fuel on a hot engine or exhaust component.

It is strongly recommended that a fire extinguisher suitable for use on fuel and electrical fires be kept handy in the garage or workshop at all times. Never try to extinguish a fuel or electrical fire with water.

Fumes

Certain fumes are highly toxic and can quickly cause unconsciousness and even death if inhaled to any extent. Gasoline vapor falls into this category, as do the vapors from some cleaning solvents. Any draining or pouring of such volatile fluids should be done in a well ventilated area.

When using cleaning fluids and solvents, read the instructions on the container carefully. Never use materials from unmarked containers.

Never run the engine in an enclosed space, such as a garage. Exhaust fumes contain carbon monoxide, which is extremely poisonous. If you need to run the engine, always do so in the open air, or at least have the rear of the vehicle outside the work area.

If you are fortunate enough to have the use of an inspection pit, never drain or pour gasoline and never run the engine while the vehicle is over the pit. The fumes, being heavier than air, will concentrate in the pit with possibly lethal results.

The battery

Never create a spark or allow a bare light bulb near a battery. They normally give off a certain amount of hydrogen gas, which is highly explosive.

Always disconnect the battery ground (–) cable *at the battery* before working on the fuel or electrical systems.

If possible, loosen the filler caps or cover when charging the battery from an external source (this does not apply to sealed or maintenance-free batteries). Do not charge at an excessive rate or the battery may burst.

Take care when adding water to a non maintenance-free battery and when carrying a battery. The electrolyte, even when diluted, is very corrosive and should not be allowed to contact clothing or skin.

Always wear eye protection when cleaning the battery to prevent the caustic deposits from entering your eyes.

Household current

When using an electric power tool, inspection light, etc., which operates on household current, always make sure that the tool is correctly connected to its plug and that, where necessary, it is properly grounded. Do not use such items in damp conditions and, again, do not create a spark or apply excessive heat in the vicinity of fuel or fuel vapor.

Secondary ignition system voltage

A severe electric shock can result from touching certain parts of the ignition system (such as the spark plug wires) when the engine is running or being cranked, particularly if components are damp or the insulation is defective. In the case of an electronic ignition system, the secondary system voltage is much higher and could prove fatal.

Conversion factors

Length (distance)

Inches (in)	X	25.4	= Millimetres (mm)	X 0.0394	= Inches (in)
Feet (ft)	X	0.305	= Metres (m)	X 3.281	= Feet (ft)
Miles	X	1.609	= Kilometres (km)	X 0.621	= Miles

Volume (capacity)

Cubic inches (cu in; in^3)	X	16.387	= Cubic centimetres (cc; cm^3)	X 0.061	= Cubic inches (cu in; in^3)
Imperial pints (Imp pt)	X	0.568	= Litres (l)	X 1.76	= Imperial pints (Imp pt)
Imperial quarts (Imp qt)	X	1.137	= Litres (l)	X 0.88	= Imperial quarts (Imp qt)
Imperial quarts (Imp qt)	X	1.201	= US quarts (US qt)	X 0.833	= Imperial quarts (Imp qt)
US quarts (US qt)	X	0.946	= Litres (l)	X 1.057	= US quarts (US qt)
Imperial gallons (Imp gal)	X	4.546	= Litres (l)	X 0.22	= Imperial gallons (Imp gal)
Imperial gallons (Imp gal)	X	1.201	= US gallons (US gal)	X 0.833	= Imperial gallons (Imp gal)
US gallons (US gal)	X	3.785	= Litres (l)	X 0.264	= US gallons (US gal)

Mass (weight)

Ounces (oz)	X	28.35	= Grams (g)	X 0.035	= Ounces (oz)
Pounds (lb)	X	0.454	= Kilograms (kg)	X 2.205	= Pounds (lb)

Force

Ounces-force (ozf; oz)	X	0.278	= Newtons (N)	X 3.6	= Ounces-force (ozf; oz)
Pounds-force (lbf; lb)	X	4.448	= Newtons (N)	X 0.225	= Pounds-force (lbf; lb)
Newtons (N)	X	0.1	= Kilograms-force (kgf; kg)	X 9.81	= Newtons (N)

Pressure

Pounds-force per square inch (psi; lbf/in^2; lb/in^2)	X	0.070	= Kilograms-force per square centimetre (kgf/cm^2; kg/cm^2)	X 14.223	= Pounds-force per square inch (psi; lbf/in^2; lb/in^2)
Pounds-force per square inch (psi; lbf/in^2; lb/in^2)	X	0.068	= Atmospheres (atm)	X 14.696	= Pounds-force per square inch (psi; lbf/in^2; lb/in^2)
Pounds-force per square inch (psi; lbf/in^2; lb/in^2)	X	0.069	= Bars	X 14.5	= Pounds-force per square inch (psi; lbf/in^2; lb/in^2)
Pounds-force per square inch (psi; lbf/in^2; lb/in^2)	X	6.895	= Kilopascals (kPa)	X 0.145	= Pounds-force per square inch (psi; lbf/in^2; lb/in^2)
Kilopascals (kPa)	X	0.01	= Kilograms-force per square centimetre (kgf/cm^2; kg/cm^2)	X 98.1	= Kilopascals (kPa)

Torque (moment of force)

Pounds-force inches (lbf in; lb in)	X	1.152	= Kilograms-force centimetre (kgf cm; kg cm)	X 0.868	= Pounds-force inches (lbf in; lb in)
Pounds-force inches (lbf in; lb in)	X	0.113	= Newton metres (Nm)	X 8.85	= Pounds-force inches (lbf in; lb in)
Pounds-force inches (lbf in; lb in)	X	0.083	= Pounds-force feet (lbf ft; lb ft)	X 12	= Pounds-force inches (lbf in; lb in)
Pounds-force feet (lbf ft; lb ft)	X	0.138	= Kilograms-force metres (kgf m; kg m)	X 7.233	= Pounds-force feet (lbf ft; lb ft)
Pounds-force feet (lbf ft; lb ft)	X	1.356	= Newton metres (Nm)	X 0.738	= Pounds-force feet (lbf ft; lb ft)
Newton metres (Nm)	X	0.102	= Kilograms-force metres (kgf m; kg m)	X 9.804	= Newton metres (Nm)

Power

Horsepower (hp)	X	745.7	= Watts (W)	X 0.0013	= Horsepower (hp)

Velocity (speed)

Miles per hour (miles/hr; mph)	X	1.609	= Kilometres per hour (km/hr; kph)	X 0.621	= Miles per hour (miles/hr; mph)

Fuel consumption*

Miles per gallon, Imperial (mpg)	X	0.354	= Kilometres per litre (km/l)	X 2.825	= Miles per gallon, Imperial (mpg)
Miles per gallon, US (mpg)	X	0.425	= Kilometres per litre (km/l)	X 2.352	= Miles per gallon, US (mpg)

Temperature

Degrees Fahrenheit = ($^\circ$C x 1.8) + 32

Degrees Celsius (Degrees Centigrade; $^\circ$C) = ($^\circ$F - 32) x 0.56

*It is common practice to convert from miles per gallon (mpg) to litres/100 kilometres (l/100km), where mpg (Imperial) x l/100 km = 282 and mpg (US) x l/100 km = 235

Troubleshooting

Contents

This Section provides an easy reference guide to the more common problems that may occur during the operation of your vehicle. Various symptoms and their probable causes are grouped under headings denoting components or systems, such as Engine, Cooling system, etc. They also refer to the Chapter and/or Section that deals with the problem.

Remember that successful troubleshooting isn't a mysterious 'black art' practiced only by professional mechanics, it's simply the result of knowledge combined with an intelligent, systematic approach to a problem. Always use a process of elimination starting with the simplest solution and working through to the most complex — and never overlook the obvious. Anyone can run the gas tank dry or leave the lights on overnight, so don't assume that you're exempt from such oversights.

Finally, always establish a clear idea why a problem has occurred and take steps to ensure that it doesn't happen again. If the electrical system fails because of a poor connection, check all other connections in the system to make sure they don't fail as well. If a particular fuse continues to blow, find out why — don't just go on replacing fuses. Remember, failure of a small component can often be indicative of potential failure or incorrect functioning of a more important component or system.

Engine

1   Engine will not rotate when attempting to start

1   Battery terminal connections loose or corroded. Check the cable terminals at the battery. Tighten the cable or remove corrosion as necessary.
2   Battery discharged or faulty. If the cable connections are clean and tight on the battery posts, turn the key to the On position and switch on the headlights and/or windshield wipers. If they fail to function, the battery is discharged. On 1986 models with a 3.0 liter V6 engine and auxiliary A/C, a discharged battery may be due to excess battery demand, especially if it occurs when both A/C blowers and other accessories have been operating. Ask your dealer service department to refer to Technical Service Bulletin no. 86-22-16.
3   Automatic transmission not completely engaged in Park or clutch not completely depressed.
4   Broken, loose or disconnected wiring in the starting circuit. Inspect all wiring and connectors at the battery, starter solenoid and ignition switch.
5   Starter motor pinion jammed in flywheel ring gear. If equipped with a manual transmission, place the transmission in gear and rock the vehicle to manually turn the engine. Remove the starter and inspect the pinion and flywheel at earliest convenience.
6   Starter solenoid faulty (Chapter 5).
7   Starter motor faulty (Chapter 5).
8   Ignition switch faulty (Chapter 12).
9   On 1986 models with a 3.0 liter V6 engine and automatic transmission, a no start condition may be caused by a damaged Neutral start switch wire (especially if it's accompanied by no back-up lights or turn signals). Have your dealer service department refer to Technical Service Bulletin no. 86-23-16
10   On vehicles equipped with a 2.3 liter engine, built between 8/6/86 and 9/1/86, a no start condition may be caused by a damaged engine control wire harness. Have your dealer service department refer to Technical Service Bulletin no. 87-1-23.

2   Engine rotates but will not start

1   Fuel tank empty.
2   Battery discharged (engine rotates slowly). Check the operation of electrical components as described in previous Section.
3   Battery terminal connections loose or corroded. See previous Section.
4   Carburetor flooded and/or fuel level in carburetor incorrect. This will usually be accompanied by a strong fuel odor from under the engine cover. Wait a few minutes, depress the accelerator pedal all the way to the floor and attempt to start the engine.
5   Choke control inoperative (Chapter 4).
6   Fuel not reaching carburetor or fuel injector(s). With the ignition switch in the Off position, remove the engine cover, remove the top

plate of the air cleaner assembly and observe the top of the carburetor (manually move the choke plate back if necessary). Depress the accelerator pedal and check that fuel spurts into the carburetor. If not, check the fuel filter (Chapter 1), fuel lines and fuel pump (Chapter 4).
7   Fuel injector(s) or fuel pump faulty (fuel injected vehicles) (Chapter 4).
8   No power to fuel pump (Chapter 4).
9   Worn, faulty or incorrectly gapped spark plugs (Chapter 1).
10   Broken, loose or disconnected wiring in the starting circuit (see previous Section).
11   Distributor loose, causing ignition timing to change. Turn the distributor as necessary to start the engine, then set the ignition timing as soon as possible (Chapter 1).
12   Broken, loose or disconnected wires at the ignition coil or faulty coil (Chapter 5).

3   Starter motor operates without rotating engine

1   Starter pinion sticking. Remove the starter (Chapter 5) and inspect.
2   Starter pinion or flywheel teeth worn or broken. Remove the cover at the rear of the engine and inspect.

4   Engine hard to start when cold

1   Battery discharged or low. Check as described in Section 1.
2   Choke control inoperative or out of adjustment (Chapter 4).
3   Carburetor flooded (see Section 2).
4   Fuel supply not reaching the carburetor (see Section 2).
5   Carburetor/fuel injection system in need of overhaul (Chapter 4).
6   Distributor rotor carbon tracked and/or damaged (Chapter 1).
7   Fuel injection malfunction (Chapter 4).
8   On 1986 models, hard starting when cold may be caused by sludge in the throttle body (2.3 liter engine). Ask your dealer service department to refer to Technical Service Bulletin no. 86-20-6.
9   On vehicles equipped with a 2.3 liter engine, built between 8/6/86 and 9/1/86, hard starting and/or stalling may be caused by a damaged engine control wire harness. Have your dealer service department refer to Technical Service Bulletin no. 87-1-23.

5   Engine hard to start when hot

1   Air filter clogged (Chapter 1).
2   Fuel not reaching the injector(s) (see Section 2).
3   Corroded electrical leads at the battery (Chapter 1).
4   Bad engine ground (Chapter 12).
5   Starter worn (Chapter 5).
6   Corroded electrical leads at the fuel injector (Chapter 4).
7   See Paragraph 9 in Section 4.

6   Starter motor noisy or excessively rough in engagement

1   Pinion or flywheel gear teeth worn or broken. Remove the cover at the rear of the engine (if so equipped) and inspect.
2   Starter motor mounting bolts loose or missing.

7   Engine starts but stops immediately

1   Loose or faulty electrical connections at distributor, coil or alternator.
2   Insufficient fuel reaching the carburetor or fuel injector(s). Disconnect the fuel line. Place a container under the disconnected fuel line and observe the flow of fuel from the line. If little or none at all, check for blockage in the lines and/or replace the fuel pump (Chapter 4).
3   Vacuum leak at the gasket surfaces of the carburetor or fuel injection unit. Make sure that all mounting bolts/nuts are tightened securely and that all vacuum hoses connected to the carburetor or fuel injection unit and manifold are positioned properly and in good condition.

8 Engine lopes while idling or idles erratically

1 Vacuum leakage. Check mounting bolts/nuts at the carburetor/fuel injection unit and intake manifold for tightness. Make sure that all vacuum hoses are connected and in good condition. Use a stethoscope or a length of fuel hose held against your ear to listen for vacuum leaks while the engine is running. A hissing sound will be heard. Check the carburetor/fuel injector and intake manifold gasket surfaces.
2 Leaking EGR valve or plugged PCV valve (see Chapters 1 and 6).
3 Air filter clogged (Chapter 1).
4 Fuel pump not delivering sufficient fuel to the carburetor/fuel injector (see Section 7).
5 Carburetor out of adjustment (Chapter 4).
6 Leaking head gasket. If this is suspected, take the vehicle to a repair shop or dealer where the engine can be pressure checked.
7 Timing chain and/or gears worn (Chapter 2).
8 Camshaft lobes worn (Chapter 2).

9 Engine misses at idle speed

1 Spark plugs worn or not gapped properly (Chapter 1).
2 Faulty spark plug wires (Chapter 1).
3 Choke not operating properly (Chapter 1).
4 Sticking or faulty emissions system components (Chapter 6).
5 Clogged fuel filter and/or foreign matter in fuel. Remove the fuel filter (Chapter 1) and inspect.
6 Vacuum leaks at the intake manifold or at hose connections. Check as described in Section 8.
7 Incorrect idle speed or idle mixture (Chapter 1).
8 Incorrect ignition timing (Chapter 1).
9 Uneven or low cylinder compression. Check compression as described in Chapter 2.
10 On 1987 models, rough idle may be caused by loose wire terminals in the fuel injector connectors. Have your dealer service department refer to Technical Service Bulletin no. 87-13-5.

10 Engine misses throughout driving speed range

1 Fuel filter clogged and/or impurities in the fuel system (Chapter 1). Also check fuel output at the carburetor/fuel injector (see Section 7).
2 Faulty or incorrectly gapped spark plugs (Chapter 1).
3 Incorrect ignition timing (Chapter 1).
4 Check for cracked distributor cap, disconnected distributor wires and damaged distributor components (Chapter 1).
5 Leaking spark plug wires (Chapter 1).
6 Faulty emissions system components (Chapter 6).
7 Low or uneven cylinder compression pressures. Remove the spark plugs and test the compression with gauge (Chapter 2).
8 Weak or faulty ignition system (Chapter 5).
9 Vacuum leaks at the carburetor/fuel injection unit or vacuum hoses (see Section 8).

11 Engine stalls

1 Idle speed incorrect (Chapter 1).
2 Fuel filter clogged and/or water and impurities in the fuel system (Chapter 1).
3 Choke improperly adjusted or sticking (Chapter 4).
4 Distributor components damp or damaged (Chapter 5).
5 Faulty emissions system components (Chapter 6).
6 Faulty or incorrectly gapped spark plugs (Chapter 1). Also check spark plug wires (Chapter 1).
7 Vacuum leak at the carburetor/fuel injection unit or vacuum hoses. Check as described in Section 8.
8 On 1986 models, stalling during idle or deceleration may be caused by sludge in the throttle body (2.3 liter engine). Ask your dealer service department to refer to Technical Service Bulletin no. 86-20-6.
9 Refer to Paragraph 9 in Section 4.
10 On 1986 and 1987 models with a 2.3 liter engine, hesitation or stalling during acceleration may be caused by carbon build-up on the intake valves. Have your dealer service department refer to Technical Service Bulletin no. 87-8-18.

12 Engine lacks power

1 Incorrect ignition timing (Chapter 1).
2 Excessive play in distributor shaft. At the same time, check for worn rotor, faulty distributor cap, wires, etc. (Chapters 1 and 5).
3 Faulty or incorrectly gapped spark plugs (Chapter 1).
4 Fuel injection unit not adjusted properly or excessively worn (Chapter 4).
5 Faulty coil (Chapter 5).
6 Brakes binding (Chapter 1).
7 Automatic transmission fluid level incorrect (Chapter 1).
8 Clutch slipping (Chapter 8).
9 Fuel filter clogged and/or impurities in the fuel system (Chapter 1).
10 Emissions control system not functioning properly (Chapter 6).
11 Use of substandard fuel. Fill tank with proper octane fuel.
12 Low or uneven cylinder compression pressures. Test with compression tester, which will detect leaking valves and/or blown head gasket (Chapter 2).

13 Engine backfires

1 Emissions system not functioning properly (Chapter 6).
2 Ignition timing incorrect (Chapter 1).
3 Faulty secondary ignition system (cracked spark plug insulator, faulty plug wires, distributor cap and/or rotor) (Chapters 1 and 5).
4 Carburetor/fuel injection unit in need of adjustment or worn excessively (Chapter 4).
5 Vacuum leak at the fuel injection unit or vacuum hoses. Check as described in Section 8.
6 Valves sticking (Chapter 2).
7 Crossed plug wires (Chapter 1).

14 Pinging or knocking engine sounds during acceleration or uphill

1 Incorrect grade of fuel. Fill tank with fuel of the proper octane rating.
2 Ignition timing incorrect (Chapter 1).
3 Carburetor/fuel injection unit in need of adjustment (Chapter 4).
4 Improper spark plugs. Check plug type against Emissions Control Information label located under hood. Also check plugs and wires for damage (Chapter 1).
5 Worn or damaged distributor components (Chapter 5).
6 Faulty emissions system (Chapter 6).
7 Vacuum leak. Check as described in Section 8.

15 Engine diesels (continues to run) after switching off

1 Idle speed too high (Chapter 1).
2 Electrical solenoid at side of carburetor not functioning properly (not all models, see Chapter 4).
3 Ignition timing incorrectly adjusted (Chapter 1).
4 Thermo-controlled air cleaner heat valve not operating properly (Chapter 1).
5 Excessive engine operating temperature. Probable causes of this are malfunctioning thermostat, clogged radiator, faulty water pump (Chapter 3).

Engine electrical system

16 Battery will not hold a charge

1 Alternator drivebelt defective or not adjusted properly (Chapter 1).
2 Electrolyte level low or battery discharged (Chapter 1).

3   Battery terminals loose or corroded (Chapter 1).
4   Alternator not charging properly (Chapter 5). A Service Bulletin has been issued for this condition (1986 models with 3.0 liter V6 engine and auxiliary A/C. See Section 1, Paragraph 2.
5   Loose, broken or faulty wiring in the charging circuit (Chapter 5).
6   Short in vehicle wiring causing a continual drain on battery.
7   Battery defective internally.

17   Alternator light stays on

1   Fault in alternator or charging circuit (Chapter 5).
2   Alternator drivebelt defective or not properly adjusted (Chapter 1).

18   Alternator light fails to come on when key is turned on

1   Warning light bulb defective (Chapter 12).
2   Alternator faulty (Chapter 5).
3   Fault in the printed circuit, dash wiring or bulb holder (Chapter 12).

19   'Check engine' light comes on

Emission system malfunction. Take the vehicle to a dealer service department.

Fuel system

20   Excessive fuel consumption

1   Dirty or clogged air filter element (Chapter 1).
2   Incorrectly set ignition timing (Chapter 1).
3   Choke sticking or improperly adjusted (Chapter 1).
4   Emissions system not functioning properly (not all vehicles, see Chapter 6).
5   Carburetor idle speed and/or mixture not adjusted properly (Chapter 1).
6   Carburetor/fuel injection internal parts excessively worn or damaged (Chapter 4).
7   Low tire pressure or incorrect tire size (Chapter 1).

21   Fuel leakage and/or fuel odor

1   Leak in a fuel feed or vent line (Chapter 4).
2   Tank overfilled. Fill only to automatic shut-off.
3   Emissions system clogged or damaged (Chapter 6).
4   Vapor leaks from system lines (Chapter 4).
5   Carburetor/fuel injection internal parts excessively worn or out of adjustment (Chapter 4).

Cooling system

22   Overheating

1   Insufficient coolant in system (Chapter 1).
2   Water pump drivebelt defective or not adjusted properly (Chapter 1).
3   Radiator core blocked or radiator grille dirty and restricted (Chapter 3).
4   Thermostat faulty (Chapter 3).
5   Fan blades broken or cracked (Chapter 3).
6   Radiator cap not maintaining proper pressure. Have cap pressure tested by gas station or repair shop.
7   Ignition timing incorrect (Chapter 1).
8   On 1986 models with a 2.3 liter engine and dealer installed accessory A/C, overheating may be caused by an incorrect cooling fan. Have your dealer service department refer to Technical Service Bulletin no. 86-22-18.

23   Overcooling

1   Thermostat faulty (Chapter 3).
2   Inaccurate temperature gauge (Chapter 12)

24   External coolant leakage

1   Deteriorated or damaged hoses or loose clamps. Replace hoses and/or tighten clamps at hose connections (Chapter 1).
2   Water pump seals defective. If this is the case, water will drip from the weep hole in the water pump body (Chapter 3).
3   Leakage from radiator core or header tank. This will require the radiator to be professionally repaired (see Chapter 3 for removal procedures).
4   Engine drain plugs or water jacket core plugs leaking (see Chapter 2).

25   Internal coolant leakage

Note: *Internal coolant leaks can usually be detected by examining the oil. Check the dipstick and inside of the rocker arm cover(s) for water deposits and an oil consistency like that of a milkshake.*
1   Leaking cylinder head gasket. Have the cooling system pressure tested.
2   Cracked cylinder bore or cylinder head. Dismantle engine and inspect (Chapter 2).

26   Coolant loss

1   Too much coolant in system (Chapter 1).
2   Coolant boiling away due to overheating (see Section 22).
3   Internal or external leakage (see Sections 24 and 25).
4   Faulty radiator cap. Have the cap pressure tested.

27   Poor coolant circulation

1   Inoperative water pump. A quick test is to pinch the top radiator hose closed with your hand while the engine is idling, then let it loose. You should feel the surge of coolant if the pump is working properly (Chapter 3).
2   Restriction in cooling system. Drain, flush and refill the system (Chapter 1). If necessary, remove the radiator (Chapter 3) and have it reverse flushed.
3   Water pump drivebelt defective or not adjusted properly (Chapter 1).
4   Thermostat sticking (Chapter 3).

Clutch

28   Fails to release (pedal pressed to the floor — shift lever does not move freely in and out of Reverse)

1   Clutch fork off ball stud. Look under the vehicle, on the left side of transmission.
2   Clutch plate warped or damaged (Chapter 8).
3   Clutch hydraulic system low or has air in system and needs to be bled (Chapter 8).

29   Clutch slips (engine speed increases with no increase in vehicle speed)

1   Clutch plate oil soaked or lining worn. Remove clutch (Chapter 8) and inspect.
2   Clutch plate not seated. It may take 30 or 40 normal starts for a new one to seat.
3   Pressure plate worn (Chapter 8).

30 Grabbing (chattering) as clutch is engaged

1 Oil on clutch plate lining. Remove (Chapter 8) and inspect. Correct any leakage source.
2 Worn or loose engine or transmission mounts. These units move slightly when clutch is released. Inspect mounts and bolts.
3 Worn splines on clutch plate hub. Remove clutch components (Chapter 8) and inspect.
4 Warped pressure plate or flywheel. Remove clutch components and inspect.

31 Squeal or rumble with clutch fully engaged (pedal released)

1 Release bearing binding on transmission bearing retainer. Remove clutch components (Chapter 8) and check bearing. Remove any burrs or nicks, clean and relubricate before reinstallation.
2 Weak linkage return spring. Replace the spring.

32 Squeal or rumble with clutch fully disengaged (pedal depressed)

1 Worn, defective or broken release bearing (Chapter 8).
2 Worn or broken pressure plate springs (or diaphragm fingers) (Chapter 8).
3 Air in hydraulic line (Chapter 8).

33 Clutch pedal stays on floor when disengaged

1 Bind in linkage or release bearing. Inspect linkage or remove clutch components as necessary.
2 Clutch hydraulic cylinder faulty or there is air in the system.

Manual transmission

Note: *All the following references are to Chapter 7, unless noted.*

34 Noisy in Neutral with engine running

1 Input shaft bearing worn.
2 Damaged main drive gear bearing.
3 Worn countershaft bearings.
4 Worn or damaged countershaft end play shims.

35 Noisy in all gears

1 Any of the above causes, and/or:
2 Insufficient lubricant (see checking procedures in Chapter 1).

36 Noisy in one particular gear

1 Worn, damaged or chipped gear teeth for that particular gear.
2 Worn or damaged synchronizer for that particular gear.

37 Slips out of high gear

1 Transmission mounting bolts loose.
2 Shift rods not working freely.
3 Damaged mainshaft pilot bushing.
4 Dirt between transmission case and engine or misalignment of transmission.

38 Difficulty in engaging gears

1 Loose, damaged or out-of-adjustment shift linkage. Make a thorough inspection, replacing parts as necessary.
2 Air in hydraulic system (Chapter 8)

39 Oil leakage

1 Excessive amount of lubricant in transmission (see Chapter 1 for correct checking procedures). Drain lubricant as required.
2 Side cover loose or gasket damaged.
3 Rear oil seal or speedometer oil seal in need of replacement.
4 Clutch hydraulic system leaking (Chapter 8).

Automatic transmission

Note: *Due to the complexity of the automatic transmission, it is difficult for the home mechanic to properly diagnose and service this component. For problems other than the following, the vehicle should be taken to a dealer or reputable repair shop.*

40 General shift mechanism problems

1 Chapter 7 deals with checking and adjusting the shift linkage on automatic transmissions. Common problems which may be attributed to poorly adjusted linkage are:

Engine starting in gears other than Park or Neutral
Indicator on shifter pointing to a gear other than the one actually being used
Vehicle moves when in Park
2 Refer to Chapter 7 to adjust the linkage.

41 Transmission will not downshift with accelerator pedal pressed to the floor

Chapter 7 deals with adjusting the TV cable to enable the transmission to downshift properly.

42 Transmission slips, shifts rough, is noisy or has no drive in forward or reverse gears

1 There are many probable causes for the above problems, but the home mechanic should be concerned with only one possibility — fluid level.
2 Before taking the vehicle to a repair shop, check the level and condition of the fluid as described in Chapter 1. Correct fluid level as necessary or change the fluid and filter if needed. If the problem persists, have a professional diagnose the probable cause.
3 A Technical Service Bulletin has been issued for several problems such as burnt fluid (after towing), leaks, engine stalling after transmission is put in gear, slipping, high shift lever effort, etc. Have your dealer service department refer to TSB no. 87-2-15.

43 Fluid leakage

1 Automatic transmission fluid is a deep red color. Fluid leaks should not be confused with engine oil, which can easily be blown by air flow to the transmission.
2 To pinpoint a leak, first remove all built-up dirt and grime from around the transmission. Degreasing agents and/or steam cleaning will achieve this. With the underside clean, drive the vehicle at low speeds so air flow will not blow the leak far from its source. Raise the vehicle and determine where the leak is coming from. Common areas of leakage are:

a) Pan: Tighten mounting bolts and/or replace pan gasket as necessary (see Chapters 1 and 7).

b) Filler pipe: Replace the rubber seal where pipe enters transmission case.
c) Transmission oil lines: Tighten connectors where lines enter transmission case and/or replace lines.
d) Vent pipe: Transmission overfilled and/or water in fluid (see checking procedures, Chapter 1).
e) Speedometer connector: Replace the O-ring where speedometer cable enters transmission case (Chapter 7).

3   On 1986 models, if fluid is leaking from the vent assembly, take the vehicle to a dealer service department to see if Technical Service Bulletin no. 86-19-11 applies.

Driveshaft

44   Oil leak at front of driveshaft

Defective transmission rear oil seal. See Chapter 7 for replacement procedures. While this is done, check the splined yoke for burrs or a rough condition which may be damaging the seal. Burrs can be removed with crocus cloth or a fine whetstone.

45   Knock or clunk when the transmission is under initial load (just after transmission is put into gear)

1   Loose or disconnected rear suspension components. Check all mounting bolts, nuts and bushings (Chapter 10).
2   Loose driveshaft bolts. Inspect all bolts and nuts and tighten them to the specified torque.
3   Worn or damaged universal joint bearings. Check for wear (Chapter 8).

46   Metallic grating sound consistent with vehicle speed

Pronounced wear in the universal joint bearings. Check as described in Chapter 8.

47   Vibration

Note: *Before assuming that the driveshaft is at fault, make sure the tires are perfectly balanced and perform the following test.*

1   Install a tachometer inside the vehicle to monitor engine speed as the vehicle is driven. Drive the vehicle and note the engine speed at which the vibration (roughness) is most pronounced. Now shift the transmission to a different gear and bring the engine speed to the same point.
2   If the vibration occurs at the same engine speed (rpm) regardless of which gear the transmission is in, the driveshaft is NOT at fault since the driveshaft speed varies.
3   If the vibration decreases or is eliminated when the transmission is in a different gear at the same engine speed, refer to the following probable causes.
4   Bent or dented driveshaft. Inspect and replace as necessary (Chapter 8).
5   Undercoating or built-up dirt, etc. on the driveshaft. Clean the shaft thoroughly and recheck.
6   Worn universal joint bearings. Remove and inspect (Chapter 8).
7   Driveshaft and/or companion flange out-of-balance. Check for missing weights on the shaft. Remove the driveshaft (Chapter 8) and reinstall 180° from original position, then retest. Have the driveshaft professionally balanced if the problem persists.

Axles

48   Noise

1   Road noise. No corrective procedures available.
2   Tire noise. Inspect the tires and check tire pressures (Chapter 1).
3   Rear wheel bearings loose, worn or damaged (Chapter 8).

4   On 1986 models, if noise is heard during turns, take the vehicle to a dealer service department to see if Technical Service Bulletin no. 86-19-8 applies.

49   Vibration

See probable causes under Driveshaft. Proceed under the guidelines listed for the driveshaft. If the problem persists, check the rear wheel bearings by raising the rear of the vehicle and spinning the wheels by hand. Listen for evidence of rough (noisy) bearings. Remove and inspect (Chapter 8).

50   Oil leakage

1   Pinion seal damaged (Chapter 8).
2   Axleshaft oil seals damaged (Chapter 8).
3   Differential inspection cover leaking. Tighten the bolts or replace the gasket as required (Chapters 1 and 8).

Brakes

Note: *Before assuming that a brake problem exists, make sure that the tires are in good condition and inflated properly (see Chapter 1), that the front end alignment is correct and that the vehicle is not loaded with weight in an unequal manner.*

51   Vehicle pulls to one side during braking

1   Defective, damaged or oil contaminated brake pads or shoes on one side. Inspect as described in Chapter 9.
2   Excessive wear of brake shoe or pad material or drum/disc on one side. Inspect and correct as necessary.
3   Loose or disconnected front suspension components. Inspect and tighten all bolts to the specified torque (Chapter 10).
4   Defective drum brake or caliper assembly. Remove the drum or caliper and inspect for a stuck piston or other damage (Chapter 9).

52   Noise (high-pitched squeal with the brakes applied)

1   Disc brake pads worn out. The noise comes from the wear sensor rubbing against the disc. Replace the pads with new ones immediately (Chapter 9).
2   On 1986 and 1987 models, if squealing occurs during the first few brake applications when the brakes are cold or in the morning after an overnight rain, the rear brake shoes may require modification. Have your dealer service department refer to Technical Service Bulletin no. 87-2-22.

53   Excessive brake pedal travel

1   Partial brake system failure. Inspect the entire system (Chapter 9) and correct as required.
2   Insufficient fluid in the master cylinder. Check (Chapter 1), add fluid and bleed the system if necessary (Chapter 9).
3   Brakes not adjusting properly. Make a series of starts and stops with the vehicle is in Reverse. If this does not correct the situation, remove the drums and inspect the self-adjusters (Chapter 9).

54   Brake pedal feels spongy when depressed

1   Air in the hydraulic lines. Bleed the brake system (Chapter 9).
2   Faulty flexible hoses. Inspect all system hoses and lines. Replace parts as necessary.
3   Master cylinder mounting bolts/nuts loose.
4   Master cylinder defective (Chapter 9).

55 Excessive effort required to stop vehicle

1 Power brake booster not operating properly (Chapter 9).
2 Excessively worn linings or pads. Inspect and replace if necessary (Chapters 1 and 9).
3 One or more caliper pistons or wheel cylinders seized or sticking. Inspect and rebuild as required (Chapter 9).
4 Brake linings or pads contaminated with oil or grease. Inspect and replace as required (Chapters 1 and 9).
5 New pads or shoes installed and not yet seated. It will take a while for the new material to seat against the drum (or rotor).

56 Pedal travels to the floor with little resistance

Little or no fluid in the master cylinder reservoir caused by leaking wheel cylinder(s), leaking caliper piston(s), loose, damaged or disconnected brake lines. Inspect the entire system and correct as necessary.

57 Brake pedal pulsates during brake application

1 Wheel bearings not adjusted properly or in need of replacement (Chapter 1).
2 Caliper not sliding properly due to improper installation or obstructions. Remove and inspect (Chapter 9).
3 Rotor or drum defective. Remove the rotor or drum (Chapter 9) and check for excessive lateral runout, out-of-round and parallelism. Have the drum or rotor resurfaced or replace it with a new one.

Suspension and steering systems

58 Vehicle pulls to one side

1 Tire pressures uneven (Chapter 1).
2 Defective tire (Chapter 1).
3 Excessive wear in suspension or steering components (Chapter 10).
4 Front end out of alignment.
5 Front brakes dragging. Inspect the brakes as described in Chapter 9.

59 Shimmy, shake or vibration

1 Tire or wheel out-of-balance or out-of-round. Have professionally balanced.
2 Loose, worn or out-of-adjustment wheel bearings (Chapters 1 and 8).
3 Shock absorbers and/or suspension components worn or damaged (Chapter 10).

60 Excessive pitching and/or rolling around corners or during braking

1 Defective shock absorbers. Replace as a set (Chapter 10).

2 Broken or weak springs and/or suspension components. Inspect as described in Chapter 10.

61 Excessively stiff steering

1 Lack of fluid in power steering fluid reservoir (Chapter 1).
2 Incorrect tire pressures (Chapter 1).
3 Lack of lubrication at steering joints (Chapter 1).
4 Front end out of alignment.
5 See Section 63.

62 Excessive play in steering

1 Loose front wheel bearings (Chapter 1).
2 Excessive wear in suspension or steering components (Chapter 10).
3 Steering gearbox out of adjustment (Chapter 10).

63 Lack of power assistance

1 Steering pump drivebelt faulty or not adjusted properly (Chapter 1).
2 Fluid level low (Chapter 1).
3 Hoses or lines restricted. Inspect and replace parts as necessary.
4 Air in power steering system. Bleed the system (Chapter 10).

64 Excessive tire wear (not specific to one area)

1 Incorrect tire pressures (Chapter 1).
2 Tires out-of-balance. Have professionally balanced.
3 Wheels damaged. Inspect and replace as necessary.
4 Suspension or steering components excessively worn (Chapter 10).

65 Excessive tire wear on outside edge

1 Inflation pressures incorrect (Chapter 1).
2 Excessive speed in turns.
3 Front end alignment incorrect (excessive toe-in). Have professionally aligned.
4 Suspension arm bent or twisted (Chapter 10).

66 Excessive tire wear on inside edge

1 Inflation pressures incorrect (Chapter 1).
2 Front end alignment incorrect (toe-out). Have professionally aligned.
3 Loose or damaged steering components (Chapter 10).

67 Tire tread worn in one place

1 Tires out-of-balance.
2 Damaged or buckled wheel. Inspect and replace if necessary.
3 Defective tire (Chapter 1).

Chapter 1 Tune-up and routine maintenance

Contents

Specifications

Recommended lubricants and fluids

Engine oil type . . . . API grade SF, SF/CC or SF/CD
Engine oil viscosity . . . . See accompanying chart
Engine oil capacity
  1987 3.0L V6 engine . . . . 4.5 qts
  All others . . . . 5.0 qts

ENGINE OIL VISCOSITY RECOMMENDATIONS

Brake fluid type . . . .   DOT 3 heavy duty brake fluid
Power steering fluid type . . . .   Motorcraft **Type F** automatic transmission fluid (part no. XT-1-QF)
Automatic transmission fluid type
    1986 and 1987 . . . .   Motorcraft **DEXRON II** automatic transmission fluid
    1988 . . . .   Motorcraft **MERCON** automatic transmission fluid (part no. AT-2-QDX)
Manual transmission lubricant type
    1986 and 1987 . . . .   Motorcraft transmission oil (part no. D8DZ-19C547-A)
    1988 . . . .   Motorcraft **MERCON** automatic transmission fluid (part no. AT-2-QDX)
Differential oil . . . .   Hypoid lubricant (part no. D8DZ-19C547-A)*
Coolant type . . . .   Ethylene glycol-based antifreeze and water
Cooling system capacity
    Four-cylinder engine . . . .   6.8 qts
    2.8L V6 engine . . . .   7.6 qts
    3.0L V6 engine . . . .   11.8 qts
* Trak-Lok axles add 4 oz. of friction modifier (part no. C8AZ-19B546-A) when oil is changed.

General

Alternator/power steering/air conditioning drivebelt tension (with tool no. T63L-8620-A)
    New belt. . . . .   150 to 190 lbs
    Used belt . . . .   140 to 160 lbs
Radiator cap pressure
    Standard . . . .   16 psi
    Lower limit (must hold pressure) . . . .   13 psi
    Upper limit (must relieve pressure) . . . .   18 psi

Brakes

Front disc brake pad thickness (minimum) . . . .   1/8 in
Rear drum brake shoe lining thickness (minimum) . . . .   1/16 in

Ignition system

Spark plug type
    Four-cylinder engine . . . .   Motorcraft AWSF44C
    2.8L V6 engine . . . .   Motorcraft AWSF44C
    3.0L V6 engine
        1986 and 1987 . . . .   Motorcraft AWSF32C
        1988 . . . .   Motorcraft AWSF32P
Spark plug gap . . . .   Refer to *Vehicle Emission Control Information label*
Idle speed . . . .   Refer to *Vehicle Emission Control Information label*

Torque specifications   Ft-lbs *(unless otherwise noted)*

Wheel lug nuts . . . .   80 to 105
Spark plugs . . . .   6 to 10
Oil pan drain plug . . . .   15 to 25
Engine block drain plug . . . .   5 to 8
Carburetor-mounted fuel filter . . . .   7 to 9
Front hub adjusting nut
    Step 1 . . . .   17 to 25
    Step 2 . . . .   back off 1/2 turn
    Step 3 . . . .   10 to 15 *in-lbs*
Automatic transmission pan bolts . . . .   8 to 10

1 Introduction

This Chapter is designed to help the home mechanic maintain the Ford Aerostar with the goals of maximum performance, economy, safety and reliability in mind.

Included is a master maintenance schedule (page 30), followed by procedures dealing specifically with each item on the schedule. Visual checks, adjustments, component replacement and other helpful items are included. Refer to the accompanying illustrations of the engine compartment and the underside of the vehicle for the locations of various components.

Servicing your vehicle in accordance with the mileage/time maintenance schedule and the step-by-step procedures will result in a planned maintenance program that should produce a long and reliable service life. Keep in mind that it is a comprehensive plan, so maintaining some items but not others at the specified intervals will not produce the same results.

As you service your vehicle, you will discover that many of the procedures can — and should — be grouped together because of the nature of the particular procedure you're performing or because of the proximity of two otherwise unrelated components to one another.

For example, if the vehicle is raised for chassis lubrication, you should inspect the exhaust, suspension, steering and fuel systems while you're under the vehicle. When you're rotating the tires, it makes good sense to check the brakes since the wheels are already removed. Finally, let's suppose you have to borrow or rent a torque wrench. Even if you only need it to tighten the spark plugs, you might as well check the torque of as many critical fasteners as time allows.

The first step in this maintenance program is to prepare yourself before the actual work begins. Read through all the procedures you're planning to do, then gather up all the parts and tools needed. If it looks like you might run into problems during a particular job, seek advice from a mechanic or an experienced do-it-yourselfer.

2 Ford Aerostar Maintenance schedule

The following maintenance intervals are based on the assumption that the vehicle owner will be doing the maintenance or service work, as opposed to having a dealer service department do the work. Although the time/mileage intervals are loosely based on factory recommendations, most have been shortened to ensure, for example, that such items as lubricants and fluids are checked/changed at intervals that promote maximum engine/driveline service life. Also, subject to the preference of the individual owner interested in keeping his or her vehicle in peak condition at all times, and with the vehicle's ultimate resale in mind, many of the maintenance procedures may be performed more often than recommended in the following schedule. We encourage such owner initiative.

When the vehicle is new it should be serviced initially by a factory authorized dealer service department to protect the factory warranty. In many cases the initial maintenance check is done at no cost to the owner.

Every 250 miles or weekly, whichever comes first

Check the engine oil level (Section 4)
Check the engine coolant level (Section 4)
Check the windshield washer fluid level (Section 4)
Check the brake and clutch fluid levels (Section 4)
Check the tires and tire pressures (Section 5)

Every 3000 miles or 3 months, whichever comes first

All items listed above plus . . .
Check the power steering fluid level (Section 6)
Check the automatic transmission fluid
   level (Section 7)
Change the engine oil and oil filter (Section 8)

Every 6000 miles or 6 months, whichever comes first

All items listed above plus . . .
Inspect/replace the underhood hoses (Section 9)
Check/adjust the drivebelts (Section 10)
Check/service the battery (Section 11)
Check/regap the spark plugs (Section 26)

Every 12,000 miles or 12 months, whichever comes first

All items listed above plus . . .
Inspect/replace the windshield wiper
   blades (Section 12)
Replace the air filter (Section 13)
Check the PCV valve and filter (Section 14)
Check the fuel system (Section 15)
Replace the fuel filter (Section 16)
Inspect the cooling system (Section 17)
Inspect the exhaust system (Section 18)
Rotate the tires (Section 19)
Inspect the steering and suspension
   components (Section 20)
Inspect the brakes (Section 21)
Lubricate the parking brake cable (Section 21)
Lubricate the automatic transmission control
   linkage (Section 22)
Check/replenish the manual transmission
   lubricant (Section 23)
Check the front wheel bearings (Section 24)
Check the rear axle (differential) oil
   level (Section 25)
Replace the spark plugs (Section 26)

Every 24,000 miles or 24 months, whichever comes first

Check/replace the spark plug wires, distributor cap
   and rotor (Section 27)
Change the automatic transmission fluid and
   filter (Section 28)
Check the choke and lubricate the
   linkage (Section 29)
Service the cooling system (drain, flush and
   refill) (Section 30)

Every 30,000 miles or 30 months, whichever comes first

Lubricate the chassis components (Section 31)
Change the rear axle (differential) oil (Section 32)

COAT GASKET WITH ENGINE OIL

FL-1A

OIL FILTER

AIR FILTER

DISTRIBUTOR

BRAKE MASTER CYLINDER

CLUTCH MASTER CYLINDER (REMOVE DIAPHRAGM-INSERT BEFORE FILLING)

POWER STEERING PUMP DIPSTICK FLUID SHOULD BE IN THE FULL COLD OR FULL HOT RANGE, DEPENDING ON TEMPERATURE

BATTERY

AUTOMATIC TRANSMISSION FLUID LEVEL DIPSTICK CHECK WITH ENGINE RUNNING AND TRANSMISSION IN PARK.

ENGINE OIL FILLER CAP

WINDSHIELD WASHER RESERVOIR

COOLANT RECOVERY RESERVOIR

ENGINE OIL LEVEL DIPSTICK

RADIATOR COOLANT LEVEL

Engine compartment component layout — four-cylinder engine

RADIATOR COOLANT LEVEL

BATTERY

COOLANT EXPANSION RESERVOIR

AIR FILTER

WINDSHIELD WASHER RESERVOIR

POWER STEERING PUMP DIPSTICK FLUID SHOULD BE BETWEEN FULL COLD AND FULL HOT MARKS, DEPENDING ON TEMPERATURE

FUEL FILTER

PCV VALVE

OIL FILTER

Motorcraft
FL-1A

CLUTCH FLUID RESERVOIR-CHECK FLUID LEVEL (REMOVE DIAPHRAGM-INSERT BEFORE FILLING)

COAT GASKET WITH ENGINE OIL

ENGINE OIL LEVEL DIPSTICK

ENGINE OIL FILLER CAP

DISTRIBUTOR

BRAKE MASTER CYLINDER-CHECK FLUID LEVEL

AUTOMATIC TRANSMISSION FLUID LEVEL DIPSTICK CHECK WITH ENGINE RUNNING AND TRANSMISSION IN PARK.

Engine compartment component layout — 2.8 liter V6 engine

Engine compartment component layout — 3.0 liter V6 engine

3   Tune-up general information

The term *tune-up* is used in this manual to represent a combination of individual operations rather than one specific procedure.

If, from the time the vehicle is new, the routine maintenance schedule is followed closely and frequent checks are made of fluid levels and high wear items, as suggested throughout this manual, the engine will be kept in relatively good running condition and the need for additional work will be minimized.

More likely than not, however, there will be times when the engine is running poorly due to lack of regular maintenance. This is even more likely if a used vehicle, which has not received regular and frequent maintenance checks, is purchased. In such cases, an engine tune-up will be needed outside of the regular routine maintenance intervals.

The first step in any tune-up or diagnostic procedure to help correct a poor running engine is a cylinder compression check. A compression check (see Chapter 2 Part C) will help determine the condition of internal engine components and should be used as a guide for tune-up and repair procedures. If, for instance, a compression check indicates serious internal engine wear, a conventional tune-up will not improve the performance of the engine and would be a waste of time and money. Because of its importance, the compression check should be done by someone with the right equipment and the knowledge to use it properly.

The following procedures are those most often needed to bring a generally poor running engine back into a proper state of tune.

Minor tune-up

Check all engine related fluids (Section 4)
Check all underhood hoses (Section 9)
Check and adjust the drivebelts (Section 10)
Clean, inspect and test the battery (Section 11)
Check the air filter (Section 13)
Check the PCV valve (Section 14)
Check the cooling system (Section 17)
Replace the spark plugs (Section 26)
Inspect the distributor cap and rotor (Section 27)
Inspect the spark plug and coil wires (Section 27)
Check and adjust the idle speed (Chapter 4)

Major tune-up

All items listed under Minor tune-up plus . . .
Check the EGR system (Chapter 6)
Check the ignition system (Chapter 5)
Check the charging system (Chapter 5)
Replace the air and PCV filters (Sections 13 and 14)
Check the fuel system (Section 15)
Replace the distributor cap and rotor (Section 27)
Replace the spark plug wires (Section 27)

4   Fluid level checks

Note: *The following are fluid level checks to be done on a 250 mile or weekly basis. Additional fluid level checks can be found in specific maintenance procedures which follow. Regardless of intervals, be alert to fluid leaks under the vehicle which would indicate a fault to be corrected immediately.*

1   Fluids are an essential part of the lubrication, cooling, brake, clutch

Underside view of engine/transmission (2.8 liter V6 engine shown)

1 Automatic transmission
  fluid pan
2 Engine oil filter
3 Engine oil drain plug
4 Steering gear boot
5 Drivebelt
6 Power steering system hoses
7 Radiator drain fitting
8 Lower radiator hose
9 Fuel lines
10 Exhaust pipe
11 Transmission shift linkage

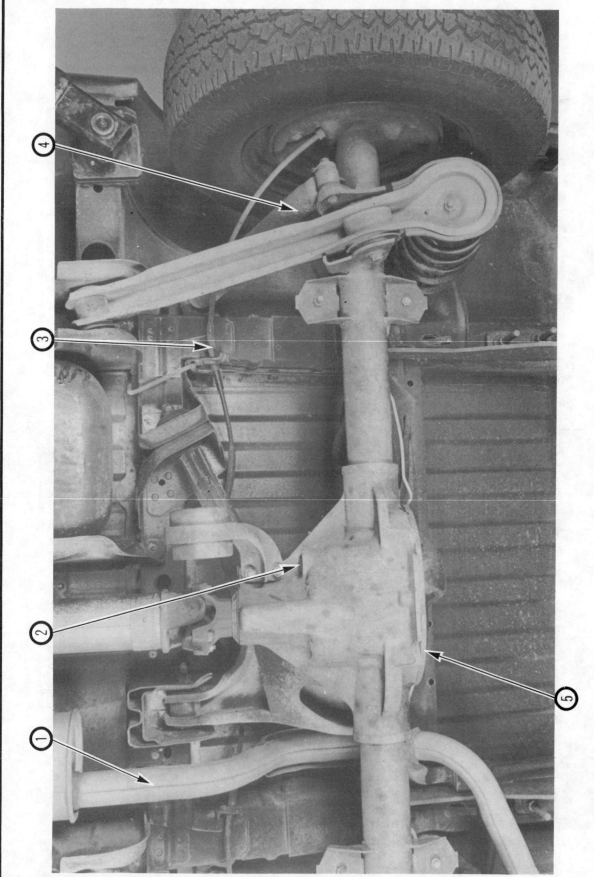

Typical rear underside component layout

1 Exhaust pipe
2 Differential oil check/fill plug
3 Parking brake cable
4 Rear shock absorber
5 Differential cover

4.2   The engine oil dipstick is located on the left (driver's) side of the engine on most models (2.8L V6 shown)

4.4   The oil level should be in the crosshatched area — if it's below the ADD line, add enough oil to bring the level into the crosshatched area (DO NOT add oil if the level is at the MAX line!)

4.6a   Oil is added to the engine through the tube near the dipstick (use a funnel to prevent spills)

4.6b   The engine oil filler tube cap is clearly marked to avoid any possibility of confusion!

and windshield washer systems. Because the fluids gradually become depleted and/or contaminated during normal operation of the vehicle, they must be periodically replenished. See *Recommended lubricants and fluids* at the beginning of this Chapter before adding fluid to any of the following components. **Note:** *The vehicle must be on level ground when fluid levels are checked.*

Engine oil

Refer to illustrations 4.2, 4.4, 4.6a and 4.6b

2   The engine oil level is checked with a dipstick **(see illustration)** that extends through a tube and into the oil pan at the bottom of the engine.

3   The oil level should be checked before the vehicle has been driven, or about 15 minutes after the engine has been shut off. If the oil is checked immediately after driving the vehicle, some of the oil will remain in the upper engine components, resulting in an inaccurate reading on the dipstick.

4   Pull the dipstick from the tube and wipe all the oil from the end with a clean rag or paper towel. Insert the clean dipstick all the way back into the tube, then pull it out again. Note the oil at the end of the dipstick. Add oil as necessary to keep the level between the ADD mark and the MAX mark on the dipstick, in the crosshatched area **(see illustration)**.

5   Don't overfill the engine by adding too much oil — it may result in oil fouled spark plugs, oil leaks or oil seal failures.

6   Oil is added to the engine after removing the filler cap **(see illustrations)**. An oil can spout or funnel may help to reduce spills.

7   Checking the oil level is an important preventive maintenance step. A consistently low oil level indicates oil leakage through damaged seals, defective gaskets or past worn rings or valve guides. If the oil looks milky in color or has water droplets in it, the cylinder head gasket(s) may be blown or the head(s) or block may be cracked. The engine should be checked immediately. The condition of the oil should also be checked. Whenever you check the oil level, slide your thumb and index finger up the dipstick before wiping off the oil. If you see small dirt or metal particles clinging to the dipstick, the oil should be changed (Section 8).

Engine coolant

Refer to illustration 4.9

Warning: *Don't allow antifreeze to come in contact with your skin or painted surfaces of the vehicle. Flush contaminated areas immediately with plenty of water. Don't store new coolant or leave old coolant lying around where it's accessible to children or pets — they're attracted by its sweet taste. Ingestion of even a small amount of coolant can be fatal! Wipe up garage floor and drip pan coolant spills immediately. Keep antifreeze containers covered and repair leaks in your cooling system as soon as they're discovered.*

8   All vehicles covered by this manual are equipped with a combined

windshield washer/coolant recovery reservoir located in the left front corner of the engine compartment. The coolant side of the reservoir is connected by a hose to the radiator filler neck. If the engine overheats, coolant escapes through a valve in the radiator cap and travels through the hose into the reservoir. As the engine cools, the coolant is automatically drawn back into the system to maintain the correct level.
9   The coolant level in the reservoir should be checked regularly. **Warning:** *Do not remove the radiator cap to check the coolant level when the engine is warm!* The level in the reservoir varies with the temperature of the engine. When the engine is cold, the coolant level should be at or slightly above the COLD mark on the reservoir. Once the engine has warmed up, the level should be at or near the HOT mark. If it isn't, allow the engine to cool, then remove the small cap from the reservoir and add a 50/50 mixture of ethylene glycol-based antifreeze and water **(see illustration)**. **Caution:** *Do not add coolant to the windshield washer reservoir!*

4.9   The combined windshield washer/coolant reservoir used on these models features separate tanks for each fluid — DO NOT add engine coolant to the windshield washer reservoir!

10   Drive the vehicle and recheck the coolant level. If only a small amount of coolant is required to bring the system up to the proper level, water can be used. However, repeated additions of water will dilute the antifreeze and water solution. In order to maintain the proper ratio of antifreeze and water, always top up the coolant level with the correct mixture. An empty plastic milk jug or bleach bottle makes an excellent container for mixing coolant. Don't use rust inhibitors or additives.
11   If the coolant level drops consistently, there may be a leak in the system. Inspect the radiator, hoses, filler cap, drain plugs and water pump (see Section 17). If no leaks are noted, have the radiator cap pressure tested by a service station.
12   If you have to remove the radiator cap, wait until the engine has cooled, then wrap a thick cloth around the cap and turn it to the first stop. If coolant or steam escapes, let the engine cool down longer, then remove the cap.
13   Check the condition of the coolant as well. It should be relatively clear. If it's brown or rust colored, the system should be drained, flushed and refilled. Even if the coolant appears to be normal, the corrosion inhibitors wear out, so it must be replaced at the specified intervals.

Windshield washer fluid
Refer to illustration 4.14
14   Fluid for the windshield washer system is located in a plastic reservoir in the engine compartment **(see illustration)**.

4.14   The windshield washer reservoir cap is clearly marked (it's also the larger of the two reservoir caps)

15   In milder climates, plain water can be used in the reservoir, but it should be kept no more than 2/3 full to allow for expansion if the water freezes. In colder climates, use windshield washer system antifreeze, available at any auto parts store, to lower the freezing point of the fluid. Mix the antifreeze with water in accordance with the manufacturer's directions on the container. **Caution:** *Don't use cooling system antifreeze — it will damage the vehicle's paint!*
16   To help prevent icing in cold weather, warm the windshield with the defroster before using the washer.

Battery electrolyte
17   All vehicles with which this manual is concerned are equipped with a battery which is permanently sealed (except for vent holes) and has no filler caps. Water doesn't have to be added to these batteries at any time. If an aftermarket battery has been installed, the caps on the top of the battery should be removed periodically to check for a low water level. This check is most critical during the warm summer months.

Brake and clutch fluid
Refer to illustrations 4.18 and 4.19
18   The brake master cylinder is mounted on the front of the power booster unit in the engine compartment. The clutch fluid reservoir used on manual transmissions is mounted to the left of the brake booster, on the inner fender panel **(see illustration)**. To check the fluid level, unscrew the cap and remove the rubber insert. The fluid level should be even with the step on the side of the reservoir.
19   The fluid inside the brake reservoir is readily visible. The level should be above the MIN mark on the reservoir **(see illustration)**. If a low level is indicated, be sure to wipe the top of the reservoir with a clean rag to prevent contamination of the brake system before removing the cap.
20   When adding fluid, pour it carefully into the reservoir to avoid spilling it onto surrounding painted surfaces. Be sure the specified fluid

4.18   Clutch fluid reservoir location — the level should be kept even with the step inside the reservoir

is used, since mixing different types of brake fluid can cause damage to the system. See *Recommended lubricants and fluids* at the front of this Chapter or your owner's manual. **Warning:** *Brake fluid can harm your eyes and damage painted surfaces, so use extreme caution when handling or pouring it. Do not use brake fluid that has been standing open or is more than one year old. Brake fluid absorbs moisture from the air. Excess moisture can cause a dangerous loss of braking effectiveness.*

21   At this time the fluid and master cylinder can be inspected for contamination. The system should be drained and refilled if deposits, dirt particles or water droplets are seen in the fluid.

22   After filling the reservoir to the proper level, make sure the cover is on tight to prevent fluid leakage.

23   The brake fluid level in the master cylinder will drop slightly as the pads and the brake shoes at each wheel wear down during normal operation. If the master cylinder requires repeated additions to keep it at the proper level, it's an indication of leakage in the brake system, which should be corrected immediately. Check all brake lines and connections (see Section 21 for more information).

24   If you discover the reservoir empty or nearly empty, the brake system should be bled (Chapter 9).

5   Tire and tire pressure checks

Refer to illustrations 5.2, 5.3, 5.4a, 5.4b and 5.8

1   Periodic inspection of the tires may spare you the inconvenience of being stranded with a flat tire. It can also provide you with vital information regarding possible problems in the steering and suspension systems before major damage occurs.

2   The original tires on this vehicle are equipped with 1/2-inch wear bands that will appear when tread depth reaches 1/16-inch, but they don't appear until the tires are worn out. Tread wear can be monitored with a simple, inexpensive device known as a tread depth indicator **(see illustration)**.

3   Note any abnormal tread wear **(see illustration)**. Tread pattern irregularities such as cupping, flat spots and more wear on one side than

4.19   The brake fluid level should be kept just above the rib on the translucent plastic reservoir (arrow)

5.2   A tire tread depth indicator should be used to monitor tire wear — they're available at auto parts stores and service stations and cost very little

Condition	Probable cause	Corrective action	Condition	Probable cause	Corrective action
Shoulder wear	• Underinflation (both sides wear) • Incorrect wheel camber (one side wear) • Hard cornering • Lack of rotation	• Measure and adjust pressure. • Repair or replace axle and suspension parts. • Reduce speed. • Rotate tires.	Feathered edge Toe wear	• Incorrect toe	• Adjust toe-in.
Center wear	• Overinflation • Lack of rotation	• Measure and adjust pressure. • Rotate tires.	Uneven wear	• Incorrect camber or caster • Malfunctioning suspension • Unbalanced wheel • Out-of-round brake drum • Lack of rotation	• Repair or replace axle and suspension parts. • Repair or replace suspension parts. • Balance or replace. • Turn or replace. • Rotate tires.

5.3   This chart will help you determine the condition of your tires, the probable cause(s) of abnormal wear and the corrective action necessary

5.4a   If a tire loses air on a steady basis, check the valve
core first to make sure it's snug (special inexpensive
wrenches are commonly available at auto parts stores)

5.4b   If the valve core is tight, raise the corner of the
vehicle with the low tire and spray a soapy water solution
on the tread as the tire is slowly turned — leaks will cause
small bubbles to appear

the other are indications of front end alignment and/or balance problems. If any of these conditions are noted, take the vehicle to a tire shop or service station to correct the problem.

4   Look closely for cuts, punctures and embedded nails or tacks. Sometimes a tire will hold air pressure for a short time or leak down very slowly after a nail has embedded itself in the tread. If a slow leak persists, check the valve stem core to make sure it is tight **(see illustration)**. Examine the tread for an object that may have embedded itself in the tire or for a "plug" that may have begun to leak (radial tire punctures are repaired with a plug that's installed in a puncture). If a puncture is suspected, it can be easily verified by spraying a solution of soapy water on the tire **(see illustration)**. The soapy solution will bubble if there is a leak. Unless the puncture is unusually large, a tire shop or service station can usually repair the tire.

5.8   To extend the life of your tires, check the air pressure
at least once a week with an accurate gauge (don't forget
the spare!)

5   Carefully inspect the inner sidewall of each tire for evidence of brake fluid leakage. If you see any, inspect the brakes immediately.

6   Correct air pressure adds miles to the lifespan of the tires, improves mileage and enhances overall ride quality. Tire pressure cannot be accurately estimated by looking at a tire, especially if it's a radial. A tire pressure gauge is essential. Keep an accurate gauge in the glovebox. The pressure gauges attached to the nozzles of air hoses at gas stations are often inaccurate.

7   Always check tire pressure when the tires are cold. Cold, in this case, means the vehicle has not been driven over a mile in the three hours preceding a tire pressure check. A pressure rise of four to eight pounds is not uncommon once the tires are warm.

8   Unscrew the valve cap protruding from the wheel or hubcap and push the gauge firmly onto the valve stem **(see illustration)**. Note the reading on the gauge and compare the figure to the recommended tire pressure shown on the tire placard on the driver's side door. Be sure to reinstall the valve cap to keep dirt and moisture out of the valve stem mechanism. Check all four tires and, if necessary, add enough air to bring them up to the recommended pressure.

9   Don't forget to keep the spare tire inflated to the specified pressure (refer to your owner's manual or the tire sidewall). Note that the pressure recommended for the compact spare is higher than for the tires on the vehicle.

---

6   Power steering fluid level check

Refer to illustration 6.5

1   Check the power steering fluid level periodically to avoid steering system problems, such as damage to the pump. **Caution:** *DO NOT hold the steering wheel against either stop (extreme left or right turn) for more than five seconds. If you do, the power steering pump could be damaged!*

2   The power steering pump, located at the front of the engine, is equipped with a twist-off cap with an integral fluid level dipstick (see the engine compartment component illustrations at the front of this Chapter if necessary).

3   Park the vehicle on level ground and apply the parking brake.

4   Run the engine until it reaches normal operating temperature. With the engine at idle, turn the steering wheel back-and-forth several times to get any air out of the steering system. Shut the engine off, remove the cap by turning it counterclockwise, wipe the dipstick clean and reinstall the cap.

6.5 Once the engine is warmed up and the wheel has been turned back-and-forth a few times to rid the system of air, pull the dipstick out and wipe it off, reinsert it and verify that the fluid level is in the FULL HOT range (be sure to use the proper range, one side is for checking the fluid cold) — if it isn't, add enough fluid to bring the level between the two lines

5   Remove the cap again and note the fluid level. It must be between the two lines designating the Full Hot range **(see illustration)** (be sure to use the proper temperature range on the dipstick when checking the fluid level — the Full Cold lines on the reverse side of the dipstick are only usable when the engine is cold).
6   Add small amounts of fluid until the level is correct. **Caution:** *Do not overfill the pump. If too much fluid is added, remove the excess with a clean syringe or suction pump.*
7   Check the power steering hoses and connections for leaks and wear (see Section 9).
8   Check the condition and tension of the power steering pump drivebelt (see Section 10).

7   Automatic transmission fluid level check

Refer to illustrations 7.4 and 7.6

1   The automatic transmission fluid level should be carefully maintained. Low fluid level can lead to slipping or loss of drive, while overfilling can cause foaming and loss of fluid. Either condition can cause transmission damage.
2   Since transmission fluid expands as it heats up, the fluid level should only be checked when the transmission is warm (at normal operating temperature). If the vehicle has just been driven over 20 miles (32 km), the transmission can be considered warm. **Caution:** *If the vehicle has just been driven for a long time at high speed or in city traffic in hot weather, or if it's been pulling a trailer, an accurate fluid level reading cannot be obtained. Allow the transmission to cool down for about 30 minutes.* You can also check the transmission fluid level when the transmission is cold. If the vehicle hasn't been driven for over five hours and the fluid is about room temperature (70 to 95°F), the transmission is cold. However, the fluid level is normally checked with the transmission warm to ensure accurate results.
3   Immediately after driving the vehicle, park it on a level surface, apply the parking brake and start the engine. While the engine is idling, depress the brake pedal and move the selector lever through all the gear ranges, beginning and ending in Park.
4   Locate the automatic transmission dipstick tube at the front of the engine compartment **(see illustration)**.
5   With the engine still idling, pull the dipstick out of the tube, wipe it off with a clean rag, push it all the way back into the tube and withdraw it again, then note the fluid level.
6   If the transmission is cold, the level should be in the room temperature range on the dipstick (between the two circles); if it's warm, the fluid level should be in the operating temperature range (between the two lines) **(see illustration)**. If the level is low, add the specified automatic transmission fluid through the dipstick tube — use a funnel to prevent spills.

7.4 The automatic transmission fluid dipstick (arrow) is accessible from under the hood — it's routed through a long tube to the transmission

7.6 If the automatic transmission fluid is cold, the level should be between the two circles; if it's at operating temperature, the level should be between the two lines

7   Add just enough of the recommended fluid to fill the transmission to the proper level. Add the fluid a little at a time and keep checking the level until it's correct.
8   The condition of the fluid should also be checked along with the level. If the fluid is black or a dark reddish-brown color, or if it smells burned, it should be changed (Section 28). If you're in doubt about its condition, purchase some new fluid and compare the two for color and smell.

8   Engine oil and filter change

Refer to illustrations 8.3, 8.9, 8.14 and 8.18

1   Frequent oil changes are the most important preventive maintenance procedure that can be done by the home mechanic. As engine oil ages, it becomes diluted and contaminated, which leads to premature engine wear.
2   Although some sources recommend oil filter changes every other oil change, the minimal cost of an oil filter and the fact that it's not hard to change dictate that a new filter be used every time the oil is changed.

8.9   Use a socket or box-end wrench to remove the engine oil drain plug — DO NOT use an open-end wrench, as the corners on the plug head can be easily rounded off!

8.3   These tools are required when changing the engine oil and filter

1   **Drain pan** — *It should be fairly shallow in depth, but wide in order to prevent spills*
2   **Rubber gloves** — *When removing the drain plug and filter it is inevitable that you will get oil on your hands (the gloves will prevent burns)*
3   **Breaker bar** — *Sometimes the oil drain plug is pretty tight and a long breaker bar is needed to loosen it*
4   **Socket** — *To be used with the breaker bar or a ratchet (must be the correct size to fit the drain plug)*
5   **Filter wrench** — *This is a metal band-type wrench, which requires clearance around the filter to be effective*
6   **Filter wrench** — *This type fits on the bottom of the filter and can be turned with a ratchet or breaker bar (different size wrenches are available for different types of filters)*

3   Gather together all necessary tools and materials before beginning this procedure (**see illustration**).
4   You should have plenty of clean rags and newspapers handy to mop up any spills. Access to the underside of the vehicle is greatly improved if the vehicle can be lifted on a hoist, driven onto ramps or supported by jackstands. **Warning:** *Do not work under a vehicle which is supported only by a bumper, hydraulic or scissors-type jack!*
5   If this is your first oil change, get under the vehicle and familiarize yourself with the locations of the oil drain plug and the oil filter. The engine and exhaust components will be warm during the actual work, so note how they are situated to avoid touching them when working under the vehicle.
6   Warm the engine to normal operating temperature. If the new oil or any tools are needed, use this warm-up time to gather everything necessary for the job. The correct type of oil for your application can be found in *Recommended lubricants and fluids* at the beginning of this Chapter.
7   With the engine oil warm (warm engine oil will drain better and

more built-up sludge will be removed with it), raise and support the vehicle — make sure it's safely supported!
8   Move all necessary tools, rags and newspapers under the vehicle. Set the drain pan under the drain plug. Keep in mind that the oil will initially flow from the pan with some force; position the pan accordingly.
9   Being careful not to touch any of the hot exhaust components, use a wrench to remove the drain plug near the bottom of the oil pan (**see illustration**). Depending on how hot the oil is, you may want to wear gloves while unscrewing the plug the final few turns.
10   Allow the old oil to drain into the pan. It may be necessary to move the pan as the oil flow slows to a trickle.
11   After all the oil has drained, wipe off the drain plug with a clean rag. Small metal particles may cling to the plug and would immediately contaminate the new oil.
12   Clean the area around the drain plug opening and reinstall the plug. Tighten the plug securely with the wrench. If a torque wrench is available, use it to tighten the plug.
13   Move the drain pan into position under the oil filter.
14   Use the filter wrench to loosen the oil filter (**see illustration**). Chain or metal band filter wrenches may distort the filter canister, but it doesn't matter since the filter will be discarded anyway.
15   Completely unscrew the old filter. Be careful; it's full of oil. Empty the oil inside the filter into the drain pan.
16   Compare the old filter with the new one to make sure they're the same type.
17   Use a clean rag to remove all oil, dirt and sludge from the area where the oil filter mounts to the engine. Check the old filter to make sure the rubber gasket isn't stuck to the engine. If the gasket is stuck to the engine, remove it.
18   Apply a light coat of clean oil to the rubber gasket on the new oil filter (**see illustration**).
19   Attach the new filter to the engine. Overtightening the filter will damage the gasket, so don't use a filter wrench. Most filter manufacturers recommend tightening the filter by hand only. Normally they should be tightened 3/4-turn after the gasket contacts the block, but be sure to follow the directions on the filter or container.
20   Remove all tools, rags, etc. from under the vehicle, being careful not to spill the oil in the drain pan, then lower the vehicle.
21   Move to the engine compartment and locate the oil filler cap.
22   If an oil can spout is used, push the spout into the top of the oil can and pour the fresh oil through the filler opening. A funnel may also be used.
23   Pour four quarts of fresh oil into the engine. Wait a few minutes to allow the oil to drain into the pan, then check the level on the oil dipstick (see Section 4 if necessary). If the oil level is above the ADD

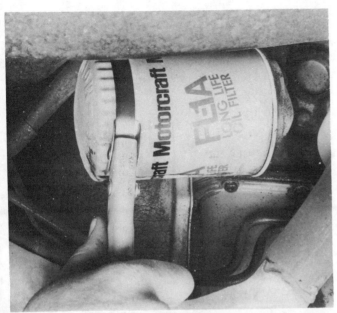

8.14 The oil filter is usually on very tight and will require a special wrench for removal — DO NOT use the wrench to tighten the new filter

8.18 Lubricate the gasket with clean engine oil before installing the filter on the engine

mark, start the engine and allow the new oil to circulate.

24 Run the engine for only about a minute and then shut it off. Immediately look under the vehicle and check for leaks at the oil pan drain plug and around the oil filter. If either is leaking, tighten with a bit more force.

25 With the new oil circulated and the filter now completely full, recheck the level on the dipstick and add more oil as necessary.

26 During the first few trips after an oil change, make it a point to check frequently for leaks and proper oil level.

27 The old oil drained from the engine cannot be reused in its present state and should be disposed of. Oil reclamation centers, auto repair shops and gas stations will normally accept the oil, which can be refined and used again. After the oil has cooled it can be drained into a suitable container (capped plastic jugs, topped bottles, milk cartons, etc.) for transport to one of these disposal sites.

9   Underhood hose check and replacement

Caution: *Replacement of air conditioning hoses must be left to a dealer service department or air conditioning shop that has the equipment to depressurize the system safely. Never remove air conditioning components or hoses until the system has been depressurized.*

General

1   High temperatures in the engine compartment can cause the deterioration of the rubber and plastic hoses used for engine, accessory and emission systems operation. Periodic inspection should be made for cracks, loose clamps, material hardening and leaks.

2   Information specific to the cooling system hoses can be found in Section 9.

3   Some, but not all, hoses are secured to the fittings with clamps. Where clamps are used, check to be sure they haven't lost their tension, allowing the hose to leak. If clamps aren't used, make sure the hose has not expanded and/or hardened where it slips over the fitting, allowing it to leak.

Vacuum hoses

4   It's quite common for vacuum hoses, especially those in the emissions system, to be color coded or identified by colored stripes molded into them. Various systems require hoses with different wall thicknesses, collapse resistance and temperature resistance. When replacing hoses, be sure the new ones are made of the same material.

5   Often the only effective way to check a hose is to remove it completely from the vehicle. If more than one hose is removed, be sure

to label the hoses and fittings to ensure correct installation.

6   When checking vacuum hoses, be sure to include any plastic T-fittings in the check. Inspect the fittings for cracks and the hose where it fits over the fitting for distortion, which could cause leakage.

7   A small piece of vacuum hose (1/4-inch inside diameter) can be used as a stethoscope to detect vacuum leaks. Hold one end of the hose to your ear and probe around vacuum hoses and fittings, listening for the ''hissing'' sound characteristic of a vacuum leak. **Warning:** *When probing with the vacuum hose stethoscope, be very careful not to come into contact with moving engine components such as the drivebelts, cooling fan, etc.*

Fuel hose

Warning: *There are certain precautions which must be taken when inspecting or servicing fuel system components. Work in a well ventilated area and do not allow open flames (cigarettes, appliance pilot lights, etc.) or bare light bulbs near the work area. Mop up any spills immediately and do not store fuel soaked rags where they could ignite. On vehicles equipped with fuel injection, the fuel system is under pressure, so if any fuel lines are to be disconnected, the pressure in the system must be relieved first (see Chapter 4 for more information).*

8   Check all rubber fuel lines for deterioration and chafing. Check especially for cracks in areas where the hose bends and just before fittings, such as where a hose attaches to the fuel filter.

9   High quality fuel line, usually identified by the word *Fluroelastomer* printed on the hose, should be used for fuel line replacement. Never, under any circumstances, use unreinforced vacuum line, clear plastic tubing or water hose for fuel lines.

10 Spring-type clamps are commonly used on fuel lines. These clamps often lose their tension over a period of time, and can be ''sprung'' during removal. Replace all spring-type clamps with screw clamps whenever a hose is replaced.

Metal lines

11 Sections of metal line are often used for fuel line between the fuel pump and carburetor or fuel injection unit. Check carefully to be sure the line has not been bent or crimped and that cracks have not started in the line.

12 If a section of metal fuel line must be replaced, only seamless steel tubing should be used, since copper and aluminum tubing don't have the strength necessary to withstand normal engine vibration.

13 Check the metal brake lines where they enter the master cylinder and brake proportioning unit (if used) for cracks in the lines or loose fittings. Any sign of brake fluid leakage calls for an immediate thorough inspection of the brake system.

10.2   Different types of drivebelts are used to power the various accessories mounted on the engine

10.3   Here are some of the common problems associated with drivebelts (check the belts very carefully to prevent an untimely breakdown)

10.4a   A drivebelt tension gauge is recommended for checking the belts on V6 engines

10.4b   On later model four-cylinder engines, the drivebelts are automatically tensioned and require no service as long as they're in good condition and the wear indicator on the tensioner is between the MIN and MAX lines

10   Drivebelt check, adjustment and replacement

Refer to illustrations 10.2, 10.3, 10.4a, 10.4b, 10.5, 10.6 and 10.13

1   The accessory drivebelts, also referred to as V-belts or simply fan belts, are located at the front of the engine. The condition and tension of the drivebelts are critical to the operation of the engine and accessories. Excessive tension causes bearing wear, while insufficient tension produces slippage, noise, component vibration and belt failure. Because of their composition and the high stresses to which they are subjected, drivebelts stretch and deteriorate as they get older. As a result, they must be periodically checked and adjusted.

Check

2   The number and type of belts used on a particular vehicle depends on the accessories installed. Various types of drivebelts are used on these models **(see illustration)**. V-ribbed belts are often referred to as *serpentine* belts because of the winding path they follow between various drive, accessory and idler pulleys.
3   With the engine off, open the hood and locate the drivebelts. Using a flashlight, check each belt for separation of the rubber plies from each side of the core, a severed core, separation of the ribs from the rubber, cracks, torn or worn ribs and cracks in the inner ridges of the ribs. Also check for fraying and glazing, which gives the belt a shiny appearance **(see illustration)**. Both sides of each belt should be inspected, which means you'll have to twist them to check the undersides. Use your fingers to feel a belt where you can't see it. If any of the above conditions are evident, replace the belt as described below.
4   To check the tension of each belt in accordance with factory recommendations, install a drivebelt tension gauge (special tool no. T63L-8620-A) **(see illustration)**. Measure the tension in accordance with the tension gauge instructions and compare your measurement

to the specified drivebelt tension for either a used or new belt. **Note:** *A ''new'' belt is defined as any belt which has not been run; a ''used'' belt is one that has been run for more than ten minutes.* Some later four-cylinder engines are equipped with an automatic tensioner which requires only that the wear indicator remain between the MIN and MAX lines on the tensioner **(see illustration)**. If the belt is damaged or the indicator is not between the lines, the belt should be replaced. This job should be done by a dealer service department because the tensioner is spring loaded.
5   The special gauge is the most accurate way to check belt tension. However, if you don't have a gauge, and cannot borrow one, the following ''rule-of-thumb'' method is recommended as an alternative. Lay a straightedge across the longest free span (the distance between two

10.5   Measuring drivebelt deflection with a straightedge and ruler

ALTERNATOR BELT
ADJUSTING
ARM

AIR
CONDITIONING

EXHAUST AIR
SUPPLY PUMP
SUPPORT

ALTERNATOR

ALTERNATOR
BRACE

BOLT

ALTERNATOR
MOUNTING
BRACKET

EXHAUST AIR
SUPPLY PUMP

POWER
STEERING

WATER PUMP
PULLEY ASSEMBLY

DRIVE
BELT

IDLER

CRANKSHAFT
PULLEY ASSEMBLY

BOLT

10.6 Typical drivebelt layout

pulleys) of the belt. Push down firmly on the belt at a point half way between the pulleys and see how much the belt moves (deflects). Measure the deflection with a ruler **(see illustration)**. The belt should deflect 1/8 to 1/4-inch if the distance from pulley center-to-pulley center is less than 12-inches; it should deflect from 1/8 to 3/8-inch if the distance from pulley center-to-pulley center is over 12-inches.

Adjustment

6   If adjustment is required to make the drivebelt tighter or looser, it's done by moving the belt driven accessory on the bracket **(see illustration)**.
7   For each component, there will be a locking bolt and pivot bolt or nut. Both must be loosened slightly to enable you to move the component.
8   After the bolts have been loosened, move the component away from the engine to tighten the belt or toward the engine to loosen the belt. Hold the accessory in position and check the belt tension. If it's correct, tighten the two bolts until snug, then recheck the tension. If it's still correct, tighten the two bolts completely.
9   To adjust the drivebelt on some components, loosen the pivot nut and the locking screw or locknut, then turn the adjusting screw to tension the belt.
10   It will often be necessary to use some sort of pry bar to move the accessory while the belt is adjusted. If this must be done to gain the proper leverage, be very careful not to damage the component being moved, or the part being pried against.
11   Run the engine for about 15 minutes, then recheck the belt tension.

Replacement

12   To replace a belt, follow the above procedures for drivebelt adjustment but slip the belt off the pulleys and remove it. If you're replacing the water pump, air pump or alternator drivebelts, the power steering pump/air conditioning compressor belt must come off first. Since belts tend to wear out more or less at the same time, it's a good idea to replace all of them at the same time. Mark each belt and the corresponding pulley grooves so the replacement belts can be installed properly.
13   Take the old belts with you when purchasing new ones in order to make a direct comparison for length, width and design. When replac-

BELT

BELT

PULLEY

PULLEY

CORRECT

INCORRECT

10.13   When installing a ribbed belt, make sure it's completely engaged in each pulley

ing a V-ribbed drivebelt (the wide one used to drive the power steering pump and A/C compressor), make sure that it fits properly into the pulley grooves — it must be completely engaged **(see illustration)**.
14   Adjust the belts as described earlier in this Section.

---

11   Battery check and maintenance

Refer to illustrations 11.1, 11.8a, 11.8b, 11.8c and 11.8d
Warning: *Certain precautions must be followed when checking and servicing the battery. Hydrogen gas, which is highly flammable, is always present in the battery cells, so keep lighted tobacco and all other open flames and sparks away from the battery. The electrolyte in the battery cells is actually dilute sulfuric acid, which will cause injury if*

11.1 Tools and materials required for battery maintenance

1 **Face shield/safety goggles** — *When removing corrosion with a brush, the acidic particles can easily fly up into your eyes*
2 **Baking soda** — *A solution of baking soda and water can be used to neutralize corrosion*
3 **Petroleum jelly** — *A layer of this on the battery posts will help prevent corrosion*
4 **Battery post/cable cleaner** — *This wire brush cleaning tool will remove all traces of corrosion from the battery posts and cable clamps*
5 **Treated felt washers** — *Placing one of these on each post, directly under the cable clamps, will help prevent corrosion*
6 **Puller** — *Sometimes the cable clamps are very difficult to pull off the posts, even after the nut/bolt has been completely loosened. This tool pulls the clamp straight up and off the post without damage*
7 **Battery post/cable cleaner** — *Here is another cleaning tool which is a slightly different version of number 4 above, but it does the same thing*
8 **Rubber gloves** — *Another safety item to consider when servicing the battery; remember that's acid inside the battery!*

splashed on your skin or in your eyes. It will also ruin clothes and painted surfaces. When removing the battery cables, always detach the negative cable first and hook it up last!

1   Battery maintenance is an important procedure which will help ensure that you're not stranded because of a dead battery. Several tools are required for this procedure **(see illustration)**.
2   Before servicing the battery, always turn the engine and all accessories off and disconnect the cable from the negative terminal.
3   A sealed (sometimes called maintenance-free) battery is standard equipment on these vehicles. The cell caps cannot be removed, no electrolyte checks are required and water cannot be added to the cells. However, if an aftermarket battery that requires regular maintenance has been installed, the following procedure can be used.

11.8a Battery terminal corrosion usually appears as light, fluffy powder

11.8b Removing a cable from the battery post with a wrench — sometimes a special battery pliers is required for this procedure if corrosion has caused deterioration of the nut hex (always remove the ground cable first and hook it up last!)

4   Check the electrolyte level in each of the battery cells. It must be above the plates. There's usually a split-ring indicator in each cell to indicate the correct level. If the level is low, add distilled water only, then install the cell caps. **Caution:** *Overfilling the cells may cause electrolyte to spill over during periods of heavy charging, causing corrosion and damage to nearby components.*
5   If the positive terminal and cable clamp on your vehicle's battery is equipped with a rubber protector, make sure that it's not torn or damaged. It should completely cover the terminal.
6   The external condition of the battery should be checked periodically. Look for damage such as a cracked case.
7   Check the tightness of the battery cable clamps to ensure good electrical connections and inspect the entire length of each cable, looking for cracked or abraded insulation and frayed conductors.
8   If corrosion (visible as white, fluffy deposits) is evident, remove the cables from the terminals, clean them with a battery brush and reinstall them **(see illustrations)**. Corrosion can be kept to a minimum by installing specially treated washers available at auto parts stores or by applying a layer of petroleum jelly or grease to the terminals and cable clamps after they are assembled.
9   Make sure that the battery carrier is in good condition and that the hold-down clamp bolt is tight. If the battery is removed (see Chapter 5 for the removal and installation procedure), make sure that no parts remain in the bottom of the carrier when it's reinstalled. When

11.8c Regardless of the type of tool used to clean the battery posts, a clean, shiny surface should be the result

11.8d When cleaning the cable clamps, all corrosion must be removed (the inside of the clamp is tapered to match the taper on the post, so don't remove too much material)

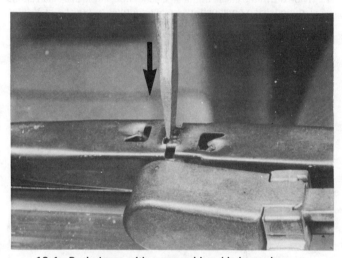

12.4 Push down with a screwdriver blade as shown to release the wiper blade from the arm

12.6 Insert the screwdriver about 1/8-inch and twist it to disengage the wiper blade

reinstalling the hold-down clamp, don't overtighten the bolt.

10 Corrosion on the carrier, battery case and surrounding areas can be removed with a solution of water and baking soda. Apply the mixture with a small brush, let it work, then rinse it off with plenty of clean water.

11 Any metal parts of the vehicle damaged by corrosion should be coated with a zinc-based primer, then painted.

12 Additional information on the battery, charging and jump starting can be found in Chapter 5 and at the front of this manual.

12   Windshield wiper blade check and replacement

Refer to illustrations 12.4, 12.6 and 12.8

1   Road film can build up on the wiper blades and affect their efficiency, so they should be washed regularly with a mild detergent solution.

Check

2   The windshield wiper and blade assembly should be inspected periodically. Even if you do not use your wipers, the sun and elements will dry out the rubber portions, causing them to crack and break apart. If inspection reveals hardened or cracked rubber, replace the wiper blades. If inspection reveals nothing unusual, wet the windshield, turn the wipers on, allow them to cycle several times, then shut them off.

An uneven wiper pattern across the glass or streaks over clean glass indicate that the blades should be replaced.

3   The operation of the wiper mechanism can loosen the fasteners, so they should be checked and tightened, as necessary, at the same time the wiper blades are checked (see Chapter 12 for further information regarding the wiper mechanism).

Blade assembly replacement

Note: *The blade assembly has a rectangular hole located directly above the wiper arm mounting pin with no apparent provision for release. The hole serves for removal, since the release is internal.*

4   Cycle the wiper assembly to a position on the windshield where removal of the blade assembly can be performed without difficulty. Turn the ignition key off at the desired position. With the blade assembly resting on the windshield, insert a small standard screwdriver into the rectangular hole on top of the blade and push down on the coil spring inside the hole. While pressing down with the screwdriver, pull the wiper blade from the wiper arm pin (**see illustration**).

5   To install the blade assembly, push it onto the pin until it snaps into place. Be sure that the blade assembly is securely attached to the wiper arm.

Blade element replacement

6   At one end of the rubber blade element, insert a standard screwdriver between the blade and the metal backing strip (**see illustration**). Press down and in, then twist the screwdriver clockwise to release

SLIDE ELEMENT STARTING   ELEMENT STOP
    AT THIS POINT   (BOTH ENDS)

**12.8   Install the blade element by
sliding the metal backing into the four
retaining tabs, then twist it into the fifth
and end tab**

**13.2   To replace the air filter, remove
the housing cover . . .**

13.3   . . . and pull the filter out

the element from the retaining tab.

7   Slide the blade element out of the remaining tabs until the element is completely detached from the frame.

8   To install the element, slide the metal backing strip into four of the retaining tabs, then twist the backing strip into the fifth and end tab **(see illustration)**.

9   Make sure that all the tabs are locked onto the metal backing strip before installing the blade on the wiper arm.

13   Air filter replacement

1   Open the hood.

Carburetor-equipped vehicles

Refer to illustrations 13.2 and 13.3

2   Remove the wingnut from the top of the housing, disconnect the

clip and lift the cover off **(see illustration)**.

3   Remove the filter element **(see illustration)**.

4   Wipe down the inside of the air cleaner housing with a clean cloth.

5   On models so equipped, use a screwdriver to pry the PCV filter element out of the housing in the air cleaner. If the PCV filter is oily or dirty, replace it with a new one.

6   Place the new air filter element in the housing. If the element is marked TOP be sure the marked side faces up.

7   Install the cover.

Fuel injected vehicles

Refer to illustrations 13.8a and 13.8b

8   Loosen the clamp and detach the tube from the air cleaner assembly **(see illustrations)**. You may have to detach or unplug vacuum hoses and wires to gain access to the cover.

9   Remove the screws and lift off the air cleaner assembly cover.

10 Lift the filter element out of the housing.

**13.8a   Four-cylinder engine air
cleaner assembly, filter and
related components —
exploded view**

13.8b 3.0L V6 engine air cleaner assembly and related components — exploded view

11   Place the new filter element in the housing. If the element is marked TOP be sure the marked side faces up.
12   Position the cover on the housing and make sure it's seated all the way around, then install and tighten the cover screws.
13   Reconnect the tube and any wires or vacuum hoses that were disconnected.

14   PCV valve check

Refer to illustration 14.1

Note: *To maintain efficient operation of the PCV system, clean the hoses and check the PCV valve at the intervals recommended in the maintenance schedule. For additional information on the PCV system, refer to Chapter 6.*

1   Locate the PCV valve **(see illustration)**.
2   To check the valve, first pull it out of the rocker arm cover or tube and shake it — if it rattles, reinstall it.
3   Start the engine and allow it to idle, then disconnect the PCV hose from the air cleaner housing and feel for vacuum at the hose. If vacuum is felt, the PCV valve/system is working properly.
4   If no vacuum is felt, the oil filler cap, hoses or rocker arm cover gasket may be leaking or the PCV valve may be bad. Check for vacuum leaks at the valve, filler cap, filter assembly (if used) and all hoses.

14.1   PCV valve mounting details

5   Pull straight up on the valve to remove it. Check the rubber grommet in the rocker arm cover for cracks and distortion. If it's damaged, replace it.
6   If the valve is clogged, the hoses are also probably plugged. Remove the hose between the valve and the intake manifold and the hose between the filter and the air cleaner housing and clean them with solvent.
7   After cleaning the hoses, inspect them for damage, wear and deterioration. Make sure the hoses fit snugly on the fittings.
8   If necessary, install a new PCV valve. **Note:** *The elbow is not part of the PCV valve. A new valve will not include the elbow. The original must be transferred to the new valve. If a new elbow is purchased, it may be necessary to soak it in warm water for up to an hour to slip it onto the new valve. Do not attempt to force the elbow onto the valve or it will break.*
9   Install the clean PCV system hoses. Make sure that the PCV valve and hoses are secure.

15   Fuel system check

Warning: *Certain precautions must be observed when inspecting or servicing the fuel system components. Work in a well ventilated area and don't allow open flames (cigarettes, appliance pilot lights, etc.) near the work area. Mop up spills immediately. Don't store fuel soaked rags where they could ignite. It's a good idea to keep a dry chemical (Class B) fire extinguisher near the work area any time the fuel system is being serviced.*

1   If you smell gasoline while driving or after the vehicle has been sitting in the sun, inspect the fuel system immediately.
2   Remove the gas filler cap and inspect it for damage and corrosion. The gasket should have an unbroken sealing imprint. If the gasket is damaged or corroded, install a new cap.
3   Inspect the fuel feed and return lines for cracks. Make sure that the connections between the fuel lines and the carburetor or fuel injection system and between the fuel lines and the in-line fuel filter are tight. **Warning:** *If your vehicle is fuel injected, you must relieve the fuel system pressure before servicing fuel system components. The fuel system pressure relief procedure is outlined in Chapter 4.*
4   Since some components of the fuel system — the fuel tank and part of the fuel feed and return lines, for example — are underneath the vehicle, they can be inspected more easily with the vehicle raised on a hoist. If that's not possible, raise the vehicle and support it on jackstands.
5   With the vehicle raised and safely supported, inspect the gas tank and filler neck for punctures, cracks and other damage. The connection between the filler neck and the tank is particularly critical. Sometimes a rubber filler neck will leak because of loose clamps or deteriorated rubber. Inspect all fuel tank mounting brackets and straps to be sure that the tank is securely attached to the vehicle. **Warning:** *Do not, under any circumstances, try to repair a fuel tank (except rubber components). A welding torch or any open flame can easily cause fuel vapors inside the tank to explode!*
6   Carefully check all rubber hoses and metal lines leading away from the fuel tank. Check for loose connections, deteriorated hoses, crimped lines and other damage. Repair or replace damaged sections as necessary (Chapter 4).

16   Fuel filter replacement

Warning: *Gasoline is extremely flammable, so extra safety precautions must be observed when working on any part of the fuel system. Do not smoke and don't allow open flames or bare light bulbs near the vehicle. Also, don't perform fuel system maintenance procedures in a garage where a natural gas type appliance, such as a water heater or clothes dryer, with a pilot light is present!*

Fuel injected vehicles
Refer to illustrations 16.1 and 16.5

Warning: *Before removing the fuel filter, the fuel system pressure must be relieved. See Chapter 4.*

1   Locate the fuel filter on the left (driver's side) frame rail, near the

16.1   The filter on fuel injected vehicles is mounted on the left (driver's side) frame rail, near the rear of the engine

16.5   Fuel filter mounting details (fuel injected vehicles)

rear of the engine **(see illustration)**. Inspect the fittings at both ends of the filter to see if they're clean. If more than a light coating of dust is present, clean the fittings before proceeding.
2   Removal of the hairpin clip from each fitting is a two-stage procedure. First, spread the two clip legs apart about 1/8-inch to disengage them, then push in on them. Pull on the other end of the clip to detach it from the fitting. **Caution:** *Do not use any tools or you may damage the plastic clips or fittings.*
3   Once both hairpin clips are released, grasp the fuel hoses, one at a time, and pull them straight off the filter.
4   After the hoses have been detached, check the clips for damage and distortion. If they were damaged in any way during removal, new ones must be used when the hoses are reattached to the new filter (if new clips are packaged with the filter, be sure to use them in place of the originals).
5   Remove the screws and detach the filter and retainer from the bracket **(see illustration)**.
6   Remove the rubber insulator ring.
7   Note that the fuel flow arrow on the filter points toward the open

APPLY ONE (1) DROP OF
THREAD SEALANT TO THE 2ND AND 3RD
THREADS FROM THE END OF THE FUEL FILTER

CARBURETOR

FRONT OF ENGINE

NOTE: USE BACKUP WRENCH
ON FUEL FILTER HEX WHEN
TIGHTENING FUEL LINE FITTING

16.13   Carburetor mounted fuel filter details

end of the retainer — the new filter must be installed in the same way.

8   Install the new filter in the retainer.

9   Install the rubber insulator ring. If the filter moves freely after installing the retainer, replace the insulators with new ones.

10   Install the filter retainer in the bracket and tighten the screws securely.

11   Carefully push each hose onto the filter until it's seated against the collar on the fitting, then install the hairpin clips. The triangular shaped side of each clip must point away from the filter. Make sure the clips are securely attached to the hose fittings — if they come off, the hoses could back off the filter and a fire could result!

12   Start the engine and check for fuel leaks.

Carburetor-equipped vehicles

Refer to illustration 16.13

13   Remove the air cleaner housing from the top of the carburetor to gain access to the filter **(see illustration)**.

14   Place a rag under the filter, then remove the fuel line from the filter while holding the filter hex with a back-up wrench. A flare nut wrench should be used if available — it will prevent rounding off the fuel line fitting hex.

15   Unscrew the filter from the carburetor. Before installation, apply one drop of thread sealant to the 2nd and 3rd threads (from the end) of the new filter.

16   Position the new filter and thread it into the carburetor — be very careful not to cross thread the fitting. Attach the fuel line to the filter and tighten the fitting securely.

17   Start the engine and check for fuel leaks at the fittings while the engine idles for two minutes. If fuel leaks are noted, tighten the appropriate fitting(s) slightly.

18   Reinstall the air cleaner housing.

17   Cooling system check

Refer to illustration 17.4

1   Many major engine failures can be attributed to a faulty cooling system. If the vehicle is equipped with an automatic transmission, the cooling system also cools the transmission fluid and thus plays an important role in prolonging transmission life.

2   The cooling system should be checked with the engine cold. Do this before the vehicle is driven for the day or after the engine has been shut off for at least three hours.

3   Remove the radiator cap by turning it to the left until it reaches a stop. If you hear a hissing sound (indicating there is still pressure in the system), wait until it stops. Now press down on the cap with the palm of your hand and continue turning to the left until the cap can be removed. Thoroughly clean the cap, inside and out, with clean water. Also clean the filler neck on the radiator. All traces of corrosion should be removed. The coolant inside the radiator should be relatively transparent. If it's rust colored, the system should be drained and refilled (Section 30). If the coolant level isn't up to the top, add additional antifreeze/coolant mixture (see Section 4).

4   Carefully check the large upper and lower radiator hoses along with the smaller diameter heater hoses which run from the engine to the firewall. Inspect each hose along its entire length, replacing any hose

ALWAYS CHECK hose for chafed or burned areas that may cause an untimely and costly failure.

SOFT hose indicates inside deterioration. This deterioration can contaminate the cooling system and cause particles to clog the radiator.

HARDENED hose can fail at any time. Tightening hose clamps will not seal the connection or stop leaks.

SWOLLEN hose or oil soaked ends indicate danger and possible failure from oil or grease contamination. Squeeze the hose to locate cracks and breaks that cause leaks.

17.4   Hoses, like drivebelts, have a habit of failing at the worst possible time — to prevent the inconvenience of a blown radiator or heater hose, inspect them carefully as shown here

which is cracked, swollen or shows signs of deterioration. Cracks may become more apparent if the hose is squeezed **(see illustration)**. Regardless of condition, it's a good idea to replace hoses with new ones every two years.

5   Make sure that all hose connections are tight. A leak in the cooling system will usually show up as white or rust colored deposits on the areas adjoining the leak. If wire-type clamps are used at the ends of the hoses, it may be a good idea to replace them with more secure screw-type clamps.

6   Use compressed air or a soft brush to remove bugs, leaves, etc. from the front of the radiator or air conditioning condenser. Be careful not to damage the delicate cooling fins or cut yourself on them.

7   Every other inspection, or at the first indication of cooling system problems, have the cap and system pressure tested. If you don't have a pressure tester, most gas stations and repair shops will do this for a minimal charge.

18   Exhaust system check

Refer to illustration 18.2

1   With the engine cold (at least three hours after the vehicle has been driven), check the complete exhaust system from the engine to the end of the tailpipe. Ideally, the inspection should be done with the vehicle on a hoist to permit unrestricted access. If a hoist isn't available, raise the vehicle and support it securely on jackstands.

2   Check the exhaust pipes and connections for evidence of leaks, severe corrosion and damage. Make sure that all brackets and hangers are in good condition and tight **(see illustration)**.

3   At the same time, inspect the underside of the body for holes, corrosion, open seams, etc. which may allow exhaust gases to enter the passenger compartment. Seal all body openings with silicone or body putty.

4   Rattles and other noises can often be traced to the exhaust system, especially the mounts and hangers. Try to move the pipes, muffler and catalytic converter. If the components can come in contact with the body or suspension parts, secure the exhaust system with new mounts.

5   Check the running condition of the engine by inspecting inside the end of the tailpipe. The exhaust deposits here are an indication of engine state-of-tune. If the pipe is black and sooty or coated with white deposits, the engine is in need of a tune-up, including a thorough fuel system inspection and adjustment.

19   Tire rotation

Refer to illustration 19.2

1   The tires should be rotated at the specified intervals and whenever uneven wear is noticed. Since the vehicle will be raised and the tires removed anyway, check the brakes also (Section 21).

2   Radial tires must be rotated in a specific pattern **(see illustration)**.

19.2   Recommended tire rotation pattern

3   Refer to the information in *Jacking and towing* at the front of this manual for the proper procedure to follow when raising the vehicle and changing a tire. If the brakes are to be checked, don't apply the parking brake.

4   The vehicle must be raised on a hoist or supported on jackstands to get all four wheels off the ground. Make sure the vehicle is safely supported!

5   After the rotation procedure is finished, check and adjust the tire pressures as necessary and be sure to check the lug nut tightness.

20   Steering and suspension check

Refer to illustrations 20.10, 20.11 and 20.12

Note: *The steering linkage and suspension components should be checked periodically. Worn or damaged suspension and steering linkage components can result in excessive and abnormal tire wear, poor ride quality and vehicle handling and reduced fuel economy. For detailed illustrations of the steering and suspension components, refer to Chapter 10.*

18.2   Inspect the exhaust system for conditions such as this — the stud broke off, creating an exhaust leak, evidenced by the carbon deposits

Shock absorber check

1   Park the vehicle on level ground, turn the engine off and set the parking brake. Check the tire pressures.

2   Push down at one corner of the vehicle, then release it while noting the movement of the body. It should stop moving and come to rest in a level position within one or two bounces.

3   If the vehicle continues to move up-and-down or if it fails to return to its original position, a worn or weak shock absorber is probably the reason.

4   Repeat the above check at each of the three remaining corners of the vehicle.

5   Raise the vehicle and support it on jackstands. The front jackstands should be positioned under the suspension (control) arms.

6   Check the shock absorbers for evidence of fluid leakage. A light film of fluid is no cause for concern. Make sure that any fluid noted is from the shocks and not from some other source. If leakage is noted, replace the shocks as a set.

7   Check the shock absorbers to be sure they're securely mounted and undamaged. Check the upper mounts for damage and wear. If damage or wear is noted, replace the shocks as a set.

8   If shock absorbers must be replaced, refer to Chapter 10 for the procedure.

Steering and suspension check

9   Visually inspect the steering system components for damage and distortion. Look for leaks and damaged seals, boots and fittings.

10   Have an assistant grasp the lower edge of the tire and move the wheel in-and-out while you look for movement at the balljoints **(see illustration)**. If there's any movement, the suspension balljoints must be replaced.

11   Grasp each front tire at the front and rear edges, push in at the rear, pull out at the front and feel for play in the steering system components **(see illustration)**. If any free play is noted, check the steering gear mounts and the tie-rod balljoints for looseness. If the steering gear mounts are loose, tighten them. If the tie-rods are loose, the balljoints may be worn (check to make sure the nuts are tight). Additional steering and suspension system information and illustrations can be found in Chapter 10.

12   Check the steering gear for leaks at the fittings, damaged boots and loose boot clamps **(see illustration)**.

21   Brake check

Refer to illustrations 21.11, 21.15a, 21.15b and 21.22

Note: *In addition to the specified intervals, the brake system should be inspected each time the wheels are removed or a malfunction is indicated. Because of the obvious safety implications, the following brake system checks are some of the most important maintenance procedures you can perform on your vehicle.*

20.10 To check the suspension balljoints, try to move the lower edge of each front tire in-and-out while watching/feeling for movement at the top of the tire and balljoints

20.11 To check the steering gear mounts and tie-rod connections for play, grasp each front tire like this and try to move it back-and-forth — if play is noted, check the steering gear mounts and make sure that they're tight; if either tie-rod is worn or bent, replace it

Symptoms of brake system problems

1   Some disc brake pads have built-in wear indicators which should make a high pitched squealing or scraping noise when they're worn to the replacement point. When you hear this noise, replace the pads immediately or expensive damage to the discs could result.

2   Any of the following symptoms could indicate a potential brake system defect. The vehicle pulls to one side when the brake pedal is depressed, the brakes make squealing or dragging noises when applied, brake travel is excessive, the pedal pulsates and brake fluid leaks are noted (usually on the inner side of the tire or wheel). If any of these conditions are noted, inspect the brake system immediately.

Brake lines and hoses

Note: *Steel tubing is used throughout the brake system, with the exception of flexible, reinforced hoses at the front wheels and as connectors at the rear axle. Periodic inspection of these lines is very important.*

3   Park the vehicle on level ground and turn the engine off.

4   Remove the wheel covers. Loosen, but do not remove, the lug nuts on all four wheels.

5   Raise the vehicle and support it securely on jackstands.

6   Remove the wheels (see *Jacking and towing* at the front of this manual, or refer to your owner's manual, if necessary).

7   Check all brake hoses and lines for cracks, chafing of the outer cover, leaks, blisters and distortion. Check all threaded fittings for leaks and make sure the brake hose mounting bolts and clips are secure.

8   If leaks or damage are discovered, they must be fixed immediately. Refer to Chapter 9 for detailed repair procedures.

Front disc brakes

9   If it hasn't already been done, raise the front of the vehicle and support it securely on jackstands. Apply the parking brake and remove the front wheels.

10 The disc brake calipers, which contain the pads, are now visible. Each caliper has an outer and an inner pad — all pads should be checked.

11 Note the pad thickness by looking through the inspection hole in the caliper **(see illustration)**. If the lining material is 1/8-inch thick or

20.12 Check the steering gear hydraulic line fittings and boots for leaks and damage (arrows) and make sure the mounting bolts are tight

21.11 The front disc brake pad lining thickness (arrows) can be checked through the caliper inspection hole

21.15a   The rear brake shoe lining thickness (A) is measured from the outer surface of the lining to the metal shoe

21.15b   The lining thickness measured to the rivet head can be checked with a tire tread depth gauge

less, or if it is tapered from end-to-end, the pads should be replaced (see Chapter 9). Keep in mind that the lining material is riveted or bonded to a metal plate or shoe — the metal portion is not included in the measurement.

12 Check the condition of the brake disc. Look for score marks, deep scratches and overheated areas (they will appear blue or discolored). If damage or wear is noted, the disc can be removed and resurfaced by an automotive machine shop or replaced with a new one. Refer to Chapter 9 for more detailed inspection and repair procedures.

Rear drum brakes

13 Refer to Chapter 9 and remove the rear brake drums.

14 **Warning:** *Brake dust produced by lining wear and deposited on brake components contains asbestos, which is hazardous to your health. DO NOT blow it out with compressed air and DO NOT inhale it! DO NOT use gasoline or solvents to remove the dust. Brake system cleaner should be used to flush the dust into a drain pan. After the brake components are wiped clean with a damp rag, dispose of the contaminated rag(s) and solvent in a covered and labelled container. Try to use non-asbestos replacement parts whenever possible.*

15 Note the thickness of the lining material on the rear brake shoes **(see illustrations)** and look for signs of contamination by brake fluid and grease. If the lining material is within 1/16-inch of the recessed rivets or metal shoes, replace the brake shoes with new ones. The shoes should also be replaced if they are cracked, glazed (shiny lining surfaces) or contaminated with brake fluid or grease. See Chapter 9 for the replacement procedure.

16 Check the shoe return and hold-down springs and the adjusting mechanism to make sure they're installed correctly and in good con-

dition. Deteriorated or distorted springs, if not replaced, could allow the linings to drag and wear prematurely.

17 Check the wheel cylinders for leakage by carefully peeling back the rubber boots. If brake fluid is noted behind the boots, the wheel cylinders must be replaced (see Chapter 9).

18 Check the drums for cracks, score marks, deep scratches and hard spots, which will appear as small discolored areas. If imperfections cannot be removed with emery cloth, the drums must be resurfaced by an automotive machine shop (see Chapter 9 for more detailed information).

19 Refer to Chapter 9 and install the brake drums.

20 Install the wheels, but don't lower the vehicle yet.

Parking brake

Note: *The parking brake cable and linkage should be periodically checked and lubricated. This maintenance procedure helps prevent the parking brake cable adjuster or the linkage from binding and adversely affecting the operation or adjustment of the parking brake.*

Lubrication

21 Set the parking brake.

22 Apply multi-purpose grease to the parking brake linkage, adjuster assembly, connectors and the areas of the parking brake cable that come in contact with the other parts of the vehicle **(see illustration)**.

21.22   Lubricate the parking brake cable linkage, adjuster assembly, connectors and the areas of the parking brake cable that come in contact with the other parts of the vehicle as shown here

22.3 Lubricate the shift linkage cable ends (automatic transmision) with multi-purpose grease

23 Release the parking brake and repeat the lubrication procedure.
24 Remove the jackstands and lower the vehicle.
25 Tighten the wheel lug nuts to the specified torque and install the wheel covers.

Check
26 The easiest, and perhaps most obvious, method of checking the parking brake is to park the vehicle on a steep hill with the parking brake set and the transmission in Neutral. If the parking brake cannot prevent the vehicle from rolling, refer to Chapter 9 and adjust it.

22 Automatic transmission control linkage lubrication

Refer to illustration 22.3

1 Raise the vehicle, support it securely on jackstands and locate the shift cable on the left side of the transmission..
2 Clean the linkage and pivot points at the upper end of the cable.
3 Lubricate the shift linkage and pivot points with multi-purpose grease **(see illustration)**.

23 Manual transmission lubricant level check

Refer to illustration 23.1

Note: *The transmission lubricant level and quality shouldn't deteriorate under normal driving conditions. However, it's recommended that you check the level occasionally. The most convenient time would be when the vehicle is raised for another reason, such as an engine oil change.*

1 The transmission has a check/fill plug which must be removed to check the lubricant level **(see illustration)**. If the vehicle is raised to

23.1 The manual transmission lubricant check/fill plug is located on the side of the case

24.1 Tools and materials needed for front wheel bearing maintenance

1 **Hammer** — *A common hammer will do just fine*
2 **Grease** — *High-temperature grease which is formulated specially for front wheel bearings should be used*
3 **Wood block** — *If you have a scrap piece of 2x4, it can be used to drive the new seal into the hub*
4 **Needle-nose pliers** — *Used to straighten and remove the cotter pin in the spindle*
5 **Torque wrench** — *This is very important in this procedure; if the bearing is too tight, the wheel won't turn freely — if it is too loose, the wheel will 'wobble' on the spindle. Either way, it could mean extensive damage*
6 **Screwdriver** — *Used to remove the seal from the hub (a long screwdriver would be preferred)*
7 **Socket/breaker bar** — *Needed to loosen the nut on the spindle if it is extremely tight*
8 **Brush** — *Together with some clean solvent, this will be used to remove old grease from the hub and spindle*

gain access to the plug, be sure to support it safely on jackstands — DO NOT crawl under a vehicle which is supported only by a jack!
2 Remove the plug from the transmission and use your little finger to reach inside the housing and feel the lubricant level. It should be at or very near the bottom of the plug hole.
3 If it isn't, add the recommended lubricant through the plug hole with a syringe or squeeze bottle.
4 Install and tighten the plug securely and check for leaks after the first few miles of driving.

24 Front wheel bearing check, repack and adjustment

Refer to illustrations 24.1, 24.3, 24.7, 24.15, 24.16 and 24.23

1 In most cases the front wheel bearings will not need servicing until the brake pads are changed. However, the bearings should be checked whenever the front of the vehicle is raised for any reason. Several items, including a torque wrench and special grease, are required for this procedure **(see illustration)**.
2 With the vehicle securely supported on jackstands, spin each wheel and check for noise, rolling resistance and free play.

24.3   To check the wheel bearings, try to move the tire in-and-out — if play is noted, or if the bearings feel rough or sound noisy when the tire is rotated, replace them

3   Move the wheel in-and-out on the spindle **(see illustration)**. If there's any noticable movement, the bearings should be checked and then repacked with grease or replaced if necessary.
4   Remove the wheel.
5   Remove the brake caliper (Chapter 9) and hang it out of the way on a piece of wire. **Warning:** *DO NOT allow the brake caliper to hang by the rubber hose!*
6   Pry the grease cap out of the hub with a screwdriver or hammer and chisel.
7   Straighten the bent ends of the cotter pin, then pull the cotter pin out of the retainer and spindle **(see illustration)**. Discard the cotter pin and use a new one during reassembly.
8   Remove the adjusting nut and washer from the end of the spindle.
9   Pull the hub assembly out slightly, then push it back into its original position. This should force the outer bearing off the spindle enough so it can be removed.
10   Pull the hub off the spindle.
11   Use a screwdriver to pry the grease seal out of the rear of the hub. As this is done, note how the seal is installed.
12   Remove the inner wheel bearing from the hub.
13   Use solvent to remove all traces of old grease from the bearings, hub and spindle. A small brush may prove helpful; however make sure no bristles from the brush embed themselves inside the bearing rollers. Allow the parts to air dry.
14   Carefully inspect the bearings for cracks, heat discoloration, worn rollers, etc. Check the bearing races inside the hub for wear and damage. If the bearing races are defective, the hubs should be taken to a machine shop with the facilities to remove the old races and press new ones in. Note that the bearings and races come as matched sets and old bearings should never be installed on new races.
15   Use high-temperature front wheel bearing grease to pack the bearings. Work the grease completely into the bearings, forcing it between the rollers, cone and cage from the back side **(see illustration)**.
16   Apply a thin coat of grease to the spindle at the outer bearing seat, inner bearing seat, shoulder and seal seat **(see illustration)**.
17   Put a small quantity of grease inboard of each bearing race inside the hub. Using your finger, form a dam at these points to provide extra grease availability and to keep thinned grease from flowing out of the bearing.
18   Place the grease-packed inner bearing into the rear of the hub and put a little more grease outboard of the bearing.
19   Place a new seal over the inner bearing and tap the seal evenly

24.7   Front hub and wheel bearing components — exploded view

24.15   Pack the wheel bearing by working the grease into the rollers from the back side

24.16   Apply a thin coat of grease to the spindle

into place with a hammer and block of wood until it's flush with the hub.
20   Carefully place the hub assembly onto the spindle and push the grease-packed outer bearing into position.
21   Install the washer and adjusting nut. Tighten the nut only slightly.
22   Spin the hub in a forward direction to seat the bearings and remove any grease or burrs which could cause excessive bearing play later.
23   While spinning the wheel, tighten the adjusting nut to the specified torque (step 1 in the Specifications) **(see illustration)**.
24   Loosen the nut 1/2 turn, no more.
25   Tighten the nut to the specified torque (step 3 in the Specifications). Install a new cotter pin through the hole in the spindle and retainer.

If the nut slots don't line up, loosen the nut slightly until they do. From the hand-tight position, the nut should not be loosened more than one-half flat to install the cotter pin.
26   Bend the ends of the cotter pin until they're flat against the nut. Cut off any extra length which could interfere with the grease cap.
27   Install the grease cap, tapping it into place with a hammer.
28   Install the caliper (Chapter 9).
29   Install the tire/wheel assembly on the hub and tighten the lug nuts.
30   Check the bearings in the manner described earlier in this Section.
31   Lower the vehicle.

25   Rear axle (differential) oil level check

Refer to illustration 25.2
1   The differential has a check/fill plug which must be removed to check the oil level. If the vehicle is raised to gain access to the plug, be sure to support it safely on jackstands — DO NOT crawl under the vehicle when it's supported only by the jack.
2   Remove the oil check/fill plug from the side of the differential **(see illustration)**.

24.23   Wheel bearing adjustment details

25.2   Use a 1/2-inch drive breaker bar or ratchet to remove the rear axle check/fill plug

3   Use your little finger as a dipstick to make sure the oil level is even with the bottom of the plug hole. If not, use a syringe to add the recommended lubricant until it just starts to run out of the opening. On some models a tag is located in the area of the plug which gives information regarding lubricant type, particularly on models equipped with a limited slip differential.

4   Install the plug and tighten it securely.

26.2   Tools required for changing spark plugs

1   **Spark plug socket** — *This will have special padding inside to protect the spark plug porcelain insulator*
2   **Torque wrench** — *Although not mandatory, use of this tool is the best way to ensure that the plugs are tightened properly*
3   **Ratchet** — *Standard hand tool to fit the plug socket*
4   **Extension** — *Depending on model and accessories, you may need special extensions and universal joints to reach one or more of the plugs*
5   **Spark plug gap gauge** — *This gauge for checking the gap comes in a variety of styles. Make sure the gap for your engine is included*

---

26   Spark plug replacement

Refer to illustrations 26.2, 26.5a, 26.5b, 26.6 and 26.10

1   The spark plugs are located on the side(s) of the engine.
2   In most cases, the tools necessary for spark plug replacement include a spark plug socket which fits onto a ratchet (spark plug sockets are padded inside to prevent damage to the porcelain insulators on the new plugs), various extensions and a gap gauge to check and adjust the gaps on the new plugs **(see illustration)**. A special plug wire removal tool is available for separating the wire boots from the spark plugs, but it isn't absolutely necessary. A torque wrench should be used to tighten the new plugs.
3   The best approach when replacing the spark plugs is to purchase the new ones in advance, adjust them to the proper gap and replace the plugs one at a time. When buying the new spark plugs, be sure to obtain the correct plug type for your particular engine. This information can be found on the *Emission Control Information label* located under the hood and in the factory owner's manual. If differences exist between the plug specified on the emissions label and in the owner's manual, assume that the emissions label is correct.
4   Allow the engine to cool completely before attempting to remove any of the plugs. While you're waiting for the engine to cool, check the new plugs for defects and adjust the gaps.
5   The gap is checked by inserting a wire type gauge between the electrodes at the tip of the plug **(see illustration)**. The gap between the electrodes should be the same as the one specified on the *Emissions Control Information label*. The wire should just slide between the elec-

26.5a   Spark plug manufacturers recommend using a wire-type gauge when checking the gap — if the wire doesn't slide between the electrodes with a slight drag, adjustment is required

26.5b   To change the gap, bend the *side* electrode only, as indicated by the arrows, and be very careful not to crack or chip the porcelain insulator surrounding the center electrode

trodes with a slight amount of drag. If the gap is incorrect, use the adjuster on the gauge body to bend the curved side electrode slightly until the proper gap is obtained **(see illustration)**. If the side electrode is not exactly over the center electrode, bend it with the adjuster until it is. Check for cracks in the porcelain insulator (if any are found, the plug should not be used).

CARBON DEPOSITS

Symptoms: Dry sooty deposits indicate a rich mixture or weak ignition. Causes misfiring, hard starting and hesitation.

Recommendation: Check for a clogged air cleaner, high float level, sticky choke and worn ignition points. Use a spark plug with a longer core nose for greater anti-fouling protection.

NORMAL

Symptoms: Brown to grayish-tan color and slight electrode wear. Correct heat range for engine and operating conditions.

Recommendation: When new spark plugs are installed, replace with plugs of the same heat range.

OIL DEPOSITS

Symptoms: Oily coating caused by poor oil control. Oil is leaking past worn valve guides or piston rings into the combustion chamber. Causes hard starting, misfiring and hesition.

Recommendation: Correct the mechanical condition with necessary repairs and install new plugs.

ASH DEPOSITS

Symptoms: Light brown deposits encrusted on the side or center electrodes or both. Derived from oil and/or fuel additives. Excessive amounts may mask the spark, causing misfiring and hesitation during acceleration.

Recommendation: If excessive deposits accumulate over a short time or low mileage, install new valve guide seals to prevent seepage of oil into the combustion chambers. Also try changing gasoline brands.

TOO HOT

Symptoms: Blistered, white insulator, eroded electrode and absence of deposits. Results in shortened plug life.

Recommendation: Check for the correct plug heat range, over-advanced ignition timing, lean fuel mixture, intake manifold vacuum leaks and sticking valves. Check the coolant level and make sure the radiator is not clogged.

WORN

Symptoms: Rounded electrodes with a small amount of deposits on the firing end. Normal color. Causes hard starting in damp or cold weather and poor fuel economy.

Recommendation: Replace with new plugs of the same heat range.

PREIGNITION

Symptoms: Melted electrodes. Insulators are white, but may be dirty due to misfiring or flying debris in the combustion chamber. Can lead to engine damage.

Recommendation: Check for the correct plug heat range, over-advanced ignition timing, lean fuel mixture, clogged cooling system and lack of lubrication.

DETONATION

Symptoms: Insulators may be cracked or chipped. Improper gap setting techniques can also result in a fractured insulator tip. Can lead to piston damage.

Recommendation: Make sure the fuel anti-knock values meet engine requirements. Use care when setting the gaps on new plugs. Avoid lugging the engine.

HIGH SPEED GLAZING

Symptoms: Insulator has yellowish, glazed appearance. Indicates that combustion chamber temperatures have risen suddenly during hard acceleration. Normal deposits melt to form a conductive coating. Causes misfiring at high speeds.

Recommendation: Install new plugs. Consider using a colder plug if driving habits warrant.

SPLASHED DEPOSITS

Symptoms: After long periods of misfiring, deposits can loosen when normal combustion temperature is restored by an overdue tune-up. At high speeds, deposits flake off the piston and are thrown against the hot insulator, causing misfiring.

Recommendation: Replace the plugs with new ones or clean and reinstall the originals.

GAP BRIDGING

Symptoms: Combustion deposits lodge between the electrodes. Heavy deposits accumulate and bridge the electrode gap. The plug ceases to fire, resulting in a dead cylinder.

Recommendation: Locate the faulty plug and remove the deposits from between the electrodes.

MECHANICAL DAMAGE

Symptoms: May be caused by a foreign object in the combustion chamber or the piston striking an incorrect reach (too long) plug. Causes a dead cylinder and could result in piston damage.

Recommendation: Remove the foreign object from the engine and/or install the correct reach plug.

26.6   When removing the spark plug wires, grasp the boots only and use a twisting/pulling motion

26.10   A length of 3/16-inch ID rubber hose will save time and prevent damaged threads when installing the spark plugs

6   With the engine cool, remove the spark plug wire from one spark plug. Pull only on the boot at the end of the wire — do not pull on the wire. A plug wire removal tool should be used if available **(see illustration)**.
7   If compressed air is available, use it to blow any dirt or foreign material away from the spark plug hole. A common bicycle pump will also work. The idea here is to eliminate the possibility of debris falling into the cylinder as the spark plug is removed.
8   Place the spark plug socket over the plug and remove it from the engine by turning it in a counterclockwise direction.
9   Compare the spark plug to those shown in the accompanying color photos to get an indication of the general running condition of the engine.
10   Thread one of the new plugs into the hole until you can no longer turn it with your fingers, then tighten it with a torque wrench (if available) or the ratchet. It might be a good idea to slip a short length of rubber hose over the end of the plug to use as a tool to thread it into place **(see illustration)**. The hose will grip the plug well enough to turn it, but will start to slip if the plug begins to cross-thread in the hole — this will prevent damaged threads and the accompanying repair costs.
11   Before pushing the spark plug wire onto the end of the plug, inspect it following the procedures outlined in Section 27.
12   Attach the plug wire to the new spark plug, again using a twisting motion on the boot until it's seated on the spark plug.
13   Repeat the procedure for the remaining spark plugs, replacing them one at a time to prevent mixing up the spark plug wires.

27   Spark plug wire, distributor cap and rotor check and replacement

Refer to illustrations 27.11, 27.12 and 27.13

Spark plug wires

Note: *Every time a wire is detached from a spark plug, the distributor cap or the coil, silicone dielectric compound (a white grease available at auto parts stores) must be applied to the inside of the boot before reconnection. Use a small standard screwdriver to coat the entire inside surface of each boot with a thin layer of the compound.*

1   The spark plug wires should be checked and, if necessary, replaced at the same time new spark plugs are installed.
2   The easiest way to identify bad wires is to make a visual check while the engine is running. In a dark, well-ventilated garage, start the engine and look at each plug wire. Be careful not to come into contact with any moving engine parts. If there is a break in the wire, you will see arcing or a small spark at the damaged area. If arcing is noticed, make a note to obtain new wires.
3   The spark plug wires should be inspected one at a time, beginning with the spark plug for the number one cylinder to prevent confusion. On the four-cylinder engine, the number one cylinder is at the front of the engine. On V6 engines, it's at the front of the right (passenger side) bank. Clearly label each original plug wire with a piece of tape marked with the correct number. The plug wires must be reinstalled in the correct order to ensure proper engine operation.
4   Disconnect the plug wire from the first spark plug. A removal tool can be used **(see illustration 26.6)**, or you can grab the wire boot, twist

it slightly and pull the wire free. *Don't pull on the wire itself, only on the rubber boot.*
5   Push the wire and boot back onto the end of the spark plug. It should fit snugly. If it doesn't, detach the wire and boot once more and use a pair of pliers to carefully crimp the metal connector inside the wire boot until it does.
6   Using a clean rag, wipe the entire length of the wire to remove built-up dirt and grease.
7   Once the wire is clean, check for burns, cracks and other damage. Don't bend the wire sharply or you might break the conductor.
8   Disconnect the wire from the distributor. Again, pull only on the rubber boot. Check for corrosion and a tight fit. Replace the wire in the distributor.
9   Inspect the remaining spark plug wires, making sure that each one is securely fastened at the distributor and spark plug when the check is complete.
10   If new spark plug wires are required, purchase a set for your specific engine model. Pre-cut wire sets with the boots already installed are available. Remove and replace the wires one at a time to avoid mix-ups in the firing order.

Distributor cap and rotor

Note: *It's common practice to install a new distributor cap and rotor each time new spark plug wires are installed. If you're planning to install new wires, install a new cap and rotor also. But if you are planning to reuse the existing wires, be sure to inspect the cap and rotor to make sure they're in good condition.*

11   Remove the mounting screws and detach the cap from the distributor. Check it for cracks, carbon tracks and worn, burned or loose terminals **(see illustration)**
12   Check the rotor for cracks and carbon tracks. Make sure the center terminal spring tension is adequate and look for corrosion and wear on the rotor tip **(see illustration)**.
13   Replace the cap and rotor if damage or defects are found. Note that on some models the rotor is held on the shaft by two screws and is indexed so it can be installed only one way. Before installing the cap, apply silicone dielectric compound to the rotor tip **(see illustration)** (see **Note** at beginning of this Section).
14   When installing a new cap, remove the wires from the old cap one at a time and attach them to the new cap in the exact same location — don't simultaneously remove all the wires from the old cap or firing order mix-ups may occur.

28   Automatic transmission fluid and filter change

Refer to illustrations 28.7 and 28.10
Caution: *The use of transmission fluid other than the type listed in the Specifications could result in transmission malfunctions or failure.*

1   At the specified intervals, the transmission fluid should be drained and replaced. Since the fluid will remain hot long after driving, perform this procedure only after the engine has cooled down completely.
2   Before beginning work, purchase the specified transmission fluid (see *Recommended lubricants and fluids* at the front of this Chapter), a new filter and gaskets.
3   Other tools necessary for this job include jackstands to support

27.12 The ignition rotor should be checked for wear and corrosion as indicated here (if in doubt about its condition, buy a new one)

27.11 Shown here are some of the common defects to look for when inspecting the distributor cap (if in doubt about its condition, install a new one)

27.13 Apply silicone dielectric compound (grease) to the rotor as shown here before installing the distributor cap

28.7 With the rear bolts loosened and holding it in place, lower the front of the transmission pan and allow the fluid to drain

the vehicle in a raised position, a drain pan capable of holding at least eight pints, newspapers and clean rags.

4   Raise the vehicle and support it securely on jackstands.

5   With the drain pan in place, remove the front and side transmission pan mounting bolts.

6   Loosen the rear pan bolts approximately four turns.

7   Carefully pry the transmission pan loose with a screwdriver, allowing the fluid to drain (see illustration). Don't damage the pan or transmission gasket surfaces or leaks could develop.

8   Remove the remaining bolts, pan and gasket. Carefully clean the gasket surface of the transmission to remove all traces of the old gasket and sealant.

9   Drain the fluid from the transmission pan, clean it with solvent and dry it with compressed air.

28.10   The transmission filter is held in place with small bolts

10   Remove the filter from the mount inside the transmission **(see illustration)**.
11   Install a new filter and gasket. Tighten the mounting bolts securely.
12   Make sure the gasket surface on the transmission pan is clean, then install a new gasket. Put the pan in place against the transmission and install the bolts. Working around the pan, tighten each bolt a little at a time until the final torque figure is reached. Don't overtighten the bolts!
13   Lower the vehicle and add about four or five pints of automatic transmission fluid through the filler tube (Section 7).
14   With the transmission in Park and the parking brake set, run the engine at a fast idle, but don't race it.
15   Move the gear selector through each range and back to Park. Check the fluid level.
16   Check under the vehicle for leaks during the first few trips.

29   Carburetor choke check

Refer to illustration 29.3

1   The choke only operates when the engine is cold, so this check should be performed before the engine has been started for the day.
2   Open the hood and remove the air cleaner housing cover and filter.
3   Locate the choke plate (the flat plate attached by small screws to a pivot shaft) in the carburetor throat **(see illustration)**.

4   Operate the throttle linkage and make sure the plate closes completely. Start the engine and watch the plate — when the engine starts, the choke plate should open slightly.
5   Allow the engine to continue running at idle speed. As the engine warms up to operating temperature, the plate should slowly open.
6   After a few minutes, the choke plate should be fully open to the vertical position.
7   Note that the engine speed corresponds to the plate opening angle. With the plate closed, the engine should run at a fast idle speed. As the plate opens, the engine speed will decrease. The fast idle speed is controlled by the fast idle cam, and even though the choke plate is open completely, the idle speed will remain high until the throttle is opened, releasing the fast idle cam. Check the drop in idle speed as the choke plate opens by occasionally ''blipping'' the throttle.
8   If the choke doesn't work as described, shut off the engine and check the shaft and linkage for deposits which could cause binding. Use a spray-on choke cleaning solvent to remove the deposits as you operate the linkage. This should loosen up the linkage and the shaft and allow the choke to work properly. If the choke still fails to function correctly, the choke bimetal assembly is malfunctioning and the carburetor may have to be overhauled. Refer to Chapter 4 for further information.
9   At regular intervals, clean and lubricate the choke shaft, the fast idle cam and linkage and the vacuum diaphragm pulldown rod to ensure good choke performance.

30   Cooling system servicing (draining, flushing and refilling)

Refer to illustration 30.4

Warning: *Antifreeze is a corrosive and poisonous solution, so be careful not to spill any of the coolant mixture on the vehicle's paint or your skin. If this happens, rinse immediately with plenty of clean water. Consult local authorities regarding proper disposal procedures for antifreeze before draining the cooling system. In many areas, reclamation centers have been established to collect used oil and coolant mixtures.*

1   Periodically, the cooling system should be drained, flushed and refilled to replenish the antifreeze mixture and prevent formation of rust and corrosion, which can impair the performance of the cooling system and cause engine damage. When the cooling system is serviced, all hoses and the radiator cap should be checked and replaced if necessary.

Draining

2   Apply the parking brake and block the wheels. If the vehicle has just been driven, wait several hours to allow the engine to cool down before beginning this procedure.
3   Once the engine is completely cool, remove the radiator cap.
4   Move a large container under the radiator drain to catch the coolant **(see illustration)**. Attach a 3/8-inch diameter hose to the drain fitting

29.3   With the air cleaner cover removed, the choke plate can be checked for proper operation

30.4   The radiator drain fitting (arrow) is located at the right rear corner of the radiator — before opening the valve, push a short section of 3/8-inch diameter rubber hose onto the plastic fitting to prevent the coolant from splashing as it drains

to direct the coolant into the container, then open the drain fitting (a pair of pliers may be required to turn it).

5   After the coolant stops flowing out of the radiator, move the container under the engine block drain plug. Remove the plug and allow the coolant in the block to drain.

6   While the coolant is draining, check the condition of the radiator hoses, heater hoses and clamps (refer to Section 17 if necessary).

7   Replace any damaged clamps or hoses (refer to Chapter 3 for detailed replacement procedures).

Flushing

8   Once the system is completely drained, flush the radiator with fresh water from a garden hose until water runs clear at the drain. The flushing action of the water will remove sediments from the radiator but will not remove rust and scale from the engine and cooling tube surfaces.

9   These deposits can be removed by the chemical action of a cleaner such as Ford *Cooling System Fast Flush*. Follow the procedure outlined in the manufacturer's instructions. If the radiator is severely corroded, damaged or leaking, it should be removed (Chapter 3) and taken to a radiator repair shop.

10   Remove the overflow hose from the coolant recovery reservoir. Drain the reservoir and flush it with clean water, then reconnect the hose.

Refilling

11   Close and tighten the radiator drain. Install and tighten the block drain plug.

12   Place the heater temperature control in the maximum heat position.

13   Slowly add new coolant (a 50/50 mixture of water and antifreeze) to the radiator until it's full. Add coolant to the reservoir up to the lower mark.

14   Leave the radiator cap off and run the engine in a well-ventilated area until the thermostat opens (coolant will begin flowing through the radiator and the upper radiator hose will become hot).

15   Turn the engine off and let it cool. Add more coolant mixture to bring the level back up to the lip on the radiator filler neck.

16   Squeeze the upper radiator hose to expel air, then add more coolant mixture if necessary. Replace the radiator cap.

17   Start the engine, allow it to reach normal operating temperature and check for leaks.

31.1   Materials required for chassis and body lubrication

1   **Engine oil** — *Light engine oil in a can like this can be used for door and hood hinges*
2   **Graphite spray** — *Used to lubricate lock cylinders*
3   **Grease** — *Grease, in a variety of types and weights, is available for use in a grease gun. Check the Specifications for your requirements*
4   **Grease gun** — *A common grease gun, shown here with a detachable hose and nozzle, is needed for chassis lubrication. After use, clean it thoroughly!*

---

31   Chassis lubrication

Refer to illustrations 31.1 and 31.6

1   Refer to *Recommended lubricants and fluids* at the front of this Chapter to obtain the necessary grease, etc. You'll also need a grease gun **(see illustration)**. Occasionally plugs will be installed rather than grease fittings. If so, grease fittings will have to be purchased and installed.

2   Look under the vehicle and see if grease fittings or plugs are installed. If there are plugs, remove them and buy grease fittings, which will thread into the component. A dealer or auto parts store will be able to supply the correct fittings. Straight, as well as angled, fittings are available.

3   For easier access under the vehicle, raise it with a jack and place jackstands under the frame. Make sure it's safely supported by the stands. If the wheels are to be removed at this interval for tire rotation or brake inspection, loosen the lug nuts slightly while the vehicle is still on the ground.

4   Before beginning, force a little grease out of the nozzle to remove any dirt from the end of the gun. Wipe the nozzle clean with a rag.

5   With the grease gun and plenty of clean rags, crawl under the vehicle and begin lubricating the components.

6   Wipe the suspension balljoint grease fitting nipple clean and push the nozzle firmly over it **(see illustration)**. Squeeze the trigger on the grease gun to force grease into the component. The upper balljoints should be lubricated until the rubber seal is firm to the touch. Don't pump too much grease into the fitting as it could rupture the seal. For all other suspension and steering components, continue pumping grease into the fitting until it oozes out of the joint between the two components. If it escapes around the grease gun nozzle, the nipple is clogged or the nozzle is not completely seated on the fitting. Resecure

31.6   After wiping the grease fitting clean, push the nozzle firmly into place and pump the grease into the component — usually about two pumps of the gun will be sufficient

the gun nozzle to the fitting and try again. If necessary, replace the fitting with a new one.

7   Wipe the excess grease from the components and the grease fitting. Repeat the procedure for the remaining fittings.

8   While you're under the vehicle, clean and lubricate the parking brake cable, along with the cable guides and levers. This can be done by smearing some of the chassis grease onto the cable and its related parts with your fingers.

9   Open the hood and smear a little chassis grease on the hood latch mechanism. Have an assistant pull the hood release lever from inside the vehicle as you lubricate the cable at the latch.
10   Lubricate all the hinges (door, hood, etc.) with engine oil to keep them in proper working order.
11   The key lock cylinders can be lubricated with spray graphite or silicone lubricant, which is available at auto parts stores.
12   Lubricate the door weatherstripping with silicone spray. This will reduce chafing and retard wear.

32   Rear axle (differential) oil change

Refer to illustration 32.6

1   Some differentials can be drained by removing the drain plug, while on others it's necessary to remove the cover plate on the differential housing. As an alternative, a hand suction pump can be used to remove the differential lubricant through the filler hole. If there is no drain plug and a suction pump isn't available, be sure to obtain a new gasket at the same time the gear lubricant is purchased.
2   Raise the vehicle and support it securely on jackstands. Move a drain pan, rags, newspapers and wrenches under the vehicle.
3   Remove the check/fill plug from the differential **(see illustration 25.2)**.
4   If equipped with a drain plug, remove the plug and allow the differential oil to drain completely. After the oil has drained, install the plug and tighten it securely.
5   If a suction pump is being used, insert the flexible hose. Work the hose down to the bottom of the differential housing and pump the oil out.
6   If the differential is being drained by removing the cover plate, remove the bolts on the lower half of the plate. Loosen the bolts on the upper half and use them to keep the cover loosely attached **(see illustration)**. Allow the oil to drain into the pan, then completely remove the cover.
7   Using a lint-free rag, clean the inside of the cover and the accessible areas of the differential housing. As this is done, check for chipped gears and metal particles in the lubricant, indicating that the differential

32.6   With the differential cover retained by two loosened bolts at the top, pry it loose and allow the oil to drain — don't damage the gasket sealing surfaces in the process!

should be more thoroughly inspected and/or repaired.
8   Thoroughly clean the gasket mating surfaces of the differential housing and the cover plate. Use a gasket scraper or putty knife to remove all traces of the old gasket.
9   Apply a thin layer of RTV sealant to the cover flange, then press a new gasket into position on the cover. Make sure the bolt holes align properly.
10   Place the cover on the differential housing and install the bolts. Tighten the bolts securely.
11   On all models, use a hand pump, syringe or funnel to fill the differential housing with the specified lubricant until it's level with the bottom of the plug hole.
12   Install the check/fill plug and tighten it securely.

Chapter 2 Part A Four-cylinder engine

Contents

Specifications

General
Cylinder numbers (front-to-rear)	1–2–3–4
Firing order	1-3-4-2

Camshaft
Bearing journal diameter	1.7713 to 1.7720 in
Bearing clearance	0.001 to 0.003 in
End play	0.001 to 0.007 in

Torque specifications
	Ft-lbs
Camshaft sprocket bolt	50 to 71
Crankshaft pulley/sprocket bolt	28 to 40
Rear camshaft retaining plate bolt	6 to 9
Auxiliary shaft sprocket bolt	28 to 40
Auxiliary shaft retaining plate screws	6 to 9
Timing belt outer cover bolts	6 to 9
Timing belt tensioner adjustment bolt	14 to 21
Timing belt tensioner pivot bolt	28 to 40
Camshaft cover bolts	6 to 8
Cylinder head bolts	
Step 1	50 to 60
Step 2	80 to 90
Flywheel/driveplate bolts	56 to 64
Intake manifold bolts	
Step 1	5 to 7
Step 2	14 to 21
Exhaust manifold bolts	
Step 1	5 to 7
Step 2	16 to 23
Oil pan-to-engine block bolts	8 to 10
Oil pan-to-transmission bolts	29 to 40
Oil pump bolts	14 to 21
Oil pump pick-up tube bolts	14 to 21
Engine mount-to-block bolts	45 to 60
Engine mount-to-frame bolts	
Left side	71 to 94
Right side	52 to 67

FRONT OF VEHICLE

DISTRIBUTOR

FIRING ORDER AND POSITION CLOCKWISE

FRONT OF VEHICLE

POSITION OF CAP ATTACHING SCREWS

Cylinder locations and firing order

1 General information

This Part of Chapter 2 is devoted to in-vehicle repair procedures for the 2.3L OHC four-cylinder engine.

Information concerning engine removal and installation, as well as engine block and cylinder head overhaul, is in Part D of this Chapter.

The following repair procedures are based on the assumption that the engine is installed in the vehicle. If the engine has been removed from the vehicle and mounted on a stand, many of the steps included in this Part of Chapter 2 will not apply.

The specifications included in this Part of Chapter 2 apply only to the engine and procedures in this Part. The specifications necessary for rebuilding the block and cylinder head are found in Part D.

2 Repair operations possible with the engine in the vehicle

Many major repair operations can be accomplished without removing the engine from the vehicle.

Clean the engine compartment and the exterior of the engine with some type of pressure washer before any work is done. A clean engine will make the job easier and will help keep dirt out of the internal areas of the engine.

Depending on the components involved, it may be a good idea to remove the hood and engine cover to improve access to the engine as repairs are performed (refer to Chapter 11 if necessary).

If vacuum, exhaust, oil or coolant leaks develop, indicating a need for gasket or seal replacement, the repairs can generally be made with the engine in the vehicle. The intake and exhaust manifold gaskets, oil pan gasket and cylinder head gasket are all accessible with the engine in place.

Engine components such as the intake and exhaust manifolds, the oil pan, the oil pump, the auxiliary shaft, the water pump, the starter motor, the alternator, the distributor and the fuel system components can be removed for repair with the engine in place.

Since the cylinder head can be removed without pulling the engine, camshaft and valve component servicing can also be accomplished with the engine in the vehicle.

In extreme cases caused by a lack of necessary equipment, repair or replacement of piston rings, pistons, connecting rods and rod bearings is possible with the engine in the vehicle. However, this practice is not recommended because of the cleaning and preparation work that must be done to the components involved.

3 Camshaft cover — removal and installation

Refer to illustration 3.6

1   Disconnect the negative cable from the battery.
2   Remove the air cleaner (Chapter 4).
3   Remove the engine cover from inside the vehicle (Chapter 11).
4   Identify and tag the various wires and hoses which cross over the camshaft cover, including the spark plug wires. Do this carefully as they all must be repositioned correctly during installation.
5   Remove the throttle linkage, the throttle body assembly and the upper intake manifold (Chapter 4).
6   Remove the bolts and one stud and separate the cover from the engine (see illustration). It may be necessary to break the gasket seal by tapping the cover with a soft-face hammer. If it's really stuck, use a knife, gasket scraper or chisel to remove it, but be very careful not to damage the gasket sealing surfaces of the cover or head.
7   Place clean rags in the camshaft gallery to keep foreign material out of the engine.
8   Remove all traces of gasket material from the cover and head. Be careful not to nick or gouge the surfaces. Clean the mating surfaces with lacquer thinner or acetone.
9   Reinstall the cover with a new gasket — no sealant is required. Install the bolts and tighten them to the specified torque in a criss-cross pattern.
10 Reinstall the intake manifold (Chapter 4) and the remaining components previously removed or disconnected.

4 Valve train components — removal and installation

Refer to illustrations 4.7, 4.8 and 4.17

Note: *Broken valve springs and defective valve stem seals can be replaced without removing the cylinder head. Two special tools and a compressed air source are normally required to perform this operation, so read through this Section carefully and rent or buy the tools before beginning the job. If compressed air isn't available, a length of nylon rope can be used to keep the valves from falling into the cylinder during this procedure.*

1   Refer to Section 3 and remove the camshaft cover.
2   Remove the spark plug from the cylinder which has the defective component. If all of the valve stem seals are being replaced, all of the spark plugs should be removed (Chapter 1).
3   Turn the crankshaft until the piston in the affected cylinder is at top dead center on the compression stroke (refer to Section 16 for instructions). If you're replacing all of the valve stem seals, begin with cylinder number one and work on the valves for one cylinder at a time. Move from cylinder-to-cylinder following the firing order sequence (1-3-4-2).
4   Thread an adapter into the spark plug hole and connect an air hose from a compressed air source to it. Most auto parts stores can supply the air hose adapter. **Note:** *Many cylinder compression gauges utilize a screw-in fitting that may work with your air hose quick-disconnect fitting.*
5   Apply compressed air to the cylinder. The valves for that cylinder should be held in place by the air pressure. If the valve faces or seats are in poor condition, leaks may prevent the air pressure from retaining the valves — refer to the alternative procedure below.
6   If you don't have access to compressed air, an alternative method can be used. Position the piston at a point just before TDC on the compression stroke, then feed a long piece of nylon rope through the spark plug hole until it fills the combustion chamber. Be sure to leave the end of the rope hanging out of the engine so it can be removed easily. Use a large breaker bar and socket to rotate the crankshaft in the normal direction of rotation until **slight** resistance is felt.
7   Stuff shop rags into the cylinder head holes above and below the valves to prevent parts and tools from falling into the engine, then use

3.6 **Exploded view of camshaft cover and related components**

4.7   While compressed air holds the valve closed, a special compressor is used to collapse the spring so the cam follower and lash adjuster can be removed

4.8   Valve components — note that in this view the camshaft lobe is contacting the cam follower (arrow) which compresses the valve spring and opens the valve — for work described in Section 4 the valve should be closed, with the cam lobe pointing up — away from the follower

A Cam follower   D Valve spring
B Lash adjuster   E Valve keepers
C Valve

a valve spring compressor to compress the spring (see illustration).
8   With the spring compressed, slide the cam follower over the lash adjuster to remove it (see illustration). Also remove the lash adjuster.
9   Still compressing the spring, remove the keepers. Release the valve spring tool and remove the spring retainer, damper assembly and valve spring.
10   Remove and discard the valve stem seal. Note: If air pressure fails to hold the valve in the closed position during this operation, the valve face or seat is probably damaged. If so, the cylinder head will have to be removed for additional repair operations.
11   Wrap a rubber band or tape around the top of the valve stem so the valve will not fall into the cylinder, then release the air pressure.
12   Inspect the valve stem for damage. Rotate the valve in the guide and check the end for eccentric movement, which would indicate that the valve is bent.
13   Move the valve up-and-down in the guide and make sure it doesn't bind. If the valve stem binds, either the valve is bent or the guide is damaged. In either case, the head will have to be removed for repair.
14   Reapply air pressure to the cylinder to retain the valve in the closed position, then remove the tape or rubber band from the valve stem. Lubricate the valve stem with engine oil and install a new umbrella type guide seal, if used.
15   Place the plastic installation cap over the end of the valve stem.
16   Start the valve stem seal carefully over the cap and push the seal down until the jacket touches the top of the guide.
17   Remove the plastic cap and use the installation tool (see illustration) or two screwdrivers to bottom the seal on the valve guide.
18   Install the valve spring, damper and retainer, compress the spring and install the keepers.
19   Install the lash adjuster and cam follower.
20   Disconnect the air hose and remove the adapter from the spark plug hole. If a rope was used in place of air pressure, pull it out of the cylinder. Caution: Do not turn the crankshaft backwards to release the rope. Turning the crankshaft backwards will cause the timing belt to jump time.
21   Reinstall the various components previously removed.
22   Start and run the engine, then check for oil leaks and unusual sounds coming from the camshaft cover area.

VALVE STEM INSTALLATION TOOL

4.17   Ford valve stem seal tool

5   Timing belt — removal, installation and adjustment

Refer to illustrations 5.10, 5.11a, 5.11b and 5.23
1   Disconnect the negative cable from the battery.
2   Remove the fan shroud (Chapter 3).
3   Remove the fan and the water pump pulley (Chapter 3).

5.10 Timing belt cover assembly

4   Remove the drivebelts.
5   Drain the cooling system (Chapter 1) and remove the upper radiator hose (Chapter 3).
6   Remove the thermostat housing and gasket (Chapter 3).
7   Position the number one piston at top dead center on the compression stroke (Section 16). **Caution:** *Always turn the crankshaft in the direction of normal rotation (clockwise, viewed from the front). Backward rotation may cause the timing belt to jump teeth. DO NOT turn the crankshaft during this procedure, after the number one piston is at TDC, until after the timing belt is reinstalled!*
8   Make sure the distributor rotor is pointing at the number one plug wire terminal.
9   Remove the crankshaft drivebelt pulley and belt guide.
10 Remove the four bolts and one screw and detach the outer timing belt cover (**see illustration**).
11 Loosen the belt tensioner adjustment bolt, then position spreader tool no. T74P-6254-A or a breaker bar on the tensioner roll pin and retract the belt tensioner (**see illustrations**). Tighten the adjustment bolt to hold the tensioner in the retracted position.
12 Remove the timing belt and inspect it for wear and damage. If it's worn or damaged, replace the belt. **Caution:** *If in doubt about the belt condition, install a new one. If the belt breaks during engine operation, extensive damage may occur!*

5.11a Timing belt and related components — exploded view

13 Check the sprockets for wear, cracks and burrs on the teeth. If the sprockets are worn or damaged, they can be detached after removing the mounting bolts. Make sure the new sprockets are installed correctly (see illustration 5.11a). Tighten the mounting bolts to the specified torque. **Note:** *Install a new camshaft sprocket bolt or use Teflon sealing tape on the old bolt.*
14 Make sure the valve timing mark on the camshaft sprocket is aligned with the pointer. Install the timing belt over the crankshaft sprocket, then over the auxiliary shaft sprocket.
15 Pull the belt up (pulling slack from between the auxiliary and camshaft sprockets) and install it on the camshaft sprocket in a counterclockwise direction so no slack will be between the two sprockets. Align the belt fore and aft on the sprockets.
16 Loosen the tensioner adjustment bolt to allow the tensioner to move against the belt. If the spring does not have enough tension to move the roller against the belt (the belt hangs loose), it may be necessary to insert tool no. T74P-6254-A or a breaker bar between the tensioner and roll pin and push the roller against the belt. Tighten the bolt to the specified torque. **Note:** *The spring cannot be used to set belt tension. A wrench must be used on the tensioner assembly.*
17 Remove the spark plugs. Slowly rotate the crankshaft two complete turns in the direction of normal rotation to make sure the belt is seated and to remove any slack. While turning the crankshaft, feel and listen for valve-to-piston contact. Don't force the crankshaft — if binding is felt, recheck all work or seek professional advice!
18 Tighten the tensioner adjustment and pivot bolts to the specified torque. Recheck the alignment of the valve timing marks.
19 Install the timing belt cover and tighten the mounting bolts to the specified torque.
20 The remaining installation steps are the reverse of removal. Be sure to tighten the crankshaft pulley/sprocket bolt to the specified torque.
21 Bring the number one piston to top dead center on the compression stroke (Section 16).
22 Remove the distributor cap and make sure the distributor rotor is pointing at the number one spark plug wire terminal.
23 Remove the access plug from the timing belt cover (see illustration).
24 Look through the access hole in the belt cover to be sure that the timing mark on the camshaft sprocket is lined up with the pointer.
25 Make sure the timing mark on the crankshaft pulley aligns with the TDC mark on the belt cover.
26 Reinstall the belt cover access plug.

6 Camshaft — removal, inspection and installation

Refer to illustrations 6.9 and 6.12

Removal

1 Disconnect the negative cable at the battery and remove the engine cover (Chapter 11).
2 Remove the camshaft cover, the timing belt cover and the timing belt (Sections 3 and 5).
3 Remove the spring clip from the hydraulic valve lash adjuster end of each cam follower.
4 Using a valve spring compressor, compress the valve spring and slide out the cam follower (see Section 4 if necessary). Keep the cam followers in order so they can be reinstalled in their original locations.
5 Lift out the hydraulic lash adjusters, keeping each one with its respective cam follower.
6 Remove the camshaft sprocket mounting bolt and washer. A long screwdriver placed through one of the holes in the sprocket will prevent the camshaft from turning.
7 Draw off the sprocket with a puller, then remove the belt guide.
8 Remove the sprocket locating pin from the end of the camshaft.
9 Remove the camshaft retaining plate from the rear bearing pedestal (see illustration).
10 Raise the vehicle and support it securely on jackstands.
11 Position a floor jack under the engine. Place a block of wood on the jack pad. Remove the left and right engine mount bolts and nuts. Raise the engine as high as it will go. Place blocks of wood between the engine mounts and frame brackets and remove the jack. **Warning:** *DO NOT place your hands under the engine where they would be crushed if the jack failed!*
12 Using a hammer and a brass or aluminum drift, drive the camshaft

5.11b A special Ford tool, or a standard breaker bar, can be used to release the tension on the timing belt

BELT TENSION RELEASING TOOL T74P-6254-A

5.23 Before starting the engine, remove the plug from the belt cover and recheck the timing marks

RETAINING PLATE

PLUG

SCREW AND WASHER

6.9 The camshaft retaining plate is held in place with two screws

FOLLOW ARM

LASH ADJUSTER

DIP IN OIL PRIOR TO INSTALLATION

FRONT OF ENGINE

VIEW A

VIEW B

CAMSHAFT

CYLINDER HEAD

CAMSHAFT BEARING

SEAL

6.12 Camshaft and related components — exploded view

out toward the front of the engine, taking the front seal with it **(see illustration)**. Be very careful not to damage the camshaft bearings and journals as it's pushed out.

Inspection

Camshaft and bearings
13 After the camshaft has been removed from the engine, cleaned with solvent and dried, inspect the bearing journals for uneven wear, pits and galling. If the journals are damaged, the bearing inserts in the head are probably damaged as well. Both the camshaft and bearings will have to be replaced with new ones. Measure the inside diameter of each camshaft bearing and record the results (take two measurements, 90° apart, at each bearing).
14 Measure the camshaft bearing journals with a micrometer to determine if they're excessively worn or out-of-round. If they're more than 0.005-inch out-of-round, the camshaft should be replaced with a new one. Subtract the bearing journal diameters from the corresponding bearing inside diameter measurements to obtain the oil clearance. If it's excessive, new bearings must be installed. **Note:** *Camshaft bearing replacement requires special tools and expertise that place it outside the scope of the do-it-yourselfer. Take the head to an automotive machine shop to ensure that the job is done correctly.*
15 Check the camshaft lobes for heat discoloration, score marks, chipped areas, pitting and uneven wear. If the lobes are in good condition the camshaft can be reused.
16 Make sure the camshaft oil passages are clear and clean.
17 To check the thrust plate for wear, install the camshaft in the cylinder head and position the thrust plate at the rear. Using a dial indicator, check the total end play by tapping the camshaft carefully back-and-forth. If the end play is outside the specified limit, replace the thrust plate with a new one.

Cam followers
18 Check the faces of the cam followers (which bear on the cam lobes) for signs of pitting, score marks and other forms of wear. They should fit snugly on the pivot bolt.
19 Inspect the face which bears on the valve stem. If it's pitted, the cam follower must be replaced with a new one.
20 If excessive cam follower wear is evident (and possibly excessive cam lobe wear), it may be due to a malfunction of the valve drive lubrication tube. If this has occurred, replace the tube and the cam follower. If more than one cam follower is excessively worn, replace the camshaft, all the cam followers and the lubrication tube. This also applies where excessive cam lobe wear is found.

21 During any operation which requires removal of the camshaft cover, make sure that oil is being discharged from the lubrication tube nozzles by cranking the engine with the starter motor.

Installation
22 Liberally coat the camshaft journals and bearings with engine assembly lube or moly-base grease, then carefully install the camshaft in the cylinder head.
23 Install the retaining plate and screws.
24 Lubricate the new camshaft oil seal with engine oil and carefully tap it into place at the front of the cylinder head with a large socket and a hammer. Make sure it enters the bore squarely and seats completely.
25 Install the belt guide and pin at the front end of the camshaft, then carefully tap on the sprocket.
26 Install a new sprocket bolt or use Teflon sealing tape on the threads of the old one.
27 Coat the hydraulic lash adjusters with engine assembly lube or moly-base grease, then install them in their original locations.
28 Coat the camshaft lobes and cam followers with engine assembly lube or moly-base grease.
29 Install the timing belt (Section 5).
30 Compress each valve spring and position each cam follower on its respective valve end and adjuster. Install the retaining spring clips.
31 Install the remaining components previously removed.

---

7   Auxiliary shaft — removal, inspection and installation

Refer to illustration 7.4

1   Detach the negative battery cable from the battery. Remove the large bolt from the front of the crankshaft and pull the drivebelt pulley off. Remove the bolts/screws and detach the outer timing belt cover **(see illustration 5.10)**.
2   Loosen the auxiliary shaft sprocket bolt **(see illustration 5.11a)**. If the shaft turns, immobilize the sprocket by inserting a large screwdriver or 3/8-inch drive extension through one of the sprocket holes. Detach the timing belt (Section 5).
3   Pull off the sprocket (a puller may be required), and remove the pin from the shaft.
4   Remove the three bolts and detach the auxiliary shaft cover **(see illustration)**.

COVER ALIGNMENT PADS
3 PLACES

VIEW A

GEAR AND FUEL PUMP ECCENTRIC
MUST NOT BE ALLOWED TO
TOUCH BEARING SURFACES
DURING INSTALLATION

AUXILIARY
SHAFT

RETAINING
PLATE

BEARING

DIP SHAFT
COMPLETELY
IN ENGINE OIL
BEFORE INSTALLING

PIN

NOTE: CUT GASKET
FOR SEPARATE
REMOVAL OR
INSTALLATION OF
COVERS

AUXILIARY
SHAFT
COVER

FRONT COVER
ALIGNMENT TOOL

VIEW A

GASKET

SCREW AND WASHER

CYLINDER
FRONT COVER

7.4 Auxiliary shaft and related components — exploded view

5   Remove the screws and detach the retaining plate.
6   Withdraw the shaft. If it's tight, reinstall the bolt and washer. Use a pry bar and spacer block to pry out the shaft. Be extremely careful not to damage the bearings as you pull the shaft out of the block.
7   Examine the auxiliary shaft bearing for pits and score marks. Replacement must be done by a shop (although it's easy to remove the old bearing, correct installation of the new one requires special tools). The auxiliary shaft may show signs of wear on the bearing journal or the eccentric. Score marks and damage to the bearing journals *cannot* be removed by grinding. If in doubt, ask a dealer service department to check the auxiliary shaft and give advice on replacement. Examine the gear teeth for wear and damage. If either is evident, a replacement shaft must be obtained.
8   Dip the auxiliary shaft in engine oil before installing it in the block. Tap it in gently with a soft-face hammer to ensure that it's seated. Install the retaining plate and the auxiliary shaft cover.
9   The remainder of the procedure is the reverse of removal. Make sure that the auxiliary shaft pin is in place before installing the sprocket. Tighten the sprocket mounting bolt to the specified torque.

8   Front oil seals — replacement

Note: *The camshaft, crankshaft and auxiliary shaft oil seals are all replaced the same way, using the same tools, after the appropriate sprocket has been removed.*

1   Disconnect the negative battery cable from the battery.
2   To remove the camshaft or auxiliary shaft sprockets, refer to Section 6 or 7. Ford manufactures a special puller designed for this purpose.
3   To remove the crankshaft sprocket, use Ford tool no. T6256B or a gear puller.
4   Ford tool no. T74P-6700-B or equivalent may be used to remove all the seals. When using the tool, be sure the jaws are gripping the thin edge of the seal very tightly before operating the screw portion of the tool. If the tool isn't available, a hammer and chisel may be used to remove the seal(s) if care is exercised.
5   Clean the seal bore and shaft surface prior to installation of the new seal. Apply a thin layer of grease to the outer edge of the new seal(s).
6   Install the seal(s) with Ford tool no. T74P-6150A. If the special tool isn't available, you may be able to use a large deep socket and a hammer or a short piece of pipe, the sprocket bolt and a large flat washer.
7   Install the components removed to gain access to the seals.

9   Intake manifold — removal and installation

Refer to illustrations 9.11 and 9.16
1   Relieve the fuel system pressure (Chapter 4).
2   Disconnect the negative battery cable from the battery.
3   Drain the cooling system (Chapter 1).
4   Remove the engine cover (Chapter 11).
5   Remove the air cleaner and ducts (Chapter 4).
6   Label and disconnect the vacuum hoses from the throttle body and emissions devices attached to the intake manifold.
7   Remove the throttle body, fuel injection wiring harness, fuel supply manifold, throttle cable, speed control cable (if equipped) and upper intake manifold (Chapter 4).
8   Disconnect the coolant bypass hose from the lower intake manifold.
9   Remove the engine oil dipstick bracket retaining bolt.
10   Remove the four bottom mounting bolts from the intake manifold.
11   Remove the four upper mounting bolts from the manifold. Note that the front two bolts also secure the engine lifting "eye" **(see illustration).**
12   Detach the manifold from the engine.
13   Clean the manifold and head mating surfaces and check the manifold for cracks. **Note:** *The mating surfaces of the head and manifold must be perfectly clean when the manifold is installed. Gasket removal solvents in aerosol cans are available at most auto parts stores and may be helpful when removing old gasket material that's stuck to the head and manifold. Be careful not to scrape or gouge the sealing surfaces.*

14   Clean and oil the manifold mounting bolts.
15   Position the new intake manifold gasket on the head, using a light coat of gasket sealant to hold it in place.
16   Position the intake manifold, along with the lifting "eye", on the head, install the fasteners and tighten them in sequence, reaching the specified torque in two steps **(see illustration).**
17   The remainder of installation is the reverse of removal.
18   Reconnect the battery and refill the cooling system.
19   Start the engine and let it run while checking for coolant, fuel and vacuum leaks.
20   Reinstall the engine cover.

9.11   Exploded view of intake manifold components

9.16   Intake manifold bolt TIGHTENING sequence

10   Exhaust manifold — removal and installation

Refer to illustrations 10.8 and 10.10
Removal
1   Disconnect the negative battery cable from the battery.
2   Remove the air cleaner and duct assembly if needed to gain working room.
3   Remove the engine cover (Chapter 11).
4   Remove the EGR line bolts at the exhaust manifold and loosen at the EGR tube (Chapter 6).
5   Disconnect the oxygen sensor wire.
6   Remove the bolt attaching the heater hoses to the camshaft cover.
7   Raise the vehicle and support it securely on jackstands. Remove the two bolts attaching the exhaust pipe to the manifold (Chapter 4).
8   Remove the eight exhaust manifold mounting bolts **(see illustration).** A special Allen head socket will be needed to remove the bolts.
9   Remove the exhaust manifold out through the bottom of the vehicle.

10.8   **Exhaust manifold mounting details**

10.10   **Exhaust manifold bolt TIGHTENING sequence**

Installation

10 Using a new gasket, install the manifold and the eight bolts attaching it to the cylinder head. Tighten the bolts (in two or three steps) to the specified torque in the sequence shown (see illustration).

11 Install the bolts attaching the exhaust pipe to the exhaust manifold.

12 Position the heater hoses on the camshaft cover.

13 Reconnect the oxygen sensor wire.

14 Install the EGR line at the exhaust manifold.

15 Install the air cleaner and duct assembly.

16 Reconnect the battery cable.

17 Reinstall the engine cover.

---

11   Cylinder head — removal and installation

Refer to illustrations 11.31 and 11.33

Removal

1   Begin the procedure by positioning the number one piston at top dead center (TDC) on the compression stroke (see Section 16). Remove the engine cover (Chapter 11).

2   Drain the cooling system (Chapter 1). Remove the air cleaner assembly and the air duct.

3   Remove the bolt retaining the heater hose to the camshaft cover.

4   Detach the distributor cap from the distributor.

5   Remove the spark plug wires from the spark plugs and remove the distributor cap and wires as an assembly. Remove the spark plugs.

6   Label and disconnect all vacuum hoses attached to the components on the head.

7   Remove the dipstick tube.

8   Remove the camshaft cover (Section 3).

9   Remove the intake manifold bolts (Section 9).

10 Loosen the alternator mounting bolts, remove the belt from the pulley and remove the bracket bolts.

11 Disconnect the upper radiator hose at both ends and remove it from the engine.

12 Remove the timing belt front cover.

13 Make sure the valve timing is correct (Section 5, Paragraphs 21 through 25), then loosen the timing belt tensioner (Section 5).

14 Remove the timing belt from the camshaft and auxiliary shaft sprockets.

15 Remove the heat stove from the exhaust manifold.

16 Remove the exhaust manifold mounting bolts (Section 10). The manifold itself can remain in place.

17 Remove the timing belt tensioner bolts.

18 Remove the timing belt tensioner spring stop from the cylinder head.

19 Disconnect the oil pressure sending unit lead wire.

20 Refer to Section 9 and remove the intake manifold.

21 Using a new head gasket, outline the cylinders and bolt pattern on a piece of cardboard. Be sure to indicate the front of the engine for reference. Punch holes at the bolt locations.

22 Loosen the cylinder head mounting bolts in 1/4-turn increments until they can be removed by hand. Store the bolts in the cardboard holder as they're removed — this will ensure that they're reinstalled in their original locations.

23 Lift the head off the engine. If it's stuck, don't pry between the head and block. Instead, rap the head with a soft-face hammer or a block of wood and a hammer to break the gasket seal.

24 Place the head on a block of wood to prevent damage to the gasket surface. Refer to Part D for cylinder head disassembly and valve service procedures.

Installation

25 If a new cylinder head is being installed, transfer all external parts from the old cylinder head to the new one.

26 The mating surfaces of the cylinder head and block must be perfectly clean when the head is installed.

27 Use a gasket scraper to remove all traces of carbon and old gasket material, then clean the mating surfaces with lacquer thinner or acetone. If there's oil on the mating surfaces when the head is installed, the gasket may not seal correctly and leaks may develop. Use a vacuum cleaner to remove any debris that falls into the cylinders.

28 Check the block and head mating surfaces for nicks, deep scratches and other damage. If damage is slight, it can be removed with a file; if it's excessive, machining may be the only alternative.

29 Use a tap of the correct size to chase the threads in the head bolt holes. Mount each bolt in a vise and run a die down the threads to remove corrosion and restore the threads. Dirt, corrosion, sealant and damaged threads will affect critical head bolt torque readings.

30 Position the new gasket over the dowel pins in the block.

CAMSHAFT 90°
TO PAN RAIL

CAMSHAFT
6250

30.9°
38.9°

VIEW A

14.0-14.5 mm
(0.55-0.57 INCH)

SECTION B

NOTE: PRIOR TO CYLINDER HEAD INSTALLATION,
CAMSHAFT MUST BE POSITIONED AS SHOWN
TO PROTECT PROTRUDING VALVES

**11.31   Be sure to turn the camshaft until the pin is in the
5 o'clock position as shown here before installing the head**

31 Make a mark on the cylinder head indicating the position of the
pin in the end of the camshaft. Turn the camshaft until the pin is in
the five o'clock position — this must be done to avoid damage to the
valves when the head is installed **(see illustration)**.
32 Carefully position the head on the block without disturbing the
gasket.
33 Install the cylinder head bolts and tighten them in sequence **(see
illustration)** to the specified torque.
34 Return the camshaft to its original position (with the pin aligned
with the mark you made on the head).
35 The remainder of installation is the reverse of the removal
procedure.
36 Change the engine oil and filter (Chapter 1).

12 Oil pan — removal and installation

Refer to illustration 12.30
Note: *Vehicles equipped with an automatic transmission have an oil
pan which can be removed out the front of the engine compartment.
Those with a manual transmission must be removed out the rear.*

1   Disconnect the negative battery cable from the battery.
2   Remove the air cleaner and hoses as an assembly.
3   Remove the oil dipstick.
4   Remove the engine mount nuts.
5   Remove the oil cooler lines at the radiator, if so equipped.
6   Remove the two bolts retaining the fan shroud to the radiator and
remove the shroud.
7   Remove the radiator mounting bolts (automatic transmission only).
8   Drain the radiator and remove the hoses. Move the radiator up and
wire it to the hood to provide working clearance (automatic transmission only).
9   Raise and support the vehicle on jackstands.
10 Drain the oil and remove the oil filter.
11 Remove the starter motor (Chapter 5).
12 Disconnect the exhaust manifold tube at the inlet pipe bracket
(Chapter 4).
13 Remove the transmission mount-to-crossmember nuts.
14 Remove the bellcrank from the converter housing (automatic
transmission only).
15 Remove the oil cooler lines from the retainer at the engine block
(automatic transmission only).
16 Remove the front crossmember (automatic transmission only).
17 Disconnect the right front lower shock absorber mount (manual
transmission only).
18 Position a jack under the engine, raise the engine and block it with
a piece of wood approximately 2-1/2 inches thick between the motor
mount and the frame rail. **Warning:** *Do not place any part of your body
under the engine where it could be crushed if the jack failed.*
19 Remove the jack.
20 Position the jack under the transmission and raise it slightly
(automatic transmission only).
21 Remove the oil pan mounting bolts and lower the pan.
22 Remove the oil pump and pick-up tube assembly and drop them
into the oil pan. Note how the intermediate shaft is installed!
23 Remove the oil pan (out the front on automatics — out the rear
on manual).
24 Clean the oil pan and inspect for damage. Remove spacers, if any,
that are attached to the oil pan transmission mounting pad.

FRONT OF ENGINE

11.33   Cylinder head bolt TIGHTENING sequence

25 Clean the oil pan gasket surface on the cylinder block and the oil
pan flange. These surfaces must be perfectly clean to prevent oil leaks.
26 Clean the oil pump exterior and oil pump pick-up tube screen.
27 To install, follow the instructions which will come with the new
gasket to apply RTV sealant. Position the gasket inside the channel
of the pan.
28 Place the oil pump and pick-up tube assembly inside the oil pan.
29 Position the oil pan under the engine, reach inside and install the
oil pump and pick-up tube assembly, tightening the bolts to the specified
torque (see Section 13).
30 Install the oil pan mounting bolts **(see illustration)** and hand tighten
them only at this time.

FRONT OF ENGINE

OIL PAN
ASSEMBLY

GASKET

USE RTV SEALER

(6 PLACES) AS SHOWN

12.30   Oil pan and related components

FRONT OF ENGINE

NOTE: OIL PUMP MUST BE FREE TO ROTATE AFTER INSTALLATION

OIL PUMP

SHAFT ASSEMBLY OIL PUMP INTERMEDIATE

13.1 Oil pump mounting details

31 Tighten the two oil pan-to-transmission bolts to the specified tor-que, then loosen them 1/2 turn.
32 Tighten the oil pan-to-engine block bolts to the specified torque, working around the pan, tightening each bolt a little at a time.
33 Retighten the remaining two bolts. **Note:** *If the oil pan is installed while the transmission is removed, either reinstall the transmission or*

use a special fixture to insure the oil pan is installed flush with the rear of the block.
34 The remainder of the installation is the reverse of the removal procedure.
35 Be sure to refill the engine with the proper quantity, grade and viscosity oil.

13 Oil pump — removal and installation

Refer to illustration 13.1

1 Remove the oil pan as described in Section 12. The pump must be removed as a part of the oil pan removal procedure **(see illustration)**.
2 If there is any possibility that the pump is faulty or if an engine overhaul is being performed, replace the pump. A faulty pump can ruin an otherwise good engine.
3 Prime the pump before installation. Hold it with the pick-up tube up and pour a few ounces of clean oil into the inlet screen. Turn the pump driveshaft by hand until oil comes out the outlet.
4 Install the pump intermediate shaft with the collar end in the engine block. Be sure the shaft seats in the distributor. Hold the shaft in place and install the pump assembly as the oil pan is installed (see Section 12). Be sure to tighten the bolts to the specified torque.
5 Add oil to the engine (Chapter 1), then start it and be sure the oil pressure comes up. If it doesn't come up within 10 or 15 seconds, shut off the engine immediately and find the cause of the problem. **Caution:** *Continued running of the engine without oil pressure will severely damage the moving parts!*
6 Check for oil leaks.

14 Flywheel/driveplate — removal and installation

Refer to illustration 14.3

1 Remove the transmission (Chapter 7).
2 Remove the pressure plate and the clutch disc from the rear of the flywheel as described in Chapter 8 (manual transmission models).
3 Lock the flywheel/driveplate using a large screwdriver in mesh with the starter ring gear and remove the six bolts securing the flywheel to the crankshaft **(see illustration)**. The bolts should be removed a

APPLY FORD POLYETHYLENE GREASE DOAZ-19584-A OR EQUIVALENT TO CRANKSHAFT PILOT HOLE

FLYWHEEL AND PRESSURE PLATE FRICTION SURFACES MUST BE FREE OF DIRT, GREASE AND OIL PRIOR TO INSTALLTION

ROLLER PILOT BEARING

FLYWHEEL

BOLTS

REAR COVER PLATE

REINFORCING PLATE

AUTOMATIC TRANSMISSION

REAR COVER PLATE

FLYWHEEL AND PRESSURE PLATE FRICTION SURFACES MUST BE FREE OF DIRT, GREASE AND OIL PRIOR TO INSTALLTION

INSTALL WITH SEAL TOWARD TRANSMISSION

FLYWHEEL

CLUTCH DISC

PRESSURE PLATE

DOWEL

MANUAL TRANSMISSION

14.3 Exploded view of flywheel/driveplate components

quarter turn at a time in a diagonal and progressive manner.

4   Mark the mating position of the flywheel/driveplate and crankshaft flange and then remove the flywheel.

5   Remove the engine rear cover plate bolts and ease the rear cover plate over the two dowel pins. Remove the cover plate.

6   If the flywheel ring gear is badly worn or has teeth missing, it should be replaced by an automotive machine shop.

7   Check for cracks and other damage.

8   Installation of the flywheel/driveplate and clutch is the reverse of the removal procedure. Apply oil-resistant sealer sparingly to the bolt threads. Be sure to tighten all bolts to the specified torque. For further information on clutch servicing and pilot bearing replacement, see Chapter 8.

15   Rear crankshaft oil seal — replacement

Refer to illustration 15.5

1   Remove the transmission and all other components necessary, such as the clutch and pressure plate, to get at the oil seal in the back of the engine (Chapters 7 and 8).

2   Remove the flywheel or driveplate (Section 14).

3   Use a small punch to make two holes on opposite sides of the seal and install small sheet metal screws in the seal. Pry on the screws with two large screwdrivers until the seal is removed from the engine. It may be necessary to place small blocks of wood against the block to provide a fulcrum point for prying. **Caution:** *Be careful not to scratch or otherwise damage the crankshaft oil seal surface.*

4   Apply a thin film of engine oil to the mating edges of the seal and the seal bore in the block, as well as the seal lips.

5   Position the seal on seal installer tool T82L-6701-A or its equivalent, then position the tool and seal at the rear of engine **(see Illustration)**. Install the seal with the spring side toward the engine. Alternate tightening of the bolts to seat the seal properly.

6   If the special seal installer is not available, gently tap the seal into place with a soft-face hammer.

7   The remainder of the installation is the reverse of the removal procedure.

16   Top Dead Center (TDC) for number one piston — locating

1   Top Dead Center (TDC) is the highest point in the cylinder that each piston reaches as it travels up-and-down when the crankshaft turns. Each piston reaches TDC on the compression stroke and again on the exhaust stroke, but TDC generally refers to piston position on the compression stroke. The timing marks are referenced to the number one piston at TDC on the compression stroke.

2   Positioning the piston(s) at TDC is an essential part of many procedures such as in-vehicle valve train service, timing belt replacement and distributor removal.

3   In order to bring any piston to TDC, the crankshaft must be turned using one of the methods outlined below. When looking at the front of the engine, normal crankshaft rotation is clockwise. **Caution:** *Turning the crankshaft backwards may cause the timing belt to jump time.*

   a) The preferred method is to turn the crankshaft with a large socket and breaker bar attached to the large bolt that's threaded into the front of the crankshaft.

   b) A remote starter switch, which may save some time, can also be used. Attach the switch leads to the switch and battery terminals on the solenoid. Once the piston is close to TDC, use a socket and breaker bar as described in the previous paragraph.

   c) If an assistant is available to turn the ignition switch to the Start position in short bursts, you can get the piston close to TDC without a remote starter switch. Use a socket and breaker bar as described in Paragraph a) to complete the procedure.

4   Locate the number one spark plug wire terminal in the distributor cap, then mark the distributor base directly under the terminal.

5   Remove the distributor cap as described in Chapter 1.

6   Turn the crankshaft (see Paragraph 3 above) until the ignition timing mark for TDC on the crankshaft pulley is aligned with the timing mark on the belt cover..

7   The rotor should now be pointing directly at the mark you made earlier. If it isn't, the piston is at TDC on the exhaust stroke.

8   To get the piston to TDC on the compression stroke, turn the crankshaft one complete turn (360°) clockwise. The rotor should now be pointing at the mark. When the rotor is pointing at the number one spark plug wire terminal in the distributor cap (which is indicated by

15.5   **A special Ford tool is used to install the rear main oil seal**

17.3   **Engine mount assemblies for the four-cylinder engine**

the mark on the distributor) and the ignition timing marks are aligned, the number one piston is at TDC on the compression stroke.

9   After the number one piston has been positioned at TDC on the compression stroke, TDC for any of the remaining cylinders can be located by turning the crankshaft and following the firing order (refer to the Specifications).

17   Engine mounts — removal and installation

Refer to illustration 17.3

1   Remove the fan shroud mounting screws.

2   Using a floor jack and a block of wood between the jack head and oil pan, support the engine.

3   Remove the nuts and washers securing the insulator assemblies (engine mounts) to the frame brackets **(see illustration)**.

4   Lift the engine sufficiently to disengage the front insulator studs from the crossmember bracket.

5   Remove the insulator assembly-to-block bolts and remove the insulators and brackets.

6   To install, mount the insulators on the block, lower the engine until the insulator stud and locking pin engages and bottoms in the slots in the crossmember and install the nuts and washers.

7   Remove the floor jack and reinstall the fan shroud mounting screws.

Chapter 2 Part B   2.8L V6 engine

Contents

Specifications

General
Cylinder numbers
  Left (driver's) side 4–5–6
  Right side 1–2–3
Firing order 1-4-2-5-3-6

Camshaft
Camshaft end play .... 0.0008 to 0.004 in
Valve clearance
  Intake .... 0.014 in
  Exhaust .... 0.016 in

Torque specifications   Ft-lbs *(unless otherwise noted)*
Camshaft gear bolt................................. 30 to 36
Camshaft thrust plate bolts.......................... 13 to 16
Crankshaft damper/pulley bolt........................ 85 to 96
Cylinder head bolts
  Step 1 .... 29 to 40
  Step 2 .... 40 to 51
  Step 3 .... 70 to 85
Exhaust manifold bolts .... 20 to 30
Flywheel-to-crankshaft bolts .... 47 to 52
Front cover bolts .... 13 to 16
Intake manifold bolt/nut
  Step 1 .... 36 to 72 in-lbs
  Step 2 .... 72 to 132 in-lbs
  Step 3 .... 11 to 15
  Step 4 .... 15 to 18
Intake manifold stud .... 10 to 12
Oil pump pick-up tube-to-pump .... 72 to 120 in-lbs
Oil pump pick-up tube to main bearing cap .... 12 to 15
Oil pan bolts .... 60 to 96 in-lbs
Rocker arm cover bolts .... 36 to 60 in-lbs
Rocker arm shaft support bolts .... 43 to 50

1 General information

This Part of Chapter 2 is devoted to in-vehicle repair procedures for the 2.8 liter V6 engine. Information concerning engine removal and installation, as well as engine block and cylinder head overhaul, is in Part D of this Chapter.

The following repair procedures are based on the assumption that the engine is installed in the vehicle. If the engine has been removed from the vehicle and mounted on a stand, many of the steps included in this Part of Chapter 2 will not apply.

The Specifications included in this Part of Chapter 2 apply only to the engine and procedures in this Part. The Specifications necessary for rebuilding the block and cylinder head are found in Part D.

2 Repair operations possible with the engine in the vehicle

Many major repair operations can be accomplished without removing the engine from the vehicle. However, due to limited access, extra time

Left side view of engine (removed from vehicle for clarity)

Front view of engine (removed from vehicle for clarity)

and patience will be required!

Clean the engine compartment and the exterior of the engine with some type of pressure washer before any work is done. A clean engine will make the job easier and will help keep dirt out of the internal areas of the engine.

Depending on the components involved, remove the engine cover, the lower instrument trim panel and, if necessary, the hood to improve access to the engine as repairs are performed (refer to Chapter 11 if necessary).

If vacuum, exhaust, oil or coolant leaks develop, indicating a need for gasket or seal replacement, the repairs can generally be made with the engine in the vehicle. The intake and exhaust manifold gaskets, oil pan gasket and cylinder head gaskets are all accessible with the engine in place.

Exterior engine components such as the intake and exhaust manifolds, the oil pan (and the oil pump), the water pump, the starter motor, the alternator, the distributor and the fuel system components can be removed for repair with the engine in place.

Since the cylinder heads can be removed without pulling the engine, valve component servicing can also be accomplished with the engine in the vehicle.

In extreme cases caused by a lack of necessary equipment, repair or replacement of piston rings, pistons, connecting rods and rod bearings is possible with the engine in the vehicle. However, this practice is not recommended because of the cleaning and preparation work that must be done to the components involved.

3 Rocker arm covers — removal and installation

Refer to illustrations 3.11 and 3.19

Removal

1   Disconnect the battery, negative cable first, then positive.
2   Remove the engine cover (Chapter 11).
3   Remove the air cleaner and air duct.
4   Remove the spark plug wires after labelling them for reinstallation.
5   Remove the PCV valve and hose from the right rocker arm cover.
6   Remove the carburetor choke air deflector plate.
7   Remove the A/C compressor (Chapter 3) and brackets (if so equipped). Set the compressor aside without disconnecting the hoses. **Warning:** *The air conditioning system contains refrigerant under high pressure. Air conditioning hoses should never be loosened or disconnected unless the system has been depressurized by a dealer service department or air conditioning shop.*
8   Remove the rocker arm cover bolts and load distribution washers. Lay out the washers so they can be reinstalled in their original positions.

Right side view of engine (removed from vehicle for clarity)

3.11   Loosening the hose clamp (A) and removing the bracket nut (B) will allow the oil filler tube to be removed from the rocker arm cover

9   Disconnect the kickdown linkage and transmission dipstick tube (automatic transmission only).
10   Position the thermactor air hose and wiring harness away from the right rocker arm cover.
11   Remove the engine oil filler tube and bracket **(see illustration)**.
12   Disconnect the vacuum line at the canister purge solenoid (Chapter 6) and disconnect the line routed from the canister to the purge solenoid.
13   Disconnect the power brake booster hose from the firewall mounted booster, if so equipped.
14   Tap the cover with a light plastic hammer to break the seal or gently pry the cover up with a screwdriver.
15   Remove the rocker arm cover.

Installation

16   Clean all old gasket material and sealer from the cylinder head and rocker arm cover gasket surfaces.
17   Apply a thin layer of gasket sealer to the rocker arm cover mating surface and lay the gasket in the cover. Put the rocker arm cover in place and install the mounting bolts and load distrubution washers.
18   Connect the kickdown linkage and transmission dipstick tube (automatic transmission only).
19   After ensuring that all rocker arm cover load distribution washers are installed in their original positions **(see illustration)**, tighten the rocker arm cover bolts to the specified torque.
20   Install the spark plug wires.
21   Install the PCV valve and hose.
22   Install the carburetor choke air deflector plate.
23   Reposition the thermactor air hose and wiring harness in their original positions.
24   Install the engine oil filler tube.
25   Connect the vacuum line at canister purge solenoid and connect the line routed from the canister to the purge solenoid.
26   Connect the power brake hose, if so equipped.
27   Install the air cleaner.
28   Reconnect the battery cables, positive cable first, then negative.
29   Start the engine and check for oil leaks.
30   Reinstall the engine cover.

---

4   Rocker arm assembly and pushrods — removal, installation and adjustment

---

Refer to illustrations 4.2, 4.4 and 4.12

Removal

1   Remove the rocker arm cover (Section 3)

**CAUTION:
IF ROCKER COVER IS TIGHTENED WITHOUT REINFORCEMENT PIECE, DEFORMATION OF THE ROCKER COVER WILL OCCUR. INSTALLING REINFORCEMENT PIECE AFTERWARD WILL NO LONGER PREVENT LEAKS.**

3.19   The load distribution washers must be installed in their proper locations to prevent warping the rocker arm cover

2   Remove the rocker arm shaft support bolts, loosening the bolts two turns at a time until free **(see illustration)**.
3   Lift off the rocker arm shaft assembly and oil baffle.
4   Pull the pushrods out and store them in order **(see illustration)**.

Installation

5   Loosen the valve lash adjusting bolts several turns.
6   Thoroughly lubricate all components with engine oil.
7   Install the pushrods, making sure they are properly seated in the lifters.

4.2   Remove the three rocker shaft support bolts (arrows) by loosening them two turns at a time

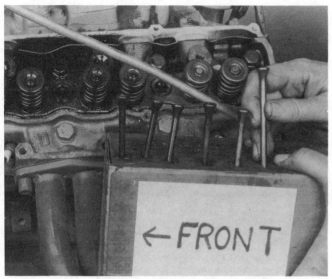

4.4 The pushrods should be stored in order of removal so they can be returned to their original locations

4.12 Turn the adjuster clockwise to decrease clearance between the rocker arm and valve stem

8   Install the oil baffle and rocker arm shaft assembly onto the head, lining up the pushrods and adjusting screws.

9   Starting in the middle and working out, tighten the rocker arm shaft support bolts two turns at a time to the specified torque.

Adjustment

10 Place your finger on the intake valve rocker arm for the number five cylinder.

11 Turn the engine over until the pushrod just starts to lift.

12 Using a feeler gauge to check the clearance, turn the self-locking adjusting bolt until the clearance on the number one intake valve is as specified (see illustration).

13 Repeat the procedure on the number one exhaust valve. Note that the clearance (valve lash) is *NOT* the same for the intake and exhaust valves.

14 Turn the engine over until the number three cylinder intake valve pushrod just starts to lift, then adjust the valves for the number *four* cylinder.

15 Turn the engine over until the number six cylinder intake valve pushrod just starts to lift, then adjust the valves for the number *two* cylinder.

16 Turn the engine over until the number one cylinder intake valve pushrod just starts to lift, then adjust the valves for the number *five* cylinder.

17 Turn the engine over until the number four cylinder intake valve pushrod just starts to lift, then adjust the valves for the number *three* cylinder.

18 Turn the engine over until the number two cylinder intake valve pushrod just starts to lift, then adjust the valves for the number *six* cylinder.

---

5   Valve spring, retainer and seals — replacement

Refer to illustrations 5.6, 5.8, 5.15, 5.17a, 5.17b and 5.17c

Note: *Broken valve springs and defective valve stem seals can be replaced without removing the cylinder head. Two special tools and a compressed air source are normally required to perform this operation, so read through this Section carefully and rent or buy the tools before beginning the job. If compressed air is not available, a length of nylon rope can be used to keep the valves from falling into the cylinder during this procedure.*

1   Refer to Section 3 and remove the rocker arm cover from the affected cylinder head. If all of the valve stem seals are being replaced, remove both rocker arm covers.

2   Remove the spark plug from the cylinder which has the defective component. If all of the valve stem seals are being replaced, all of the

spark plugs should be removed.

3   Turn the crankshaft until the piston in the affected cylinder is at top dead center on the compression stroke (refer to Section 11 for instructions). If you are replacing all of the valve stem seals, begin with cylinder number one and work on the valves for one cylinder at a time. Move from cylinder-to-cylinder following the firing order sequence (1-4-2-5-3-6).

4   Thread an adapter into the spark plug hole and connect an air hose from a compressed air source to it. Most auto parts stores can supply the air hose adapter. **Note:** *Many cylinder compression gauges utilize a screw-in fitting that may work with your air hose quick-disconnect fitting.*

5   Remove the rocker arm assembly for the head with the defective part and pull out the pushrod. If all of the valve stem seals are being replaced, all of the pushrods should be removed (refer to Section 4).

6   Apply compressed air to the cylinder (see illustration). The valves should be held in place by the air pressure. If the valve faces or seats are in poor condition, leaks may prevent the air pressure from retaining the valves — refer to the alternative procedure below.

7   If you do not have access to compressed air, an alternative method can be used. Position the piston at a point just before TDC on the com-

5.6 An adapter is used to attach the compressed air source to the cylinder

5.8   Use needle-nose pliers (shown) or a small magnet to remove the valve spring keepers. Be careful you don't drop them down into the engine!

5.15   Note that the closely wound coils (arrow) go on the bottom (against the cylinder head)

pression stroke, then feed a long piece of nylon rope through the spark plug hole until it fills the combustion chamber. Be sure to leave the end of the rope hanging out of the engine so it can be removed easily. Use a large breaker bar and socket to rotate the crankshaft in the normal direction of rotation until slight resistance is felt.

8   Stuff shop rags into the cylinder head holes above and below the valves to prevent parts and tools from falling into the engine, then use a valve spring compressor to compress the spring/damper assembly. Remove the keepers with small needle-nose pliers or a magnet (see illustration). Note: *A couple of different types of tools are available for compressing the valve springs with the head in place. One type grips the lower spring coils and presses on the retainer as the knob is turned, as shown here.*

9   Remove the spring retainer valve spring assembly, then remove the umbrella-type guide seal. Note: *If air pressure fails to hold the valve in the closed position during this operation, the valve face or seat is probably damaged. If so, the cylinder head will have to be removed for additional repair operations.*

10   Wrap a rubber band or tape around the top of the valve stem so the valve will not fall into the cylinder, then release the air pressure. Note: *If a rope was used instead of air pressure, turn the crankshaft slightly in the direction opposite normal rotation.*

11   Inspect the valve stem for damage. Rotate the valve in the guide and check the end for eccentric movement, which would indicate that the valve is bent.

12   Move the valve up-and-down in the guide and make sure it doesn't bind. If the valve stem binds, either the valve is bent or the guide is damaged. In either case, the head will have to be removed for repair.

13   Reapply air pressure to the cylinder to retain the valve in the closed position, then remove the tape or rubber band from the valve stem. If a rope was used instead of air pressure, rotate the crankshaft in the normal direction of rotation until slight resistance is felt.

14   Lubricate the valve stem with engine oil and install a new umbrella-type guide seal.

15   Install the spring/damper assembly and shield in position over the valve. Note that the close wound coils must be against the head (see illustration).

16   Install the valve spring retainer. Compress the valve spring assembly.

17   Position the keepers in the upper groove. Note the difference between intake and exhaust (see illustrations). Apply a small dab of grease to the inside of each keeper to hold it in place if necessary (see illustration). Remove the pressure from the spring tool and make sure the keepers are seated.

18   Disconnect the air hose and remove the adapter from the spark plug hole. If a rope was used in place of air pressure, pull it out of the cylinder.

19   Refer to Section 4 and install the rocker arm assembly and push-rod(s).

20   Install the spark plug(s) and hook up the wire(s).

21   Refer to Section 3 and install the rocker arm cover(s).

22   Start and run the engine, then check for oil leaks and unusual sounds coming from the rocker arm cover area.

5.17a   Note that the exhaust and intake valves have different style keepers

5.17b   The grooves in the intake valves (A) and exhaust valves (B) require that the correct keepers be used

5.17c   Apply a small dab of grease to each keeper before installation to hold them in place on the valve stem until the spring is released

6 Intake manifold — removal and installation

Refer to illustrations 6.5, 6.12, 6.13, 6.14a, 6.14b, 6.16a and 6.16b

1 Disconnect the negative cable from the battery.
2 Remove the air cleaner and air ducts.
3 Remove the engine cover under the dash (Chapter 11).
4 Disconnect the throttle cable (Chapter 4).
5 Drain the coolant (Chapter 1). Disconnect and remove the hose from water outlet to radiator (bottom hose). Disconnect the bypass hose from the intake manifold to the water pump housing rear cover **(see illustration)**.
6 Label the spark plug wires (if not already marked by the factory) and remove the distributor cap and plug wires as an assembly. Disconnect the distributor wiring harness.
7 Remove the distributor (Chapter 5).
8 Remove the rocker arm covers (Section 3).
9 Disconnect the fuel line from the fuel filter (Chapter 4).
10 Disconnect and label all wires and hoses that will interfere with manifold removal.
11 Remove the carburetor and EGR spacer (Chapters 4 and 6).
12 Remove the intake manifold bolts and nuts by backing off on the bolts/nuts two turns apiece until loose. **Note:** *During removal of the bolts note the length and location of the bolts so they can be installed in their original location* **(see illustration)**.
13 Tap the manifold lightly with a plastic hammer or wrap a rag around the tip of a screwdriver and very gently pry up on the manifold to break the seal **(see illustration)**.

14 Remove all old gasket material and sealing compound from the manifold and mating surfaces on the heads and engine block. Place a rag in the cavity to prevent debris from falling into the engine **(see illustrations)**.

6.5   Disconnect the bypass hose (arrow) at the rear of the water pump housing

6.12   A cardboard box can be used to keep the manifold bolts in the proper sequence

6.13   Use a screwdriver wrapped with a rag to carefully pry on the manifold and break the gasket seal

6.14a   Scrape all old gasket material off the mating surfaces

6.14b   A rag will help keep pieces of gasket material out of the engine during the cleaning process

6.16a Apply sealing compound to the bolt bosses
prior to installation

6.16b Intake manifold bolt tightening sequence

Installation

15 Apply sealing compound to the joining surfaces and place the intake
manifold gasket into position, making sure the tab on the right cylinder
bank fits into the cutout of the manifold gasket.

16 Apply sealing compound to the attaching bolt bosses on the intake
manifold **(see illustration)** and position the intake manifold. The length
of the bolts, using torque sequence numbers is: 1 and 2 — 3-1/4 inches;
3 and 4 — nut; 5, 6 and 7 — 4-1/2 inches; 8 — 4-3/4 inches. Follow
the tightening sequence **(see illustration)** and tighten the bolts to the
specified torque.

17 The remainder of the installation is the reverse of the removal
procedures.

18 Refill the cooling system and reconnect the battery.

19 Run the engine and check for leaks.

20 Reinstall the engine cover.

7 Exhaust manifolds — removal and installation

Refer to illustrations 7.2, 7.3 and 7.6

1 Remove the air cleaner and air duct (Chapter 4).

2 Remove the attaching nuts from the exhaust manifold shroud on
the right side **(see illustration)**.

3 Disconnect the attaching nuts from the exhaust pipe at the
manifold, then remove the thermactor by unbolting the attaching bolt
and pulling the tube out of the way **(see illustration)**.

4 Unplug the electrical connector from the choke or disconnect choke
(Chapter 4).

7.2   Right exhaust manifold

A Heat shield mounting nuts   C Thermactor tube bolt
B Hot air tube   D Manifold mounting bolts

7.3   Left exhaust manifold

A Thermactor tube bolt   B Manifold mounting bolts

7.6   An 8 mm Allen wrench is required for removal and
installation of the exhaust manifold bolts

5 Disconnect the EGO sensor wire on the left side exhaust manifold (Chapter 4).
6 Remove the manifold attaching bolts (see illustration).
7 Remove the manifold from the cylinder head.
8 Position the manifold in place with new gaskets and install and tighten the attaching bolts to the specified torque. Tighten the bolts two turns at a time, drawing the manifold to the head evenly.
9 Install a new exhaust pipe gasket, then install the exhaust pipe to the exhaust manifold.
10 Position the exhaust manifold shroud on the manifold (right side) and install and tighten the nuts securely.
11 Install the thermactor tube.
12 Install the air cleaner and choke electrical connector.
13 Connect the EGO sensor wire.

---

8 Cylinder heads — removal and installation

Refer to illustrations 8.5, 8.7, 8.8, 8.9a, 8.9b, 8.10 and 8.12

Removal

1 Disconnect the negative cable at the battery.
2 Drain the coolant (Chapter 1).
3 Refer to Section 6 and remove the intake manifold.
4 Remove the rocker arm covers, rocker arm shafts and oil baffles (Sections 3 and 4).
5 Remove the pushrods and keep them in sequence for proper assembly (see illustration).
6 Remove the exhaust manifold(s) (Section 7).
7 Remove the cylinder head attaching bolts and lift off the cylinder head. Discard the head gasket. It may be necessary to wrap a rag around a screwdriver and carefully pry up on the cylinder head to break the seal (see illustration).

8 **Note:** *It may be necessary to remove the cylinder head studs in order to lift up and back on the cylinder head to clear the front cover retainer. To remove the stud, run a nut down to the end of the threads and back it up with another nut, then use the first nut to unscrew the stud* (see illustration).

Installation

9 Clean the cylinder heads, intake manifold, rocker arm cover and cylinder block gasket surfaces (see illustrations).

8.5 Keep the pushrods in their original order

8.7 A rag-wrapped screwdriver can be used to break the gasket seal — be careful that the head does not fall as this is done

8.8 A back-up nut and two wrenches can be used to remove the head studs

8.9a Scrape all old gasket material from the head mounting surfaces

8.9b Be sure to remove all foreign matter (including fluid) from the head bolt holes (arrows)

8.10   Be sure the correct head gasket is used for the side
you are working on and that the marks face up (arrow)

10 Place new cylinder head gaskets in position on cylinder block.
Gaskets are marked with the words *front* and *top* for correct positioning.
Left and right head gaskets are not interchangeable **(see illustration)**.
11 A new head gasket set comes with alignment dowels to make the
installation of the head easier. Install alignment dowels in cylinder block
and install cylinder head assemblies on the engine block.
12 Remove the alignment dowels and install cylinder head attaching
bolts and studs and tighten in sequence **(see illustration)** to specified
torque.
13 Install the intake manifold.
14 Install the exhaust manifolds.
15 Apply engine oil to both ends of the pushrods and install them.
16 Install the oil baffles and rocker arm assemblies.

8.12   Cylinder head bolt tightening sequence

17 The remainder of the installation is the reverse of the removal
procedure.
18 Adjust the valves (Section 4).
19 Refill the cooling system (Chapter 1).
20 Change the oil and filter (Chapter 1).
21 Run the engine and check for leaks.

9   Front crankshaft oil seal — replacement

Refer to illustrations 9.2a, 9.2b, 9.4a and 9.4b

1   To replace the front oil seal, drain the coolant and remove the
radiator (Chapter 3). Remove the crankshaft hub, pulley and drivebelts.
Note: *It is not necessary to remove the front cover.*
2   Remove the front cover seal by using Seal Remover Tool 1175-AC,
or its equivalent and Impact Slide Hammer T59L-100-B or its equivalent
(see illustrations).

9.2a   Removing the front oil seal using Ford tool

9.2b   Removing the front oil seal with a seal puller

9.4a   Installing the front seal using a Ford tool

9.4b   If you lack the special seal installer, you can use a
socket and hammer to tap it into place

10.8   When removing the timing gear cover without taking off the oil pan, you must remove the five front oil pan mounting bolts (arrows)

10.9   The spacer plate is held in place by two bolts (arrows)

3   To replace, coat the new seal with engine oil.
4   Slide the new seal onto the crankshaft and, using a front seal installer T74P-6700-A or a socket the same diameter as the seal, drive the seal in until the tool butts against the front cover (see illustrations).
5   Replace crankshaft hub and bolt and tighten to the specified torque.
6   Install the drivebelt pulley.
7   Install the radiator and drivebelts.
8   Fill the cooling system (Chapter 1).
9   Operate the engine at a fast idle and check for coolant and oil leaks.

10   Timing gear cover — removal and installation

Refer to illustrations 10.8, 10.9, 10.12 and 10.14
Note: *Ford recommends that the oil pan be removed before beginning this procedure. However, we found that the cover could be removed for gasket replacement or timing gear inspection without removing the oil pan, as described in the steps which follow. A new pan gasket will be required, however. If removing the cover to replace the timing gears it will be necessary to remove the oil pan.*

Removal

1   Drain the coolant and remove the radiator (Chapter 3).
2   Unbolt the air conditioner compressor (Chapter 3) and power steering pump and bracket, if so equipped (refer to Chapter 10). Tie the compressor out of the way. Do not loosen or disconnect the refrigerant hoses!

3   Loosen the alternator and thermactor pump adjusting bolts and remove the drivebelt (Chapter 1). Remove the alternator (Chapter 5).
4   Remove the fan (Chapter 3).
5   Remove the coolant hoses connected to the water pump, then remove the water pump (Chapter 3).
6   Remove the crankshaft hub from the crankshaft (Section 9).
7   Raise the vehicle and support it securely on jackstands.
8   From under the vehicle remove the five front oil pan bolts (see illustration).
9   Remove the seven front cover bolts and carefully remove the cover by prying the top of the cover loose with a screwdriver. Carefully pry the front cover away from the oil pan. If necessary, remove the guide sleeves from cylinder block and then the spacer plate (see illustration).

Installation

10   Clean the mating surfaces of all gasket material and apply sealing compound to the gasket surfaces on the block and back of the cover. Be sure to clean the front section of the oil pan.
11   Cut a section of the new pan gasket to match the removed section, coat with sealant and install.
12   If removed, install the guide sleeves with new seal rings lubricated with engine oil, the chamfered end towards the front cover (see illustration).
13   With sealing compound applied, place the new gasket in position on the front cover.
14   Place the cover on the engine and start all the retaining bolts. The cover must be centered by inserting Front Cover Aligner tool T74P-6019-A or equivalent in the oil seal (see illustration). If the tool is not available, use the crankshaft hub to align the cover.
15   Tighten the attaching bolts to the specified torque.
16   Remove the aligner, install the hub and tighten the attaching bolt to the specified torque.
17   If removed, install the oil pan as described in Section 16.
18   The remainder of the installation is the reverse of the removal procedure.

10.12   Always use new seals on the guide sleeves (arrows)

TOOL–T74P 6019-A

10.14   An alignment tool should be used when installing the timing gear cover

11.4a If your engine still has original-type spark plug wires, they are helpful for locating the number one terminal on the distributor — arrow indicates mark for number one TDC

11.4b Firing order and cylinder numbering

11   Top Dead Center (TDC) for number one piston — locating

Refer to illustrations 11.4a, 11.4b and 11.6

1   Top Dead Center (TDC) is the highest point in the cylinder that each piston reaches as it travels up-and-down when the crankshaft turns. Each piston reaches TDC on the compression stroke and again on the exhaust stroke, but TDC generally refers to piston position on the compression stroke. The timing marks on the vibration damper installed on the front of the crankshaft are referenced to the number one piston at TDC on the compression stroke.

2   Positioning the piston(s) at TDC is an essential part of many procedures such as rocker arm removal, valve adjustment, timing gear replacement and distributor removal.

3   In order to bring any piston to TDC, the crankshaft must be turned using one of the methods outlined below. When looking at the front of the engine, normal crankshaft rotation is *clockwise*. **Warning:** *Before beginning this procedure, be sure to place the transmission in Neutral and disconnect the coil wire at the distributor cap and ground it to disable the ignition system.*

   a) The preferred method is to turn the crankshaft with a large socket and breaker bar attached to the crankshaft hub bolt that is threaded into the front of the crankshaft.

   b) A remote starter switch, which may save some time, can also be used. Attach the switch leads to the S (switch) and battery terminals on the starter solenoid. Once the piston is close to TDC, use a socket and breaker bar as described in the previous paragraph.

   c) If an assistant is available to turn the ignition switch to the Start position in short bursts, you can get the piston close to TDC without a remote starter switch. Use a socket and breaker bar as described in Paragraph a) to complete the procedure.

4   Make a mark on the distributor housing directly below the number one spark plug wire terminal on the distributor. If the numbers are missing from the spark plug wires **(see illustration)**, refer to the firing order diagram **(see illustration)**.

5   Remove the distributor cap as described in Chapter 1.

6   Turn the crankshaft (see Step 3 above) until the TDC mark on the crankshaft hub is aligned with the timing pointer **(see illustration)**.

7   The rotor should now be pointing directly at the mark on the distributor housing. If it is 180° off, the piston is at TDC on the exhaust stroke.

8   To get the piston to TDC on the compression stroke, turn the crankshaft one complete turn (360°) clockwise. The rotor should now be pointing at the mark. When the rotor is pointing at the number one spark plug wire terminal in the distributor cap (which is indicated by the mark on the housing) and the timing marks are aligned, the number one piston is at TDC on the compression stroke.

9   After the number one piston has been positioned at TDC on the

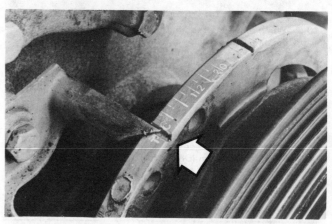

11.6   The timing pointer (arrow) should be aligned with the Top Dead Center (TDC) mark on the crankshaft hub

compression stroke, TDC for any of the remaining cylinders can be located by turning the crankshaft 120° at a time and following the firing order (refer to the Specifications).

12   Timing gears — removal and installation

Refer to illustrations 12.5, 12.6a, 12.6b and 12.7

Note: *Any time a component is to be removed which could effect the timing of the engine, begin the procedure by putting the number one piston at TDC (top dead center) on the compression stroke. Check the alignment of all the timing marks. Remove the distributor cap and see that the rotor is pointing towards the number one spark plug wire. Do not rotate engine while the timing gears are off.*

1   Remove the oil pan (Section 16).

2   Remove the timing gear cover (Section 10).

3   Remove the radiator (Chapter 3).

4   Remove the bolt retaining the camshaft gear to the camshaft and remove the camshaft gear.

5   Using gear puller T71P-19703-B and shaft protector T71P-7137-H or a two jaw gear puller, remove the crankshaft gear **(see illustration)**.

6   To install the crankshaft gear, align the keyway in the gear with the Woodruff key, then slide the gear onto the shaft. **Note:** *To install the crankshaft gear we fabricated an installing tool by using a piece of 1-7/8 inch diameter pipe, 3-3/4 inches long and inserted a bolt and washer through the pipe* **(see illustrations)**.

7   With the Woodruff key in the camshaft aligned with the gear keyway and the timing marks (dot to dot) on both gears aligned, install the cam gear **(see illustration)**.

8   Install the cam gear retaining bolt and washer and tighten to the specified torque.

9   Check camshaft end play (Section 14). If not within specifications replace the thrust plate.

10 Install the timing gear cover, oil pan and radiator.

11 Fill the cooling system with coolant and the crankcase with oil.

12 Operate the engine at a fast idle and check all hose connections and gaskets for leaks.

12.5   Removing the crankshaft gear with a Ford puller

12.6b   As you tighten the bolt the gear slides into place

12.6a   We fabricated this tool to install the crankshaft timing gear

12.7   Align the gears so that the dots are next to each other

---

13   Valve lifters — removal, inspection and installation

Refer to illustrations 13.2a and 13.2b

Removal and installation

1   Remove the cylinder head and related parts (Section 8).
2   Remove the lifters with a magnet and place them in a rack in sequence so they can be replaced in their original order **(see illustrations)**.

3   Clean the lifters and apply engine oil to both the lifters and bores before installing. Be sure to install the lifters in their original bores.
4   Install the cylinder head and related parts.

Lifter inspection

5   The faces of the lifters which bear on the camshaft should show no signs of pitting, scoring or other forms of wear. They should also not be a loose fit in the lifter bore. Wear is only normally encountered

13.2a   Work the lifters out of the block with a magnet

13.2b   Keep the lifters in order and replace them in their original locations

14.4   Mount the dial indicator with the plunger registering on the cam gear mounting bolt washer

at very high mileages or in cases of neglected engine lubrication.

6   If the lifters show signs of wear they must be replaced as a complete set and the camshaft must be replaced as well. See Chapter 2 Part D for further information.

14   Camshaft end play — check

Refer to illustration 14.4

Caution: *Prying against the camshaft gear, with the valve train load on the camshaft, can break or damage the gear and camshaft.*

1   Remove the rocker arm cover and timing gear cover (Sections 3 and 10).

2   Back off on rocker arm adjusting bolts or loosen the rocker arm shaft stands sufficiently to remove the valve spring loading on the camshaft (Section 4).

3   Push the camshaft toward the rear of the engine.

4   Install a dial indicator so that the indicator plunger is on the camshaft gear attaching bolt washer **(see illustration)**. Zero the dial indicator.

5   Position a large screwdriver between the camshaft gear and the block.

6   Pull the camshaft forward and release it.

7   Compare the dial indicator reading with specifications. If end play is excessive, replace the thrust plate **(see illustration 15.14)**.

8   Remove the dial indicator.

9   After checking the camshaft end play, adjust the valve clearance (Section 4).

10 Install the rocker arm covers and timing gear cover.

15   Camshaft — removal and installation

Refer to illustrations 15.9, 15.14 and 15.15

Removal

1   Disconnect the negative cable at the battery.

2   Remove the rocker arm covers (Section 3) and the rocker arm assembly (Section 4).

3   Remove the timing gear cover (Section 10). Stuff a rag in the oil pan opening.

4   Label and disconnect the spark plug wires from the spark plugs.

5   Remove the distributor cap and spark plug wires as an assembly.

6   Disconnect the distributor wiring harness connector and remove the distributor (Chapter 5).

7   Remove the alternator (Chapter 5).

8   Remove the thermactor pump (Chapter 6).

9   Disconnect the fuel line at the carburetor and remove the carburetor (Chapter 4). Remove the two bolts retaining the fuel pump and set the pump out of the way, then remove the fuel pump rod **(see illustration)**.

10 Remove the intake manifold (Section 6).

11 Lift out push rods and lifters and place them in a marked rack so they can be installed in the same location (Section 13).

12 Remove the camshaft gear attaching bolt and washer.

13 Slide the gear off the camshaft and remove the Woodruff key from the camshaft.

14 Remove the camshaft thrust plate **(see illustration)**.

15 Carefully remove the camshaft from the block, avoiding damage to the camshaft bearings **(see illustration)**.

Installation

16 Oil the camshaft journals and cam lobes with engine oil. Install the spacer ring with the chamfered side toward the camshaft and insert the camshaft Woodruff key.

17 Insert the camshaft into the block, carefully avoiding damage to the bearing surfaces.

18 Install the thrust plate so that it covers the main oil gallery and tighten the attaching bolts to the specified torque.

19 Install the camshaft gear and tighten the attaching bolt to the

15.9   Remove the fuel pump rod from the block

15.14   Unbolt the camshaft thrust plate (the spacer ring and thrust plate are available in two thicknesses for end play adjustment)

15.15 Carefully support the camshaft as you remove it from the block

16.18 Be sure the wedge seals are in place and engage the oil pan side gaskets properly

specified torque.
20 Check the camshaft end play (Section 14). The spacer ring and thrust plate are available in two thicknesses to permit adjusting the end play.
21 The remainder of the installation is the reverse of the removal procedures.

16 Oil pan — removal and installation

Refer to illustration 16.18
1 Disconnect negative cable at the battery.
2 Remove the air cleaner assembly (Chapter 4).
3 Remove the fan shroud and position it over the fan.
4 Remove the engine cover (Chapter 11).
5 Raise the vehicle and support it securely on jackstands.
6 Drain the engine oil (Chapter 1).
7 Remove the oil filter (Chapter 1)
8 Disconnect the exhaust pipes from the exhaust manifolds.
9 Disconnect the oil cooler bracket and lower it out of way (if so equipped).
10 Remove the starter cable from the starter.
11 Remove the two attaching bolts and remove the starter motor (Chapter 5)
12 Disconnect and position out of way the transmission oil cooler lines (if so equipped).
13 Disconnect the engine mounts by taking off each of the top nuts (Section 19).
14 Position a jack under the engine oil pan. Place a block of wood between the jack and oil pan so as not to damage the oil pan. Raise engine and install wooden blocks between the front insulator mounts and the crossmember. **Warning:** *Do not place any part of your body under the engine.*
15 Lower the engine onto the blocks and remove the jack.
16 Remove the oil pan bolts and lower the pan out the rear.
17 Clean the gasket surfaces of the engine and oil pan.
18 Apply sealer to the gasket mating surfaces and install the oil pan gaskets. Be sure the wedge seals are in place **(see illustration)**.
19 Install the oil pan, tightening the bolts to the specified torque.
20 The remainder of installation is the reverse of removal.

17 Oil pump — removal and installation

Refer to illustration 17.2
1 Remove the oil pan as described in Section 16.
2 Remove the oil pickup-to-main bearing cap mounting nuts **(see illustration)**.

3 Remove the oil pump mounting bolts. This requires a TORX bit, available in many auto parts and tool stores.
4 Lift out the oil pump assembly and withdraw the oil pump driveshaft.
5 Prior to installation prime the oil pump by pouring motor oil into the oil pickup and turning the pump shaft by hand.
6 If you are replacing the oil pickup, use a new gasket and tighten the bolts to the specified torque.
7 Insert the oil pump driveshaft into the block with the pointed end facing inward (the pointed end is closest to the pressed on flange).
8 Install the oil pump with a new gasket and tighten the bolts to the specified torque.
9 Install the oil pickup nuts and tighten them to the specified torque.
10 Install the oil pan (Section 16).
11 Change the oil filter and add oil.
12 Run the engine and check for leaks.

18 Rear crankshaft oil seal — replacement

Refer to illustrations 18.6, 18.9a and 18.9b
1 Remove the transmission by following the appropriate procedures in Chapter 7.
2 Remove the clutch and pressure plate, if so equipped (Chapter 8).
3 Remove the flywheel/driveplate.

17.2 The oil pump Torx-head attaching bolts (A) and oil pickup mounting nuts (B)

18.6   Pry the seal out carefully with a screwdriver

18.9a   Installing rear seal using Ford tool and hammer

18.9b   The installed seal should look like this

19.6   Engine mounts — exploded view

4   Remove the bolts and spring washers securing the flywheel housing and rear plate where fitted.
5   Clean the area surrounding the seal thoroughly.
6   Carefully pry the seal out with a screwdriver by working around it a little at a time (see illustration). Caution: *During this operation avoid scratching or otherwise damaging the crankshaft and oil seal bore surface.*
7   Coat the oil seal to cylinder block surface of the oil seal with sealer.
8   Coat the seal contact surface of the oil seal and crankshaft with engine oil.
9   Start the seal in the recess and install it with tool T72C-6165 (see illustration) or an equivalent such as a hammer and socket. Drive the seal into position until it is firmly seated (see illustration).
10   The remainder of the installation is the reverse of the removal procedures.

19   Engine mounts — removal and installation

Refer to illustration 19.6
1   Disconnect the negative cable at the battery.
2   Remove the fan shroud attaching bolts.
3   Support the engine using a wood block and a jack placed under the oil pan.
4   Remove the engine cover (Chapter 11).
5   Raise the vehicle and support it securely on jackstands.
6   Remove the nuts and washers attaching the insulators to the cross-

member brackets and lift the engine enough to disengage the insulator stud from the crossmember (see illustration). Warning: *Do not place any part of your body under the engine.*
7   Remove the bolt attaching the fuel pump shield to the left engine bracket, if equipped.
8   Remove the engine insulator assembly to cylinder block attaching bolts and lockwashers and remove the engine mount assembly.
9   To install, position the engine mount assembly to the cylinder block and install the bracket bolts.
10   Install the bolt attaching the fuel pump shield to the left bracket, if equipped.
11   Lower the engine until the insulator stud engages and bottoms in the slot on the crossmember pedestal. Tighten the nuts securely.
12   Remove the block of wood and jack from the engine oil pan.
13   Install the fan shroud attaching bolts.
14   Connect the battery and install the engine cover.

Chapter 2 Part C 3.0L V6 engine

Contents

Specifications

General

Cylinder numbers (front-to-rear)

Left (driver's) side	4–5–6
Right side	1–2–3
Firing order	1-4-2-5-3-6

Valves

Valve stem-to-rocker arm clearance..................	0.088 to 0.189 in (2.23 to 4.77 mm)

Torque specifications

	Ft-lbs
Camshaft sprocket bolt	40 to 51
Camshaft thrust plate bolts........................	6 to 8
Timing chain cover bolts...........................	15 to 22
Cylinder head bolts (in sequence)	
Step 1	48 to 54
Step 2	63 to 80
Vibration damper bolt	141 to 169
Intake manifold bolts (in sequence)	
Step 1	11
Step 2	18
Exhaust manifold bolts	
Step 1	15 to 17
Step 2	20 to 30
Oil pan bolts	7 to 9
Rocker arm cover bolts............................	7 to 9
Rocker arm fulcrum bolts	
Step 1	5 to 11
Step 2	18 to 26
Oil pump-to-block bolts............................	15 to 22
Oil pump pickup tube-to-oil pump	15 to 22
Engine mount-to-block bolts........................	33 to 44
Engine mount-to-crossmember nuts	52 to 54

1   General information

This Part of Chapter 2 is devoted to in-vehicle repair procedures. Part D covers the removal and installation procedures for the 3.0 liter V6 engines. All information concerning engine block and cylinder head servicing can also be found in Part D of this Chapter.

The repair procedures included in this Part are based on the assumption that the engine is still installed in the vehicle. Therefore, if this information is being used during a complete engine overhaul — with the engine already out of the vehicle and on a stand — many of the steps included here will not apply.

The specifications included in this Part of Chapter 2 apply only to the engine and procedures found here. For specifications regarding engines other than the 3.0 liter V6, see Part A or B, whichever applies. Part D of Chapter 2 contains the specifications necessary for engine block and cylinder head rebuilding procedures.

2   Repair operations possible with the engine in the vehicle

Many major repair operations can be accomplished without removing the engine from the vehicle.

Clean the engine compartment and the exterior of the engine with some type of pressure washer before any work is done. A clean engine will make the job easier and will help keep dirt out of the internal areas of the engine.

If oil or coolant leaks develop, indicating a need for gasket or seal replacement, the repairs can generally be made with the engine in the vehicle. The oil pan gasket, the cylinder head gaskets, intake and exhaust manifold gaskets, timing cover gaskets and the crankshaft oil seals are accessible with the engine in place.

Exterior engine components, such as the water pump, the starter motor, the alternator, the distributor and the EFI components, as well as the intake and exhaust manifolds, can be removed for repair with the engine in place.

Since the cylinder heads can be removed without pulling the engine, valve component servicing can also be accomplished with the engine in the vehicle.

Replacement of, repairs to or inspection of the timing chain and sprockets and the oil pump are all possible with the engine in place.

In extreme cases caused by a lack of necessary equipment, repair or replacement of piston rings, pistons, connecting rods and rod bearings is possible with the engine in the vehicle. However, this practice is not recommended because of the cleaning and preparation work that must be done to the components involved.

3   Rocker arm covers — removal and installation

Refer to illustration 3.9

1   Disconnect the negative cable at the battery.
2   Remove the engine cover under the dash (Chapter 11).
3   Disconnect the spark plug wires on the side(s) you are taking off, leaving them attached to the wire separators.
4   Remove the spark plug wire separators from the rocker arm cover studs.
5   If the right rocker arm cover is being removed, remove the PCV valve (Chapter 6), EGR tube and heater hoses from the valve cover.
6   If the left cover is being removed, take off the oil filler tube and PCV tube.
7   Remove the rocker cover attaching screws and remove the cover. If you must pry the cover off, be careful not to bend the sealing flange.
8   Clean all gasket sealing surfaces thoroughly and lightly oil all fastener threads.
9   Apply a bead of RTV sealant at the cylinder head to intake manifold rail step, two places per rail **(see illustration)**. Put a new gasket in place.
10 Place the cover on the head and install the attaching bolts and

3.9   Rocker arm cover components — exploded view

studs, noting the location of the spark plug wire separators. Tighten all fasteners to the specified torque.
11 The remainder of the installation is the reverse of removal.
12 Reconnect the battery, start the engine and check for leaks.
13 Reinstall the engine cover.

---

4   Rocker arms and pushrods — removal, inspection, installation and adjustment

Refer to illustrations 4.2, 4.3a, 4.3b, 4.17 and 4.20

Removal

1   Remove the rocker arm covers as described in Section 3.
2   Remove the rocker arm fulcrum bolts **(see illustration)**.

4.2   Rocker arm attaching bolt and fulcrum

3   Remove the rocker arms. If only the pushrods are being removed, loosen the fulcrum bolts and rotate the rocker arms out of the way of the pushrods **(see illustration)**. Keep the pushrods organized to ensure that they are reinstalled in their original locations **(see illustration)**.

Inspection

4   Check the rocker arms for excessive wear, cracks and other damage, especially where the pushrods and valve stems contact the rocker arm faces.
5   Make sure the hole at the pushrod end of the rocker arm is open.
6   Check the rocker arm fulcrum contact area for wear and galling. If the rocker arms are worn or damaged, replace them with new ones and use new fulcrum seats as well.
7   Inspect the pushrods for cracks and excessive wear at the ends. Roll each pushrod across a flat surface to see if they are bent.

Installation

8   Apply engine oil or assembly lube to the top of the valve stem and the pushrod guide in the cylinder head.
9   Apply engine oil to the rocker arm fulcrum seat and the fulcrum seat socket in the rocker arm.
10 Install the pushrods.
11 Install the rocker arms, fulcrums, and fulcrum bolts.
12 Turn the crankshaft until the lifter is all the way down.
13 Tighten the fulcrum bolts to the specified torque in two stages.
14 Replace the rocker arm covers and gaskets as described in Section 3.
15 Start the engine and check for roughness and/or noise.
16 Reinstall the engine cover.

Adjustment

Note: *Adjustment is normally only needed when valves and/or seats have been ground a considerable amount.*

17 Set the engine at Top Dead Center (TDC) on number 1 cylinder. This is position 1 **(see illustration)**.
18 Using Ford lifter bleed-down tool T70P-6513-A or equivalent, press on the rocker arm until the lifter leaks down.
19 Check the following valves:
    Intake — 1, 3 and 6
    Exhaust — 1, 2 and 4

4.3a   Loosen the bolt (arrow) and pivot the rocker arm to the side to remove the pushrod

4.3b   A perforated cardboard box can be used to store the pushrods to ensure installation in their original locations

4.17   Positioning the crankshaft for a valve clearance check

Position 1: Piston #1 at TDC on compression stroke
Position 2: Turn crankshaft 360° (one full turn) clockwise

4.20 With the lifter completely collapsed, check the clearance between the valve stem and rocker arm

5.8 Apply air pressure to the cylinder, compress the valve spring and remove the keepers

20 Check the clearance between the valve stem and rocker arm with a feeler gauge **(see illustration)**. Compare this to the Specifications and write it down. **Note:** *The arrangement of intake and exhaust valves is as follows:*
    Left side — E-I-E-I-E-I
    Right side — I-E-I-E-I-E
21 Rotate the crankshaft 360 degrees to position 2 and check the following valves:
    Intake — 2, 4 and 5
    Exhaust — 3, 5 and 6
22 Clearance may be varied by using different length pushrods, available from your dealer. If there is not enough clearance, use a shorter pushrod; too much clearance, use a longer one.

5 Valve springs, retainers and seals — replacement

Refer to illustrations 5.8, 5.14 and 5.15

Note: *Broken valve springs and defective valve stem seals can be replaced without removing the cylinder head. Two special tools and a compressed air source are normally required to perform this operation, so read through this Section carefully and rent or buy the tools before beginning the job. If compressed air is not available, a length of nylon rope can be used to keep the valves from falling into the cylinder during this procedure.*

1 Refer to Section 3 and remove the rocker arm cover from the affected cylinder head. If all of the valve stem seals are being replaced, remove both rocker arm covers.
2 Remove the spark plug from the cylinder which has the defective component. If all of the valve stem seals are being replaced, all of the spark plugs should be removed.
3 Turn the crankshaft until the piston in the affected cylinder is at top dead center on the compression stroke (refer to Section 11 for instructions). If you are replacing all of the valve stem seals, begin with cylinder number one and work on the valves for one cylinder at a time. Move from cylinder-to-cylinder following the firing order sequence (1-4-2-5-3-6).
4 Thread an adapter into the spark plug hole and connect an air hose from a compressed air source to it. Most auto parts stores can supply the air hose adapter. **Note:** *Many cylinder compression gauges utilize a screw-in fitting that may work with your air hose quick-disconnect fitting.*
5 Remove the bolt, pivot ball and rocker arm for the valve with the defective part and pull out the pushrod. If all of the valve stem seals are being replaced, all of the rocker arms and pushrods should be removed (refer to Section 4).
6 Apply compressed air to the cylinder. The valves should be held in place by the air pressure. If the valve faces or seats are in poor condition, leaks may prevent the air pressure from retaining the valves — refer to the alternative procedure below.
7 If you do not have access to compressed air, an alternative method can be used. Position the piston at a point just before TDC on the compression stroke, then feed a long piece of nylon rope through the spark plug hole until it fills the combustion chamber. Be sure to leave the

end of the rope hanging out of the engine so it can be removed easily. Use a large breaker bar and socket to rotate the crankshaft in the normal direction of rotation until slight resistance is felt.
8 Stuff shop rags into the cylinder head holes above and below the valves to prevent parts and tools from falling into the engine, then use a valve spring compressor to compress the spring/damper assembly **(see illustration)**. Remove the keepers with small needle-nose pliers or a magnet. **Note:** *A couple of different types of tools are available for compressing the valve springs with the head in place. One type grips the lower spring coils and presses on the retainer as the knob is turned, while the other type utilizes the rocker arm bolt for leverage. Both types work very well, although the lever type is usually less expensive.*
9 Remove the spring retainer and valve spring assembly, then remove the umbrella-type guide seal **Note:** *If air pressure fails to hold the valve in the closed position during this operation, the valve face or seat is probably damaged. If so, the cylinder head will have to be removed for additional repair operations.*
10 Wrap a rubber band or tape around the top of the valve stem so the valve will not fall into the combustion chamber, then release the air pressure. **Note:** *If a rope was used instead of air pressure, turn the crankshaft slightly in the direction opposite normal rotation.*
11 Inspect the valve stem for damage. Rotate the valve in the guide and check the end for eccentric movement, which would indicate that the valve is bent.
12 Move the valve up-and-down in the guide and make sure it doesn't bind. If the valve stem binds, either the valve is bent or the guide is damaged. In either case, the head will have to be removed for repair.
13 Reapply air pressure to the cylinder to retain the valve in the closed position, then remove the tape or rubber band from the valve stem. If a rope was used instead of air pressure, rotate the crankshaft in the normal direction of rotation until slight resistance is felt.
14 Lubricate the valve stem with engine oil and install a new umbrella-type guide seal **(see illustration)**.

5.14 Carefully place the seal in position, then tap it into place with a deep socket and hammer

VALVE SPRING RETAINER (6 REQ'D)

VALVE SPRING DAMPER ASSEMBLY (6 REQ'D)

VALVE KEEPERS

FRONT OF ENGINE

VALVE STEM SEAL (6 REQ'D)

CYLINDER HEAD

NOTE: THREE INTAKE AND THREE EXHAUST SEALS ARE DIFFERENT

5.15 Valve spring components — exploded view

15 Install the spring/damper assembly in position over the valve (see illustration).
16 Install the valve spring retainer. Compress the valve spring assembly.
17 Position the keepers in the upper groove. Apply a small dab of grease to the inside of each keeper to hold it in place if necessary. Remove the pressure from the spring tool and make sure the keepers are seated.
18 Disconnect the air hose and remove the adapter from the spark plug hole. If a rope was used in place of air pressure, pull it out of the cylinder.
19 Refer to Section 4 and install the rocker arm(s) and pushrod(s).
20 Install the spark plug(s) and hook up the wire(s).
21 Refer to Section 3 and install the rocker arm cover(s).
22 Start and run the engine, then check for oil leaks and unusual sounds coming from the rocker arm cover area.

TORX HEAD BOLT (8 REQ'D)

LOWER INTAKE MANIFOLD ASSEMBLY

FRONT OF ENGINE

6.14 Intake manifold bolt tightening sequence

FRONT OF ENGINE

SEAL-INTAKE MANIFOLD REAR

SECTION B

SEAL-INTAKE MANIFOLD FRONT

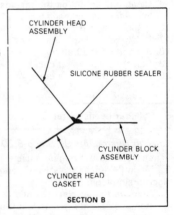

CYLINDER HEAD ASSEMBLY

SILICONE RUBBER SEALER

CYLINDER BLOCK ASSEMBLY

CYLINDER HEAD GASKET

SECTION B

6.9 Apply RTV sealer in the four locations shown before installing the end seals

6 Intake manifold — removal and installation

Refer to illustrations 6.9 and 6.14

1   Relieve the fuel pressure (Chapter 4).
2   Disconnect the negative cable at the battery.
3   Drain the cooling system (Chapter 1).
4   Disconnect the fuel lines and remove the throttle body (Chapter 4).
5   Remove the upper radiator hose and water outlet heater hose.
6   Remove the distributor as described in Chapter 5.
7   Remove the manifold attaching bolts/studs. The fuel rails and injectors may remain in place. Lift the manifold out of the engine compartment.
8   Clean all traces of old gasket material from the mating surfaces. Lightly oil all threaded fasteners prior to assembly.
9   Apply RTV sealant to the intersections of the cylinder head and block (see illustration).
10 Install the front and rear manifold seals.
11 Position the intake manifold gaskets in place over the tabs on the cylinder heads. Note: *Do not allow the sealer to dry prior to installation.*
12 Apply RTV sealer on top of the end seals.
13 Carefully lower the manifold into place. Avoid displacing the seals and gaskets.
14 Install the bolts and studs, tightening them in the sequence shown (see illustration) to the specified torque.
15 Install the thermostat housing with a new gasket (Chapter 3).
16 The remainder of the installation is the reverse of the removal procedure.
17 Refill the cooling system and connect the battery.
18 Run the engine and check for vacuum and fluid leaks.

7 Exhaust manifolds — removal and installation

1   Disconnect the negative cable at the battery.
2   Raise the vehicle and support it securely on jackstands.

3   Remove the engine cover under the dash (Chapter 11).
4   Unbolt the exhaust pipe(s) from the appropriate manifold(s) as described in Chapter 4.

Left side

5   Remove the oil dipstick tube bracket.
6   Remove the power steering hoses (when equipped).

Right side

7   Remove the heater hose support bracket.
8   Drain the cooling system (Chapter 1).
9   Remove the heater hoses and set aside.
10 Disconnect the oxygen sensor.
11 Remove the EGR tube.

Both sides

12 Unbolt and remove the manifold(s).
13 Clean the mating surfaces of the head and manifold.
14 Clean and lightly oil the threads of all fasteners.
15 Install the manifold and tighten all fasteners to the specified torque.
16 Reinstall all parts removed for access.
17 Refill the cooling system if it was drained.
18 Reconnect the battery.
19 Run the engine and check for leaks.
20 Reinstall the engine cover.

---

8   Cylinder heads — removal and installation

Refer to illustrations 8.19 and 8.20

1   Disconnect the negative cable at the battery.
2   Drain the cooling system (Chapter 1), including removing engine block drain plugs.
3   Remove the air cleaner outlet tube (Chapter 4).
4   Remove the intake manifold (Section 6).
5   Remove the drivebelts (Chapter 1).

8.19   Installation dowels are used to locate the head gaskets

Left head

6   Remove the accessory drivebelt idler bracket.
7   If equipped with power steering, remove the pump mounting bracket bolts. Leave the pump hoses connected and tie the pump aside.
8   Remove the ignition coil bracket and dipstick tube.

Right head

9   Remove the alternator adjusting arm.
10 Remove the ground strap and throttle cable bracket.

8.20   Head bolt tightening sequence

9.4   Remove the vibration damper with a puller

9.8   A piece of pipe, a bolt and several large washers can be used to fabricate a seal installation tool

Both heads

11   Remove the exhaust manifold(s) (Section 7).
12   Remove the rocker arm cover(s) (Section 3).
13   Remove the pushrods (Section 4).
14   Unbolt and remove the cylinder heads.
15   Thoroughly clean and inspect the gasket mating surfaces for cracks and warpage.
16   Service the head(s) as needed (Chapter 2 Part D).
17   Be sure all bolt and bolt hole threads are clean, dry and in good condition.
18   Lightly oil all bolt and stud threads prior to installation.
19   Carefully position the head gaskets on the block using the dowels for alignment **(see illustration)**.

20   Install the heads and head bolts and tighten them in two steps following the sequence shown **(see illustration)** to the specified torque. **Note:** *When head bolts have been tightened using the above procedure it is not necessary to retighten them after engine warm-up.*
21   Installation of the remaining parts is the reverse of removal.
22   Refill cooling system (Chapter 1).
23   Run the engine and check for leaks and proper operation.

9   Front crankshaft oil seal — replacement

Refer to illustrations 9.4 and 9.8

1   Disconnect the negative cable at the battery.
2   Remove the radiator (Chapter 3).
3   Remove the drivebelts (Chapter 1) and the crankshaft pulley.
4   Remove the vibration damper bolt. Install a puller **(see illustration)** and remove the vibration damper.
5   Carefully pry the old seal from the cover using a seal remover or a screwdriver. Do not nick or scratch the crankshaft or seal bore.
6   Thoroughly clean the seal area.
7   Apply engine oil to the seal lips. Slide the seal into place with the spring side facing the engine.
8   Press the seal into place using a seal installer **(see illustration)** or a large socket and hammer. Be sure the seal seats against the timing chain cover.
9   Reinstall the vibration damper and tighten the bolt to the specified torque.
10   The remainder of the installation is the reverse of removal.
11   Refill the cooling system and run the engine, checking for leaks.

10   Timing chain cover — removal and installation

Refer to illustration 10.6

1   Remove the radiator and lower hose (Chapter 3).
2   Remove the idler pulley and bracket assembly.
3   Remove the drivebelts (Chapter 1) and water pump (Chapter 3).
4   Remove the crankshaft pulley and damper (Section 9).
5   Remove the oil pan-to-timing cover bolts (front of oil pan).
6   Unbolt the cover and remove it **(see illustration)**.
7   While the cover is off, replace the front oil seal. Drive the old one out from the rear. Place the cover on a block of wood and install a new seal using a hammer and a suitable driver.
8   Carefully cut and remove the exposed part of the old oil pan gasket. Clean off all traces of old gasket material from the cover and block.
9   Cut the required section of gasket from a new oil pan gasket and position it and the timing cover gasket with RTV sealer.
10   Install the cover and tighten all fasteners to the specified torque. **Note:** *Use sealant on all cover bolts which go into the water jacket.*
11   The remainder of the installation is the reverse of removal.
12   Refill the cooling system and run the engine, checking for leaks.

FRONT OF ENGINE

ADD PIPE SEALANT TO THIS BOLT

STUD BOLT

DOWEL (2 REQ'D)

SEAL PROTECTOR AS REQ'D

FRONT COVER GASKET

LOCATING PINS

CYLINDER BLOCK ASSEMBLY

10.6   Timing chain cover components — exploded view

FIRING ORDER — 1-4-2-5-3-6

11.4   Cylinder numbering and plug wire sequence on the distributor cap

11   Top Dead Center (TDC) for number one piston — locating

Refer to illustration 11.4

1   Top Dead Center (TDC) is the highest point in the cylinder that each piston reaches as it travels up-and-down when the crankshaft turns. Each piston reaches TDC on the compression stroke and again on the exhaust stroke, but TDC generally refers to piston position on the compression stroke. The timing marks on the vibration damper installed on the front of the crankshaft are referenced to the number one piston at TDC on the compression stroke.

2   Positioning the piston(s) at TDC is an essential part of many procedures such as rocker arm removal, valve adjustment, timing chain and sprocket replacement and distributor removal.

3   In order to bring any piston to TDC, the crankshaft must be turned using one of the methods outlined below. When looking at the front of the engine, normal crankshaft rotation is *clockwise*. **Warning:** *Before beginning this procedure, be sure to place the transmission in Neutral and disconnect and ground the coil wire at the distributor cap to disable the ignition system.*

   a) The preferred method is to turn the crankshaft with a large socket and breaker bar attached to the vibration damper bolt that is threaded into the front of the crankshaft.

   b) A remote starter switch, which may save some time, can also be used. Attach the switch leads to the switch and battery terminals on the solenoid. Once the piston is close to TDC, use a socket and breaker bar as described in the previous paragraph.

   c) If an assistant is available to turn the ignition switch to the Start position in short bursts, you can get the piston close to TDC without a remote starter switch. Use a socket and breaker bar as described in Paragraph a to complete the procedure.

4   Using a felt tip pen, make a mark on the distributor housing directly below the number one spark plug wire terminal on the distributor cap **(see illustration)**.

5   Remove the distributor cap as described in Chapter 1.

6   Turn the crankshaft (see Paragraph 3 above) until the zero on the vibration damper is aligned with the pointer on the timing cover. The timing pointer and vibration damper are located low on the front of the engine, near the pulley that turns the drivebelt.

7   The rotor should now be pointing directly at the mark on the distributor housing. If it is 180° off, the piston is at TDC on the exhaust stroke.

8   To get the piston to TDC on the compression stroke, turn the crankshaft one complete turn (360°) clockwise. The rotor should now be pointing at the mark. When the rotor is pointing at the number one spark plug wire terminal in the distributor cap (which is indicated by the mark on the housing) and the timing marks are aligned, the number one piston is at TDC on the compression stroke.

9   After the number one piston has been positioned at TDC on the compression stroke, TDC for any of the remaining cylinders can be located by turning the crankshaft 120° at a time and following the firing order (refer to the Specifications).

12   Timing chain and sprockets — checking, removal and installation

Refer to illustrations 12.3, 12.4, 12.11, 12.12 and 12.14

Checking

1   Remove the left rocker arm cover (Section 3).

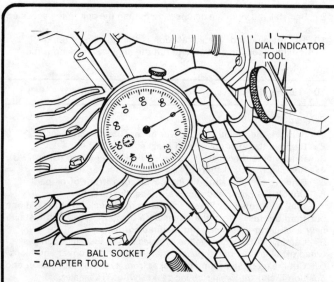

12.3   Mount a dial indicator on the pushrod to detect valve lifter movement

12.4   Turn the crankshaft clockwise to TDC (view shows chain exposed for clarity)

12.11 **Timing chain components — exploded view**

12.12 **Use two screwdrivers to "walk" the sprocket off the crankshaft**

2   Loosen the number 5 cylinder exhaust valve rocker arm (4th one back) and rotate it aside.
3   Mount a dial indicator on the end of the pushrod **(see illustration)**.
4   Turn the crankshaft clockwise until the number 1 piston is at Top Dead Center (Section 11). The damper timing mark should point to TDC on the timing degree indicator. This will take up slack on the right side of the chain **(see illustration)**.
5   Zero the dial indicator.
6   Slowly turn the crankshaft *counterclockwise* until the slightest movement is seen on the dial indicator. Check to see how far the damper TDC timing mark has moved away from the pointer.
7   If the reading on the timing indicator exceeds 6 degrees, replace the timing chain and sprockets.

Removal

8   Turn the crankshaft clockwise until the number one piston is at Top Dead Center (Section 11).
9   Remove the timing chain cover (Section 10).
10   Stuff a clean rag into the oil pan opening.
11   Unbolt the camshaft sprocket **(see illustration)**. Be sure the engine does not turn during bolt removal. Carefully remove the sprocket with the chain still on it.
12   Pry the crankshaft sprocket off **(see illustration)**. Do not lose the

small crankshaft key.
13   Check the timing chain and sprockets for visible wear and damage. Replace as a set if necessary.

Installation

14   Slide both sprockets and the chain onto the camshaft and crankshaft with the timing marks aligned **(see illustration)**. Tap the crankshaft sprocket into place with a brass drift and hammer.
15   Install the camshaft bolt and washer and tighten to the specified torque. **Caution:** *The camshaft bolt has a drilled oil passage. Be sure that passage is open before installation. DO NOT substitute any other type bolt.*
16   Apply oil to the timing chain and sprockets.
17   Install the timing chain cover (Section 10).

13   Valve lifters — removal, inspection and installation

Refer to illustrations 13.2 and 13.3
Removal and installation

1   Remove the intake manifold (Section 6) and pushrods (Section 4).
2   Remove the lifters with a magnet and place them in a rack in sequence so they can be replaced in their original order **(see illustration)**.

12.14 **Align the timing marks on the camshaft and crankshaft sprockets**

13.2 **A clearly labelled box with subdividers is a handy way to keep the lifters in order so that they can be reinstalled in the same lifter bores**

13.3 The lifters in an engine that has accumulated many miles may have to be removed with a special tool

3   If stuck carefully use a lifter puller tool to remove them by rotating them back and forth to loosen them from gum or varnish deposits **(see illustration)**.
4   Clean the lifters and apply engine oil to both the lifters and bores before installing. Be sure to install the lifters in their original bores.
5   Install the manifold and pushrods.

Lifter inspection

6   The faces of the lifters which bear on the camshaft should show no signs of pitting, scoring or other forms of wear. They should also not be a loose fit in the lifter bore. Wear is only normally encountered at very high mileages or in cases of neglected engine lubrication.
7   If the lifters show signs of wear they must be replaced as a complete set and the camshaft must be replaced as well.
8   Press down on the plunger using a phillips screwdriver to check for freeness of operation. Replace the entire lifter if the plunger is not free in the body.
9   See Chapter 2 Part D for further information.

14 Camshaft — removal and installation

Note: *Refer to Chapter 2, Part D and check the camshaft lobe lift as described there before removing the camshaft.*

Removal

1   Open the hood and remove the engine cover, then cover the seats to avoid damage to the upholstery.
2   Remove the intake manifold (see Section 6).
3   Remove the rocker arm covers (see Section 3).
4   Loosen the rocker arm bolts and rotate the rocker arms to the side.
5   If the pushrods are to be reused, remove them from the engine and place them in a holder to keep them in order (Section 4).
6   Remove the valve lifters from the engine using a special tool designed for this purpose (Section 13). Sometimes they can be removed with a magnet if there is no varnish build-up or wear. If they are stuck in their bores you will have to obtain the special tool designed for grasping lifters internally and work them out. Do not use pliers as the surface will be damaged.
7   Remove the timing chain cover (Section 10).
8   Unbolt the camshaft sprocket. Be sure you do not turn the engine while doing so.
9   Remove the timing chain and sprockets (Section 12).
10   Remove the bolts securing the camshaft thrust plate to the engine block.
11   Slowly withdraw the camshaft from the engine, being careful not to nick, scrape or otherwise damage the bearings with the cam lobes.
12   See Chapter 2, Part D for camshaft and lifter inspection procedures.

Installation

13   Lubricate the camshaft journals with engine oil and apply engine assembly lube to the cam lobes.
14   Slide the camshaft into position, being careful not to scrape or nick the bearings.
15   Install the camshaft thrust plate. Tighten the thrust plate retaining bolts to the specified torque. Install the timing chain and sprockets.
16   Check the timing chain deflection as described in Section 12.
17   Install the hydraulic valve lifters in their original bores if the old ones are being used. Make sure they are coated with engine assembly lube. Never use old lifters with a new camshaft or new lifters with an old camshaft.
18   The remainder of the installation procedure is the reverse of removal.

15 Oil pan — removal and installation

Refer to illustration 15.4

1   Disconnect the negative cable at the battery.
2   Remove the oil dipstick.
3   Raise the vehicle and support it securely on jackstands.
4   If equipped, disconnect the low oil level sensor **(see illustration)** by removing the retainer clip at the sensor and then separating the connector from the sensor.
5   Drain the oil and remove the oil filter (Chapter 1).
6   Remove the starter motor (Chapter 5).
7   Remove the bellhousing dust cover.
8   Unbolt and remove the oil pan. If it is stuck on, gently pry it off, taking care not to bend or distort the pan sealing flange.
9   Thoroughly clean the gasket surfaces of the block and pan.
10   Apply a 4 to 5 mm (1/4-inch) bead of RTV sealer to the junctions of the rear main bearing cap and engine block and also to the timing chain cover-to-block.
11   Attach the oil pan gasket to oil pan with sealer and position the pan on the engine.
12   Install the oil pan bolts and tighten to the specified torque.
13   Reinstall any parts removed and refill with engine oil.
14   Run the engine and check for leaks.

16 Oil pump and pickup — removal and installation

Refer to illustration 16.5
Note: *We recommend oil pump replacement any time the engine is rebuilt and when the pump has high mileage or is otherwise suspect.*

1   Remove the oil pan as described in Section 15.
2   While supporting the oil pump, remove the pump-to-rear main bearing cap bolt. The oil pan baffle may then be removed.
3   Lower the pump and remove it along with the pump driveshaft.
4   If a new oil pump is installed, make sure the pump driveshaft is mated with the shaft inside the pump.
5   Position the pump on the engine and make sure the hex in the upper end of the driveshaft is aligned with the lower end of the distributor shaft. The distributor drives the oil pump, so it is absolutely essential that the components mate properly **(see illustration)**.
6   Install the mounting bolt and tighten it to the specified torque.
7   Install the oil pan and add oil.

17 Rear crankshaft oil seal — replacement

Refer to illustration 17.8

1   Remove the transmission (Chapter 7).
2   On manual transmission equipped vehicles, remove the clutch assembly (Chapter 8).
3   Remove the flywheel/driveplate.
4   Carefully pry out the old seal using a seal remover or screwdriver. Take care to prevent nicking or scratching the seal bore or crankshaft.
5   Clean and inspect the oil seal area.
6   Lubricate the new seal with engine oil.
7   Start the seal into its recess with the spring side facing the engine.
8   Press the seal into place with the Ford tool no. T82L-6701-A **(see illustration)** or a large socket and hammer.

FRONT OF ENGINE

OIL LEVEL SENSOR

SCREW AND WASHER
ASSEMBLY

OIL LEVEL
SENSOR
GASKET

OIL PAN
GASKET

OIL PAN
ASSEMBLY

SILICONE SEALER

SILICONE SEALER

15.4 Oil pan components — exploded view

BOLT

OIL PUMP
ASSEMBLY

RETAINER

VIEW A

OIL PUMP
INTERMEDIATE SHAFT

NUT

OIL PUMP BAFFLE

FRONT OF ENGINE

RETAINER-OIL PUMP
INTERMEDIATE SHAFT

OIL PUMP
INTERMEDIATE
SHAFT

VIEW A

16.5 Oil pump components — exploded view

REAR OIL
SEAL ASSEMBLY

REAR SEAL
INSTALLATION TOOL

17.8 Rear seal installation using a special Ford tool

SCREW AND WASHER ASSEMBLY

RH BRACKET AND INSULATOR ASSEMBLY

STUD

LH BRACKET AND INSULATOR ASSEMBLY

NUT AND WASHER ASSEMBLY

FRONT OF VEHICLE

INSTALLATION OF FRONT ENGINE MOUNTS

18.3 Engine mount assemblies — exploded view

9   Install the flywheel/driveplate.
10   The remainder of installation is the reverse of removal.
11   Run the engine and check for leaks.

18 Front engine mounts — removal and installation

Refer to illustration 18.3
1   Remove the fan shroud attaching bolts.
2   Support the engine using a wood block and a jack placed under the oil pan.

3   Remove the nuts and washers attaching the insulators to the cross-member and lift the engine enough to disengage the insulator stud from the crossmember (see illustration).
4   Remove the engine insulator assembly to cylinder block attaching bolts and lockwashers and remove the engine mount assembly.
5   To install, position the engine mount assembly to the cylinder block, install the bracket bolts and tighten to the specified torque.
6   Lower the engine until the insulator stud engages and bottoms in the slot on the crossmember pedestal. Tighten the nuts to the specified torque.
7   Remove the block of wood and jack from the engine oil pan.
8   Install the fan shroud attaching bolts and tighten.

Chapter 2 Part D
General engine overhaul procedures

Contents

Specifications

2.3L four-cylinder engine
General

Oil pressure	40 to 60 psi @ 2000 rpm
Compression pressure	Lowest reading cylinder must be within 75% of highest reading cylinder (100 psi minimum)

Valves and related components

Valve face angle	44°
Valve seat angle	45°
Valve margin width	1/32-in
Valve stem diameter	
Intake	0.3416 to 0.3423 in
Exhaust	0.3411 to 0.3418 in
Valve stem-to-guide clearance	
Intake	0.0010 to 0.0027 in
Exhaust	0.0015 to 0.0032 in
Valve seat width	
Intake	0.060 to 0.080 in
Exhaust	0.070 to 0.090 in
Valve spring free length	1.877 in
Valve spring installed height	1.49 to 1.55 in
Head surface warpage limit	0.006 in over the length of the head

2.3L four-cylinder engine (continued)
Crankshaft and connecting rods
Crankshaft end play	0.004 to 0.008 in
Connecting rod side clearance	0.0035 to 0.0105 in
Main bearing journal diameter	2.399 to 2.3982 in
Out-of-round limit	0.0006 in maximum
Taper limit	0.0006 in per in
Journal runout limit	0.002 in maximum
Runout service limit	0.005 in
Main bearing oil clearance	
Nominal	0.0008 to 0.0015 in
Allowable	0.0008 to 0.0026 in
Rear oil seal installed depth	0.005 in maximum
Connecting rod bearing journal diameter	2.0462 to 2.0472 in
Connecting rod bearing oil clearance	
Nominal	0.0008 to 0.0015 in
Allowable	0.0008 to 0.0026 in

Engine block
Cylinder bore	3.7795 to 3.7825 in
Out-of-round limit	0.0015 in
Taper limit	0.010 in

Pistons and rings
Compression ring side clearance	0.0020 to 0.0040 in
Piston diameter	3.7780 to 3.7786 in
Piston-to-bore clearance (select fit)	0.0014 to 0.0022 in
Piston ring groove width	
Top and bottom compression	0.080 to 0.081 in
Oil ring	0.189 to 0.190 in
Piston ring end gap	
Compression	0.010 to 0.020 in
Oil ring	0.015 to 0.055 in

Camshaft
Lobe lift (intake and exhaust)	0.2381 in
Bearing journal diameter	1.7713 to 1.7720 in
Bearing oil clearance	0.001 to 0.003 in
Camshaft end play	0.001 to 0.007 in

Torque specifications*
	Ft-lbs
Main bearing cap bolts	
Step 1	50 to 60
Step 2	80 to 90
Connecting rod nuts	
Step 1	25 to 30
Step 2	30 to 36

* **Note:** *Refer to Part A for additional torque specifications.*

2.8L V6 engine
General
Oil pressure	40 to 60 psi @ 2000 rpm
Compression pressure	Lowest reading cylinder must be within 75% of highest reading cylinder (100 psi minimum)

Valves and related components
Valve face angle	44°
Valve seat angle	45°
Valve margin width	1/32-in
Valve stem-to-guide clearance	
Intake	0.0008 to 0.0025 in
Exhaust	0.0018 to 0.0035 in
Valve seat width	0.060 to 0.079 in
Valve spring installed height	1-37/64 to 1-39/64-in
Valve spring free length	1.91 in
Head warpage limit	0.006 in over the length of the head

Crankshaft and connecting rods

Crankshaft end play	0.004 to 0.008 in
Connecting rod side clearance	0.004 to 0.011 in
Main bearing journal	
Diameter	2.2433 to 2.2441 in
Out-of-round limit	0.0006 in
Taper limit	0.0006 in
Runout limit	0.002 in
Main bearing oil clearance	
Nominal	0.0008 to 0.0015 in
Allowable	0.0005 to 0.0019 in
Connecting rod journal	
Diameter	2.1252 to 2.1260 in
Out-of-round limit	0.0006 in
Taper limit	0.0006 in
Connecting rod bearing oil clearance	
Nominal	0.0006 to 0.0016 in
Allowable	0.0005 to 0.0022 in

Engine block

Cylinder bore diameter	3.6614 to 3.6630 in
Out-of-round	
Nominal	0.0015 in
Service limit	0.005 in
Taper limit	0.010 in

Pistons and rings

Compression ring side clearance	0.0020 to 0.0033 in
Oil ring side clearance	Snug fit
Piston-to-bore clearance	0.0011 to 0.0019 in
Piston ring end gap	
Compression rings	0.015 to 0.023 in
Oil ring	0.015 to 0.055 in

Camshaft

Lobe lift	0.2555 in
Bearing journal diameter	
Number 1	1.7285 to 1.7293 in
Number 2	1.7135 to 1.7143 in
Number 3	1.6985 to 1.6992 in
Number 4	1.6835 to 1.6842 in
Bearing oil clearance	0.0017 in

Torque specifications*

	Ft-lbs
Connecting rod nuts	19 to 24
Main bearing cap bolts	65 to 75
Subframe-to-frame bolts	187 to 260

* **Note:** *Refer to Part B for additional torque specifications*

3.0L V6 engine

General

Oil pressure	40 to 60 psi @ 2500 rpm
Compression pressure	Lowest reading cylinder must be within 75% of highest reading cylinder (100 psi minimum)

Valves and related components

Valve face angle	44°
Valve seat angle	45°
Valve margin width	1/32-in
Valve stem-to-guide clearance	
Intake	0.001 to 0.0027 in
Exhaust	0.0015 to 0.0032 in
Valve seat width	0.060 to 0.080 in
Valve spring installed height	
1987	1.58 in
1988	1.85 in
Valve spring free length (1987 only)	1.84 in
Head warpage limit	0.006 in over the length of the head

3.0L V6 engine (continued)
Crankshaft and connecting rods
Crankshaft end play	0.004 to 0.008 in
Connecting rod side clearance	0.006 to 0.014 in
Main bearing journal	
Diameter	2.5190 to 2.5198 in
Out-of-round limit	0.0003 in
Taper limit	0.0006 in
Runout limit	0.002 in
Main bearing oil clearance	
Nominal	0.001 to 0.0014 in
Allowable	0.0005 to 0.0023 in
Connecting rod journal	
Diameter	2.1253 to 2.1261 in
Out-of-round limit	0.0003 in
Taper limit	0.0006 in
Connecting rod bearing oil clearance	
Nominal	0.001 to 0.0014 in
Allowable	0.00086 to 0.0027 in

Engine block
Cylinder bore diameter	3.504 in
Out-of-round	
Nominal	0.001 in
Service limit	0.002 in
Taper limit	0.002 in

Pistons and rings
Compression ring side clearance	0.0016 to 0.0037 in
Oil ring side clearance	Snug fit
Piston-to-bore clearance	0.0012 to 0.0023 in
Piston ring end gap	
Compression rings	0.010 to 0.020 in
Oil ring	0.010 to 0.049 in

Camshaft
Lobe lift	0.260 in
Bearing journal diameter	2.0074 to 2.0084 in
Bearing oil clearance	
Standard	0.001 to 0.0026 in
Service limit	0.006 in

Torque specifications*
	Ft-lbs
Connecting rod nuts	
Step 1	20 to 28
Step 2	Back off two full turns
Step 3	20 to 25
Main bearing cap bolts	65 to 81

* **Note:** *Refer to Part C for additional torque specifications.*

1   General information

Included in this portion of Chapter 2 are the general overhaul procedures for the cylinder heads and internal engine components. The information ranges from advice concerning preparation for an overhaul and the purchase of replacement parts to detailed, step-by-step procedures covering removal and installation of internal engine components and the inspection of parts.

The following Sections have been written based on the assumption that the engine has been removed from the vehicle. For information concerning in-vehicle engine repair, as well as removal and installation of the external components necessary for the overhaul, see Part A, B or C of Chapter 2 (depending on engine type) and Section 7 of this Part.

The Specifications included here in Part D are only those necessary for the inspection and overhaul procedures which follow. Refer to Part A, B or C for additional Specifications related to the various engines covered in this manual.

2   Cylinder compression check

Refer to illustration 2.4

1   A compression check will tell you what mechanical condition the upper end (pistons, rings, valves, head gaskets) of the engine is in. Specifically, it can tell you if the compression is down due to leakage caused by worn piston rings, defective valves and seats or a blown head gasket. **Note:** *The engine must be at normal operating temperature*

2.4   Access for compression check is through wheel wells on V6 engines (the gauge shows a low reading cylinder)

for this check and the battery must be fully charged.

2   Begin by cleaning the area around the spark plugs before you remove them (compressed air works best for this). This will prevent dirt from getting into the cylinders as the compression check is being done. Remove all of the spark plugs from the engine.

3   Block the throttle wide open. Disconnect the coil wire from the distributor cap and ground it.

4   With the compression gauge in the number one spark plug hole (**see illustration**), crank the engine over at least four compression strokes and watch the gauge. The compression should build up quickly in a healthy engine. Low compression on the first stroke, followed by gradually increasing pressure on successive strokes, indicates worn piston rings. A low compression reading on the first stroke, which does not build up during successive strokes, indicates leaking valves or a blown head gasket (a cracked head could also be the cause). Record the highest gauge reading obtained.

5   Repeat the procedure for the remaining cylinders. The lowest reading cylinder should be within 75-percent of the highest reading cylinder.

6   Add some engine oil (about three squirts from a plunger-type oil can) to each cylinder, through the spark plug hole, and repeat the test.

7   If the compression increases after the oil is added, the piston rings are definitely worn. If the compression does not increase significantly, the leakage is occurring at the valves or head gasket. Leakage past the valves may be caused by burned valve seats and/or faces or warped, cracked or bent valves.

8   If two adjacent cylinders have equally low compression, there is a strong possibility that the head gasket between them is blown. The appearance of coolant in the combustion chambers or the crankcase would verify this condition.

9   If the compression is unusually high, the combustion chambers are probably coated with carbon deposits. If that is the case, the cylinder heads should be removed and decarbonized.

10   If compression is way down or varies greatly between cylinders, it would be a good idea to have a leak-down test performed by an automotive repair shop. This test will pinpoint exactly where the leakage is occurring and how severe it is.

---

3   Engine overhaul — general information

Refer to illustrations 3.4a, 3.4b and 3.4c

It's not always easy to determine when, or if, an engine should be completely overhauled, as a number of factors must be considered.

High mileage is not necessarily an indication that an overhaul is needed, while low mileage doesn't preclude the need for an overhaul. Frequency of servicing is probably the most important consideration. An engine that's had regular and frequent oil and filter changes, as well as other required maintenance, will most likely give many thou-

sands of miles of reliable service. Conversely, a neglected engine may require an overhaul very early in its life.

Excessive oil consumption is an indication that piston rings, valve seals and/or valve guides are in need of attention. Make sure that oil leaks aren't responsible before deciding that the rings and/or guides are bad. Have a cylinder compression or leakdown test performed by an experienced tune-up mechanic to determine the extent of the work required.

If the engine is making obvious knocking or rumbling noises, the connecting rod and/or main bearings may be at fault. Check the oil pressure with a gauge installed in place of the oil pressure sending unit (**see illustrations**) and compare it to the Specifications. If it's extremely low, the bearings and/or oil pump are probably worn out.

Loss of power, rough running, excessive valve train noise and high fuel consumption rates may also point to the need for an overhaul, especially if they're all present at the same time. If a complete tune-up doesn't remedy the situation, major mechanical work is the only solution.

An engine overhaul involves restoring the internal parts to the specifications of a new engine. During an overhaul, the piston rings are replaced and the cylinder walls are reconditioned (rebored and/or honed). If a rebore is done, new pistons are required. The main bearings, connecting rod bearings and camshaft bearings are generally replaced with new ones and, if necessary, the crankshaft may be reground to restore the journals. Generally, the valves are serviced as well, since they're usually in less-than-perfect condition at this point. While the engine is being overhauled, other components, such as the distributor,

3.4a   The oil pressure switch (warning light type shown) is located at the left rear of the four-cylinder engine

3.4b   The oil pressure sending unit (arrow) on the 2.8L V6 is located adjacent to the fuel pump

OIL PRESSURE
SWITCH

OIL PRESSURE
SENDER

3.4c   The oil pressure switch or sending unit (depending on type of gauges) is located at the right rear corner of the 3.0L V6 engine

starter and alternator, can be rebuilt as well. The end result should be a like new engine that will give many trouble free miles. **Note:** *Critical cooling system components such as the hoses, drivebelts, thermostat and water pump MUST be replaced with new parts when an engine is overhauled. The radiator should be checked carefully to ensure that it isn't clogged or leaking; if in doubt, replace it with a new one. Also, we don't recommend overhauling the oil pump — always install a new one when an engine is rebuilt.*

Before beginning the engine overhaul, read through the entire procedure to familiarize yourself with the scope and requirements of the job. Overhauling an engine isn't difficult, but it is time consuming. Plan on the vehicle being tied up for a minimum of two weeks, especially if parts must be taken to an automotive machine shop for repair or reconditioning. Check on availability of parts and make sure that any necessary special tools and equipment are obtained in advance. Most work can be done with typical hand tools, although a number of precision measuring tools are required for inspecting parts to determine if they must be replaced. Often an automotive machine shop will handle the inspection of parts and offer advice concerning reconditioning and replacement. **Note:** *Always wait until the engine has been completely disassembled and all components, especially the engine block, have been inspected before deciding what service and repair operations must be performed by an automotive machine shop.* Since the block's condition will be the major factor to consider when determining whether to overhaul the original engine or buy a rebuilt one, never purchase parts or have machine work done on other components until the block has been thoroughly inspected. As a general rule, time is the primary cost of an overhaul, so it doesn't pay to install worn or substandard parts.

As a final note, to ensure maximum life and minimum trouble from a rebuilt engine, everything must be assembled with care in a spotlessly clean environment.

4   Engine rebuilding alternatives

The do-it-yourselfer is faced with a number of options when performing an engine overhaul. The decision to replace the engine block, piston/connecting rod assemblies and crankshaft depends on a number of factors, with the number one consideration being the condition of the block. Other considerations are cost, access to machine shop facilities, parts availability, time required to complete the project and experience.

Some of the rebuilding alternatives include:

Individual parts — If the inspection procedures reveal that the engine block and most engine components are in reusable condition, pur-

chasing individual parts may be the most economical alternative. The block, crankshaft and piston/connecting rod assemblies should all be inspected carefully. Even if the block shows little wear, the cylinder bores should receive a finish hone.

Crankshaft kit — This rebuild package usually consists of a reground crankshaft, main and rod bearings, and a matched set of pistons with rings and connecting rods. The pistons will already be installed on the connecting rods. These kits are commonly available for standard cylinder bores, as well as for engine blocks which have been bored to a regular oversize.

Short block — A short block consists of an engine block with a crankshaft and piston/connecting rod assemblies already installed. All new bearings are incorporated and all clearances will be correct. Depending on where the short block is purchased, a guarantee may be included. The existing camshaft, valve train components, cylinder head and external parts can be bolted to the short block with little or no machine shop work necessary.

Long block — A long block consists of a short block plus an oil pump, oil pan, cylinder head, rocker arm cover, camshaft and valve train components, timing sprockets and chain and timing chain cover. All components are installed with new bearings, seals and gaskets incorporated throughout. The installation of manifolds and external parts is all that is necessary. Some form of guarantee is usually included with the purchase.

Give careful thought to which alternative is best for you and discuss the situation with local automotive machine shops, auto parts dealers and experienced rebuilders before ordering or purchasing replacement parts.

5   Engine removal — methods and precautions

If it has been decided that an engine must be removed for overhaul or major repair work, certain preliminary steps should be taken.

It is important to note that all engines installed in the Aerostar are removed from the bottom — dropping the engine/subframe assembly and lifting away the vehicle body. For this reason, the removal and installation process is somewhat unconventional and requires lifting devices and tools not common to a home mechanic. If it is decided to attempt this procedure, read through the instructions in Section 6 and ensure that the job can be performed safely before beginning.

Locating a suitable work area is extremely important. A shop is, of course, the most desirable place to work. Adequate work space, along with storage space for the vehicle, is very important.

Cleaning the engine compartment and engine prior to removal will help keep tools clean and organized.

A vehicle hoist will also be necessary. Make sure that the equipment is rated in excess of the combined weight of the vehicle and its contents. Safety is of primary importance, considering the potential hazards involved in lifting the vehicle off of the engine and subframe.

If the engine is being removed by a novice, a helper should be available. Advice and aid from someone more experienced would also be helpful. There are many instances when one person cannot simultaneously perform all of the operations required when lifting the vehicle away from the engine and subframe.

Plan the operation ahead of time. Arrange for or obtain all of the tools and equipment you will need prior to beginning the job. Some of the equipment necessary to perform engine removal and installation safely and with relative ease are (in addition to a vehicle hoist) a heavy duty floor jack, complete sets of wrenches and sockets as described in the front of this manual, wooden blocks, a heavy duty dolly and plenty of rags and cleaning solvent for mopping up the inevitable spills. You will also need a way to lift the engine from the subframe to an engine stand.

Plan for the vehicle to be out of use for a considerable amount of time. A machine shop will be required to perform some of the work which the do-it-yourselfer cannot accomplish due to a lack of special equipment. These shops often have a busy schedule, so it would be wise to consult them before removing the engine in order to accurately estimate the amount of time required to rebuild or repair components that may need work.

Always use extreme caution when removing and installing the engine. Serious injury can result from careless actions. Plan ahead. Take your time and a job of this nature, although major, can be accomplished successfully.

6.17   Remove all ground wires, such as this one behind the dipstick bracket (2.8L V6) — hoses and wires can be difficult to see so search carefully

6   Engine — removal and installation

Refer to illustrations 6.17, 6.21, 6.23, 6.29, 6.31 and 6.32

Warning: *Have a dealer or air conditioning shop discharge the system prior to disconnecting any a/c components.*

1   On a/c equipped four-cylinder models only, have the refrigerant discharged by a professional.
2   Place the van on a hoist designed to lift vehicles for servicing. It must be configured to allow engine/subframe removal out the bottom of the vehicle. Drive-on ramp and axle lift (twin post) hoists won't work. Center post hoists may work if the transmission is removed first.
3   Relieve the fuel system pressure (Chapter 4).
4   Disconnect and remove the battery (Chapter 5).
5   Drain the cooling system (Chapter 1).
6   Remove the engine cover under the dash (Chapter 11).
7   Remove the right front seat for access (Chapter 11).
8   Remove the air cleaner assembly (Chapter 4).
9   Remove the upper and lower radiator hoses and disconnect the heater hoses.
10   Remove the radiator and shroud (Chapter 3).
11   Disconnect the optional auxilliary transmisssion cooler lines.
12   Remove the drivebelts (Chapter 1).
13   Remove the engine cooling fan (Chapter 3).
14   On a/c equipped four-cylinder models, disconnect the refrigerant lines from the compressor and plug the open fittings. On V6 models, unplug the wiring connector and unbolt the compressor from the engine without disconnecting the lines. Tie the compressor up out of the way.
15   Disconnect the throttle cable, transmission kickdown linkage and cruise control cable (as equipped), from the carburetor or throttle body and unbolt its retaining bracket (Chapter 4).
16   Label the vacuum lines, emission and coolant hoses, wiring connectors, ground straps and fuel lines to ensure correct reinstallation.
17   Carefully disconnect the vacuum lines, coolant and emission hoses, fuel lines, ground straps **(see illustration)** and electrical connectors which connect the engine to the vehicle. Refer to Chapters 4, 5 and 6 as needed.
18   Remove the starter motor (Chapter 5).
19   Set the front wheels and steering wheel in the straight ahead position (centered). Remove the bolt holding the intermediate steering shaft to the steering gear and separate the shaft from the gear (Chapter 10).
20   Remove the front wheels.
21   Remove the front brake calipers (Chapter 9) without disconnecting the hoses. Unbolt the brake line brackets from the subframe **(see illustration)** and tie the calipers out of the way.

6.21   Unbolt the brake line brackets prior to sub-frame removal

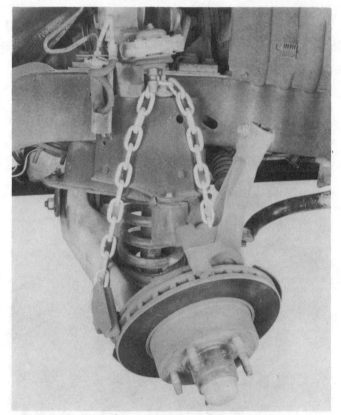

6.23   Wrap the lower control arm with a safety chain to keep the coil spring caged

22   Remove the front stabilizer bar end nuts (Chapter 10).
23   Wrap the lower control arms with safety chains **(see illustration)** and separate the upper balljoints from the spindles (Chapter 10).
24   On manual transmission models, remove the floorshift (Chapter 7) and disconnect the hydraulic hose at the slave cylinder.
25   Remove the catalytic converter (Chapter 4).
26   Disconnect the transmission linkage, wiring harness and speedometer cable, cooling lines (automatic transmission only) and

6.29   Gently lower the vehicle until the subframe rests on a strong dolly or wooden platform

driveshaft. Refer to Chapter 7 or 8 as needed.
27 The engine may be removed with the transmission still attached, although you may want to reduce the overall weight by removing the transmission at this time.
28 Carefully check to be sure everything connecting the engine/subframe to the vehicle has been disconnected except the engine mounts (and crossmember, if transmission is still attached).
29 Position a wheeled dolly (or wooden cradle) under the engine/subframe and lower the vehicle until the subframe just rests on the dolly (see illustration). Place wooden blocks between the engine (and transmission, if attached) and dolly to keep it level. Secure the subframe to the dolly with safety chains.
30 If the transmission is still attached, place a jack under it and remove the crossmember.
31 With the engine/subframe securely supported, remove the three nuts from the mounting bolts which attach the subframe to the frame on each side of the vehicle (see illustration).

6.32   Carefully raise the vehicle off the engine/subframe, making sure that nothing is still connected

6.31   The engine/subframe is attached to the frame with three mounting bolts on each side

32 Carefully raise the vehicle, making sure nothing is still connected or snagged (see illustration).
33 With the vehicle fully raised, unbolt the power steering pump and remove the torque converter and transmission (Chapter 7), if applicable. Remove the flywheel/driveplate. Attach a shop crane or other safe lifting device to the engine.
34 Unbolt the engine mounts from the block and lift the engine from the subframe.
35 Attach the engine to an engine stand or place it on a sturdy workbench.
36 Upon installation, bolt the engine to the subframe and position the engine/subframe unit correctly under the raised vehicle. Slowly and carefully lower the vehicle and bolt the unit to the frame. Ensure that the engine/transmission/subframe assembly is secure before connecting and installing the various components to complete the installation.
37 Add coolant, oil, power steering and transmission fluids as needed.
38 Run the engine and check for proper operation and leaks. Correct as needed.
39 Reinstall the engine cover and seat.
40 If the a/c system was discharged, take the vehicle to an air conditioning shop or service station for evacuation, recharging and leak testing.
41 Have the wheel alignment checked.

7   Engine overhaul — disassembly sequence

1   It is much easier to disassemble and work on the engine if it is mounted on an engine stand. These stands can often be rented for

a reasonable fee from an equipment rental yard. Before the engine is mounted on a stand, the flywheel/driveplate should be removed from the engine.

2   If a stand is not available, it is possible to disassemble the engine with it blocked up on a sturdy workbench or on the floor. Be extra careful not to tip or drop the engine when working without a stand.

3   If you are going to obtain a rebuilt engine, all external components must come off your old engine first in order to be transferred to the replacement engine (just as they will if you are doing a complete engine overhaul yourself). These include:

Alternator and brackets
Emissions control components
Distributor, spark plug wires and spark plugs
Thermostat and housing
Water pump
Carburetor/fuel injection components
Intake/exhaust manifolds
Oil filter
Fuel pump
Engine mounts
Flywheel/driveplate

Note: *When removing the external components from the engine, pay close attention to details that may be helpful or important during installation. Note the installed position of gaskets, seals, spacers, pins, washers, bolts and other small items.*

4   If you are obtaining a short block, which consists of the engine block, crankshaft, pistons and connecting rods all assembled, then the cylinder head, oil pan and oil pump will have to be removed as well. See Section 4, *Engine rebuilding alternatives*, for additional information regarding the different possibilities to be considered.

5   If you are planning a complete overhaul, the engine should be dismantled to the basic "short block" stage, which includes the removal of:

Four-cylinder engine
Cam cover
Timing belt/sprocket cover
Timing belt and sprockets
Cylinder head
Oil pan

V6 engines
Rocker arm covers
Cylinder heads and pushrods
Timing cover
Oil pan

6   Before beginning the disassembly and overhaul procedures, make sure the following items are available:

Common hand tools
Small cardboard boxes or plastic bags for storing parts
Gasket scraper
Ridge reamer
Vibration damper puller
Micrometers and/or vernier caliper
Telescoping (snap) gauge
Dial indicator set
Valve spring compressor
Cylinder surfacing hone
Electric drill motor
Tap and die set
Wire brushes
Cleaning solvent

---

8   Cylinder head — disassembly

Refer to illustrations 8.3, 8.4 and 8.5

Note: *New and rebuilt cylinder heads are commonly available for most engines at dealerships and auto parts stores. Due to the fact that some specialized tools are necessary for the disassembly and inspection procedures, and replacement parts may not be readily available, it may be more practical and economical for the home mechanic to purchase a replacement head rather than taking the time to disassemble, inspect and recondition the original.*

1   On four cylinder engines, the camshaft, followers and lash adjusters must be removed prior to cylinder head disassembly (see Part A). On V6 engines, the rocker arm shaft assemblies or rocker arms must be removed (see Part B or C).

2   Remove the deposits from the combustion chambers and valve heads with a scraper and a wire brush before removing the valves. **Caution:** *Be careful not to scratch the gasket surfaces.*

3   Compress the valve springs with a valve spring compressor. Remove the keepers and release the springs **(see illustration).**

4   Remove the retainer, spring assembly and seal from the valve. The valve can now be removed through the bottom of the head. If the valve binds in the guide (will not pull through), push it back into the head and deburr the area around the head of the stem with a fine file or whetstone **(see illustration).**

5   Repeat the procedure for the remaining valves. Remember to keep all the parts for each valve together so they can be reinstalled in the

8.3   Use a valve spring compressor to compress the spring, then remove the keepers from the valve stem

8.4   If the tips of the valves are mushroomed, they must be filed down prior to valve removal

same locations (see illustration).

6   Once the valves have been removed and stored in an organized manner, the head should be thoroughly cleaned and inspected. If a complete engine overhaul is being done, finish the engine disassembly procedures before beginning the cylinder head cleaning and inspection process.

9   Cylinder head — cleaning and inspection

Refer to illustrations 9.12a, 9.12b, 9.14, 9.21, 9.22a and 9.22b

1   Thorough cleaning of the cylinder head(s) and related valve train components, followed by a detailed inspection, will enable you to decide how much valve service work must be done during the engine overhaul.

Cleaning

2   Scrape all traces of old gasket material and sealing compound off the head gasket, intake manifold and exhaust manifold sealing surfaces.
3   Remove built-up scale from the coolant passages.
4   Run a stiff wire brush through the oil holes to remove any deposits that may have formed in them.
5   Run a tap into each of the threaded holes to remove corrosion and thread sealant that may be present. If compressed air is available, use it to clear the holes of debris produced by this operation.
6   Clean the exhaust and intake manifold stud threads (V6 engine) with a die. Clean the rocker arm pivot bolt or stud threads, if applicable, with a wire brush.
7   Clean the cylinder head with solvent and dry it thoroughly. Compressed air will speed the drying process and ensure that all holes and recessed areas are clean. **Note:** *Decarbonizing chemicals are available and may prove very useful when cleaning cylinder heads and valve train components. They are very caustic and should be used with caution. Be sure to follow the instructions on the container.*
8   Clean the rocker arms and pushrods (V6 engine) with solvent and dry them thoroughly. Compressed air will speed the drying process and can be used to clean out the oil passages.
9   Clean all the valve springs, keepers, retainers, shields and shims with solvent and dry them thoroughly. Do the components from one valve at a time to avoid mixing up the parts.
10   Scrape off any heavy deposits that may have formed on the valves, then use a motorized wire brush to remove deposits from the valve heads and stems. Again, make sure the valves do not get mixed up.

Inspection

Cylinder head

11   Inspect the head very carefully for cracks, evidence of coolant leakage and other damage. If cracks are found, a new cylinder head should be obtained.
12   Using a straightedge and feeler gauge, check the head gasket

8.5   A small plastic bag, with an appropriate label, can be used to store the valve train components so they can be kept together and reinstalled in the correct guide

mating surfaces for warpage (see illustrations). If the warpage exceeds specifications, the head can be resurfaced at an automotive machine shop.
13   Examine the valve seats in each of the combustion chambers. If they are pitted, cracked or burned, the head will require valve service that is beyond the scope of the home mechanic.
14   Check the valve stem-to-valve guide clearance. Use a dial indicator to measure the lateral movement of each valve stem with the valve in the guide and approximately 1/16-inch off the seat (see illustration). The valve stem-to-guide clearance is one-half the dial indicator reading. Compare the reading to the desired stem-to-guide clearance in the Specifications. If, after this check, there is still some doubt as to the condition of the valve guides, the exact clearance and condition of the guides can be checked by an automotive machine shop, usually for a very small fee.

Cam followers (four-cylinder engine)

15   Clean all the parts thoroughly. Make sure that all oil passages are open.
16   Inspect the pad at the valve end of the follower and the camshaft end pad for indications of scuffing or abnormal wear. If the pad is grooved replace the follower. Do not attempt to true the surface by grinding.

9.12a   Check for head warpage with a straightedge and feeler gauge both diagonally and straight across

9.12b   Check for head-to-manifold mating surface warpage with a straightedge and feeler gauge

9.14   To measure valve guide clearance with a dial indicator, rock the valve back and forth (arrows)

VALVE MARGIN WIDTH

NO MARGIN

9.21   The margin width on each valve must be as specified (if no margin exists, the valve cannot be reused)

Rocker arm components (V6 engine)

17   Check the rocker arm faces for pits, wear and rough spots. Check the pivot contact areas as well.

18   Inspect the pushrod ends for scuffing and excessive wear. Roll the pushrod on a flat surface, such as a piece of glass, to determine if it is bent.

19   Any damaged or excessively worn parts must be replaced with new ones.

Valves

20   Carefully inspect each valve face for cracks, pits and burned spots. Check the valve stem and neck for cracks. Rotate the valve and check for any obvious indication that it is bent. Check the end of the stem for pits and excessive wear. The presence of any of these conditions indicates the need for valve service by a machine shop.

21   Measure the width of the valve margin on each valve (see illustration) and compare it to the Specifications. Any valve with a margin narrower than specified will have to be replaced with a new one.

Valve train components

22   Check each valve spring for wear on the ends and pits. Measure the free length (see illustration) and compare it to the Specifications. Any springs that are shorter than specified have sagged and should not be reused. Check each valve spring for squareness (see illustration).

23   Check the spring retainers and keepers for obvious wear and cracks. Any questionable parts should be replaced with new ones, as extensive damage will occur in the event of failure during engine operation.

24   If the inspection process indicates that the valve components are in generally poor condition and worn beyond the limits specified, which is usually the case in an engine that is being overhauled, reassemble the valves in the cylinder head and refer to Section 10 for valve servicing recommendations.

25   If the inspection turns up no excessively worn parts, and if the valve faces and seats are in good condition, the valve train components can be reinstalled in the cylinder head without major servicing. Refer to the appropriate Section for cylinder head reassembly procedures.

9.22a   Measure the free length of each valve spring and replace any that have sagged or collapsed

9.22b   Check each valve spring for squareness

11.3a   Using a deep socket and hammer to install a valve guide seal (V6 engines)

11.3b   Make sure each seal is seated properly on the guide

10   Valves — servicing

1   Because of the complex nature of the job and the special tools and equipment needed, servicing of the valves, the valve seats and the valve guides, commonly known as a valve job, is best left to a shop.
2   The home mechanic can remove and disassemble the head, do the initial cleaning and inspection, then reassemble and deliver the head to a dealer service department or an automotive machine shop for the actual valve servicing.
3   The dealer service department, or automotive machine shop, will remove the valves and springs, recondition or replace the valves and valve seats (four-cylinder engine), recondition the valve guides, check and replace the valve springs, spring retainers and keepers (as necessary), replace the valve seals with new ones (four-cylinder engines require a plastic installation cap), reassemble the valve components and make sure the installed spring height is correct. The cylinder head gasket surface will also be resurfaced if it is warped.
4   After the valve job has been performed by a shop the head will be in like new condition. When the head is returned, be sure to clean it again before installation on the engine to remove any metal particles and abrasive grit that may still be present from the valve service or head resurfacing operations. Use compressed air, if available, to blow out all the oil holes and passages.

11   Cylinder head — reassembly

Refer to illustrations 11.3a, 11.3b, 11.4, 11.6 and 11.7
1   Regardless of whether or not the head was sent to an automotive repair shop for valve servicing, make sure it is clean before beginning reassembly.
2   If the head was sent out for valve servicing, the valves and related components will already be in place.
3   On V6 engines, lubricate and install the valves, then install new seals on each of the valve guides. Using a hammer and a deep socket, gently tap each seal into place until it is properly seated on the guide (see illustrations). Do not twist or cock the seals during installation or they will not seal properly on the valve stems.
4   On four-cylinder engines install the valves, then install the valve seals. Install the plastic installation cap (see illustration) over the end of the valve stem to allow the seal to pass over the ridges on valve stem. After installation remove the plastic cap and push the seal down until it is fully seated.
5   Install the valve spring shim(s) (if required) around the valve guide boss and set the valve spring, cap and retainer in place.
6   Compress the spring with a compressor and install the keepers. Release the compressor, making sure the keepers are seated properly in the valve stem groove(s). If necessary, grease can be used to hold the keepers in place until the compressor is released (see illustration).

PLASTIC INSTALLATION CAP
(OIL SURFACE OF CAP TO
FACILITATE SEAL INSTALLATION)

TOOL—T73P-6571-A
SHOULD CONTACT
SHOULDER

SEAL JACKET

VALVE GUIDE

STEP NO. 1   STEP NO. 2   STEP NO. 3

STEP NO. 1— WITH VALVES IN HEAD. PLACE PLASTIC INSTALLATION CAP OVER END OF VALVE STEM.
STEP NO. 2— START VALVE STEM SEAL CAREFULLY OVER CAP. PUSH SEAL DOWN UNTIL JACKET TOUCHES TOP OF GUIDE.
STEP NO. 3— REMOVE PLASTIC INSTALLATION CAP. USE INSTALLATION TOOL—T73P-6571-A OR SCREWDRIVERS TO BOTTOM SEAL ON VALVE GUIDE.

11.4   A plastic installation cap covers the valve stem on four-cylinder engines when installing the new valve seals

11.6   Apply a small dab of grease to each keeper before installation — it will hold them in place on the valve stem until the spring is released

11.7   Be sure to check the valve spring installed height (the distance from the top of the seat/shims to the top of the shield)

12.1   A ridge reamer is required to remove the ridge from the top of each cylinder — do this before removing the pistons!

7   Check the installed valve spring height (**see illustration**). If it was correct before reassembly it should still be within the specified limits. If it is not, install additional valve spring shims (available from a dealer) to bring the height to within the specified limit.

8   Install the rocker arm and shaft (2.8L V6) and tighten the nuts to the specified torque. Be sure to lubricate the ball pivots with moly base grease or engine assembly lube.

9   On four-cylinder engines install the camshaft, lash adjusters and followers.

12   Piston/connecting rod assembly — removal

Refer to illustrations 12.1, 12.2a, 12.2b and 12.3

1   Using a ridge reamer, completely remove the ridge at the top of each cylinder (follow the manufacturer's instructions provided with the ridge reaming tool) (**see illustration**). Failure to remove the ridge before attempting to remove the piston/connecting rod assemblies may result in piston breakage.

2   Check the connecting rods and connecting rod caps for identification marks (**see illustration**). If they are not plainly marked, identify each rod and cap, using a small punch to make the appropriate number of indentations to indicate the cylinders they are associated with (**see illustration**).

3   Loosen each of the connecting rod cap nuts 1/2-turn. Remove the number one connecting rod cap and bearing insert. Do not drop the bearing insert out of the cap. Slip a short length of plastic or rubber hose over each connecting rod cap bolt to protect the crankshaft journal and cylinder wall when the piston is removed (**see illustration**) and push

12.2a   Some manufacturers mark the connecting rods and caps with numbers

12.2b   If the rods and caps are not identified, use a hammer and punch to mark them

12.3   To prevent damage to the crankshaft journals and cylinder walls, slip sections of hose over the rod bolts before removing the pistons

13.2   Main bearing caps usually have a cast-in number to indicate position in the block and an arrow which should point to the front of the engine when the cap is installed

13.3   If the main bearing caps aren't numbered, use a hammer and punch to mark them

14.1a   Use a hammer and a large punch to knock the soft plugs into the block

14.1b   Grab the plug with pliers, turn it sideways and pull it out of the block

the connecting rod/piston assembly out through the top of the engine. Use a wooden tool to push on the upper bearing insert in the connecting rod. If resistance is felt, double-check to make sure that all of the ridge was removed from the cylinder.

4   Repeat the procedure for the remaining cylinders. After removal, reassemble the connecting rod caps and bearing inserts in their respective connecting rods and install the cap nuts finger tight. Leaving the old bearing inserts in place until reassembly will help prevent the connecting rod bearing surfaces from being accidentally nicked or gouged.

13   Crankshaft — removal

Refer to illustrations 13.2 and 13.3

1   Loosen each of the main bearing cap bolts 1/4-turn at a time, until they can be removed by hand.
2   Check the main bearing caps to see if they are marked as to their locations. They are usually numbered consecutively (beginning with 1) from the front of the engine to the rear **(see illustration)**.
3   If they are not, mark them with number stamping dies or a center-punch **(see illustration)**.
4   Gently tap the caps with a soft face hammer, then separate them from the engine block. If necessary, use the main bearing cap bolts as levers to remove the caps. Try not to drop the bearing insert if it comes out with the cap.
5   Carefully lift the crankshaft out of the engine. You may want to have an assistant available, since the crankshaft is quite heavy. With the bearing inserts in place in the engine block and in the main bearing caps, return the caps to their respective locations on the engine block and tighten the bolts finger tight.

14   Engine block — cleaning

Refer to illustrations 14.1a, 14.1b, 14.8 and 14.10

1   Remove the soft plugs from the engine block. To do this, knock the plugs into the block (using a hammer and punch), then grasp them with large pliers and pull them back through the holes **(see illustrations)**.
2   Using a gasket scraper, remove all traces of gasket material from the engine block. Be very careful not to nick or gouge the gasket sealing surfaces.
3   Remove the main bearing caps and separate the bearing inserts from the caps and the engine block. Tag the bearings according to which journal they removed from (and whether they were in the cap or the block) and set them aside.
4   Remove the threaded oil gallery plugs from the block.
5   If the engine is extremely dirty it should be taken to an automotive machine shop to be steam cleaned or hot tanked. Any bearings left in the block (such as the camshaft bearings in V6 engines) will be

14.8   All bolt holes in the block — particularly the main bearing cap and head bolt holes — should be cleaned and restored with a tap (be sure to remove debris from the holes after this is done)

14.10   A large socket on an extension and a hammer can be used to install the new soft plugs in the block

15.4a   Measure the diameter of each cylinder just under the wear ridge (A), at the center (B) and at the bottom (C)

damaged by the cleaning process, so plan on having new ones installed while the block is at the machine shop.

6   After the block is returned, clean all oil holes and oil galleries one more time. Brushes for cleaning oil holes and galleries are available at most auto parts stores. Flush the passages with warm water until the water runs clear, dry the block thoroughly and wipe all machined surfaces with a light, rust preventative oil. If you have access to compressed air, use it to speed the drying process and to blow out all the oil holes and galleries.

7   If the block is not extremely dirty or sludged up, you can do an adequate cleaning job with warm soapy water and a stiff brush. Take plenty of time and do a thorough job. Regardless of the cleaning method used, be sure to thoroughly clean all oil holes and galleries, dry the block completely and coat all machined surfaces with light oil.

8   The threaded holes in the block must be clean to ensure accurate torque readings during reassembly. Run the proper size tap into each of the holes to remove any rust, corrosion, thread sealant or sludge and to restore any damaged threads (see illustration). If possible, use compressed air to clear the holes of debris produced by this operation. Now is a good time to thoroughly clean the threads on the head bolts and the main bearing cap bolts.

9   Reinstall the main bearing caps and tighten the bolts finger tight.

10   After coating the sealing surfaces of the new soft plugs with a good quality gasket sealer, install them in the engine block (see illustration). Make sure they are driven in straight and seated properly or leakage could result. Special tools are available for this purpose, but good results can be obtained using a large socket (with an outside diameter that will just slip into the soft plug) and a hammer.

11   If the engine is not going to be reassembled right away, cover it with a large plastic trash bag to keep it clean.

15   Engine block — inspection

Refer to illustrations 15.4a, 15.4b and 15.4c

1   Before the block is inspected, it should be cleaned as described in Section 14. Double-check to make sure the ridge at the top of each cylinder has been completely removed.

2   Visually check the block for cracks, rust and corrosion. Look for stripped threads in the threaded holes. It's also a good idea to have the block checked for hidden cracks by an automotive machine shop that has the special equipment to do this type of work. If defects are found, have the block repaired, if possible, or replaced.

3   Check the cylinder bores for scuffing and scoring.

4   Measure the diameter of each cylinder at the top (just under the ridge area), center and bottom of the cylinder bore, parallel to the crankshaft axis (see illustrations). Next, measure each cylinder's

15.4b   The ability to ''feel'' when the telescoping gauge is at the correct point will be developed over time, so work slowly and repeat the check until you're satisfied that the bore measurement is accurate

15.4c   The gauge is then measured with a micrometer to determine the bore size

16.3a   A ''bottle-brush'' hone will produce better results if
you've never done cylinder honing before

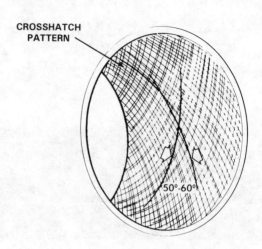

16.3b   The cylinder hone should leave a smooth,
crosshatch pattern with the lines intersecting at
approximately a 60° angle

diameter at the same three locations *across* the crankshaft axis. Compare the results to the Specifications. If the cylinder walls are badly
scuffed or scored, or if they're out-of-round or tapered beyond the limits
given in the Specifications, have the engine block rebored and honed
at an automotive machine shop. If a rebore is done, oversize pistons
and rings will be required.

5   If the cylinders are in reasonably good condition and not worn to
the outside of the limits, and if the piston-to-cylinder clearances can
be maintained properly, then they don't have to be rebored. Honing
is all that's necessary (Section 16).

16   Cylinder honing

Refer to illustrations 16.3a and 16.3b

1   Prior to engine reassembly, the cylinder bores must be honed so
the new piston rings will seat correctly and provide the best possible
combustion chamber seal. **Note:** *If you don't have the tools or don't
want to tackle the honing operation, most automotive machine shops
will do it for a reasonable fee.*

2   Before honing the cylinders, install the main bearing caps and
tighten the bolts to the specified torque.

3   Two types of cylinder hones are commonly available — the flex
hone or ''bottle brush'' type and the more traditional surfacing hone
with spring-loaded stones. Both will do the job, but for the less experienced mechanic the ''bottle brush'' hone will probably be easier to
use. You'll also need plenty of light oil or honing oil, some rags and
an electric drill motor. Proceed as follows:

   a) Mount the hone in the drill motor, compress the stones and slip
       it into the first cylinder (**see illustration**). Be sure to wear safety
       goggles or a face shield!

   b) Lubricate the cylinder with plenty of oil, turn on the drill and move
       the hone up-and-down in the cylinder at a pace that will produce
       a fine crosshatch pattern on the cylinder walls. Ideally, the cross-
       hatch lines should intersect at approximately a 60° angle (**see
       illustration**). Be sure to use plenty of lubricant and don't take off
       any more material than is absolutely necessary to produce the
       desired finish. **Note:** *Piston ring manufacturers may specify a
       smaller crosshatch angle than the traditional 60° — read and
       follow any instructions included with the new rings.*

   c) Don't withdraw the hone from the cylinder while it's running.
       Instead, shut off the drill and continue moving the hone up-and-
       down in the cylinder until it comes to a complete stop, then com-
       press the stones and withdraw the hone. If you're using a ''bottle
       brush'' type hone, stop the drill motor, then turn the chuck in

the normal direction of rotation while withdrawing the hone from
the cylinder.

   d) Wipe the oil out of the cylinder and repeat the procedure for the
       remaining cylinders.

4   After the honing job is complete, chamfer the top edges of the
cylinder bores with a small file so the rings won't catch when the
pistons are installed. **Be very careful not to nick the cylinder walls with
the end of the file.**

5   The entire engine block must be washed again very thoroughly
with warm, soapy water to remove all traces of the abrasive grit produced during the honing operation. **Note:** *The bores can be considered
clean when a white cloth — dampened with clean engine oil — used
to wipe them out doesn't pick up any more honing residue, which will
show up as gray areas on the cloth.* Be sure to run a brush through
all oil holes and galleries and flush them with running water.

6   After rinsing, dry the block and apply a coat of light rust preventive
oil to all machined surfaces. Wrap the block in a plastic trash bag to
keep it clean and set it aside until reassembly.

17   Piston/connecting rod assembly — inspection

Refer to illustrations 17.2, 17.4a, 17.4b, 17.5, 17.10 and 17.11

1   Before the inspection process can be carried out, the piston/con-
necting rod assemblies must be cleaned and the original piston rings
removed from the pistons. **Note:** *Always use new piston rings when
the engine is reassembled.*

2   Using a piston ring installation tool, carefully remove the rings from
the pistons (**see illustration**). Do not nick or gouge the pistons in the
process.

3   Scrape all traces of carbon from the top (or crown) of the piston.
A hand held wire brush or a piece of fine emery cloth can be used once
the majority of the deposits have been scraped away. Do not, under
any circumstances, use a wire brush mounted in a drill motor to remove
deposits from the pistons. The piston material is soft and may be eroded
away by the wire brush.

4   Use a piston ring groove cleaning tool to remove any carbon
deposits from the ring grooves (**see illustration**). If a tool is not available,
a piece broken off an old ring will do the job (**see illustration**). Be very
careful to remove only the carbon deposits. Do not remove any metal
and do not nick or scratch the sides of the ring grooves.

5   Once the deposits have been removed, clean the piston/rod
assemblies with solvent and dry them thoroughly. Make sure that the
oil return holes or slots in the back sides of the ring grooves are clear
(**see illustration**).

6   If the pistons are not damaged or worn excessively, and if the
engine block is not rebored, new pistons will not be necessary. Normal piston wear appears as even vertical wear on the piston thrust
surfaces and slight looseness of the top ring in its groove. New piston
rings should always be used when an engine is rebuilt.

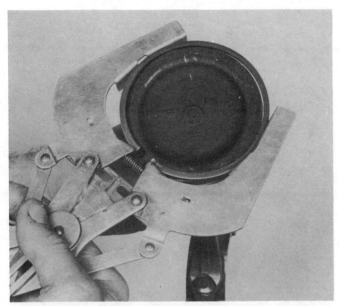

17.2   Use a piston ring tool to remove the old rings without scratching the pistons

17.4a   The piston ring grooves can be cleaned with a special tool, as shown here . . .

17.4b   . . . or a section of broken ring

17.5   Make sure the oil return slots (arrow) are clear

7   Carefully inspect each piston for cracks around the skirt, at the pin bosses and at the ring lands.

8   Look for scoring and scuffing on the thrust faces of the skirt, holes in the piston crown and burned areas at the edge of the crown. If the skirt is scored or scuffed, the engine may have been suffering from overheating and/or abnormal combustion, which caused excessively high operating temperatures. The cooling and lubrication systems should be checked thoroughly. A hole in the piston crown is an indication that abnormal combustion (preignition) was occurring. Burned areas at the edge of the piston crown are usually evidence of spark knock (detonation). If any of the above problems exist, the causes must be corrected or the damage will occur again.

9   Corrosion of the piston (evidenced by pitting) indicates that coolant is leaking into the combustion chamber and/or the crankcase. Again, the cause must be corrected or the problem may persist in the rebuilt engine.

10   Measure the piston ring side clearance by laying a new piston ring in each ring groove and slipping a feeler gauge in between the ring and the edge of the ring groove (see illustration). Check the clearance at three or four locations around each groove. If the side clearance is greater than specified, new pistons will have to be used.

17.10   Check the ring side clearance with a feeler gauge at several points around the groove

17.11   Measure the piston diameter at a 90° angle to the piston pin and in line with it

18.2   Measure the diameter of each crankshaft journal at several points to detect taper and out-of-round conditions

11 Check the piston-to-bore clearance by measuring the bore (see Section 15) and the piston diameter. Make sure that the pistons and bores are correctly matched. Measure the piston across the skirt **(see illustration)**. Subtract the piston diameter from the bore diameter to obtain the clearance. If it is greater than specified, the block will have to be rebored and new pistons and rings installed. Check the piston-to-rod clearance by twisting the piston and rod in opposite directions. Any noticeable play indicates that there is excessive wear, which must be corrected. The piston/connecting rod assemblies should be taken to an automotive machine shop to have new piston pins installed and the pistons and connecting rods rebored.

12 If the pistons must be removed from the connecting rods, such as when new pistons must be installed, or if the piston pins have too much play in them, they should be taken to an automotive machine shop. While they are there, have the connecting rods checked for bend and twist, as automotive machine shops have special equipment for this purpose. Unless new pistons or connecting rods must be installed, do not disassemble the pistons from the connecting rods.

13 Check the connecting rods for cracks and other damage. Temporarily remove the rod caps, lift out the old bearing inserts, wipe the rod and cap bearing surfaces clean and inspect them for nicks, gouges or scratches. After checking the rods, replace the old bearings, slip the caps into place and tighten the nuts finger tight.

18   Crankshaft — inspection

Refer to illustration 18.2

1   Clean the crankshaft with solvent and dry it thoroughly. Be sure to clean the oil holes with a stiff brush and flush them with solvent. Check the main and connecting rod bearing journals for uneven wear, scoring, pitting or cracks. Check the crankshaft for cracks and damage.

2   Using a micrometer, measure the diameter of the main and connecting rod journals **(see illustration)** and compare the results to the Specifications. By measuring the diameter at a number of points around the journal's circumference, you will be able to determine whether or not the journal is out of round. Take the measurement at each end of the journal, near the crank counterweights, to determine whether the journal is tapered.

3   If the crankshaft journals are damaged, tapered, out of round or worn beyond the limits given in the Specifications, have the crankshaft reground by an automotive machine shop. Be sure to use the correct oversize bearing inserts if the crankshaft is reconditioned.

4   Refer to Section 19 and examine the main and rod bearing inserts.

5   New main and connecting rod bearings should be installed whenever the engine is disassembled.

19   Main and connecting rod bearings — inspection

Refer to illustration 19.2

1   Even though the main and connecting rod bearings should be replaced with new ones during the engine overhaul, the old bearings should be retained for close examination, as they may reveal valuable information about the condition of the engine.

2   Bearing failure occurs mainly because of lack of lubrication, the presence of dirt or other foreign particles, overloading the engine and corrosion **(see illustration)**. Regardless of the cause of bearing failure, it must be corrected before the engine is reassembled to prevent it from happening again.

3   When examining the bearings, remove them from the engine block, the main bearing caps, the connecting rods and the rod caps and lay them out on a clean surface in the same general position as their location in the engine. This will enable you to match any noted bearing problems with the corresponding crankshaft journal.

4   Dirt and other foreign particles get into the engine in a variety of ways. It may be left in the engine during assembly, or it may pass through filters or breathers. It may get into the oil, and from there into the bearings. Metal chips from machining operations and normal engine wear are often present. Abrasives are sometimes left in engine components after reconditioning, especially when parts are not thoroughly cleaned using the proper cleaning methods. Whatever the source, these foreign objects often end up embedded in the soft bearing material and are easily recognized. Large particles will not embed in the bearing and will score or gouge the bearing and shaft. The best prevention for this cause of bearing failure is to clean all parts thoroughly and keep everything spotlessly clean during engine assembly. Frequent and regular engine oil and filter changes are also recommended.

5   Lack of lubrication or lubrication breakdown has a number of interrelated causes. Excessive heat, which thins the oil, overloading, which squeezes the oil from the bearing face, and oil leakage or throw off from excessive bearing clearances, worn oil pump or high engine speeds, all contribute to lubrication breakdown. Blocked oil passages, which usually are the result of misaligned oil holes in a bearing shell, will also oil starve a bearing and destroy it. When lack of lubrication is the cause of bearing failure, the bearing material is wiped or extruded from the steel backing of the bearing. Temperatures may increase to the point where the steel backing turns blue from overheating.

19.2   Six common types of bearing problems

20.1   To verify camshaft lobe lift, measure the major (A) and minor (B) diameters of each lobe with a micrometer or vernier caliper — subtract each minor diameter form the major diameter to arrive at the lobe lift

6   Driving habits can have a definite effect on bearing life. Full throttle, low speed operation in too high a gear (or lugging the engine) puts very high loads on bearings, which tends to squeeze out the oil film. These loads cause the bearings to flex, which produces fine cracks in the bearing face (fatigue failure). Eventually the bearing material will loosen in pieces and tear away from the steel backing. Short trip driving leads to corrosion of bearings because insufficient engine heat is produced to drive off the condensed water and corrosive gases. These products collect in the engine oil, forming acid and sludge. As the oil is carried to the engine bearings, the acid attacks and corrodes the bearing material.

7   Incorrect bearing installation during engine assembly will lead to bearing failure as well. Tight fitting bearings leave insufficient bearing oil clearance and will result in oil starvation. Dirt or foreign particles trapped behind a bearing insert result in high spots on the bearing which lead to failure.

20   Camshaft, lifters and bearings — inspection and replacement

Camshaft inspection
Four-cylinder engine
Refer to illustration 20.1

1   Measure the major (A) and minor (B) diameters **(see illustration)** of each cam lobe and compare the readings to the Specifications. The difference between the readings is the lobe lift.

2   If the lobe lift is not as specified, replace the camshaft and all the followers.

3   After the camshaft is removed from the engine, cleaned with solvent and dried, inspect the bearing journals for uneven wear, pitting and evidence of seizure. If the journals are damaged, the bearing inserts are probably damaged as well. Both the camshaft and bearings will have to be replaced with new ones.

V6 engines
Refer to illustrations 20.6 and 20.12

4   The lobe lift measurement on the V6 can be made with the camshaft still installed in the engine or as in Step 1 above.

20.6   Mount a dial indicator on the rocker arm over the pushrod to measure camshaft lobe lift on V6 engines

5   Remove the rocker arm cover.

6   Beginning with the number one cylinder, mount a dial indicator with the stem resting on the rocker arm directly in line with the pushrod **(see illustration)**.

7   Rotate the crankshaft very slowly in the direction of normal rotation (clockwise) until the lifter is on the heel of the cam lobe. At this point the pushrod will be at its lowest position.

8   Zero the dial indicator, then very slowly rotate the crankshaft in the direction of rotation until the pushrod is at its highest position. Note and record the reading on the dial indicator, then compare it to the lobe lift specifications.

9   Repeat the procedure for each of the remaining valves.

10   If the lobe lift measurements are not as specified, a new camshaft and lifters should be installed.

11   After the camshaft has been removed from the engine, cleaned with solvent and dried, inspect the bearing journals for uneven wear, pitting or evidence of seizure. If the journals are damaged, the bearing inserts are probably damaged as well. Both the camshaft and bearings will have to be replaced with new ones.

20.12   Use a micrometer to check the camshaft journals for wear, taper and out-of-round conditions

20.16a   Check the pushrod seat (arrow) in the top of each lifter for excessive wear

20.16b   A concave wear pattern on the base of this lifter indicates the need for a new camshaft and a complete set of lifters

20.16c   The foot of each lifter should be slightly convex — the side of another lifter can be used as a straightedge to check it; if it appears flat, it's worn and must not be reused

12 Measure the camshaft bearing journals with a micrometer (see illustration) to determine if they are excessively worn or out-of-round. If they are more than 0.001-inch out-of-round, the camshaft should be replaced with a new one.
13 Check the camshaft lobes for heat discoloration, score marks, chipped areas, pitting and uneven wear.
14 If the lobes are in good condition and if the lobe lift measurements are as specified, the camshaft can be reused.

Lifter inspection

Refer to illustrations 20.16a, 20.16b and 20.16c
15 Clean the lifters with solvent and dry them thoroughly without mixing them up.
16 Check each lifter wall, pushrod seat and foot for scuffing, score marks and uneven wear (see illustration). Each lifter foot (the surface that rides on the cam lobe) must be slightly convex — if they are concave (see illustrations) the lifters and camshaft must be replaced with new ones. If the lifter walls are damaged or worn (which is not very likely), inspect the lifter bores in the engine block as well.
17 If new lifters are being installed, a new camshaft must also be installed. If a new camshaft is installed, then use new lifters as well. Never install used lifters unless the original camshaft is used and the lifters can be installed in their original locations.

Bearing replacement

18 Camshaft bearing replacement requires special tools and expertise that place it outside the scope of the do-it-yourselfer. Take the block

(V6) or head (four-cylinder) to an automotive machine shop to ensure that the job is done correctly.

---

21   Engine overhaul — reassembly sequence

1   Before beginning engine reassembly, make sure you have all the necessary new parts, gaskets and seals as well as the following items on hand:

Common hand tools
Torque wrench
Piston ring installation tool
Piston ring compressor
Short lengths of rubber or plastic hose
  to fit over connecting rod bolts
Plastigage
Feeler gauges
A fine-tooth file
New engine oil
Engine assembly lube or moly-base grease
RTV-type gasket sealant
Anaerobic-type gasket sealant
Thread locking compound

2   In order to save time and avoid problems, engine reassembly must be done in the following general order:

22.3a When checking piston ring end gap, the ring must be square in the cylinder bore (this is done by pushing the ring down with the top of a piston as shown)

22.3b With the ring square in the cylinder, measure the end gap with a feeler gauge

22.5 If the end gap is too small, clamp a file in a vise and file the ring ends (from the outside in only) to enlarge the gap slightly

22.9a Installing the spacer/expander in the oil control ring groove

New camshaft bearings (must be done by automotive machine shop)
Piston rings
Crankshaft and main bearings
Piston/connecting rod assemblies
Oil pump
Camshaft and lifters
Cylinder heads, pushrods and rocker arms
Camshaft drive components
Oil pan
Camshaft drive cover
Intake and exhaust manifolds
Rocker arm covers
Flywheel/driveplate

22 Piston rings — installation

Refer to illustrations 22.3a, 22.3b, 22.5, 22.9a, 22.9b and 22.12

1   Before installing the new piston rings, the ring end gaps must be checked. It is assumed that the piston ring side clearance has been checked and verified correct (Section 17).
2   Lay out the piston/connecting rod assemblies and the new ring sets so the ring sets will be matched with the same piston and cylinder during the end gap measurement and engine assembly.

3   Insert the top (number one) ring into the first cylinder and square it up with the cylinder walls by pushing it in with the top of the piston (see illustration). To measure the end gap, slip a feeler gauge between the ends of the ring (see illustration). Compare the measurement to the Specifications.
4   If the gap is larger or smaller than specified, double-check to make sure that you have the correct rings before proceeding.
5   If the gap is too small, it must be enlarged or the ring ends may come in contact with each other during engine operation, which can cause serious damage to the engine. The end gap can be increased by filing the ring ends very carefully with a fine file. Mount the file in a vise, slip the ring over the file with the ends contacting the file face and slowly move the ring to remove material from the ends. When performing this operation, file only from the outside in (see illustration).
6   Excess end gap is not critical unless it is greater than 0.040-inch (1 mm). Again, double-check to make sure you have the correct rings for your engine.
7   Repeat the procedure for each ring that will be installed in the first cylinder and for each ring in the remaining cylinders. Remember to keep rings, pistons and cylinders matched up.
8   Once the ring end gaps have been checked/corrected, the rings can be installed on the pistons.
9   The oil control ring (lowest one on the piston) is installed first. It is composed of three separate components. Slip the spacer/expander into the groove (see illustration), then install the side rails. Do not use

22.9b   DO NOT use a piston ring installation tool when installing the oil ring side rails

22.12   When installing the compression rings, always use a ring expander tool, don't mix up the top and second rings, and make sure the mark (if applicable) is on top of the ring when installed — arrow visible on top of piston points to front of engine when installed

a piston ring installation tool on the oil ring side rails, as they may be damaged. Instead, place one end of the side rail into the groove between the spacer/expander and the ring land, hold it firmly in place and slide a finger around the piston while pushing the rail into the groove (see illustration).

10 After the three oil ring components have been installed, check to make sure that both the upper and lower side rails can be turned smoothly in the ring groove.

11 The number two (middle) ring is installed next. It should be stamped with a mark so it can be readily distinguished from the top ring. **Note:** *Always follow the instructions printed on the ring package or box — different manufacturers may require different approaches.* Do not mix up the top and middle rings, as they have different cross sections.

12 Use a piston ring installation tool and make sure that the identification mark is facing the top of the piston, then slip the ring into the middle groove on the piston (see illustration). Do not expand the ring any more than is necessary to slide it over the piston.

13 Finally, install the number one (top) ring in the same manner. Make sure the identifying mark is facing up.

14 Repeat the procedure for the remaining pistons and rings.

23 Crankshaft — installation and main bearing oil clearance check

Refer to illustrations 23.10, 23.14, 23.24 and 23.26

1 Crankshaft installation is generally one of the first steps in engine reassembly. It is assumed at this point that the engine block and crankshaft have been cleaned, inspected and repaired or reconditioned.

2 Remove the main bearing cap bolts and lift out the caps. Lay them out in the proper order to help ensure that they are installed correctly.

3 If they are still in place, remove the old bearing inserts from the block and the main bearing caps. Wipe the main bearing surfaces of the block and caps with a clean, lint-free cloth. They must be kept spotlessly clean.

4 Clean the back sides of the new main bearing inserts and lay one bearing half in each main bearing saddle in the block. Lay the other bearing half from each bearing set in the corresponding main bearing cap. Make sure the tab on the bearing insert fits into the recess in the block or cap.

5 The oil hole in the block must line up with the oil hole in the bearing insert. Do not hammer the bearing into place and do not nick or gouge the bearing faces. No lubrication should be used at this time.

23.10   Lay the Plastigage strips (arrow) on the main bearing journals, parallel to the crankshaft centerline

6 The flanged thrust bearing must be installed in the number three cap main bearing position on both the 4 and 6 cylinder engines (third position back from front of engine).

7 Clean the faces of the bearings in the block and the crankshaft main bearing journals with a clean, lint-free cloth. Check or clean the oil holes in the crankshaft, as any dirt here can go only one way — straight through the new bearings.

8 Once you are certain that the crankshaft is clean, carefully lay it in position (an assistant would be very helpful here) in the main bearings.

9 Before the crankshaft can be permanently installed, the main bearing oil clearance must be checked.

10 Trim several pieces of the appropriate size of Plastigage (so they are slightly shorter than the width of the main bearings) and place one

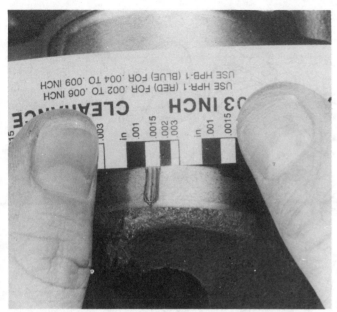

23.14   Compare the width of the crushed Plastigage to the scale on the container to determine the main bearing oil clearance (always take the measurement at the widest point of the Plastigage); be sure to use the correct scale — standard and metric scales are included

23.24   Pry back and forth slowly while watching the dial indicator reading

23.26   A feeler gauge blade inserted between the crankshaft and the thrust bearing can be used to check crankshaft end play

piece on each crankshaft main bearing journal, parallel with the journal axis (see illustration).

11 Clean the faces of the bearings in the caps and install the caps in their respective positions (do not mix them up) with the arrows pointing toward the front of the engine. Do not disturb the Plastigage.

12 Starting with the center main and working out toward the ends, tighten the main bearing cap bolts, in three steps, to the specified torque. Do not rotate the crankshaft at any time during this operation.

13 Remove the bolts and carefully lift off the main bearing caps. Keep them in order. Do not disturb the Plastigage or rotate the crankshaft. If any of the main bearing caps are difficult to remove, tap them gently from side-to-side with a soft face hammer to loosen them.

14 Compare the width of the crushed Plastigage on each journal to the scale printed on the Plastigage container to obtain the main bearing oil clearance (see illustration). Check the Specifications to make sure it is correct.

15 If the clearance is not correct, double-check to make sure you have the right size bearing inserts. Also, make sure that no dirt or oil is between the bearing inserts and the main bearing caps or the block.

16 Carefully scrape all traces of the Plastigage material off the main bearing journals and/or the bearing faces. Do not nick or scratch the bearing faces. A fingernail or edge of a credit card works well.

17 Carefully lift the crankshaft out of the engine. Clean the bearing faces in the block, then apply a thin, uniform layer of clean, high quality moly base grease or engine assembly lube to each of the bearing surfaces. Be sure to coat the thrust flange faces as well as the journal face of the thrust bearing.

18 Make sure the crankshaft journals are clean, then lay the crankshaft back in place in the block. Clean the faces of the bearings in the caps, then apply a thin, uniform layer of clean, moly base grease to each of the bearing faces.

19 Install the caps in their respective positions with the arrows pointing toward the front of the engine.

20 Install and tighten all main bearing bolts finger tight. Then tighten all bolts by starting with the center main and working outwards. Work up to the final torque in three steps.

21 Rotate the crankshaft a number of times by hand and check for any obvious binding.

22 The final step is to check the crankshaft end play with a feeler gauge or a dial indicator.

23 To check the end play with a dial indicator, mount the indicator on the block with the plunger parallel to the crankshaft and seated against either end of the crankshaft.

24 Using a large screwdriver, pry the crankshaft to the rear in the block as far as it will go and zero the dial indicator (see illustration).

25 Pry the crankshaft forward as far as it will go and read the end play off the dial indicator.

26 To check end play with a feeler gauge, pry the crankshaft as far forward in the block as it will go, then insert progessively larger feeler gauge blades between the crankshaft and the face of the thrust bearing until the space is filled (see illustration). The thickness of feeler gauge blades required is the end play.

---

24   Rear main oil seal — installation

Four-cylinder engine
Refer to illustration 24.1

1   Position the seal on Seal Installer Tool no. T82L-6701-A (see illus-

NOTE: REAR FACE OF SEAL MUST BE WITHIN 0.127mm (0.005-INCH) OF THE REAR FACE OF THE BLOCK.

24.1   Rear main oil seal installation (four-cylinder engine)

tration) and start the bolts into the crankshaft flange.

2   To seat the seal properly, alternate the tightening of the bolts until the seal is positioned at the proper depth.

V6 engines

Refer to illustration 24.6

3   Make sure the engine block is free of all dirt, lint or foreign matter to ensure a proper fit.

4   To install coat the seal-to-cylinder block surface of the oil seal with engine oil.

5   Coat the seal surface and crankshaft with engine oil.

6   Start the seal in the recess and install it with tool T72C-6165 2.8L, or T82L-6701A for 3.0L **(see illustration)**. Alternatively, use a hammer and socket the same diameter as the seal to drive the seal into the seal bore.

7   Drive the seal into position until it is firmly seated.

---

25   Piston/connecting rod assembly — installation and rod bearing oil clearance check

---

Refer to illustrations 25.5, 25.8a, 25.8b, 25.9, 25.12, 25.13, 25.14 and 25.20

1   Before installing the piston/connecting rod assemblies the cylinder walls must be perfectly clean, the top edge of each cylinder must be chamfered, and the crankshaft must be in place.

2   Remove the connecting rod cap from the end of the number one connecting rod. Remove the old bearing inserts and wipe the bearing surfaces of the connecting rod and cap with a clean, lint-free cloth. They must be kept spotlessly clean.

3   Clean the back side of the new upper bearing half, then lay it in place in the connecting rod. Make sure that the tab on the bearing fits into the recess in the rod. Do not hammer the bearing insert into place and be very careful not to nick or gouge the bearing face. Do not lubricate the bearing at this time.

4   Clean the back side of the other bearing insert and install it in the rod cap. Again, make sure the tab on the bearing fits into the recess in the cap, and do not apply any lubricant. It is critically important that the mating surfaces of the bearing and connecting rod are perfectly clean and oil free when they are assembled.

24.6   Rear seal installation (3.0L V6 shown, 2.8L is similar)

5   Position the piston ring gaps **(see illustration)**, then slip a section of plastic or rubber hose over the connecting rod cap bolts.

6   Lubricate the piston and rings with clean engine oil and attach a piston ring compressor to the piston. Leave the skirt protruding about 1/4-inch to guide the piston into the cylinder. The rings must be compressed as far as possible.

7   Rotate the crankshaft until the number one connecting rod journal is as far from the number one cylinder as possible (bottom dead center), and apply a coat of engine oil to the cylinder walls.

8   With the notch on top of the piston facing to the front of the engine **(see illustration)**, gently place the piston/connecting rod assembly into the number one cylinder bore and rest the bottom edge of the ring compressor on the engine block **(see illustration)**. Tap the top edge of the ring compressor to make sure it is contacting the block around

25.5   Compression and oil control ring gap positioning

A) Oil ring spacer
    butt connection

B) Oil ring side rail gaps

C) Compression ring gaps

25.8a   The pistons may have a notch in the crown, or an arrow, which should point to the front of the engine when the piston is installed

25.8b   With the ring compressor installed, slide the piston and rod assembly into the cylinder

25.9   The piston can be driven (gently) into the cylinder bore with the end of a wooden hammer handle

25.12   Lay the Plastigage strips on each rod bearing journal, parallel to the crankshaft centerline

its entire circumference.

9   Carefully tap on the top of the piston with the end of a wooden hammer handle (see illustration) while guiding the end of the connecting rod into place on the crankshaft journal.

10   The piston rings may try to pop out of the ring compressor just before entering the cylinder bore, so keep some downward pressure on the ring compressor. Work slowly, and if any resistance is felt as the piston enters the cylinder, stop immediately. Find out what is hanging up and fix it before proceeding. Do not, for any reason, force the piston into the cylinder, as you will break a ring and/or the piston.

11   Once the piston/connecting rod assembly is installed, the connecting rod bearing oil clearance must be checked before the rod cap is permanently bolted in place.

12   Cut a piece of the the appropriate size Plastigage slightly shorter than the width of the connecting rod bearing and lay it in place on the number one connecting rod journal, parallel with the journal axis (it must not cross the oil hole in the journal) (see illustration).

25.13   Pull the connecting rod firmly against
the crankshaft

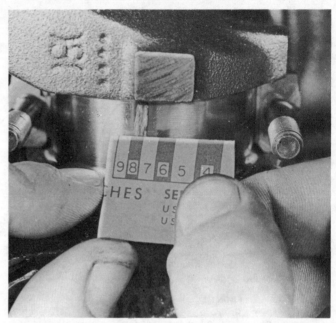

25.14   Measuring the width of the crushed Plastigage to
determine the rod bearing oil clearance (be sure to use the
correct scale — standard and metric scales are included)

13   Pull the connecting rod firmly against the crankshaft (see illus-tration), remove the protective hoses from the connecting rod bolts and install the rod cap. Make sure the mating mark on the cap is on the same side as the mark on the connecting rod. Install the nuts and tighten them to the specified torque, working up to it in three steps. Do not rotate the crankshaft at any time during this operation.
14   Remove the rod cap, being very careful not to disturb the Plastigage. Compare the width of the crushed Plastigage to the scale printed on the Plastigage container to obtain the oil clearance (see illus-tration). Compare it to the Specifications to make sure the clearance is correct. If the clearance is not correct, double-check to make sure that you have the correct size bearing inserts. Also, recheck the crankshaft connecting rod journal diameter and make sure that no dirt or oil was between the bearing inserts and the connecting rod or cap when the clearance was measured.
15   Carefully scrape all traces of the Plastigage material off the rod journal and/or bearing face. Be very careful not to scratch the bearing — use your fingernail or a piece of hardwood. Make sure the bearing faces are perfectly clean, then apply a layer of moly base grease or engine assembly lube to both of them. You will have to push the piston into the cylinder to expose the face of the bearing insert in the con-necting rod. Be sure to replace the protective hoses over the rod bolts first.
16   Slide the connecting rod back into place on the journal, remove the protective hoses from the rod cap bolts, install the rod cap and tighten the nuts to the specified torque. Again, work up to the torque in three steps.
17   Repeat the entire procedure for the remaining piston/connecting rod assemblies. Keep the back sides of the bearing inserts and the inside of the connecting rod and cap perfectly clean when assembling them. Make sure you have the correct piston for the cylinder and that the notch on the piston faces to the front of the engine when the piston is installed. Remember, use plenty of oil to lubricate the piston before installing the ring compressor. Also, when installing the rod caps for the final time, be sure to lubricate the bearing faces.
18   After all the piston/connecting rod assemblies have been properly installed, rotate the crankshaft a number of times by hand and check for any obvious binding.
19   As a final step, the connecting rod side clearance must be checked. Compare the measured side clearance to the Specifications to make sure it is correct.
20   Pry the connecting rod (4-cylinder) or rod pair (V6) all the way for-ward on the journal, then insert progressively thicker feeler gauges be-tween the rod and crankshaft until all the space is taken up (see illus-tration). The thickness of feeler gauge required is the side clearance.

25.20   Check the connecting rod side clearance with a
feeler gauge as shown

26   Pre-oiling engine after overhaul

Refer to illustration 26.3

1   After an overhaul it is a good idea to pre-oil the engine before it is installed in the vehicle and started for the first time. Pre-oiling will reveal any problems with the lubrication system at a time when cor-rections can be made easily and will prevent major engine damage. It will also allow the internal engine parts to be lubricated thoroughly in the normal fashion without the heavy loads associated with com-bustion placed on them.
2   The engine should be completely assembled with the exception of the distributor and rocker arm covers. The oil filter and oil pressure sending unit must be in place and the specified amount of oil must be in the crankcase (see Chapter 1).
3   A modified Ford distributor will be needed for this procedure — a junkyard should be able to supply one for a reasonable price. In order to function as a pre-oil tool, the distributor must have the gear on the

26.3   A typical pre-oil distributor (right) has the gear ground off and the advance weights (if equipped) removed

lower end of the shaft ground off (**see illustration**) and, if equipped, the advance weights on the upper end of the shaft removed.

4   Install the pre-oil distributor in place of the original distributor and make sure the lower end of the shaft mates with the upper end of the oil pump driveshaft. Turn the distributor shaft until they are aligned and the distributor body seats on the block. Install the distributor hold-down clamp and bolt.

5   Mount the upper end of the shaft in the chuck of an electric drill and use the drill to turn the pre-oil distributor shaft, which will drive the oil pump and circulate the oil throughout the engine. **Note:** *The drill must turn in a clockwise direction.*

6   It may take two or three minutes, but oil should soon start to flow out of all of the rocker arm holes, indicating that the oil pump is working properly. Let the oil circulate for several seconds, then shut off the drill motor.

7   Remove the pre-oil distributor, then install the rocker arm covers. The distributor should be installed after the engine is installed in the vehicle, so plug the hole with a clean cloth.

27   Initial start-up and break-in after overhaul

1   Once the engine has been properly installed in the vehicle, double-check the engine oil and coolant levels.

2   With the spark plugs out of the engine and the coil high tension lead grounded to the engine block, crank the engine over until oil pressure registers on the gauge (if so equipped) or until the oil light goes off.

3   Install the spark plugs, hook up the plug wires and the coil high tension lead.

4   Make sure the carburetor choke plate is closed, then start the engine. It may take a few moments for the gasoline to reach the carburetor, but the engine should start without a great deal of effort.

5   As soon as the engine starts it should be set at a fast idle to ensure proper oil circulation and allowed to warm up to normal operating temperature. While the engine is warming up, make a thorough check for oil and coolant leaks.

6   Shut the engine off and recheck the engine oil and coolant levels. Restart the engine and check the ignition timing and the engine idle speed (refer to Chapter 1). Make any necessary adjustments.

7   Drive the vehicle to an area with minimum traffic, accelerate at full throttle from 30 to 50 mph, then allow the vehicle to slow to 30 mph with the throttle closed. Repeat the procedure 10 or 12 times. This will load the piston rings and cause them to seat properly against the cylinder walls. Check again for oil and coolant leaks.

8   Drive the vehicle gently for the first 500 miles (no sustained high speeds) and keep a constant check on the oil level. It is not unusual for an engine to use oil during the break-in period.

9   At approximately 500 to 600 miles, change the oil and filter and retorque the cylinder head bolts.

10   For the next few hundred miles, drive the vehicle normally. Do not either pamper it or abuse it.

11   After 2000 miles, change the oil and filter again and consider the engine fully broken in.

Chapter 3 Cooling, heating and air conditioning systems

Contents

Specifications

General

Radiator cap pressure rating .... See Chapter 1
Coolant capacity .... See Chapter 1
Coolant type .... See Chapter 1
Refrigerant capacity .... 3.5 lbs

Torque specifications   Ft-lbs *(unless otherwise noted)*

Thermostat housing .... 12 to 15
Fan-to-clutch .... 4.5 to 6.0
Clutch-to-water pump
  Four-cylinder engine .... 12 to 18
  2.8L V6 engine .... 15 to 25
  3.0L V6 engine .... 30 to 100 in-lbs
Temperature sending unit .... 8 to 18
Water pump-to-front cover
  Four-cylinder engine .... 14 to 21
  2.8L V6 engine .... 84 to 108 in-lbs
  3.0L V6 engine .... 6 to 8
A/C condenser-to-body bolts....................... 8 to 12
A/C compressor-to-bracket .... 25 to 35
A/C hose manifold-to-compressor .... 13 to 27

1 General information

Engine cooling system

These vehicles employ a pressurized engine cooling system with thermostatically controlled coolant circulation. An impeller-type water pump mounted on the front of the block pumps coolant through the engine. The pump is driven by the timing belt on 4-cylinder engines and by a drivebelt on V6 engines.

The coolant flows around each cylinder and toward the rear of the engine. Cast-in coolant passages direct coolant around the intake and exhaust ports, near the spark plug areas and in close proximity to the exhaust valve guide inserts.

A wax pellet type thermostat is located in the front of the intake manifold, just ahead of the throttle body. During warm up, the closed thermostat prevents coolant from circulating through the radiator. When the engine reaches normal operating temperature, the thermostat opens and allows hot coolant to travel through the radiator, where it is cooled before returning to the engine.

The aluminum radiator is the crossflow type, with tanks on either side of the core.

The cooling system is sealed by a pressure type radiator cap. This raises the boiling point of the coolant and the higher boiling point of the coolant increases the cooling efficiency of the radiator.

If the system pressure exceeds the cap pressure relief value, the excess pressure in the system forces the spring-loaded valve inside the cap off its seat and allows the coolant to escape through the overflow tube into a coolant reservoir. When the system cools the excess coolant is automatically drawn from the reservoir back into the radiator.

The coolant reservoir maintains the proper radiator fluid level and acts as a holding tank for overheated coolant. This type of cooling system is known as a *closed* design because coolant that escapes past the pressure cap is saved and reused.

Heating system

The heating system consists of a blower fan and heater core located under the hood, the inlet and outlet hoses connecting the heater core to the engine cooling system and the heater/air conditioning control head on the dashboard. Hot engine coolant is circulated through the heater core at all times. When the heater mode is activated, a flap door opens to expose the heater box to the passenger compartment. A fan switch on the control head activates the blower motor, which forces air through the core, heating the air.

Air conditioning system

The air conditioning system consists of a condenser mounted in front of the radiator, an evaporator mounted under the hood, a compressor mounted on the engine, a filter-drier (accumulator) which contains a high pressure cycling switch and the plumbing connecting all of the above.

A blower fan forces the warmer air of the passenger compartment through the evaporator core (sort of a radiator-in-reverse), transferring the heat from the air to the refrigerant. The liquid refrigerant boils off into low pressure vapor, taking the heat with it when it leaves the evaporator.

2 Antifreeze — general information

Warning: *Do not allow antifreeze to come in contact with your skin or painted surfaces of the vehicle. Flush contacted areas immediately with plenty of water. Antifreeze can be fatal to children and pets. Wipe up any garage floor and drip pan coolant spills immediately. Keep antifreeze containers covered and repair leaks in your cooling system immediately.*

The cooling system should be drained, flushed and refilled at least every other year (see Chapter 1). The use of antifreeze solutions for periods of longer than two years is likely to cause damage and encourage the formation of rust and scale in the system.

Before adding antifreeze to the system, check all hose connections, because antifreeze tends to search out and leak through very minute openings.

The exact mixture of antifreeze to water which you should use depends on the relative weather conditions. The mixture should contain at least 50 percent antifreeze, but should never contain more than 70 percent antifreeze. Read carefully all instructions printed on the antifreeze container.

Due to the aluminum radiator, use Ford coolant E2FZ-19549-A or equivalent meeting specifications ESE-M97B44-A. Coolant may be diluted with tap water except in areas where it has high alkaline content, in which case distilled water should be used.

3 Thermostat — replacement

Refer to illustrations 3.3, 3.4, 3.6, 3.9 and 3.10

Warning: *The engine must be completely cool before beginning this procedure.*

1   Refer to the Warning in Section 2.

2   Drain the cooling system so that the coolant level is below the thermostat (Chapter 1).

3   On V6 engines the thermostat is mounted at the front of the intake manifold in an extension housing **(see illustration)**.

4   On 4-cylinder engines, disconnect the heater return hose at the thermostat housing, located on the front of the head **(see illustration)**.

ROTATE THERMOSTAT INTO WATER OUTLET CONNECTOR IN A CLOCKWISE DIRECTION TO SECURE THERMOSTAT TO CONNECTOR

NOTE: THERMOSTAT ASSEMBLY SHOWN IN PLACE IN THERMOSTAT HOUSING

3.3 Exploded view of thermostat components — 3.0L V6

3.4 Exploded view of thermostat components — 4-cylinder engine

3.6   Removing the thermostat housing
(2.8L V6)

3.9   The thermostat properly located
inside the housing — DO NOT
install it backwards!

3.10   Make sure the thermostat does
not block the entrance to the heater
tube (4-cylinder)

4.4   Exploded view of radiator
components (V6 shown,
4-cylinder similar)

5   Remove the upper radiator hose from the thermostat housing.
6   Remove the coolant outlet housing retaining bolts **(see illustration)**. Be prepared for additional coolant to flow from the engine, then pull the housing out sufficiently to provide access to the thermostat.
7   Remove the thermostat by turning counterclockwise and remove the gasket. **Caution:** *Do not pry on the thermostat to remove.*
8   Clean the thermostat housing surface and the engine surface thoroughly. All traces of gasket material must be scraped clean before proceeding.
9   Install the thermostat with the bridge section in the outlet casting **(see illustration)**. Turn the thermostat clockwise to lock it in position on the flats cast into the outlet elbow.
10   On 4-cylinder models which have a heater hose connection, make sure that the thermostat is aligned properly to allow full flow to the heater **(see illustration).**
11   Coat both sides of a new gasket with water resistant gasket sealer and position the gasket on the thermostat housing mating surface.
12   Position the thermostat housing carefully against the block or head,

making sure the gasket is not disturbed.
13   Install and tighten the retaining bolts to the specified torque.
14   On 4-cylinder models, connect the heater hose to the thermostat housing.
15   Fill the cooling system with the recommended antifreeze and water mixture as described in Chapter 1.
16   Check for leaks and proper heater operation after the engine has reached normal operation temperature. After the engine has completely cooled remove the radiator cap and check for proper coolant level (see Chapter 1).

4   Radiator — removal and installation

Refer to illustrations 4.4, 4.9 and 4.10

1   Disconnect the negative cable at the battery.
2   Drain the cooling system (Chapter 1).

4.9   Radiator components

A   Overflow hose
B   Fan shroud
　　mounting bolt
C   Transmission cooling line
　　(automatic only)
D   Radiator mounting bolt

4.10   On A/C equipped vehicles, the refrigerant line must be pushed aside (arrow) to clear the hose neck

3   Disconnect the overflow hose near the filler neck.
4   Remove the two upper fan shroud bolts (see illustration), lift up on the shroud until it pops out of the bottom locating pockets, then lay it over the fan.
5   Disconnect the upper and lower radiator hoses.
6   Disconnect the two transmission cooling lines from the radiator (automatic transmission only). Be sure to place a drain pan underneath. Cover the ends of the hoses with a plastic bag to prevent additional transmission fluid loss and contamination.
7   Unbolt the cooler tube bracket under the radiator (automatic transmission only).
8   Remove the hoses from the optional auxiliary transmission cooler (if equipped).
9   Remove the two radiator mounting bolts (see illustration).
10   Tilt the radiator back about one inch and lift up, clear of the radiator support and fan. Push the A/C hoses aside, if so equipped (see illustration), and carefully lift the radiator out of the vehicle. Caution: *Do not disconnect any of the air conditioning hoses or components without first having the system depressurized by a qualified dealer or specialist.*
11   Following radiator removal, the shroud may be lifted out if desired.
12   Do not lose the rubber insulators from the bottom of the radiator.
13   Installation is the reverse of removal.
14   Refill the radiator with coolant (Chapter 1). Fill the system slowly to ensure the radiator is completely full. After driving, allow the system to cool and then check again that the level inside the radiator is full.
15   Check and correct the transmission fluid level (automatic transmission only).

5.5   Fan and viscous clutch assembly on V6 engine

5.6a   Removing fan clutch with Ford tools

---

5   Engine cooling fan and clutch — check and replacement

Refer to illustrations 5.5, 5.6a, 5.6b and 5.14
Warning: *The engine must be completely cool before beginning this procedure.*

Check

Note: *The following checks should be done with the engine off.*

1   Check fan clutch for fluid leakage. Slight seepage is acceptable. Substantial leaking requires replacement.
2   Rock the fan blades to check for bearing play in the hub. Replace the clutch assembly if excessive play or noise when turning the fan is noted.
3   If the fan completely freewheels (no resistance) when the engine is warm, or locks up completely regardless of temperature, replace the clutch assembly with a new one.

V6 engines
4   Unbolt the fan shroud. Place the shroud over the fan, against the engine.
5   Remove the fan to clutch bolts from the inside (see illustration).
6   Remove the large nut which attaches the viscous clutch to the hub of the water pump shaft, using tools T83T-6312-A and T83T-6312-B or equivalent (see illustration). Caution: *This nut has*

5.6b If the factory tools are unavailable, remove the lower pulley for clearance. Wrap a rag around the water pump pulley, attach a chain wrench or similar tool, and turn the hex-nut on fan hub with an adjustable wrench clock-wise to loosen (left hand threads). You may have to unbolt the fan from the clutch hub for clearance.

left-hand threads and must be rotated clockwise for removal. In place of these special tools, we were able to use a chain wrench to hold the assembly stationary and adjustable wrench to loosen the nut **(see illustration)**.

7   Install the clutch/fan assembly on the water pump shaft and install the nut using the special tools or chain wrench/adjustable wrench. Remember that these are left-hand threads.

8   Attach the fan to the clutch (if separated).

9   Install the fan shroud.

4-cylinder engine

10   Disconnect the negative cable from the battery.

11   Remove the fan shroud.

12   Disconnect the overflow tube and lift the shroud off the lower retaining clips.

13   Move the shroud back over the fan in order to get to the fan bolts.

14   Remove the four bolts retaining the clutch and fan assembly to the pulley and remove the assembly from the vehicle **(see illustration)**.

15   If necessary, the fan and clutch can be separated by removing the four bolts which join them.

16   Prior to installation, attach the fan to the clutch with the four bolts (if separated).

17   Position the fan and clutch assembly to the pulley and secure with the four bolts.

18   Install the fan shroud.

19   Connect the battery cable.

---

6   Coolant temperature sending unit — check and replacement

Refer to illustrations 6.8a, 6.8b and 6.8c

Warning: *The engine must be completely cool before removing the sending unit. Antifreeze/coolant is toxic, keep it away from children and pets.*

Note: *The following procedure applies only to the standard analog instruments. The optional digital panel diagnosis requires special equipment the home mechanic is not likely to have. We recommend you take these to a dealer.*

Checking

1   If the coolant temperature gauge is inoperative, check the fuses first (Chapter 12).

2   If the temperature gauge indicates excessive temperature after running, see the Troubleshooting Section in the front of the manual.

5.14   Fan and clutch assembly on 4-cylinder engine

3   If the temperature gauge indicates ''Hot'' as soon as the engine is started cold, disconnect the wire at the coolant temperature sensor. If the gauge reading drops, replace the sending unit. If the reading remains high, the wire to the gauge may be shorted to ground or the gauge is faulty.

4   If the coolant temperature gauge fails to show any indication after the engine has been warmed up, (approximately 10 minutes) and the fuses checked out OK, shut off the engine. Disconnect the wire at the sending unit and, using a jumper wire, connect it to a clean ground on the engine. Turn on the ignition without starting the engine. If the gauge now indicates ''Hot'', replace the sending unit.

5   If the gauge still does not work, the circuit may be open or the gauge may be faulty — see Chapter 12 for additional information.

Replacement

6   Disconnect the negative cable at the battery.

7   With the engine completely cool, remove the cap from the radiator to relieve any pressure and then replace the cap. Place a drain pan under the sender.

8   Disconnect the temperature sending unit wire at the sending unit **(see illustrations)**.

6.8a   The coolant temperature sending unit (arrow) is located in left side of thermostat housing (2.8L V6). Coolant hose removed for access

FUEL
INJECTORS
(6 REQ'D)

WIRING
ASSEMBLY

6.8b Coolant temperature
sending unit location (3.0L V6)

FRONT OF VEHICLE

WIRING
ASSEMBLY

WATER
TEMPERATURE
SENDER ASSEMBLY
(MECHANICAL
CLUSTER)

WIRING
ASSEMBLY

COOLANT
TEMPERATURE
SENSOR
(ELECTRONIC
INSTRUMENTATION)

9   Prepare the new temperature sending unit for installation by applying D8AZ-19554-A or an equivalent sealer to the threads.
10 Remove the temperature sending unit. Immediately install the new sending unit to minimize coolant loss.
11 Connect the temperature sending unit wire.
12 Refill the cooling system to replace lost coolant.
13 Connect the battery cable and start the engine. Check for leaks.

7 Coolant reservoir — removal and installation

Refer to illustration 7.6

Warning: *Store coolant/antifreeze in a tightly closed, properly labeled container, out of reach of children and pets. Immediately clean up any spills and observe precautions listed on the container.*

1   The coolant reservoir is located under the battery. It is combined with the windshield washer reservoir in a common housing separated by a bulkhead.
2   Remove the battery as described in Chapter 5.
3   Unbolt the starter solenoid as described in Chapter 5.
4   Remove the four bolts retaining the battery tray and lift it out.
5   Disconnect the hoses and wiring connectors from the reservoir.
6   Remove the retaining screw from the rear of the reservoir **(see illustration)** and lift it out while disengaging the locating flange at the front of the reservoir.
7   Installation is the reverse of removal.

8 Water pump — check

Refer to illustration 8.4

1   A failure of the water pump can cause overheating and serious engine damage (the pump will not circulate coolant through the engine).
2   There are three ways to check the operation of the water pump while it is installed on the engine. If the pump is defective, it should

7.6 The combination coolant/windshield washer reservoir

A Coolant filler plug
B Coolant overflow hose
C Windshield washer hose
D Mounting screw
E Windshield washer
   filler tube clamp

be replaced with a new or rebuilt unit.
3   With the engine running and at normal operating temperature, squeeze the upper radiator hose. If the water pump is working properly, a pressure surge will be felt as the hose is released.
4   Water pumps are equipped with a 'weep' or vent hole. If a pump

8.4   Coolant seepage stains from the water pump ''weep hole'' (arrow), viewed from below

seal failure occurs, small amounts of coolant will leak from the weep hole **(see illustration)**.

5   If the water pump shaft bearing fails, there may be a squealing sound emitted from the front of the engine while it is running. Shaft or bearing wear can be felt as free play if the water pump pulley is rocked up and down by hand.

9   Water pump — removal and installation

Refer to illustrations 9.11, 9.27a, 9.27b, 9.30 and 9.31

Warning: *The engine must be completely cool before beginning this procedure. Also, see the Warning in Section 2 pertaining to antifreeze.*

4-cylinder engine

1   Disconnect the negative cable at the battery.
2   Drain the cooling system (refer to Chapter 1, if necessary).
3   Remove the shroud retaining bolts and move the shroud back over the fan.
4   Remove the four bolts retaining the fan assembly to the water pump shaft and then remove the fan (Section 5) and shroud from the engine compartment.
5   If equipped with air conditioning, loosen the air conditioner compressor idler pulley and remove the drivebelt.
6   Loosen the alternator and power steering mounting bolts and remove the alternator and power steering belts.
7   Remove the water pump pulley.
8   Disconnect the heater hose at the water pump.
9   Remove the timing belt cover.
10   Disconnect the lower radiator hose from the water pump.
11   Remove the water pump retaining bolts and remove the water pump **(see illustration)**. Pay close attention to the various types and locations of the bolts for reinstallation.
12   Clean all old gasket and sealant from the gasket surfaces.
13   Coat both sides of the new gasket with sealant and place the gasket on the water pump surface.
14   Install the water pump on the cylinder block and install the retaining bolts. Apply D8AZ-19554-A sealer or water resistant sealer to the bolt threads prior to installing.
15   Install the lower radiator hose.
16   Install the heater hose.
17   Install the timing belt cover and tighten the bolts evenly.
18   Position the water pump pulley on the pump shaft.
19   Position the power steering (if so equipped) and alternator drivebelts to their respective pulleys.
20   Position the air conditioner compressor drivebelt (if so equipped) to its pulley.
21   Put the shroud around the fan assembly and install the fan assembly onto the water pump shaft (Section 5).
22   Position the shroud on the radiator and install the retaining bolts.

9.11   Water pump, thermostat and inner timing belt cover installation assembly on the 4-cylinder engine

9.27a   Remove the coolant hose (arrow) by loosening the clamp and tapping the screw with a small hammer (2.8L V6 shown)

23   Adjust all drivebelts (Chapter 1).
24   Fill the cooling system (Chapter 1).
25   Start the engine and check for leaks.

V6 engines

26   Disconnect the negative cable at the battery.
27   To provide adequate clearance, remove the radiator (Section 4) and then the coolant hoses from the pump **(see illustrations)**.
28   Remove the fan and clutch assembly (Section 5).
29   Loosen the alternator mounting bolts and remove the belt. On some models it may be necessary to remove the idler pulley and bracket.
30   Remove the water pump pulley **(see illustration)**.
31   Remove the water pump assembly attaching bolts **(see illustration)** making note of the positions of the various length bolts. Remove the water pump (some models) from the front cover.
32   Remove all gasket material from the sealing surfaces on the front

9.27b Remove the short coolant hose from the bottom of the pump (2.8L V6 shown)

9.30 After fan removal, use the chain wrench to hold the pulley during bolt removal

9.31 Arrows show locations of typical water pump mounting bolts (2.8L V6 shown)

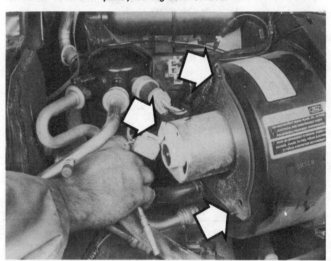

10.5 Remove the three blower retaining screws (arrows)

cover and water pump assembly.

33 Install the water pump assembly on the front cover with two bolts. Tighten the bolts only finger-tight.

34 Working around the pump, tighten all the water pump bolts to the specified torque.

35 Install the water pump pulley and the alternator and bracket if removed.

36 Install the radiator and connect all hoses.

37 Install all belts and adjust to the proper tension (Chapter 1).

38 Install the fan and clutch assembly (Section 6).

39 Connect the battery.

40 Fill the cooling system as described in Chapter 1.

41 Start the engine and check for leaks.

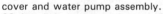

10 Heater blower motor — removal and installation

Refer to illustrations 10.5, 10.6, 10.14 and 10.15

Standard front blower

1 Disconnect the negative cable at the battery.

2 The blower motor is located on the right side of the engine compartment firewall. Depending on the engine installed, the air cleaner and/or duct may have to be removed for access to the motor.

3 Disconnect the wiring harness at the blower motor. This is done by pushing down on the tab and then pulling the connector away.

10.6 During blower removal you may have to twist the unit to clear obstructions

4 Disconnect the small rubber cooling tube at the blower motor.

5 Remove the screws which attach the motor to the heater blower assembly (see illustration).

6 Being very careful not to damage the gasket, pull the blower motor assembly out of the heater (see illustration). You may have to turn

10.14   To remove the rear air conditioner/heater panel, remove the three screws at bottom (arrows) and pull out until clips at top (arrows) disengage

10.15   Rear mounted blower

A Hose   C Hold-down screws
B Connector   (one is hidden)

11.6   Heater core removal

the motor to clear the accumulator.

7   At this point the blower wheel can be separated from the motor by removing the clamp on the motor shaft.

8   Installation is essentially the reverse of removal, however note the following points:

9   The gasket between the blower motor and the heater assembly must be in good condition. If it was damaged on removal, use a new gasket.

10   Make sure the electrical connector is fully seated.

11   Reconnect the battery.

12   Test for proper operation upon completion.

Optional rear blower

13   Disconnect the negative cable at the battery.

14   Remove the access panel **(see illustration)**.

15   The remainder of the procedure is essentially the same as for the front mounted blower — follow Steps 3 to 12 described above **(see illustration)**.

11   Heater core and hoses — removal and installation

Refer to illustrations 11.6, 11.14 and 11.18

Heater core

1   Allow the engine to completely cool before beginning.

2   Using a thick cloth, turn the radiator cap slowly to the first stop.

3   Step back and let the pressure release.

4   Once the pressure has been released, tighten the radiator cap.

5   Disconnect the heater hoses at the engine compartment firewall and plug the ends to prevent further draining of the system.

6   In the passenger compartment, remove the six screws attaching the heater core access cover to the plenum assembly. Remove the access cover **(see illustration)**.

7   Depress the retainer bracket at the top of the heater core. Pull the heater core rearward and down, removing it from the plenum assembly.

8   Position the new heater core and seal in the plenum assembly.

9   Install the heater core access cover to the plenum assembly.

10   Install the heater hoses.

11   Check the coolant level and add coolant as required (see Chapter 1).

12   Check the system for proper operation and for leaks.

Heater hoses

13   Drain the coolant from the cooling system (Chapter 1).

14   Disconnect the hoses by depressing the plastic tabs using Ford tool no. T85T-18539-AH **(see illustration)**. If you are unable to obtain this tool, you may be able to squeeze the retainer together with pliers or your fingers.

15   Pull the hoses apart until the plastic connector clears the locking tabs.

16   Damaged sections of hose may be repaired in an emergency by cutting out the damaged section and splicing in a new section using a short piece of 5/8-inch diameter tubing and hose clamps.

17   If a coupler clip is damaged, they may be purchased separately and installed.

18   Installation consists of pushing the two hose ends together until they click in, using new O-rings and silicone lubricant **(see illustration)**. Try to pull them apart to ensure that they are properly seated.

19   Refill the cooling system (Chapter 1).

20   Check for leaks and proper system operation.

CAUTION — ENGINE SHOULD BE OFF BEFORE DISCONNECTING COUPLING

11.14 Heater hose coupling disconnect procedure

11.18 Heater hose quick connect coupling tool

12 Air conditioning system — check and maintenance

Refer to illustration 12.9

Warning: *The air conditioning system is pressurized at the factory and depressurization requires special equipment. Discharging should be left to your dealer or air conditioning shop. Do not, under any circumstances, disconnect air conditioning fittings while the system is under pressure.*

1   The following maintenance steps should be performed on a regular basis to ensure that the air conditioner continues to operate at peak efficiency.

  a) Check the tension of the drivebelt and adjust if necessary (Chapter 1).

  b) Inspect the condition of the hoses. Check for cracking, hardening or other deterioration. **Warning:** *Do not replace A/C hoses until the system has been discharged by a dealer or air conditioning specialist.*

  c) Inspect the fins of the condenser for leaves, bugs and any other foreign material. A soft brush and compressed air can be used to remove them.

  d) Maintain the correct refrigerant charge.

2   The A/C compressor should be run for about 10 minutes at least once a month. This is particularly important during the winter months because long-term non-use can cause hardening of the internal seals.

12.9 Exploded view of air conditioner components shows evaporator without its housing

3   Because of the complexity of the air conditioning system and the special equipment required to effectively work on it, accurate troubleshooting and repair of the system should be left to a professional mechanic. One probable cause for poor cooling that can be determined by the home mechanic is low refrigerant charge. Should the system lose its cooling ability, the following procedure will help you pinpoint the cause.

4   Warm the engine to normal operating temperature.

5   The hood and doors should be open.

6   Set the control mode selector lever to the A/C position.

7   Set the temperature selector lever to the Cold position.

8   Set the blower control selector to the Hi position.

9   With the compressor engaged, feel the evaporator inlet pipe (**see illustration**) between the orifice and the evaporator. Put your other hand

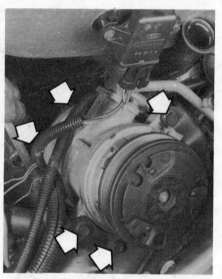

13.2   Air conditioning accumulator

A Mounting screws   C Test gauge fitting
B Refrigerant lines   D Pressure switch

14.3   Top view of compressor shows
location of refrigerant line hold down
bolts (arrows)

14.5   View of A/C compressor on 2.8L
V6 shows mounting bolt locations
(arrows). Wrench is on right rear bolt,
another is adjacent at the left rear

on the surface of the accumulator can.

10   If both surfaces feel about the same temperature and if both feel a little cooler than the ambient temperature, the freon level is probably okay. The problem is elsewhere.

11   If the inlet pipe has frost accumulation or feels cooler than the accumulator surface, the freon charge is low.

13   Air conditioning system accumulator — removal and installation

Refer to illustration 13.2

Warning: *The A/C system is under high pressure. Have the system discharged by a dealer or A/C specialist prior to repairs.*

Note: *A number of special tools are necessary to properly disconnect the A/C lines and fittings at the accumulator. For this reason, this job may be better left to a dealer or specialist equipped with these tools.*

1   Disconnect negative cable at the battery.

2   Unplug the pressure switch connector **(see illustration)**.

3   Disconnect the refrigerant line couplings using the special tool available from Ford.

4   Remove the mounting screws.

5   Installation is the reverse of removal.

6   Reconnect the refrigerant lines.

7   Have the system evacuated, recharged and leak tested by an air conditioning specialist.

14   Air conditioning system compressor — removal and installation

Refer to illustrations 14.3 and 14.5

Warning: *The A/C system is under high pressure. Have the system discharged prior to repairs by a dealer or A/C specialist.*

1   Disconnect the negative cable at the battery.

2   Remove the compressor drivebelt (Chapter 1).

3   Disconnect the refrigerant lines **(see illustration)** and cap them.

4   Disconnect the compressor wiring.

5   Remove the mounting bolts **(see illustration)** and lift the compressor out of the engine compartment.

6   Installation is the reverse of removal.

7   Have the system evacuated, recharged and leak tested by an air conditioning specialist.

15   Air conditioning system condenser — removal and installation

Refer to illustration 15.3

Warning: *The A/C system is under high pressure. Have the system discharged prior to repairs by a dealer or A/C specialist.*

1   Remove the radiator (Section 4).

2   After discharging system, disconnect the refrigerant lines from the condenser.

3   Remove the bolts from the upper corners of the condenser **(see illustration)** and lift it out of the vehicle.

4   Installation is the reverse of removal.

5   Have the system evacuated, recharged and leak tested by an air conditioning specialist.

15.3   Cutaway view of A/C condenser installation

16.3   Unplug the electrical connectors (arrows)

16.8   To replace the blower switch, pull off the control knob (A), unclip and remove the wiring connector (B), disconnect the light plug (C), and remove the screws (D)

16   Air conditioning and heater contol assembly — removal and installation

Refer to illustrations 16.3 and 16.9

Note: *Early production vehicles were equipped with manual (cable) operated controls. Later models have vacuum operated air doors.*

Dash mounted control

1   Remove the instrument cluster cowl (Chapter 11).

2   Remove the four screws attaching the face plate to the control assembly. Remove the rear screw holding the control to the dash.

3   Pull the control assembly out towards you and unplug the elec-trical (and vacuum, if equipped) connectors (**see illustration**).

4   Using pliers, carefully release the black function control cable and blue temperature control cable, as applicable.

5   Installation is the reverse of removal.

6   See Section 17 for adjustment procedures.

Optional rear mounted control

7   Remove the three cover mounting screws.

8   Lift the control out of the panel. Remove the knob, wiring and screws. Lift the switch out (**see illustration**).

9   Installation is the reverse of removal.

17.4   Function and temperature cable removal

17   Heater control cables — check and adjustment

Refer to illustrations 17.4, 17.5 and 17.6

Note: *Early production vehicles were equipped with manual (cable) operated controls. Later models have vacuum operated air doors.*

1   Remove the heater control assembly (Section 16).

2   To check the function control cable, turn the blower on High and move the function control lever to its various positions and check for airflow at the various outlets.

3   To adjust or replace either cable, remove the upper finish panel.

4   To replace a broken cable, disconnect it at both ends **(see illustra-** tion) and remove it from the vehicle. Install the cable at the control end first and adjust it using the following steps.

5   To adjust the function control cable, unclip the cable near the mode cam **(see illustration)**, place the control lever in the OFF position and align the holes in the mode cam with a Phillips screwdriver. Holding this position, snap the cable fastening clip into place.

6   To adjust the temperature control cable, unclip the cable at the temperature control cam **(see illustration)** and rotate the temperature control cam clockwise until the control lever is in the Cool position. Holding the cable in this position, snap the retaining clip into place, securing the cable housing.

7   Reinstall the control assembly and panels removed for access.

17.5   Function control cable adjustment

17.6   Temperature control cable adjustment

Chapter 4 Fuel and exhaust systems

Contents

Specifications

Fuel pump (carburetor-equipped models)
Fuel pressure (at idle) . . . . 4.5 to 6.5 psi
Fuel pump pushrod length . . . . 2.43 in (minimum)

Torque specifications   Ft-lbs (*unless otherwise noted*)
Four-cylinder engine
Air bypass valve mounting bolts . . . . 71 to 102 in-lbs
Throttle body to upper intake manifold bolts/nuts . . . . 12 to 15
Upper intake manifold to lower intake manifold bolts . . . . 14 to 21
Throttle position sensor to throttle body . . . . 14 to 15 in-lbs
Fuel pressure relief valve . . . . 48 to 84 in-lbs
Fuel pressure regulator to fuel supply manifold . . . . 27 to 40 in-lbs
Fuel supply manifold to lower intake manifold bolts . . . . 15 to 22

2.8L V6 engine
Carburetor to intake manifold . . . . 14 to 16
Fuel pump mounting bolts . . . . 11 to 19

3.0L V6 engine
Air intake throttle body assembly bolts and studs . . . . 15 to 22

1   General information

Fuel system

The fuel system consists of the fuel tank, the fuel pump(s), an air cleaner assembly, either a carburetor or a fuel injection system and the various steel, plastic and/or nylon lines and fittings connecting everything together. 1986 Aerostars powered by the 2-8L V6 are equipped with a carburetor. 1986 and 1987 vehicles with 2.3L OHC fours and all 1986 through 1988 models with 3.0L V6s are equipped with electronic fuel injection (EFI).

The fuel pump on carburetor equipped vehicles is a mechanical type mounted on the block and driven off the camshaft by a pushrod. The pumps on fuel injected vehicles are electric. A low pressure pump is mounted inside the fuel tank and a high pressure pump is mounted on the left frame rail, forward of the tank.

Exhaust system

All vehicles are equipped with a single exhaust manifold (2.3L OHC Four), or a pair of manifolds (2.8L V6 and 3.0L V6), connecting pipe between the exhaust manifold and the catalytic converter, a catalytic converter, an exhaust pipe and a muffler. Any component of the exhaust system can be replaced.

2   Fuel pressure relief procedure (fuel injected vehicles)

Refer to illustrations 2.1 and 2.5

1   The inertia switch, which shuts off fuel to the engine in the event of a collision, affords a simple and convenient means by which fuel pressure can be relieved before servicing fuel injection components. The switch is located on the toe-board to the right of the transmission hump, on the kick panel to the right of the passenger seat, or in the engine compartment **(see illustration)**.

2   Locate the switch on your vehicle, remove the mounting screws and remove the switch.

3   Unplug the inertia switch electrical connector.

4   Start the engine and allow it to idle until it eventually stops running on its own.

5   The fuel system pressure is now relieved. When finished working on the fuel system, check for fuel leaks, then simply plug the electrical connector back into the switch.

Warning: *If you see or smell gasoline, do not reset the switch until you have located the source of the leak and fixed it.*

6   Reinstall the inertia switch and tighten the two mounting nuts securely. Insure the switch is operational by depressing the reset button **(see illustration)**.

3   Fuel lines and fittings

Refer to illustrations 3.5, 3.9, 3.10, 3.13, 3.14 and 3.26

Warning: *The fuel system pressure must always be relieved before disconnecting fuel lines and fittings on fuel-injected vehicles (see Section 2). Gasoline is extremely flammable, so extra precautions must be taken when working on any part of the fuel system. DO NOT smoke or allow open flames or bare light bulbs near the work area. Also, don't work in a garage where a natural gas appliance such as a water heater or clothes dryer is present.*

Push connect fittings — disassembly and reassembly

1   Ford uses two different push connect fitting designs. Fittings used with 3/8 and 5/16-inch diameter lines have a ''hairpin'' type clip; fittings used with 1/4-inch diameter lines have a ''duck bill'' type clip. The procedure used for releasing each type of fitting is different. The clips should be replaced whenever a connector is disassembled.

2   Disconnect all push connect fittings from fuel system components such as the fuel filter, the carburetor/fuel charging assembly, the fuel tank, etc. before removing the assembly.

3/8 and 5/16-inch fittings (hairpin clip)

3   Inspect the internal portion of the fitting for accumulations of dirt.

2.1   A typical inertia switch location on a four-cylinder vehicle — other locations include the kick panel to the right of the front passenger seat and the engine compartment

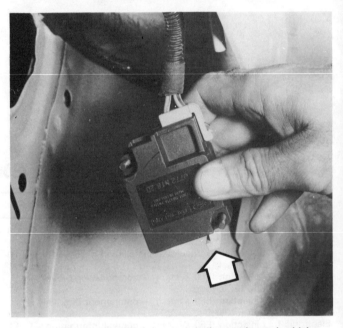

2.6   The inertia switch has a reset button (arrow) which should be pushed in after reinstalling the switch

If more than a light coating of dust is present, clean the fitting before disassembly.

4   Some adhesion between the seals in the fitting and the line will occur over a period of time. Twist the fitting on the line, then push and pull the fitting until it moves freely.

5   Remove the hairpin clip from the fitting by bending the shipping tab down until it clears the body **(see illustration)**. Then, using nothing but your hands, spread each leg about 1/8-inch to disengage the body and push the legs through the fitting. Finally, pull lightly on the triangular end of the clip and work it clear of the line and fitting. Remember, don't use any tools to perform this part of the procedure.

6   Grasp the fitting and hose and pull it straight off the line.

7   Do not reuse the original clip in the fitting. A new clip must be used.

8   Before reinstalling the fitting on the line, wipe the line end with a clean cloth. Inspect the inside of the fitting to ensure that it's free of dirt and/or obstructions.

9   To reinstall the fitting on the line, align them and push the fitting into place. When the fitting is engaged, a definite click will be heard. Pull on the fitting to ensure that it's completely engaged **(see illustration)**. To install the new clip, insert it into any two adjacent openings in the fitting with the triangular portion of the clip pointing *away* from the fitting opening. Using your index finger, push the clip in until the legs are locked on the outside of the fitting.

3.5 An exploded view of the hairpin clip type push connect fitting

PUSH UNTIL CLICK IS HEARD

3.9 Connecting push connecting fittings

3.10 A push connect fitting with a duck bill clip

HOSE

3.13 Duck bill clip fitting removal using the special Ford disassembly tool

3.14 Pulling off the duck bill clip type push connect fitting

1/4-inch fittings (duck bill clip)

10 The duck bill clip type fitting consists of a body, spacers, O-rings and the retaining clip (see illustration). The clip holds the fitting securely in place on the line. One of the two following methods must be used to disconnect this type of fitting.

11 Before attempting to disconnect the fitting, check the visible internal portion of the fitting for accumulations of dirt. If more than a light coating of dust is evident, clean the fitting before disassembly.

12 Some adhesion between the seals in the fitting and line will occur over a period of time. Twist the fitting on the line, then push and pull the fitting until it moves freely.

13 The *preferred method* used to disconnect the fitting requires a special tool. To disengage the line from the fitting, align the slot in the push connect disassembly tool (Ford Part No. T82L-9500-AH or equivalent tool) with either tab on the clip (90 degrees from the slots on the side of the fitting) and insert the tool (see illustration). This disengages the duck bill from the line. **Note:** *Some fuel lines have a secondary bead which aligns with the outer surface of the clip. The bead can make tool insertion difficult. If necessary, use the alternative disassembly method described in Step 16.*

14 Holding the tool and the line with one hand, pull the fitting off (see

illustration). **Note:** *Only moderate effort is necessary if the clip is properly disengaged. The use of anything other than your hands should not be required.*

15 After disassembly, inspect and clean the line sealing surface. Also inspect the inside of the fitting and the line for any internal parts that may have been dislodged from the fitting. Any loose internal parts should be immediately reinstalled (use the line to insert the parts).

16 The *alternative disassembly procedure* requires a pair of small Channelock pliers. The pliers must have a jaw width of 3/16-inch or less.

17 Align the jaws of the pliers with the openings in the side of the fitting and compress the portion of the retaining clip that engages the body. This disengages the retaining clip from the body (often one side of the clip will disengage before the other — both sides must be disengaged).

18 Pull the fitting off the line. **Note:** *Only moderate effort is required if the retaining clip has been properly disengaged. Do not use any tools for this procedure.*

19 Once the fitting is removed from the line end, check the fitting and line for any internal parts that may have been dislodged from the fitting. Any loose internal parts should be immediately reinstalled (use the line to insert the parts).

20 The retaining clip will remain on the line. Disengage the clip from

FEMALE FITTING

O-RINGS—SUPPLIED IN E35Y-19D690-A KIT

GARTER SPRING

MALE FITTING

CAGE

SPRING LOCK COUPLING DISCONNECTED

TO DISCONNECT COUPLING

CAUTION—DISCHARGE SYSTEM BEFORE DISCONNECTING COUPLING

NOTE:
EACH END OF TOOL T81P-19623-G IS A DIFFERENT SIZE TO FIT 3/8 AND 1/2 INCH COUPLINGS

TOOL
T81P-19623-G - 3/8 AND 1/2 INCH
T81P-19623-G1 - 3/8 INCH
T81P-19623-G2 - 1/2 INCH
T83P-19623-C - 5/8 INCH

CAGE

① FIT TOOL TO COUPLING SO THAT TOOL CAN ENTER CAGE TO RELEASE THE GARTER SPRING.

TO CONNECT COUPLING

GARTER SPRING

REPLACEMENT GARTER SPRINGS
3/8 INCH — E1ZZ-19E576-A
1/2 INCH — E1ZZ-19E576-B
5/8 INCH — E35Y-19E576-A
ALSO AVAILABLE IN
E35Y-19D690-A KIT

① CHECK FOR MISSING OR DAMAGED GARTER SPRING—REMOVE DAMAGED SPRING WITH SMALL HOOKED WIRE—INSTALL NEW SPRING IF DAMAGED OR MISSING.

PUSH TOOL INTO CAGE

② PUSH THE TOOL INTO THE CAGE OPENING TO RELEASE THE FEMALE FITTING FROM THE GARTER SPRING.

A – CLEAN FITTINGS

B – INSTALL NEW O-RINGS—USE ONLY SPECIFIED O-RINGS —SUPPLIED IN E35Y-19D690-A KIT

C – LUBRICATE WITH CLEAN REFRIGERANT OIL

D – ASSEMBLE FITTING TOGETHER BY PUSHING WITH A SLIGHT TWISTING MOTION

②

③ PULL THE COUPLING MALE AND FEMALE FITTINGS APART.

GARTER SPRING

③ TO ENSURE COUPLING ENGAGEMENT, VISUALLY CHECK TO BE SURE GARTER SPRING IS OVER FLARED END OF FEMALE FITTING.

④ REMOVE THE TOOL FROM THE DISCONNECTED SPRING LOCK COUPLING.

3.26 Connecting and disconnecting spring lock coupling fittings

the line bead to remove it. Do not reuse the retaining clip — install a new one!

21 Before reinstalling the fitting, wipe the line end with a clean cloth. Check the inside of the fitting to make sure that it's free of dirt and/or obstructions.

22 To reinstall the fitting, align it with the line and push it into place. When the fitting is engaged, a definite click will be heard. Pull on the fitting to ensure that it's fully engaged.

23 Install the new replacement clip by inserting one of the serrated edges on the duck bill portion into one of the openings. Push on the other side until the clip snaps into place.

Spring lock push connect fittings

24 The fuel supply and return lines used on EFI engines utilize spring lock couplings at the engine fuel rail end instead of plastic push connect fittings. The male end of the spring lock coupling, which is girded by two O-rings, is inserted into a female flared end engine fitting. The coupling is secured by a garter spring which prevents disengagement by gripping the flared end of the female fitting.

25 To disconnect the 1/2-inch (12.7mm) spring lock coupling supply fitting, you will need to obtain a spring lock coupling tool D87L-9280-B or its equivalent; for the 3/8-inch (9.52mm) return fitting, get tool D87L-9280-A or its equivalent.

26 Study the accompanying illustration carefully before detaching either spring lock coupling fitting (see illustration).

4 Fuel pump — check

Warning: Gasoline is extremely flammable, so extra precautions must be taken when working on any part of the fuel system. Do not smoke or allow open flames or bare light bulbs near the work area. Also, do not work in a garage if a natural gas appliance with a pilot light is present.

Mechanical fuel pump

General check

1 On carburetor-equipped engines, the fuel pump is located on the left side of the engine.

2 The fuel pump is sealed and no repairs are possible other than component replacement. However, the fuel pump can be inspected and tested on the vehicle as follows.

3 Make sure there is fuel in the fuel tank.

4 With the engine running, check for leaks at all fuel line connections between the fuel tank and the carburetor.

5 Tighten any loose connections and inspect all lines for flat spots and kinks which could restrict fuel flow. Air leaks or restrictions on the suction side of the fuel pump will greatly affect pump output.

6 Check for leaks at the fuel pump diaphragm flange.

7 Disconnect the coil wire from the distributor and fuel inlet line from the carburetor. Direct the fuel line from the pump into a metal container.

8 Crank the engine several revolutions and make sure that well defined spurts of fuel are ejected from the line. If not, the fuel line is clogged or the fuel pump is defective.

9 Disconnect the fuel line at both ends of the line and blow through it with compressed air to determine if the fuel line is clogged.

Pressure test

10 Connect a fuel pressure gauge (0 to 15 psi) to the fuel filter end of the line.

11 Start the engine — it should be able to run for over 30 seconds on the fuel in the carburetor bowl — and read the pressure after ten seconds. Compare your reading to the specified pressure.

12 If pump pressure is not as specified, install a new fuel pump.

13 Reconnect the fuel lines and install the air cleaner.

Electric fuel pump (fuel injected vehicles)

14 An electric fuel pump malfunction will usually result in a loss of fuel flow and/or pressure that is often reflected by a corresponding reduction in performance. If you suspect an electric fuel pump problem, disconnect the electrical harness from the pump(s) (see Section 7), attach a fused jumper between the battery and the pump and carefully listen to the pump. If it's not running, replace it. If it is running, then the problem lies within the fuel pump circuit or elsewhere (see Troubleshooting). Diagnosis of this circuit is beyond the scope of the home mechanic. Take the vehicle to a dealer and have the fuel pump circuit checked by a professional.

5 Fuel tank — removal and installation

Refer to illustration 5.5

Note: Don't begin this procedure until the gauge indicates that the tank is empty or nearly empty. If the tank must be removed when it's full (for example, if the fuel pump malfunctions), siphon any remaining fuel from the tank prior to removal.

Warning: Gasoline is extremely flammable so extra precautions must be taken when working on any part of the fuel system. DO NOT smoke or allow open flames or bare light bulbs in or near the work area. Also, don't work in a garage if a natural gas appliance such as a water heater or clothes dryer is present.

1 On fuel injected vehicles, relieve the fuel pressure (refer to Section 2).

2 Detach the cable from the negative terminal of the battery.

3 Raise the vehicle and support it securely on jackstands.

4 Unless the vehicle has been driven far enough to completely empty the tank, it's a good idea to siphon the residual fuel out before removing the tank from the vehicle. Siphon or pump the fuel out through the fuel filler pipe. On US vehicles, a small diameter hose may be necessary because of the small trap door installed in the fuel filler pipe to prevent vapors from escaping during refueling. Fuel injected vehicles have reservoirs inside the tank to maintain fuel near the pump pick-up during vehicle cornering maneuvers and when the fuel level is low. The reservoirs could prevent siphon tubes or hoses from reaching the bottom of the fuel tank. This situation can be overcome by repositioning the siphon hose several times.

5 Loosen the hose clamps securing the fuel filler neck hose (see illustration on next page) and detach the hose.

6 Place a floor jack under the tank and position a block of wood between the jack pad and the tank. Raise the jack until it's supporting the tank.

7 Remove the bolt from the front and rear straps. (The straps are hinged at the other end so you can swing them out of the way.)

8 Lower the tank far enough to unplug the wiring harness and to disconnect the fuel feed return and vapor hoses. Note that each of these hoses has a different diameter, making it impossible to mix them up during reassembly.

9 Slowly lower the jack while steadying the tank. Remove the tank from the vehicle and remove the shield from the tank.

10 If you're replacing the tank, or having it cleaned or repaired, remove the sender unit (carburetor equipped vehicles) or fuel pump/sending unit (fuel injected vehicles) (see Section 7). For information regarding tank cleaning and repair, see Section 6.

11 When the tank is ready to be installed, install the fuel pump/sending unit (see Section 7).

12 Install the shield.

13 Installation is the reverse of removal.

6 Fuel tank — cleaning and repair

1 Repairs to the fuel tank or filler neck should be peformed by a professional with the proper training to carry out this critical and potentially dangerous work. Even after cleaning and flushing, explosive fumes can remain and could explode during repair of the tank.

2 If the fuel tank is removed from the vehicle, it should not be placed in an area where sparks or open flames could ignite the fumes coming out of the tank. Be especially careful inside garages where a natural gas appliance is located because the pilot light could cause an explosion.

7 Fuel pump — removal and installation

Warning: Gasoline is extremely flammable so extra precautions must be taken when working on any part of the fuel system. DO NOT smoke or allow open flames or bare light bulbs in or near the work area. Also, don't work in a garage if a natural gas appliance such as a water heater or clothes dryer is present.

148

CAP ASSEMBLY

PART OF BODY

PIPE ASSEMBLY

CLAMP

VIEW E

VIEW E

VIEW E

PIPE ASSEMBLY

PIPE ASSEMBLY

VIEW E

VIEW B

VIEW P

VIEW B

VIEW N

CLAMP

TANK ASSEMBLY

SHIELD ASSEMBLY

U-NUT

U-NUT

U-NUT

STRAP

INSERT NUT

SHIELD

VIEW Y

CLAMP

NOTE: ALIGN DIMPLE ON UNDERSIDE OF PIPE WITH PAINT STRIP ON UNDERSIDE OF HOSE

VIEW ROTATED SLIGHTLY
VIEW E

STRAP

STRAP MUST BE INSTALLED IN BRACKET AS SHOWN TYPICAL 2 PLACES
VIEW P

NOTE: ALIGN TAPE STRIP ON TUBE TO BE IN LINE WITH ARROW ON FUEL TANK

VIEW FROM ABOVE
VIEW B

CLAMP

PIPE ASSEMBLY

SEAL

VIEW N

TANK ASSEMBLY

5.5 An exploded view of a typical midship fuel tank assembly

7.2   To break the fuel pump loose from the block, loosen the fuel pump mounting bolts (arrows) a couple of turns — if it still sticks to the block, have a friend turn the engine over once or twice — when the camshaft lobe actuates the fuel pump pushrod, it will break the pump loose

7.3   An exploded view of the mechanical fuel pump assembly and the line connecting it to the carburetor on the 2.8L V6 — be sure to use a backup wrench when loosening the threaded fittings at either end of the metal line

Mechanical fuel pump (carburetor equipped vehicles)
Refer to illustrations 7.2 and 7.3

1   Loosen the threaded fuel line fittings (at the pump) with the proper size wrench (a flare nut wrench is recommended), then retighten them until they're just snug. Don't remove the lines at this time. The outlet line is pressurized, so protect your eyes with safety goggles or wrap the fitting with a shop rag, then loosen it carefully.
2   Loosen the mounting bolts (see illustration) two turns. Use your hands to loosen the fuel pump. If it's stuck to the block, do not use a tool — you could damage the pump. If you cannot loosen the pump by hand, have an assistant operate the starter while you keep one hand on the pump. As the camshaft turns, the pump pushrod will operate the pump — when the pump feels loose, stop turning the engine over.
3   Disconnect the fuel lines (see illustration) from the pump. Be sure to use a back-up wrench.
4   Remove the fuel pump bolts and detach the pump and gasket. Discard the old gasket. Pull out the pushrod.
5   Inspect the pushrod for damage or excessive wear.
6   Remove all old gasket material and sealant from the engine block. If you're installing the original pump, remove all the old gasket material from the pump mating surface as well. Wipe the mating surfaces of the block and pump with a cloth saturated with lacquer thinner or acetone.
7   Install the fuel pump pushrod. Insert the bolts through the pump (to use as a guides for the new gasket) and place the gasket in position on the fuel pump mounting flange. Position the fuel pump on the block (make sure the pump arm engages the pushrod properly). Tighten the bolts a little at a time until they're at the specified torque.
8   Attach the fuel lines to the pump. Start the threaded fitting by hand to avoid cross-threading it. Tighten the outlet nut securely. If any of the hoses are cracked, hardened or otherwise deteriorated, replace them at this time.
9   Start the engine and check for fuel leaks for two minutes.
10   Stop the engine and check the fuel line connections for leaks by running a finger under each fitting. Check for oil leaks at the fuel pump mounting gasket.

Electric fuel pump (fuel injected vehicles)
Refer to illustrations 7.13, 7.16 and 7.22

In-Tank (low pressure) pump

11   Relieve the fuel system pressure (see Section 2).

7.13   Be sure to use a BRASS punch when loosening the lock ring on the electric fuel pump/sending unit (a spark from a steel punch or hammer could cause an explosion)

12   Remove the fuel tank (see Section 5).
13   Using a **brass** punch only, tap the lock ring counterclockwise until it's loose (see illustration).
14   Carefully pull the the fuel pump/sending unit assembly from the tank.
15   Remove the old lock ring gasket and discard it.

16 If you're planning to reinstall the original fuel pump/sending unit, remove the strainer by prying it off with a screwdriver (see illustration), wash it in clean solvent, then push it back onto the metal pipe on the end of the pump. If you're installing a new pump/sending unit, the assembly will include a new strainer.

17 Clean the fuel pump mounting flange and the tank mounting surface and seal ring groove.

18 Installation is the reverse of removal. Apply a thin coat of heavy grease to the new lock ring gasket to hold it in place during assembly.

Externally mounted (high pressure) pump

19 Relieve the fuel system pressure (see Section 2).

20 Raise the vehicle and place it securely on jackstands.

21 Unplug the electrical connector.

22 Disconnect the fuel line fittings from both ends of the pump. (see Section 3) (see illustration).

23 Remove the mounting bolts.

24 Remove the pump.

25 Installation is the reverse of removal.

8 Air cleaner housing — removal and installation

Refer to illustrations 8.2, 8.8 and 8.9

Four-cylinder engine

Refer to illustration 8.2

1 Detach the cable from the negative terminal of the battery.

2 Disconnect the inlet tube and idle bypass tube from the air cleaner cover (see illustration).

3 Unplug the electrical connector to the throttle air bypass valve.

4 Remove the air cleaner cover and filter element.

5 Remove the three nuts holding the air cleaner tray.

6 Remove the air cleaner tray.

7 Installation is the reverse of removal.

7.16   If you're replacing the pump, this step isn't necessary, but if you're going to reinstall the old pump, remove the strainer and clean it with solvent

3.0L V6 engine

Refer to illustration 8.8

8 Removal and installation of the air cleaner housing assembly on the 3.0L V6 is basically similar to the procedure outlined above for the 2.3L four (see illustration). Note: *Be sure that the sealing gasket is in position between the right fender apron and the air cleaner assembly when reinstalling the air cleaner assembly.*

7.22   The externally mounted high pressure fuel pump is located on the left frame rail forward of the fuel tank

HOSE CLAMP

HOSE CLAMP

HOSE CLAMP

RESONATOR BRACKET ASSEMBLY

SCREW

AIR BYPASS TUBE

AIR INTAKE RESONATOR OUTLET TUBE

HOSE CLAMP

HOSE CLAMP

FRONT OF VEHICLE

HOSE CLAMP

AIR INTAKE RESONATOR INLET TUBE

THROTTLE VALVE GASKET

THROTTLE AIR BYPASS VALVE ASSEMBLY

AIR CLEANER DUCT TUBE ADAPTER

AIR CLEANER ASSEMBLY

NUT AND WASHER ASSEMBLY

BOLT

8.2 An exploded view of the air cleaner assembly for the four-cylinder engine

R.H. FENDER APRON

GASKET

AIR CLEANER ASSEMBLY

R.H. WHEELHOUSING

RESONATOR AND TUBE ASSEMBLY

NUT AND WASHER ASSEMBLY

CLAMP

FRONT OF VEHICLE

8.8 An exploded view of the air cleaner assembly for the 3.0L V6

AIR CHARGE TEMPERATURF SENSOR ASSEMBLY

VIEW X

ELBOW

VIEW Y

SCREW

FRONT OF ENGINE

AIR CLEANER INTAKE TUBE ASSEMBLY

HOT AIR TUBE

INSTALL WITH SLEEVE AT BOTTOM

CLAMP

NUT AND WASHER ASSEMBLY

RIVET

HOT AIR TUBE

DUCT AND VALVE ASSEMBLY

DUCT AND VALVE TO AIR CLEANER GASKET

AIR CLEANER OUTER AIR DUCT SHROUD

AIR CLEANER INNER AIR DUCT SHROUD ASSEMBLY

WING NUT

VIEW X

CARBURETOR AIR CLEANER GROMMET ASSEMBLY

AIR CLEANER ASSEMBLY

VIEW Y

STUD

AIR CLEANER TO CARBURETOR

FRONT OF ENGINE

8.12 An exploded view of the air cleaner assembly for the 2.8L V6

9.2   An exploded view of a typical throttle cable assembly for the 2.3L four

2.8L V6 engine

Refer to illustration 8.12

9   Detach the cable from the negative terminal of the battery.
10   Unplug the electrical connector from the air charge temperature sensor (see Chapter 6 if necessary).
11   Detach the vacuum line from the vacuum motor (on top of the snorkel).
12   Detach the air intake tube assembly **(see illustration)**.
13   Remove the single air cleaner housing cover retaining clip on the driver's side of the housing.
14   Remove the wing nut from the top of the air cleaner housing cover.
15   Remove the housing cover.
16   Remove the filter element.
17   Remove the air cleaner housing assembly from the carburetor.
18   Installation is the reverse of removal.

9   Throttle linkage components — removal and installation

Refer to illustrations 9.2, 9.3a and 9.3b

1   Detach the cable from the negative terminal of the battery.
2   Remove the throttle linkage shield (2.3L only) **(see illustration)**.
3   Detach the throttle cable from the throttle lever at the carburetor or throttle body **(see illustrations)**.
4   Remove the throttle cable from the bracket on the intake manifold.
5   From inside the vehicle, remove the throttle cable end from the top of the accelerator pedal.
6   Collapse the retaining clips at the dash panel and push the throttle cable through the dash panel into the engine compartment. Remove the cable assembly.
7   Installation is the reverse of removal.

9.3a   An exploded view of a typical throttle cable assembly for the 2.8L V6

9.3b   An exploded view of a typical throttle cable assembly for the 3.0L V6

10   Carburetor — removal, overhaul and installation

Refer to illustration 10.15

Warning: *Gasoline is extremely flammable so extra precautions must be taken when working on any part of the fuel system. DO NOT smoke or allow open flames or bare light bulbs in or near the work area. Also, don't work in a garage if a natural gas appliance such as a water heater or clothes dryer is present.*

Diagnosis

1   A thorough road test and check of carburetor adjustments should be done before any major carburetor service work. Specifications for some adjustments are listed on the *Vehicle Emissions Control Information label* found in the engine compartment.

2   Some performance complaints directed at the carburetor are actually a result of loose, out-of-adjustment or malfunctioning engine or electrical components. Others develop when vacuum hoses leak, are disconnected or are incorrectly routed. The proper approach to analyzing carburetor problems should include a routine check of the following items.

    a)   Inspect all vacuum hoses and actuators for leaks and correct installation (see Chapter 6).
    b)   Tighten the intake manifold nuts and carburetor mounting nuts evenly and securely.
    c)   Perform a cylinder compression test.
    d)   Clean or replace the spark plugs as necessary.
    e)   Check the resistance of the spark plug wires.
    f)   Inspect the ignition primary wires and check the vacuum advance operation. Replace any defective parts.
    g)   Check the ignition timing according to the instructions printed on the *Emissions Control Information label.*

    h)   Check the fuel pump pressure.
    i)   Check the heat control valve in the air cleaner for proper operation (see Chapter 6).
    j)   Check/replace the air filter element.
    k)   Check the PCV system (see Chapter 6).

3   Carburetor problems usually show up as flooding, hard starting, stalling, severe backfiring, poor acceleration and lack of response to idle mixture screw adjustments. A carburetor that is leaking fuel and/or covered with wet looking deposits definitely needs attention.

4   Diagnosing carburetor problems may require that the engine be started and run with the air cleaner off. While running the engine without the air cleaner, backfires are possible. This situation is likely to occur if the carburetor is malfunctioning, but just the removal of the air cleaner can lean the fuel/air mixture enough to produce an engine backfire. **Warning:** *Do not position any part of your body, especially your face, directly over the carburetor during inspection and servicing procedures.*

Removal

5   Remove the air cleaner duct (see Section 8).

6   Disconnect the throttle cable from the throttle lever (see Section 9).

7   If your vehicle is equipped with an automatic transmission, disconnect the TV rod from the throttle lever (see Chapter 7).

8   **Note:** *Label all vacuum hoses and fittings before removing them to simplify installation.* Disconnect all vacuum hoses and the fuel line from the carburetor. Use a back-up wrench on the fuel inlet fitting when removing the fuel line to avoid changing the float level.

9   Label the wires and terminals, then unplug all wire harness connectors.

10   Remove the four carburetor mounting nuts and detach the carburetor from the intake manifold. Remove the carburetor mounting gasket spacer (if so equipped).

Overhaul

11 Once it's determined that the carburetor needs adjustment or an overhaul, several options are available. If you're going to attempt to overhaul the carburetor yourself, first obtain a good quality carburetor rebuild kit (which will include all necessary gaskets, internal parts, instructions and a parts list). You'll also need some special solvent and a means of blowing out the internal passages of the carburetor with air.

12 Because the vehicles covered by this book are primarily fuel injected and because carburetor designs are constantly modified by the manufacturer in order to meet increasingly more stringent emissions regulations, it isn't feasible for us to do a step-by-step overhaul of each type. You'll receive a detailed, well illustrated set of instructions with any carburetor overhaul kit; they will apply in a more specific manner to the carburetor on your vehicle.

13 Another alternative is to obtain a new or rebuilt carburetor. They are readily available from dealers and auto parts stores. Make absolutely sure the exchange carburetor is identical to the original. A tag is usually attached to the top of the carburetor. It will aid in determining the exact type of carburetor you have. When obtaining a rebuilt carburetor or a rebuild kit, take time to make sure that the kit or carburetor matches your application exactly. Seemingly insignificant differences can make a large difference in the performance of your engine.

14 If you choose to overhaul your own carburetor, allow enough time to disassemble the carburetor carefully, soak the necessary parts in the cleaning solvent (usually for at least one-half day or according to the instructions listed on the carburetor cleaner) and reassemble it, which will usually take much longer than disassembly. When disassembling the carburetor, match each part with the illustration in the carburetor kit and lay the parts out in order on a clean work surface. Overhauls by inexperienced mechanics can result in an engine which runs poorly or not at all. To avoid this, use care and patience when disassembling the carburetor so you can reassemble it correctly.

Installation

15 Clean the gasket mating surfaces of the intake manifold and the carburetor to remove all traces of the old gasket **(see illustration)**. Place

10.15 Before installing the carburetor, carefully scrape away all traces of old gasket material from the manifold

a new gasket and spacer (if so equipped) on the intake manifold. Position the carburetor on the gasket and spacer and install the four mounting nuts. To prevent distortion or damage to the carburetor body flange, tighten the nuts to the specified torque in several steps.

16 The remaining installation steps are the reverse of removal.

---

11 Electronic fuel injection (EFI) system — general information

The electronic fuel injection (EFI) system is a multi-point pulse time, speed density injection system. Fuel is metered into the air intake stream in accordance with engine demands through four (2.3L) or six (3.0L) solenoid injection valves mounted on a tuned intake manifold. Fuel is supplied from the fuel tank by a low pressure, electric fuel

pump mounted in the fuel tank. An externally mounted high pressure pump boosts fuel pressure on its way to the engine. The fuel is filtered and sent to the fuel charging manifold assembly and then to the injectors. The fuel delivery pressure is maintained by a pressure regulator connected in series with the injectors and positioned downstream from them. Excess fuel supplied by the pump but not needed by the engine is returned, through the regulator to the fuel tank by a steel fuel return line.

Air flow to the engine is controlled by a single butterfly valve mounted in a two piece, die-cast aluminum housing called a throttle body. The butterfly valve is identical in configuration to the throttle plates of a conventional carburetor and is actuated by a similar pedal and linkage arrangement.

The fuel supply manifold assembly is the component that delivers high pressure fuel from the vehicle fuel supply line to the fuel injectors. The assembly consists of two pre-formed tubes, or stampings, one for fuel supply and one for fuel return. The manifold is equipped with a fuel pressure relief valve on the fuel supply tube (2.3L four) or regulator mounting flange (3.0L V6).

Each fuel injector nozzle is an electro-mechanical device which meters and atomizes the fuel delivered to the engine. The injectors are mounted in the lower intake manifold and are positioned so that their tips are directing fuel just ahead of the engine intake valves. Each injector body consists of a solenoid actuated pintle and needle valve assembly.

An electrical control signal from the EEC electronic processor activates the solenoid, causing the pintle to move inward off the seat and allowing fuel to flow. The injector flow orifice is fixed and the fuel supply is constant. Therefore, fuel flow to the engine is controlled by how long the solenoid is energized.

---

12 Electronic Fuel Injection (EFI) system — component removal and installation (2.3L four)

Air bypass valve

Refer to illustration 12.4

Note: *Unlike any of the other fuel injection assembly components, the air bypass valve is not actually located on the throttle body or the intake manifold — it's mounted on the air cleaner housing.*

1 Detach the cable from the negative terminal of the battery.
2 Unplug the electrical connector at the air bypass valve.
3 Remove the air cleaner cover.
4 Separate the air bypass valve and gasket from the air cleaner by removing the three retaining bolts **(see illustration)**.
5 Installation is the reverse of removal.

12.4 An exploded view of the air bypass valve assembly

12.8 The throttle position sensor electrical connector is attached to the throttle body with a pair of small bolts — be sure to remove them before attempting to remove the sensor

12.9 Make scribe marks on the throttle position sensor and the throttle body casting (arrow) to ensure proper installation of the sensor — note the locating dimple (arrow) for the sensor connector

Throttle position sensor
Refer to illustrations 12.8 and 12.9

6   Detach the cable from the negative terminal of the battery.
7   Unplug the wiring harness from the throttle position sensor electrical connector.
8   Remove the two bolts which attach the throttle position sensor connector to the air intake throttle body **(see illustration)**. After the connector is detached from the throttle body, note the locating dimple on the throttle body for locating the connector properly (see next illustration).
9   Before removing the throttle position sensor, make scribe marks on the throttle body and on the throttle position sensor to insure proper alignment during reinstallation **(see illustration)**.
10 Remove the two throttle position sensor retaining screws, the sensor and the gasket.
11 When installing the throttle position sensor, make sure that the rotary tangs on the sensor are aligned with the throttle shaft blade. Slide the rotary tangs into position over the throttle shaft blade, then rotate the throttle position sensor clockwise only to its installed position. **Caution:** *Failure to install the throttle position sensor in this manner may result in excessive idle speeds.* Tighten the sensor to the specified torque.
12 The remainder of installation is the reverse of removal.

Throttle body
Refer to illustrations 12.17 and 12.18

Note: *If you are replacing the gasket between the upper intake manifold and the lower intake manifold (or if you are simply removing the entire fuel injection assembly for access to the lower intake manifold or gasket) it is not necessary to remove the throttle body from the upper intake manifold. Simply remove both as an assembly. The following procedure, however, must be used if you are replacing either the throttle body itself or the gasket between the throttle body and the upper intake manifold.*

13 Detach the cable from the negative terminal of the battery.
14 Remove the air intake resonator outlet tube (the duct between the resonator and the throttle body) (see Section 8).
15 Unplug the electrical connector from the throttle position sensor (see above).
16 Remove the throttle linkage shield, then detach the throttle cable and, if equipped, speed control cable (see Section 9).
17 Clearly label, then detach the air bypass and crankcase vent hoses **(see illustration)**.
18 Remove the two lower mounting nuts and the two upper mounting bolts **(see illustration)**.
19 Carefully separate the air throttle body from the upper intake manifold.
20 Remove and discard the gasket between the throttle body and the upper intake manifold.

12.17 If you are removing the throttle body, detach the hoses from the air bypass and crankcase vent fittings (if you are removing the throttle body and upper intake manifold as an assembly, also detach the hoses from the manifold vacuum tree and the PCV hose)

12.18 The throttle body assembly is attached to the upper intake manifold with a pair of nuts and bolts at the top and two nuts along its lower mounting flange (lower mounting nuts not visible in this illustration)

12.25 Before removing the upper intake manifold, detach the EGR tube from the EGR valve assembly

12.27 When installing the upper intake manifold, tighten the four mounting bolts to the specified torque in the sequence shown

12.29 To remove the fuel pressure regulator, detach the vacuum line and . . .

21 Installation is the reverse of removal. Be sure that the gasket surfaces are clean and tighten the mounting bolts and nuts to the specified torque.

Upper intake manifold
Refer to illustrations 12.25, 12.26 and 12.27

22 If you are replacing the gasket between the upper and lower intake manifold or between the lower intake manifold and the cylinder head, if you are replacing/servicing an injector or if you are removing the entire fuel injection assembly to service the head, simply detach the throttle cable, cruise control cable (if equipped), vacuum lines, etc. from the throttle body (see above), but do not separate the throttle body from the upper intake manifold. Unless you are replacing the upper intake manifold itself, there is no reason to detach the throttle body.

23 Unplug the knock sensor electrical connector (located on the front side of the upper intake manifold). **Note:** *If you intend to replace the upper intake manifold with a new one, remove the knock sensor and install it in the new manifold.*

12.26 An exploded view of the throttle body/upper intake manifold assembly

12.30 . . . remove the three Allen retaining screws, then lift the regulator, gasket and O-ring assembly from the fuel supply manifold

24 Detach the upper intake manifold vacuum lines from the upper intake manifold vacuum tree, disconnect the vacuum lines to the EGR valve and the fuel pressure regulator and detach the PCV hose from the fitting on the underside of the upper intake manifold **(see illustration 12.17)**. Be sure to clearly label all hoses to prevent mix-ups during reassembly.

25 Disconnect the EGR tube from the EGR valve **(see illustration)**.

26 Remove the four upper intake manifold mounting bolts and detach the upper intake manifold and gasket from the intake manifold **(see illustration)**. Be sure to discard the old gasket and use a new one for reassembly.

27 Installation is the reverse of removal. Be sure to tighten the upper intake manifold mounting bolts to the specified torque, in the sequence shown **(see illustration)**.

Fuel pressure regulator
Refer to illustrations 12.29 and 12.30

28 Relieve the fuel pressure (see Section 2). Remove the fuel tank filler cap to relieve fuel tank pressure.

29 Detach the vacuum line from the pressure regulator **(see illustration)**.

30 Remove the three Allen retaining screws from the pressure regulator housing, then remove the regulator, gasket and O-ring **(see illustration)**. Discard the gasket and inspect the O-ring for signs of cracks or deterioration.

12.36 An exploded view of the fuel supply manifold assembly

31 Before installing the regulator, make sure that the gasket surfaces of the fuel pressure regulator and the fuel supply manifold are clean. Then lubricate the O-ring with light oil ESF-M6C2-A or equivalent. **Caution:** *Do not use silicone grease. It will clog the injectors.*
32 Installation is the reverse of removal. Be sure to use a new gasket and tighten the regulator Allen screws to the specified torque.

Fuel supply manifold assembly

Refer to illustration 12.36
33 Relieve the fuel pressure (see Section 2). Remove the fuel tank filler cap to relieve the fuel tank pressure.
34 Remove the air intake throttle body and the upper intake manifold (see above).
35 Unplug the four injector electrical connectors and set the harness aside.
36 Remove the two fuel supply manifold mounting bolts **(see illustration)**.
37 Carefully disengage the manifold and fuel injectors from the engine and remove the assembly.
38 If you are replacing an injector, or injectors, or injector O-rings, see below.
39 Installation is the reverse of removal. Be sure to tighten the fuel supply manifold mounting bolts to the specified torque.

Fuel injector

Refer to illustrations 12.42 and 12.43
40 Relieve the fuel pressure (see Section 2). Remove the fuel tank filler cap to relieve the fuel tank pressure.
41 Remove the fuel supply manifold assembly (see above).
42 Grasping the injector body, pull it out of the fuel supply manifold while gently rocking the injector from side-to-side **(see illustration)**.
43 Inspect the two injector O-rings and the injector plastic hat (covering the injector pintle) and washer **(see illustration)** for deterioration. Replace as necessary. **Note:** *If the hat is missing, look for it in the intake manifold.*
44 Before inserting the injector into the fuel supply manifold, be sure to lubricate the new O-rings with light grade oil ESF-M6C2-A or equivalent and install them on the injector. **Caution:** *Do not use silicone grease. It will clog the injectors.*
45 Install the injector(s) into the the fuel supply manifold using a light, twisting, pushing motion.
46 The remainder of installation is the reverse of removal. Be sure to tighten the fuel supply manifold mounting bolts to the specified torque.

12.42 To remove an injector from the fuel supply manifold, grasp it firmly and gently pull on it while twisting it from side-to-side

12.43 If you are planning to reinstall an old injector, inspect the two O-rings and the plastic hat which protects the pintle for signs of deterioration and replace if necessary (it's a good practice to simply replace the O-rings and hat anytime you remove the injector)

13.2 To remove the air bypass valve, simply unplug the electrical connector and remove the two retaining screws

13.9 Before removing the throttle position sensor, make scribe marks on the sensor housing and the throttle body to ensure proper realignment, then simply remove the two retaining screws

13 Electronic fuel injection (EFI) system — component removal and installation (3.0L V6)

Air bypass valve
Refer to illustration 13.2

1   Detach the cable from the negative terminal of the battery.
2   Unplug the wiring harness electrical connector from the air bypass valve assembly **(see illustration)**.
3   Remove the two air bypass valve retaining screws and the air bypass valve and gasket.
4   Make sure that both the throttle body and the air bypass valve gasket mating surfaces are clean. **Caution:** *Should it be necessary to scrape either surface, be extremely careful not to damage the air bypass valve or throttle body gasket surfaces or drop material into the throttle body.*
5   Installation is the reverse of removal. Be sure to tighten the air bypass retaining screws to the specified torque.

Throttle position sensor
Refer to illustration 13.9

6   Detach the cable from the negative terminal of the battery.
7   Unplug the wiring harness electrical connector from the throttle position sensor.
8   Make scribe marks on the air throttle body and on the throttle position sensor to indicate the proper alignment during installation.
9   Remove the two throttle position sensor retaining screws and remove the throttle position sensor **(see illustration)**.
10 When installing the throttle position sensor, make sure that the rotary tangs on the sensor are aligned with the throttle shaft blade and that the red seal is inside the connector housing. Slide the rotary tangs into position over the throttle shaft blade, then rotate the throttle position sensor clockwise only to its installed position. **Caution:** *Failure to install the throttle position sensor in this manner may result in excessive idle speeds.* Tighten the sensor to the specified torque.
11 The remainder of installation is the reverse of removal.

13.14 To remove the air cleaner outlet tube between the air cleaner and the air throttle body, loosen the hose clamps at either end of the outlet tube

Fuel metering and air intake/throttle body components
Refer to illustrations 13.14, 13.15 and 13.20

12 Relieve the fuel pressure (see Section 2). Remove the fuel tank filler cap to relieve fuel tank pressure.
13 Detach the cable from the negative terminal of the battery.
14 Remove the engine air cleaner outlet tube between the air cleaner and the air throttle body by loosening the two clamps **(see illustration)**.

15 Unplug the injector wiring harness electrical connectors from the throttle position sensor, air bypass valve and air charge temperature sensor **(see illustration)**.

16 Disconnect the push connect fuel supply and return lines (see Section 3).

17 Clearly label, then detach, the vacuum hoses from the vacuum fittings on the intake manifold.

18 Detach and remove the throttle cable and, if equipped, cruise control cable (see Section 9) from the throttle linkage.

19 If your vehicle is equipped with an automatic transmission, remove the transmission (TV) linkage from the throttle lever (see Chapter 7B).

20 Remove the four retaining bolts and two stud bolts in the indicated sequence **(see illustration)** and lift the air intake throttle body assembly from the guide pins on the lower intake assembly. Remove the gasket from the lower intake assembly and discard it.

21 Clean and inspect the mounting surfaces of the air intake throttle body assembly and the lower intake manifold assembly. They must be clean and flat. Also clean and oil the threads in the manifold stud bores.

22 Install a new gasket and, using the guide pins as locators, install the air intake throttle body assembly on the lower intake manifold and tighten the mounting bolts and stud bolts, in the same sequence previously indicated, to the specified torque.

23 The remainder of the installation is the reverse of removal.

Fuel pressure regulator
Refer to illustration 13.28

24 Relieve the fuel pressure (see Section 2). Remove the fuel tank filler cap to relieve the fuel tank pressure.

25 Detach the cable from the negative terminal of the battery.

26 Detach the vacuum line from the pressure regulator.

27 Remove the three Allen retaining screws from the regulator housing.

28 Remove the pressure regulator assembly, gasket and O-ring **(see illustration)**. Discard the gasket and inspect the O-ring for signs of cracks or deterioration.

29 Before installing the fuel pressure regulator, make sure that the gasket surfaces of the regulator and the fuel rail assembly are clean. Lubricate the new O-ring with clean engine oil and install it on the regulator.

30 Install the regulator and a new gasket on the fuel rail assembly and tighten the regulator retaining screws to the specified torque.

31 The remainder of installation is the reverse of removal.

Fuel injector manifold assembly
Refer to illustrations 13.34 and 13.36

32 Relieve the fuel pressure.

33 Remove the air intake throttle body (see above).

13.15 Before removing the air intake/throttle body, unplug the fuel injection wiring harness from the throttle position sensor, air bypass valve and air charge temperature sensor

13.20 To remove the air intake throttle body assembly, remove the four retaining bolts and two stud bolts in the indicated sequence and lift the assembly off the guide pins on the lower intake assembly

13.28 The fuel pressure regulator assembly consists of the regulator itself, a gasket and three retaining screws

34 Carefully unplug the wiring harness electrical connectors from the injectors **(see illustration)**.
35 Detach the vacuum line from the fuel pressure regulator.
36 Remove the four fuel injector manifold retaining bolts (two on each side) **(see illustration)**.
37 Carefully disengage the fuel rail assembly from the fuel injectors by lifting and gently rocking the rail.

38 Remove the injectors by lifting while gently rocking from side to side.
39 Place the removed components in a clean container to avoid dirt or other contamination. The injector(s) and fuel rail must be handled with extreme care to prevent damage to sealing areas and sensitive fuel metering orifices.

14 Exhaust system components — replacement

Warning: *Never attempt to service any part of the exhaust system until it has cooled. Be especially careful when working around the catalytic converter. The temperature of the converter rises to a high level after only a few minutes of engine operation and, once the engine reaches its operating temperature, can remain high enough to cause burns for a long time after the engine is shut off.*

1 Detach the cable from the negative terminal of the battery.
2 Raise the vehicle and place it securely on jackstands.

Converter assembly — four-cylinder engine
Refer to illustration 14.3

3 Remove the two nuts attaching the converter pipe assembly to the muffler and the outlet pipe **(see illustration on next page)**.
4 Remove the two nuts attaching the converter pipe assembly to the exhaust manifold.
5 Apply a soapy solution to the support slide of the converter support bracket at the support insulator.
6 Remove the converter pipe assembly from the vehicle.
Installation is the reverse of removal.

13.34 The fuel injector wiring harness

13.36 An exploded view of the fuel supply manifold assembly

14.3 An exploded view of a typical exhaust system on the 2.3L four-cylinder engines

Converter assembly — V6 engines

Refer to illustration 14.7

7   Remove the two nuts attaching the converter pipe assembly to the muffler and outlet pipe **(see illustration)**. On the 2.8L engine, remove the clamp securing the Managed Thermactor Air (MTA) tube to the catalytic converter. Remove the screw holding the MTA tube bracket to the forward converter and separate the MTA tube from the converter.

8   On the 2.8L engine, disconnect the hose from the top of the MTA and check valve. It may be necessary to heat the MTA tube slightly to detach it from the nipple on the converter. Remove the MTA tube and check valve. To facilitate removal, rotate the assembly as it is being lowered.

9   Loosen and remove the exhaust manifold stud nuts. Slide the muffler and outlet pipe rearward. Remove the gasket. Move the converter assembly rearward, rotate it to clear the studs and remove it.

10 Installation is the reverse of removal.

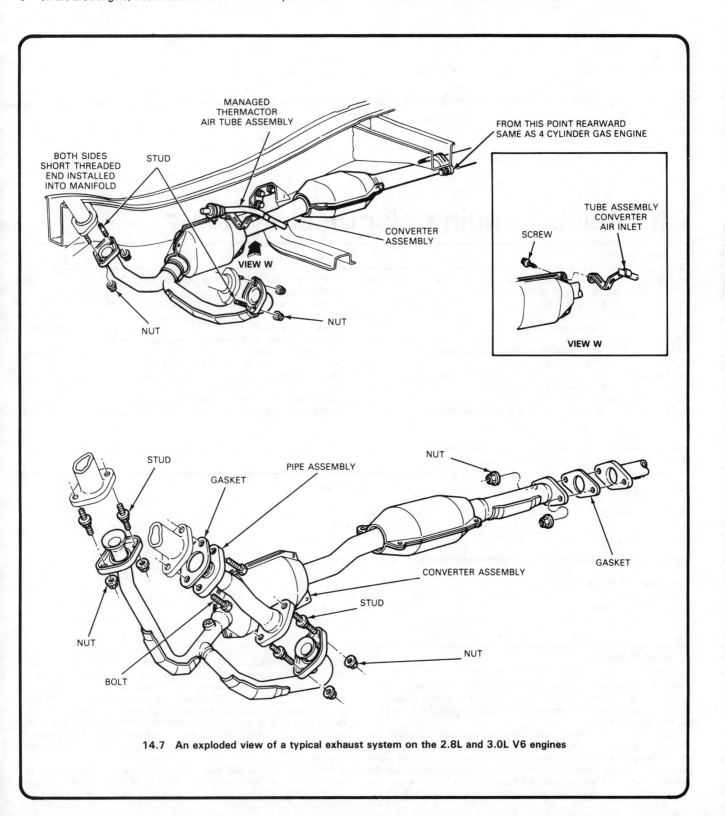

14.7   An exploded view of a typical exhaust system on the 2.8L and 3.0L V6 engines

Chapter 5 Engine electrical systems

Contents

Specifications

Drivebelt deflection . . . . See Chapter 1

Battery voltage
Engine off 12-volts
Engine running . . . . 14-to-15 volts

Ignition coil-to-distributor cap wire resistance . . . . 5000 ohms per foot

Ignition coil resistance
Primary resistance . . . . 0.3 to 1.0 ohms
Secondary resistance . . . . 8.0 to 11.5 K-ohms

---

1 General information

The engine electrical systems include all ignition, charging and starting components. Because of their engine-related functions, these components are considered separately from chassis electrical devices such as the lights, instruments, etc.

Access to the distributor, distributor cap and coil is through the engine access panel inside the vehicle. Be very careful when working on the engine electrical components. They are easily damaged if checked, connected or handled improperly. The alternator is driven by an engine drivebelt which could cause serious injury if your hands, hair or clothes become entangled in it with the engine running. Both the starter and alternator are connected directly to the battery and could arc or even cause a fire if mishandled, overloaded or shorted out.

Never leave the ignition switch on for long periods of time with the engine off. Don't disconnect the battery cables while the engine is running. Correct polarity must be maintained when connecting battery cables from another source, such as another vehicle, during jump starting. Always disconnect the negative cable first and hook it up last or the battery may be shorted by the tool being used to loosen the cable clamps.

Additional safety related information on the engine electrical systems can be found in *Safety first* near the front of this manual. It should be referred to before beginning any operation included in this Chapter.

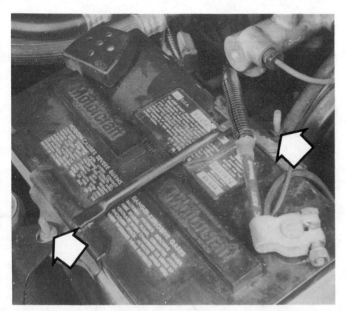

2.2 To remove the battery, detach the cables from the negative, then the positive, terminals, remove the hold down clamp nuts (arrows) and the clamp, then carefully lift out the battery

2 Battery — removal and installation

Refer to illustration 2.2

1 Disconnect both cables from the battery terminals. **Caution:** *Always disconnect the negative cable first and hook it up last or the battery may be shorted by the tool being used to loosen the cable clamps.*
2 Remove both battery hold-down clamp nuts and the clamp **(see illustration)**.
3 Lift out the battery. Special straps that attach to the battery posts are available — lifting and moving the battery is much easier if you use one.
4 Installation is the reverse of removal.

3 Battery — emergency jump starting

Refer to the *Booster battery (jump) starting* procedure at the front of this manual.

4 Battery cables — check and replacement

Note: *Additional information and illustrations on battery servicing can be found in Chapter 1.*

1 Periodically inspect the entire length of each battery cable for damage, cracked or burned insulation and corrosion. Poor battery cable connections can cause starting problems and decreased engine performance.
2 Check the cable-to-terminal connections at the ends of the cables for cracks, loose wire strands and corrosion. The presence of white, fluffy deposits under the insulation at the cable terminal connection is a sign that the cable is corroded and should be replaced. Check the terminals for distortion, missing mounting bolts and corrosion.
3 When replacing the cables, *always disconnect the negative cable first and hook it up last* or the battery may be shorted by the tool used to loosen the cable clamps. Even if only the positive cable is being replaced, be sure to disconnect the negative cable from the battery first.
4 Disconnect and remove the cable. Make sure the replacement cable is the same length and diameter.
5 Clean the threads of the relay or ground connection with a wire

brush to remove rust and corrosion. Apply a light coat of petroleum jelly to the threads to prevent future corrosion.
6 Attach the cable to the relay or ground connection and tighten the mounting nut/bolt securely.
7 Before connecting the new cable to the battery, make sure that it reaches the battery post without having to be stretched.
8 Connect the positive cable first, followed by the negative cable.

5 Ignition system — general information

The ignition system is a solid state electronic design consisting of an ignition module, a coil, a distributor, the spark plug wires and the spark plugs.
All models use the Thick Film Integrated IV (TFI-IV) ignition module, which is housed in a molded thermoplastic box mounted on the base of the distributor. The TFI-IV module is controlled by the Electronic Engine Control IV (EEC-IV).
The TFI-IV/EEC-IV type distributor has neither a centrifugal nor a vacuum advance mechanism (advance is handled by the computer instead). The TFI-IV module does, however, include a "push start" mode that allows push starting of the vehicle if necessary.
A Hall Effect stator assembly consisting of a Hall sensor, a permanent magnet and a rotary vane cup, causes the ignition coil to be switched off and on by the EEC-IV and the TFI-IV models.

6 Ignition system — check

Refer to illustration 6.2
Warning: *Because of the very high secondary (spark plug) voltage generated by the ignition system, extreme care should be taken when this check is done.*

Calibrated ignition tester method

1 If the engine turns over but won't start, disconnect the spark plug lead from any spark plug and attach it to a calibrated ignition tester (available at most auto parts stores). Make sure the tester is designed for Ford ignition systems if a universal tester isn't available.
2 Connect the clip on the tester to a bolt or metal bracket on the engine **(see illustration)**, crank the engine and watch the end of the tester to see if bright blue, well-defined sparks occur.

6.2 To use a calibrated ignition tester (available at most auto parts stores), simply disconnect a spark plug wire, attach the wire to the tester, clip the tester to a convenient ground (like a rocker arm cover bolt) and operate the starter — if there's enough power to fire the plug, sparks will be visible between the electrode tip and the tester body

3   If sparks occur, sufficient voltage is reaching the plug to fire it. Repeat the check at the remaining plug wires to verify that the distributor cap and rotor are OK. However, the plugs themselves may be fouled, so remove and check them as described in Chapter 1 or install new ones.

4   If no sparks or intermittent sparks occur, remove the distributor cap and check the cap and rotor as described in Chapter 1. If moisture is present, dry out the cap and rotor, then reinstall the cap and repeat the spark test.

5   If there's still no spark, detach the secondary coil wire from the distributor cap and hook it up to the tester (reattach the plug wire to the spark plug), then repeat the spark check.

6   If no sparks occur, check the primary (small) wire connections at the coil to make sure they're clean and tight. Refer to Section 7 and check the ignition coil supply voltage circuit. Make any necessary repairs, then repeat the check.

7   If sparks now occur, the distributor cap, rotor, plug wire(s) or spark plug(s) (or all of them) may be defective.

8   If there's still no spark, the coil-to-cap wire may be bad. Check the resistance with an ohmmeter and compare it to the Specifications. If a known good wire doesn't make any difference in the test results, the ignition coil, module or other internal components may be defective.

Alternative method

Note: If you're unable to obtain a calibrated ignition tester, the following method will allow you to determine if the ignition system has spark, but it won't tell you if there's enough voltage produced to actually initiate combustion in the cylinders.

9   Remove the wire from one of the spark plugs. Using an insulated tool, hold the wire about 1/4-inch from a good ground and have an assistant crank the engine.

10   If bright blue, well-defined sparks occur, sufficient voltage is reaching the plug to fire it. However, the plug(s) may be fouled, so remove and check them as described in Chapter 1 or install new ones.

11   If there's no spark, check the remaining wires in the same manner. A few sparks followed by no spark is the same condition as no spark at all.

12   If no sparks occur, remove the distributor cap and check the cap and rotor as described in Chapter 1. If moisture is present, dry out the cap and rotor, then reinstall the cap and repeat the spark test.

13   If there's still no spark, disconnect the secondary coil wire from the distributor cap, hold it about 1/4-inch from a good engine ground and crank the engine again.

14   If no sparks occur, check the primary (small) wire connections at the coil to make sure they're clean and tight. Refer to Section 7 and check the ignition coil supply voltage circuit. Make any necessary repairs, then repeat the check again.

15   If sparks now occur, the distributor cap, rotor, plug wire(s) or spark plug(s) (or all of them) may be defective.

16   If there's still no spark, the coil-to-cap wire may be bad. Check the resistance with an ohmmeter and compare it to the Specifications. If a known good wire doesn't make any difference in the test results, the ignition coil, module or other internal components may be defective.

7   Ignition coil and circuits — check and coil replacement

Refer to illustrations 7.2, 7.9, 7.12, 7.19, 7.29a, 7.29b, 7.38 and 7.46

Ignition coil primary circuit

1   Unplug the wiring harness connector from the ignition module. Inspect it for dirt, corrosion and damage (refer to Section 10 for a detailed illustration of the connector terminals), then plug it back in.

2   Attach a 12-volt DC test light between the coil TACH terminal and a good engine ground **(see illustration)**.

7.2   Checking ignition coil primary circuit switching

3   Crank the engine.

4   If the light flashes, or comes on but doesn't flash, refer to Step 7.

5   If the light stays off or is very dim, refer to Step 16.

6   Remove the test light.

Ignition coil primary resistance

7   Turn the ignition switch to Off.

8   Unplug the ignition coil wire harness connector. Inspect it for dirt, corrosion and damage.

9   Measure the resistance between the primary terminals of the ignition coil **(see illustration)**.

10   If the resistance is within the specified limits, proceed to Step 12.

11   If the resistance is less or more than specified, replace the ignition coil (Step 49).

Ignition coil secondary resistance

12   Measure the resistance from the negative primary terminal to the secondary terminal of the ignition coil **(see illustration)**.

13   If the resistance is within the specified limits, proceed to Step 25.

7.9   Measuring ignition coil primary resistance

7.12   Measuring ignition coil secondary resistance

7.19 Checking primary circuit continuity

CONNECTOR TERMINAL	WIRE/CIRCUIT	IGNITION SWITCH TEST POSITION
#2	TO IGNITION COIL (−) TERMINAL	RUN
#3	RUN CIRCUIT	RUN AND START
#4	START CIRCUIT	START

7.29a Check the wire harness connector voltage with the switch in each of the above positions

7.29b Check the wiring harness between the coil and the module

14 If the resistance is less or more than the specified resistance, replace the ignition coil (Step 49).
15 Reconnect the ignition coil wires.

Primary circuit continuity

16 Unplug the wiring harness connector from the ignition module. Inspect it for dirt, corrosion and damage.
17 Attach the negative lead of a VOM to the distributor base.
18 Measure battery voltage and record it for future reference.
19 Attach the positive lead of the VOM to a small straight pin inserted into connector terminal 2 (see illustration). Caution: *Do not allow the straight pin to ground against anything.*
20 Turn the ignition switch to the Run position and measure the terminal 2 voltage.
21 If the voltage is 90 percent of battery voltage, proceed to the wiring harness check (Step 25).
22 If the voltage is less than 90 percent of battery voltage, proceed to Step 35.
23 Turn the ignition switch to the Off position.
24 Remove the straight pin.

Wiring harness

25 Unplug the wiring harness connector from the ignition module. In-

spect it for dirt, corrosion and damage.
26 Disconnect the wire at the S terminal of the starter relay.
27 Attach the negative lead of a VOM to the distributor base.
28 Measure battery voltage and record it for future reference.
29 Using the accompanying table (see illustration), measure the connector terminal voltage by attaching the positive lead of the VOM to a small straight pin inserted into the connector terminals, one at a time, with the ignition switch in the indicated positions (see illustration).
30 If the voltage is 90 percent of battery voltage at all three terminals, refer to the EEC-IV check in Section 10.
31 If the voltage is less than 90 percent of battery voltage, inspect the wiring harness and the connectors (refer to the wiring diagrams at the end of this book for the appropriate circuits). Check the ignition switch for damage or wear (refer to Chapter 12).
32 Turn the ignition switch to the Off position.
33 Remove the straight pin.
34 Reconnect the wire to the S terminal of the starter relay.

Ignition coil primary voltage

35 Attach the negative lead of a VOM to the distributor base.
36 Measure battery voltage and record it.
37 Turn the ignition switch to the Run position.

7.38   Measuring ignition coil primary voltage

7.46   Measuring ignition coil supply voltage

38 Measure the voltage at the negative terminal of the ignition coil (see illustration).
39 If the voltage is 90 percent of battery voltage, inspect the wiring harness between the ignition module and the coil negative terminal.
40 If the voltage is less than 90 percent of battery voltage, inspect the wiring harness between the ignition module and the coil negative terminal, then proceed to Step 42.
41 Turn the ignition switch to the Off position.

Ignition coil supply voltage

42 Unplug the ignition coil wire harness.
43 Attach the negative lead of a VOM to the distributor base.
44 Measure battery voltage.
45 Turn the ignition switch to the Run position.
46 Measure the voltage at the positive terminal of the ignition coil (see illustration).
47 If the voltage is 90 percent of battery voltage, inspect the ignition coil connector and terminals for dirt, corrosion and damage. If both the connector and terminals are clean, replace the ignition coil (Step 49).
48 If the voltage is less than 90 percent of battery voltage, inspect and repair the circuit between the ignition coil and the ignition switch (refer to the wiring diagrams at the end of the book). Check the igni-

tion switch for damage and wear (refer to Chapter 12).

Ignition coil replacement

49 Detach the cable from the negative terminal of the battery.
50 Detach the wires from the primary terminals on the coil (some coils have a single connector for the primary wires).
51 Unplug the coil secondary lead.
52 Remove both bracket bolts (see illustration) and detach the coil.
53 Installation is the reverse of removal.

---

8   Distributor — removal and installation

Refer to illustrations 8.3, 8.4a and 8.4b

Removal

1   Detach the cable from the negative terminal of the battery.
2   Detach the coil secondary lead from the coil and the wires from the plugs, then remove the distributor cap and wires as an assembly (refer to Chapter 1).
3   Unplug the module electrical connector (see illustration).

7.52   A typical coil assembly (2.8L V6 shown) — to remove it, unplug the coil primary leads (terminal obscured by the high tension lead in photo) and the boot on the high tension terminal, then remove the four mounting bolts (arrows)

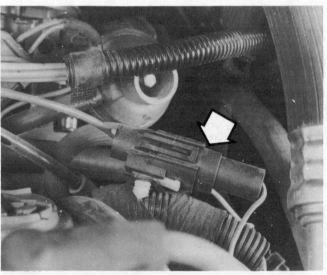

8.3   Before removing (or timing) the distributor, always unplug this connector (arrow) to detach the single wire lead from the ignition module

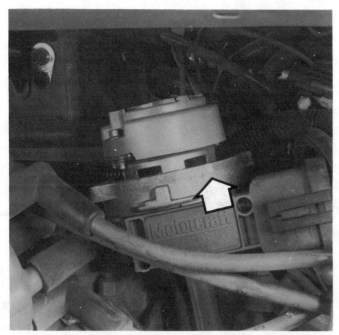

8.4a Before removing the distributor, remove the spark plug cap (see Chapter 1), mark the direction in which the rotor is pointing by scribing or painting an alignment mark on the edge of the distributor base (arrow) immediately below the rotor tip . . .

8.4b . . . and paint or scribe an alignment mark on the distributor base and the block (arrow) to ensure proper reinstallation, then remove the distributor hold down bolt and clamp (arrow) and lift out the distributor assembly

4 Make a mark on the edge of the distributor base **(see illustration)** directly below the rotor tip and in line with it (if the rotor on your engine has more than one tip, use the center one for reference). Mark the distributor base and the engine block to ensure that the distributor is installed correctly **(see illustration)**.

5 Remove the distributor hold down bolt and clamp, then pull the distributor straight up to remove it. Be careful not to disturb the intermediate driveshaft. **Note:** *If the crankshaft is turned while the distributor is removed, or if a new distributor is required, the alignment marks will be useless.*

Installation (crankshaft not turned after distributor removal)

6 Insert the distributor into the engine in exactly the same relationship to the block that it was in when removed.

7 To mesh the helical gears on the camshaft and the distributor it may be necessary to turn the rotor slightly. If the distributor doesn't seat completely, the hex shaped recess in the lower end of the distributor shaft is not mating properly with the oil pump shaft. Recheck the alignment marks between the distributor base and the block to verify that the distributor is in the same position it was in before removal. Also check the rotor to see if it is aligned with the mark you made on the edge of the distributor base. Then, using a socket and a breaker bar on the crankshaft pulley bolt, turn the crankshaft in the normal direction of rotation. Because the gear on the distributor shaft is engaged with the gear on the camshaft, their relationship to one another will not change as long as the distributor is not lifted from the engine. When the hex shaped recess in the end of the distributor shaft and the oil pump shaft are aligned, the distributor will drop down over the pump shaft and the distributor housing will seat against the block.

Installation (crankshaft turned after distributor removal)

8 Position the number one piston at TDC on the compression stroke (see Chapter 2).

9 Position the rotor so it is pointing to the number one spark plug tower on the distributor cap.

10 Lower the distributor into place.

11 To mesh the helical gears on the camshaft and the distributor, it may be necessary to turn the rotor slightly.

12 If the distributor doesn't seat completely against the block, the lower end of the distributor shaft is not mating properly with the oil pump shaft. Recheck the alignment marks between the distributor housing and the block to verify that the distributor is in the same position it was in before removal. Then, using a socket and a breaker bar on the crankshaft pulley bolt, turn the crankshaft in the normal direction of rotation. Because the gear on the distributor shaft is engaged with the gear on the camshaft, their relationship to one another will not change as long as the distributor is not lifted from the engine. When the hex shaped recess in the end of the distributor shaft and the oil pump shaft are aligned, the distributor will drop down over the pump shaft and the distributor housing will seat against the block.

Final installation

13 Place the hold down clamp in position and loosely install the bolt.

14 Install the distributor cap and tighten the cap screws securely.

15 Plug in the module electrical connector.

16 Reattach the spark plug wires to the plugs.

17 Connect the cable to the negative terminal of the battery.

18 Check the ignition timing (refer to Section 9) and tighten the distributor hold down bolt securely.

---

9 Ignition timing — check and adjustment

Refer to illustrations 9.6a and 9.6b

Note: *Check the Vehicle Emission Control Information label on your vehicle to see if a different procedure and/or ignition timing specification is given. If so, follow the information on the VECI label, as it contains information specific to your vehicle.*

1 Apply the parking brake and block the wheels. Place the transmission in Park (automatic) or Neutral (manual). Turn off all accessories (heater, air conditioner, etc.).

2 Start the engine and warm it up. Once it has reached operating temperature, turn it off.

3 Unplug the single wire connector located immediately above the harness connector for the module **(see illustration 8.3)**.

4 Connect an inductive timing light and a tachometer in accordance with the manufacturer's instructions. **Caution:** *Make sure that the timing light and tach wires don't hang anywhere near the electric cooling*

9.6a On the 2.8L and 3.0L V6 engines, the timing marks are located on the crankshaft vibration damper (2.8L V6 shown) — verify that the 10° mark (arrow) — or whatever mark is specified by the VECI label on your vehicle — is aligned with the stationary pointer on the front of the water pump housing

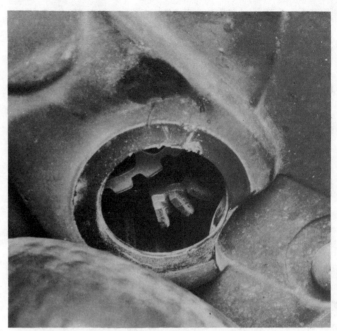

9.6b On the 2.3L engine, the timing marks are located on the edge of the camshaft pulley — to see the marks, remove the small access cover in the front of the timing belt cover

fan or they may become entangled in the fan blades when it comes on.
5   Start the engine.
6   Point the timing light at the timing marks on the crankshaft pulley/vibration damper or camshaft pulley (2.3L engine) and note whether the timing mark **(see illustrations)** is aligned with the timing pointer.
7   If the mark indicating the number of degrees advance called for on the VECI label isn't aligned with the stationary pointer, loosen the distributor hold down bolt just enough so that the distributor can be rotated. Turn the distributor until the desired mark is aligned with the pointer. Tighten the distributor hold down bolt securely when the timing is correct and recheck it to make sure it didn't change when the bolt was tightened.
8   Turn off the engine.
9   Plug in the single wire connector.
10 Remove the timing light and tachometer.
11 The universal distributor used in all vehicles incorporates an octane adjustment feature. The adjustment is accomplished by replacing the standard zero degree rod located in the distributor with a three-degree or six-degree retard rod. Consult your local Ford dealer for additional information on this feature.

10 Ignition module — check and replacement

Refer to illustrations 10.12, 10.13 and 10.14
Caution: *The ignition module is a delicate and relatively expensive electronic component. The following tests must be done with the right equipment by someone who knows how to use it properly. Failure to follow the step-by-step procedures could result in damage to the module and/or other electronic devices, including the EEC-IV microprocessor itself. Moreover, all devices under computer control are protected by a Federally mandated extended warranty. Check with your dealer before attempting to diagnose them yourself.*

Check
1   Unplug the wiring harness connector from the ignition module. Inspect it for dirt, corrosion and/or damage, then plug it back in.
2   Unplug the single wire connector located immediately above the ignition module connector (see Section 8).

3   Using a calibrated spark tester, check for spark (see Section 6).
4   If there is no spark, proceed to the distributor/TFI-IV module check (Step 7).
5   If there is spark, the problem lies either with the inferred mileage sensor (IMS) or within the EEC-IV electronic control module (ECM). Diagnosis of these items is beyond the scope of the home mechanic. Take the vehicle to a dealer service department.
6   Remove the spark tester and reconnect the single wire connector.

Distributor/TFI-IV module
Note: *You must purchase a new ignition module before performing the following check. Since the check can result in only one of two possibilities (you will need a new module, or you won't), the odds are 50/50 that you'll be buying a new module that you may not need. Electronic components can't be returned once they're purchased, so if you're unwilling to invest in a new module that you may not need until later take the vehicle to a dealer and have the module checked.*

7   Remove the distributor (see Section 8).
8   Install a new module on the distributor. Connect the body harness to the TFI-IV. Make sure the unit is grounded with a jumper lead from the distributor to the engine. Rotate the distributor shaft by hand and check for spark with the ignition tester (see Section 6).
9   If there is spark, the old module has failed. Leave the new module on the distributor and install the distributor (see Section 8).
10 If there is no spark, the sensor has failed. Your old module is okay but you need a new or rebuilt distributor. Install the new/rebuilt distributor with the old module.

Replacement
11 Disconnect the negative battery cable and the wiring connector at the side of the module.
12 Remove the two module mounting screws **(see illustration)**.
13 Pull straight down on the module to disconnect the spade connectors from the stator connector **(see illustration)**.
14 Whether you are installing the old module or a new one, wipe the back of the module clean with a soft, clean rag and apply a film of silicone dielectric grease to the back of the module **(see illustration)**.
15 Installation is the reverse of removal. Wipe a thin film of dielectric grease on the rear of the module before installation. When plugging in the module, make sure that the three terminals are inserted all the way into the stator connector.

10.12 To remove the TFI-IV ignition module from the distributor base, remove the two screws (arrows) . . .

10.13 . . . then pull the module straight down to detach the spade terminals from the stator connector

10.14 Be sure to wipe the back of the module clean and apply a film of dielectric grease (essential for cool operation of the module) — DO NOT use any other type of grease!

11.9 With the distributor shaft housing locked securely in a vise lined with several shop rags (to prevent damage to the housing), drive out the roll pin

11 Distributor stator assembly — check and replacement

Refer to illustrations 11.9, 11.11, 11.12, 11.13, 11.14, 11.15, 11.19, 11.28a and 11.28b

Check

1 The factory doesn't specify a check for the TFI-IV system stator (sensor). If the ignition module is good, but the system won't function normally, the stator must be replaced.

Replacement

2 Remove the distributor cap and position it out of the way with the wires attached.
3 Disconnect the TFI module from the wire harness.
4 Remove the distributor (see Section 8).

5 Remove the rotor (see Chapter 1).
6 Although not absolutely necessary, it's a good idea to remove the ignition module (see Section 10) to prevent possible damage to the module while the distributor is being disassembled.
7 Clamp the lower end of the distributor housing in a vise. Place a shop rag in the vise jaws to prevent damage to the distributor and don't overtighten the vise.
8 Before removing the drive gear, note that the roll pin is slightly offset. When the distributor is reassembled, the roll pin cannot be reinstalled through the drive gear and distributor shaft holes unless the holes are perfectly lined up. Use a bit of paint to mark the positions of these components
9 With an assistant holding the distributor steady in the vise, use a pin punch to drive the roll pin out of the shaft (see illustration).
10 Loosen the vise and reposition the distributor with the drive gear facing up.

11.11   With the distributor shaft pointing up, use a small puller to separate the drive gear from the shaft

11.12   Inspect the distributor shaft for burrs or residue buildup in the vicinity of the hole for the drive gear roll pin — remove it with emery cloth to prevent damage to the distributor shaft bushing when removing and installing the shaft

11.13   As soon as you remove the distributor shaft, note how the washer is installed before removing it (or it can easily fall out and be lost)

11.14   To detach the octane rod from the distributor, remove the retaining screw — note the condition of the small square rubber grommet that seals the octane rod hole when you pull the rod out (it seals the interior of the distributor to prevent moisture from damaging the electronics)

11.15   To remove the octane rod, lift the inner end of the rod off the stator assembly post (A) — to remove the stator assembly, remove both mounting screws (B) and lift the stator straight up and off the posts

11   Remove the drive gear with a small puller (see illustration).
12   Before removing it from the distributor, check the shaft for burrs or built up residue, particularly around the drive gear roll pin hole (see illustration). If burrs or residue are evident, polish the shaft with emery cloth and wipe it clean to prevent damage to the lip seal and bushing in the distributor base.
13   After removing any burrs/residue, remove the shaft assembly by gently pulling on the plate. Note the relationship of the spacer washer to the distributor base before removing the washer (see illustration).
14   Remove the octane rod retaining screw (see illustration).
15   Lift the inner end of the rod off the stator retaining post (see illustration) and pull the octane rod from the distributor base. Note: Don't lose the grommet installed in the octane rod hole. The grommet protects the electronic components of the distributor from moisture.
16   Remove the two stator screws (see illustration 11.15).
17   Gently lift it straight up and remove the stator assembly from the distributor.
18   Check the shaft bushing in the distributor base for wear or signs of excessive heat buildup. If signs of wear and/or damage are evident, replace the complete distributor assembly.
19   Inspect the O-ring at the base of the distributor. If it's damaged

11.19   If the O-ring at the base of the distributor is worn
or damaged, replace it with a new one

11.28a   After securing the distributor assembly upside
down in a vise, ''eyeball'' the roll pin holes in the drive
gear and the shaft, then tap the drive gear onto the shaft
with a deep socket and hammer

11.28b   If the drive gear and shaft roll pin hole are
misaligned, the roll pin cannot be driven through the drive
gear and shaft holes — this drive gear must now be pulled
off the shaft and realigned

or worn, remove it and install a new one **(see illustration)**.
20 Inspect the base casting for cracks and wear. If any damage is
evident, replace the distributor assembly.
21 Place the stator assembly in position over the shaft bushing and
press it down onto the distributor base until it's completely seated on
the posts.
22 Install the stator screws and tighten them securely.
23 Insert the octane rod through the hole in the distributor base and
push the inner end of the rod onto the post. **Note:** *Make sure that the
octane rod hole is properly sealed by the grommet.*
24 Reinstall the octane rod screw and tighten it securely.
25 Apply a light coat of engine oil to the distributor shaft and insert
the shaft through the bushing.
26 Mount the distributor in the vise with the lower end up. Be sure
to line the vise jaws with a few clean shop rags to protect the distributor
base. Place a block of wood under the distributor shaft to support it
and prevent it from falling out while the drive gear is being installed.
27 Using the paint marks you made on on the drive gear and the
distributor shaft housing, turn the shaft until the drive gear hole (and
paint mark), the shaft hole and the paint mark on the distributor shaft
housing are aligned.
28 Using a deep socket and hammer, carefully tap the drive gear back

onto the distributor shaft **(see illustration)**. Make sure the hole in the
drive gear and the hole in the shaft are lined up. Because the holes
were drilled off center by the factory, they must be perfectly aligned
or the roll pin cannot be installed **(see illustration)**.
29 Once the drive gear is seated and the holes are lined up, turn the
distributor sideways in the vise and, with an assistant steadying it,
drive a new roll pin into the drive gear with a pin punch. Make sure
that neither end of the roll pin protrudes from the drive gear.
30 Check the distributor shaft for smooth rotation, then remove the
distributor assembly from the vise.
31 Install the TFI-IV module (refer to Section 10).
32 Install the rotor (refer to Chapter 1 if necessary).
33 Install the distributor.

12   Charging system — general information and precautions

The charging system includes the alternator, either an internal or an
external voltage regulator, a charge indicator, the battery, a fusible
link and the wiring between all the components. The charging system
supplies electrical power for the ignition system, the lights, the radio,
etc. The alternator is driven by a drivebelt at the front (right end) of
the engine.

The purpose of the voltage regulator is to limit the alternator's voltage
to a preset value. This prevents power surges, circuit overloads, etc.,
during peak voltage output.

The fusible link is a short length of insulated wire integral with the
engine compartment wiring harness. The link is four wire gauges smaller
in diameter than the circuit it protects. Production fusible links and their
identification flags are identified by the flag color. See Chapter 12 for
additional information regarding fusible links.

The charging system doesn't ordinarily require periodic maintenance.
However, the drivebelt, battery and wires and connections should be
inspected at the intervals outlined in Chapter 1.

Be very careful when making electrical circuit connections to a vehicle
equipped with an alternator and note the following:

a) When reconnecting wires to the alternator from the battery, be
sure to note the polarity.
b) Before using arc welding equipment to repair any part of the vehicle, disconnect the wires from the alternator and the battery
terminals.
c) Never start the engine with a battery charger connected.
d) Always disconnect both battery leads before using a battery
charger.

13.9   To check the voltage at the regulator wiring harness plug, touch the positive lead of a VOM to the I terminal, then the S terminal while touching the negative lead to the rear of the alternator housing

14.3a   To remove the alternator, remove the adjustment bolt (arrow), remove the drivebelt, unplug both the voltage regulator (arrow) and alternator (not shown) wire harness connectors . . .

13   Charging system — check

Refer to illustration 13.9

1   If a malfunction occurs in the charging circuit, don't automatically assume that the alternator is causing the problem. First check the following items:

   a) The battery cables where they connect to the battery. Make sure the connections are clean and tight (refer to Chapter 1).

   b) Check the external alternator wiring harness and the connectors at the alternator and voltage regulator. They must be in good condition, clean and tight.

   c) Check the drivebelt condition and tension (refer to Chapter 1).

   d) Make sure the alternator mounting and adjustment bolts are tight.

   e) Check the fusible link located between the starter relay (refer to Section 19) and the alternator. If it's burned, determine the cause, repair the circuit and replace the link (refer to Chapter 12).

   f) Run the engine and check the alternator for abnormal noise.

2   Using a voltmeter, check the battery voltage with the engine off. It should be approximately 12-volts.

3   Start the engine and check the battery voltage again. It should now be approximately 14-to-15 volts.

4   If the voltage reading is less or more than the specified charging voltage, replace the voltage regulator (refer to Section 15).

5   Locate the regulator terminal (screw F) on the back of the alternator.

6   With the ignition switch in the Off position, touch the F screw with the voltmeter positive lead while touching the alternator housing with the negative lead.

7   The meter should indicate battery voltage if the system is operating normally.

8   If less than battery voltage is indicated, proceed to the next Step to determine the cause of the current drain.

9   Disconnect the wire harness from the *regulator* and connect the voltmeter positive lead to terminal I in the plug **(see illustration)**. No voltage should be indicated.

10   If voltage is indicated, check the I lead from the ignition switch to identify and eliminate the voltage source (refer to the wiring diagrams at the end of this book).

11   If no voltage is indicated, contact the voltmeter positive lead to terminal S. No voltage should be indicated.

12   If voltage is indicated, disconnect the wire harness from the *alternator*. Again, connect the positive voltmeter lead to terminal S in the wiring harness connector.

13   If voltage is still indicated, repair the S lead to the alternator plug to eliminate the voltage source.

14   If no voltage is indicated, the problem is with the rectifier. Replace the alternator (refer to Section 14).

14.3b   . . . then remove the alternator pivot through bolt (arrow) and carefully lift the alternator from the vehicle (2.8L V6 shown — other engines similar)

14   Alternator — removal and installation

Refer to illustrations 14.3a and 14.3b

1   Detach the cable from the negative terminal of the battery.

2   Unplug the electrical connectors from the alternator and the voltage regulator.

3   Loosen the alternator adjustment and pivot bolts and detach the drivebelt **(see illustrations)**.

4   Remove the adjustment and pivot bolts and separate the alternator from the engine.

5   Installation is the reverse of removal.

6   After the alternator is installed, adjust the drivebelt tension (see Chapter 1).

15.3 To detach the voltage regulator/brush holder assembly, remove the four screws (arrows)

15.5 To remove the brushes from the voltage regulator/brush holder assembly, detach the rubber plugs from the two brush lead wire screws and remove both screws (arrows)

15.9 Before installing the voltage regulator/brush holder assembly, insert a paper clip to hold the brushes in place during installation — after installation, pull out the paper clip

15 Voltage regulator/alternator brushes — replacement

Integral regulator

Refer to illustrations 15.3, 15.5 and 15.9

1 Remove the alternator (see Section 14).
2 Set the alternator on a clean workbench.
3 Remove the four voltage regulator mounting screws **(see illustration)**.
4 Detach the voltage regulator.
5 Detach the rubber plugs and remove the brush lead retaining screws and nuts to separate the brush leads from the holder **(see illustration)**. Note that the screws have Torx heads and require a special screwdriver.
6 After noting the relationship of the brushes to the brush holder assembly, remove both brushes. Don't lose the springs.
7 If you're installing a new voltage regulator, insert the old brushes into the brush holder of the new regulator. If you're installing new brushes, insert them into the brush holder of the old regulator. Make sure the springs are properly compressed and the brushes are properly inserted into the recesses in the brush holder.
8 Install the brush lead retaining screws and nuts.
9 Insert a short section of wire, such as a paper clip, through the

CONNECTOR TO REGULATOR

15.14 To detach the wire harness from the remote voltage regulator, position the tip of a screwdriver as shown and twist it — the screwdriver will push the connector off the regulator

hole in the voltage regulator **(see illustration)** to hold the brushes in the retracted position during regulator installation.
10 Carefully install the regulator. Make sure the brushes don't hang up on the rotor.
11 Install the voltage regulator screws and tighten them securely.
12 Remove the wire or paper clip.
13 Install the alternator (see Section 14).

Remote regulator

Refer to illustration 15.14

14 Remove the negative cable from the battery terminal, then disconnect the wire harness from the regulator. Use a screwdriver to unplug the harness connector — do not pull on the wires **(see illustration)**.
15 Remove the mounting bolts and detach the regulator.
16 Installation is the reverse of removal.

16   Starting system — general information

The function of the starting system is to crank the engine to start it. The system is composed of the starter motor, starter relay, battery, switch and connecting wires.

Turning the ignition key to the Start position actuates the starter relay through the starter control circuit. The starter relay then connects the battery to the starter. The battery supplies the electrical energy to the starter motor, which does the actual work of cranking the engine.

Vehicles equipped with an automatic transmission have a Neutral start switch in the starter control circuit, which prevents operation of the starter unless the shift lever is in Neutral or Park. The circuit on vehicles with a manual transmission prevents operation of the starter motor unless the clutch pedal is depressed.

Never operate the starter motor for more than 30 seconds at a time without pausing to allow it to cool for at least two minutes. Excessive cranking can cause overheating, which can seriously damage the starter.

17   Starter motor and circuit — in-vehicle check

Note: *Before diagnosing starter problems, make sure the battery is fully charged.*

General check

1   If the starter motor doesn't turn at all when the switch is operated, make sure the shift lever is in Neutral or Park (automatic transmission) or the clutch pedal is depressed (manual transmission).

2   Make sure the battery is charged and that all cables at the battery and starter relay terminals are clean and secure (see Chapter 1).

3   If the starter motor spins but the engine doesn't turn over, then the drive assembly in the starter motor is slipping and the starter motor must be replaced (see Section 19).

4   If, when the switch is actuated, the starter motor doesn't operate at all but the starter relay operates (clicks), then the problem lies with either the battery (Chapter 1), the starter relay contacts or the starter motor connections.

5   If the starter relay doesn't click when the ignition switch is actuated, either the starter relay circuit is open or the relay itself is defective. Check the starter relay circuit (refer to the wiring diagrams at the end of this book) or replace the relay (see Section 19).

6   To check the starter relay circuit, remove the push-on connector from the relay wire (the red one with a blue stripe). Make sure that the connection is clean and secure and the relay bracket is grounded. If the connections are good, check the operation of the relay with a jumper wire. To do this, place the transmission in Park (automatic) or Neutral (manual). Remove the push-on connector from the relay. Connect a jumper wire between the battery positive terminal and the exposed terminal on the relay. If the starter motor now operates, the starter relay is okay. The problem is in the ignition switch, Neutral start switch or in the starting circuit wiring (look for open or loose connections).

7   If the starter motor still doesn't operate, replace the starter relay (see Section 19).

8   If the starter motor cranks the engine at an abnormally slow speed, first make sure the battery is fully charged and all terminal connections are clean and tight. Also check the connections at the starter relay and battery ground. Eyelet terminals should not be easily rotated by hand. Also check for a short to ground. If the engine is partially seized, or has the wrong viscosity oil in it, it will crank slowly.

Starter cranking circuit test

Refer to illustration 17.12

Note: *To determine the location of excessive resistance in the starter circuit, perform the following simple series of tests.*

9   Disconnect the ignition coil wire from the distributor cap and ground it on the engine.

10   Connect a remote control starter switch from the battery terminal of the starter relay to the S terminal of the relay.

11   Connect a voltmeter positive lead to the starter motor terminal of the starter relay, then connect the negative lead to ground.

12   Make the test connections as shown (**see illustration**). Refer to this illustration as you perform the following four tests.

17.12   Cranking circuit test connections number 1 through 4 (see text)

13   Operate the ignition switch and take the voltmeter readings as soon as a steady figure is indicated. Don't allow the starter motor to turn for more than 30 seconds at a time.

14   The voltage drop in the circuit will be indicated by the voltmeter (put the voltmeter on the 0-to-2 volt range). The maximum allowable voltage drop should be:

a)   0.5-volt with the voltmeter negative lead connected to the starter terminal and the positive lead connected to the battery positive

19.2   The starter relay (arrow) is located behind and below the battery (battery removed for clarity) — to replace it, clearly label then detach the electrical leads and remove the two relay bracket mounting bolts (not visible in this photo)

terminal (Connection 1 in illustration 17.12).

b) 0.1-volt with the voltmeter negative lead connected to the starter relay (battery side) and the positive lead connected to the positive terminal of the battery (Connection 2).

c) 0.3-volt with the voltmeter negative lead connected to the starter relay (starter side) and the positive lead connected to the positive terminal of the battery (Connection 3).

d) 0.3-volt with the voltmeter negative lead connected to the negative terminal of the battery and the positive lead connected to the engine ground (Connection 4).

18 Starter motor — removal and installation

1 Detach the cable from the negative terminal of the battery.

2 Raise the vehicle and support it securely on jackstands.
3 Disconnect the large cable from the terminal on the starter motor.
4 Remove the two starter motor mounting bolts. Remove the starter.
5 Installation is the reverse of removal.

19 Starter relay — removal and installation

Refer to illustration 19.2

1 Detach the cable from the negative terminal of the battery.
2 Label the wires and the terminals then disconnect the Neutral safety switch wire (automatics only), the battery cable, the fusible link and the starter cable from the relay terminals **(see illustration)**.
3 Remove the mounting bolts and detach the relay.
4 Installation is the reverse of removal.

Chapter 6 Emissions control systems

Contents

Specifications

Torque specifications   Ft-lbs
Air pump pulley bolts .... 10 to 12.5
Air pump mounting bolt 25

---

1 General information

Refer to illustration 1.7

To prevent pollution of the atmosphere from incompletely burned and evaporating gases, and to maintain good driveability and fuel economy, a number of emission control systems are incorporated. They include the:

Electronic Engine Control (EEC-IV) system
Exhaust Gas Recirculation (EGR) system
Managed air thermactor system
Fuel evaporative emission control system
Positive Crankcase Ventilation (PCV) system
Inlet air temperature control system
Catalytic converter

All of these systems are linked, directly or indirectly, to the EEC-IV system.

The Sections in this Chapter include general descriptions, checking procedures within the scope of the home mechanic and component replacement procedures (when possible) for each of the systems listed above.

Before assuming that an emissions control system is malfunctioning, check the fuel and ignition systems carefully. The diagnosis of some emission control devices requires specialized tools, equipment and training. If checking and servicing become too difficult or if a procedure is beyond your ability, consult a dealer service department.

This doesn't mean, however, that emission control systems are particularly difficult to maintain and repair. You can quickly and easily perform many checks and do most (if not all) of the regular maintenance at home with common tune-up and hand tools. **Note:** *The most frequent cause of emissions problems is simply a loose or broken vacuum hose or wire, so always check the hose and wiring connections first.*

Pay close attention to any special precautions outlined in this Chapter. It should be noted that the illustrations of the various systems may not exactly match the system installed on your vehicle because of changes made by the manufacturer during production or from year-to-year.

A Vehicle Emissions Control Information label is located in the engine compartment **(see illustration)**. This label contains important emissions specifications and adjustment information, as well as a vacuum hose schematic with emissions components identified. When servicing the engine or emissions systems, the VECI label in your particular vehicle should always be checked for up-to-date information.

1.7 The Vehicle Emission Control Information (VECI) label located on the underside of the hood contains essential information such as spark plug type, the ignition timing procedure, fast idle speed adjustment, etc. — always defer to the information contained on the VECI label as the "last word" on the devices installed on your vehicle

2   Electronic Engine Control (EEC-IV) system

Refer to illustrations 2.4, 2.5, 2.6, 2.7, 2.8 and 2.13

General description

1   The Electronic Engine Control (EEC-IV) system consists of an on-board computer, known as the Electronic Control Assembly (ECA), and the information sensors, which monitor various functions of the engine and send data to the ECA. Based on the data and the information programmed into the computer's memory, the ECA generates output signals to control various engine functions.

2   The ECA, located behind the left side dash panel in the passenger compartment is the "brain" of the EEC-IV system. It receives data from a number of sensors and other electronic components (switches, relays, etc.). Based on the information it receives, the ECA generates output signals to control various relays, solenoids and other actuators. The ECA is specifically calibrated to optimize the emissions, fuel economy and driveability of your vehicle.

2.4 The Manifold Absolute Pressure (MAP) sensor is located on the firewall (2.8L V6 shown) — to replace it, simply label, then detach, the vacuum hoses and remove the sensor bracket mounting screws

3   Because of a Federally-mandated extended warranty which covers the ECA, the information sensors and all components under its control, and because any damage to the ECA, the sensors and/or the control devices may void the warranty, it isn't a good idea to attempt diagnosis or replacement of the ECA at home. Take your vehicle to a dealer service department if the ECA or a system component malfunctions.

Information input sensors

4   The Manifold Absolute Pressure (MAP) sensor, mounted on the firewall **(see illustration)**, measures the absolute pressure of the mixture in the intake manifold and sends a signal to the ECA that is proportional to absolute pressure.

5   The Air Charge Temperature (ACT) sensor, located on the front of the air cleaner housing (2.8L), the rear of the intake manifold (2.3L) or the side of the throttle body (3.0L), provides the ECA with fuel/air mixture temperature information. The ECA uses this information to correct fuel flow and control fuel flow during cold enrichment (cold starts) **(see illustration)**.

6   The EGR Valve Position (EVP) sensor, located on the EGR valve **(see illustration)**, tells the ECA the position of the EGR valve.

2.5 The Air Charge Temperature (ACT) sensor is located either on the air cleaner housing as shown (2.8L V6), the rear of the intake manifold (2.3L four) or the throttle body (3.0L V6)

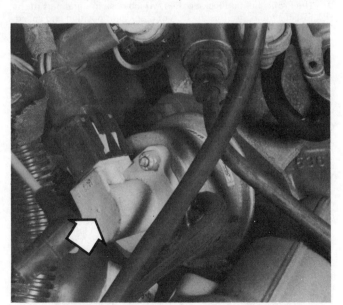

2.6 The EGR valve position (EVP) sensor is located on top of the EGR valve — to replace it, simply unplug the connector and remove the mounting bolts

2.7   To replace the engine coolant temperature (ECT) sensor (center of the intake manifold on 2.3L four, adjacent to water outlet on front end of 3.0L V6), unplug the electrical connector and unscrew the sensor (be sure to coat the threads of the new sensor with teflon tape to prevent coolant leakage)

2.8   The exhaust gas oxygen (EGO) sensor is screwed into the exhaust manifold — to replace it, raise the vehicle, unplug the connector at the pigtail lead and unscrew the sensor (be sure to coat the threads of the new sensor with anti-seize compound to prevent it from welding itself to the manifold)

7   The Engine Coolant Temperature (ECT) sensor, which is threaded into the center of the intake manifold (2.3L models) or adjacent to the water outlet at the front of the engine (3.0L vehicles), (see illustration), monitors engine coolant temperature. The ECT sends the ECA a constantly varying voltage signal which influences ECA control of the fuel mixture, ignition timing and EGR operation.

8   The Exhaust Gas Oxygen (EGO) sensor, which is threaded into the exhaust manifold (see illustration), constantly monitors the oxygen content of the exhaust gases. A voltage signal which varies in accordance with the difference between the oxygen content of the exhaust gases and the surrounding atmosphere is sent to the ECA. The ECA translates this exhaust gas oxygen content signal to fuel/air ratio, then alters it to the ideal ratio for current engine operating conditions.

9   The Profile Ignition Pick-up (PIP), which is an integral part of the Hall Effect switch, informs the ECA of crankshaft position and speed. The PIP assembly consists of a rotary vane plate that rotates past a permanent magnet.

10   The Throttle Position Sensor (TPS), which is mounted on the side of the throttle body (Chapter 4) and connected directly to the throttle shaft, senses throttle movement and position, then transmits an electrical signal to the ECA. This signal enables the ECA to determine when the throttle is closed, in its normal cruise condition or wide open. Further information regarding the TPS can be found in Chapter 4.

Output devices

Note: Your engine will be equipped with some, but not all, of the following devices. Refer to the VECI label to determine which of the following devices are on your vehicle.

11   The A/C and cooling fan controller module is operated by the ECA, the coolant temperature switch and the the brake light switch. The controller module provides an output signal which controls operation of the A/C compressor clutch and the engine cooling fan.

12   The EEC power relay, which is activated by the ignition switch, supplies battery voltage to the ECA when the switch is on.

13   The Canister purge solenoid (CANP), located on the front of the intake manifold, switches manifold vacuum to operate the canister purge valve when a signal is received from the ECA. Vacuum opens the purge valve when the solenoid is energized (see illustration).

14   The solenoid-operated fuel injectors are located in the intake manifold (2.3L and 3.0L). The ECA controls the length of time the injectors are open. The "open" time of the injectors determines the amount of fuel delivered. For information regarding injector replacement, see Chapter 4.

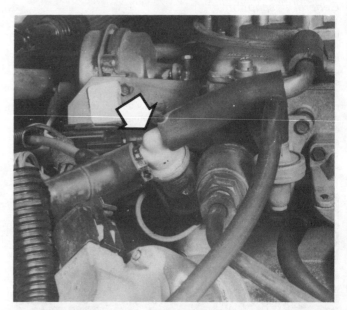

2.13   To replace the canister purge solenoid valve (arrow), unplug the electrical connector and detach the vacuum lines from the T-fitting

15   The fuel pump relay (used on fuel injected vehicles) is activated by the ECA with the ignition switch in the On position. When the ignition switch is turned to the On position, the relay is activated to supply initial line pressure to the system. For information regarding fuel pump checking and replacement, see Chapter 4.

16   The Idle Speed Control (ISC) motor changes idle speed in accordance with signals from the ECA. For information regarding ISC replacement, see Chapter 4.

17   The shift indicator light tells the driver when to shift gears for optimum fuel economy. The ECA signals it in accordance with the information it receives regarding engine speed and manifold vacuum levels.

18   The Thermactor Air Bypass (TAB) solenoid provides a vacuum

signal to the bypass valve in response to signals from the ECA. The TAB valve then bypasses the thermactor air pump to the atmosphere. For information regarding the thermactor system, see Section 4 in this Chapter.

19 The Thermactor Air Diverter (TAD) solenoid provides a vacuum signal to the diverter valve in response to signals from the ECA. The TAD valve then diverts thermactor pump air to either the exhaust manifold or the catalytic converter. For more information regarding the thermactor system, see Section 4 in this Chapter.

20 The TFI-IV ignition module, mounted on the side of the distributor base, triggers the ignition coil and determines dwell. The ECA uses a signal from the Profile Ignition Pick-Up to determine crankshaft position. Ignition timing is determined by the ECA, which then signals the module to fire the coil. For further information regarding the TFI-IV module, see the appropriate Section in Chapter 5.

21 The throttle kicker solenoid is a two-port valve with an atmospheric vent. A vacuum diaphragm is used to maintain nominal idle speed on command from the ECA. For further information regarding the throttle kicker, see the appropriate Section in Chapter 4.

22 The Wide Open Throttle (WOT) A/C cut-out circuit is energized by the ECA when a wide open throttle condition is detected. During wide open throttle, power to the A/C compressor clutch is disconnected until sometime after partial throttle operation resumes. For further information regarding the WOT A/C cut-out, see Chapter 4.

Checking

23 Because of the specialized test equipment needed to check the sensors and output devices, diagnosis is well beyond the scope of the home mechanic. If engine driveability deteriorates, take the vehicle to a dealer service department to have the EEC-IV system checked.

Component replacement

Note: *Because of the Federally-mandated extended warranty which covers the ECA, the information sensors and the devices it controls, there's no point in replacing any of the following components yourself unless the warranty has expired. However, once the warranty has expired, you may wish to perform some of the following component replacement procedures yourself after having the problem diagnosed by a dealer service department or repair shop.*

Air Charge Temperature (ACT) sensor
24 Detach the cable from the negative terminal of the battery.
25 Locate the ACT sensor in the intake manifold **(see illustration 2.5)**.
26 Unplug the electrical connector from the sensor.
27 Remove the sensor with a wrench.
28 Wrap the threads of the new sensor with teflon tape to prevent air leaks.
29 Installation is the reverse of removal.

EGR Valve Position (EVP) sensor
30 Detach the cable from the negative terminal of the battery.
31 Locate the EVP sensor on the EGR valve **(see illustration 2.6)**.
32 Unplug the electrical connector from the sensor.
33 Remove the three mounting bolts and detach the sensor.
34 Installation is the reverse of removal.

Engine Coolant Temperature (ECT) sensor
35 Detach the cable from the negative terminal of the battery.
36 Locate the ECT sensor on the thermostat housing **(see illustration 2.7)**.
37 Unplug the electrical connector from the sensor.
38 Remove the sensor with a wrench.
39 Wrap the threads of the new sensor with teflon tape to prevent coolant leakage.
40 Installation is the reverse of removal.

Manifold Absolute Pressure (MAP) sensor
41 Detach the cable from the negative terminal of the battery.
42 Locate the MAP sensor on the firewall **(see illustration 2.4)**.
43 Unplug the electrical connector from the sensor.
44 Detach the vacuum line from the sensor.
45 Remove the two mounting bolts and detach the sensor.
46 Installation is the reverse of removal.

Exhaust Gas Oxygen (EGO) sensor
47 Detach the cable from the negative terminal of the battery.
48 Raise the vehicle and support it securely on jackstands.
49 Locate the EGO sensor on the exhaust manifold **(see illustration 2.8)**.

50 Unplug the electrical connector from the sensor.
51 Remove the sensor with a wrench.
52 Coat the threads of the new sensor with anti-seize compound to prevent the threads from welding themselves to the manifold.
53 Installation is the reverse of removal.

Throttle Position Sensor (TPS) switch
54 Don't attempt to replace the TPS switch! Specialized calibration equipment is necessary to adjust the switch once it's installed, making replacement beyond the scope of the home mechanic.

Canister Purge Solenoid
55 Detach the cable from the negative terminal of the battery.
56 Locate the canister purge solenoid on the left side of the engine compartment, next to the left wheel well **(see illustration 2.13)**.
57 Unplug the electrical connector from the solenoid.
58 Label the vacuum hoses and ports, then detach the hoses.
59 Remove the solenoid.
60 Installation is the reverse of removal.

Vacuum control solenoid
61 Detach the cable from the negative terminal of the battery.
62 Locate the vacuum control solenoid on the left strut tower.
63 Unplug the electrical connector from the solenoid.
64 Label the vacuum hoses and ports, then detach the hoses.
65 Remove the solenoid/bracket screws and detach the solenoid.
66 Installation is the reverse of removal.

---

3 Exhaust Gas Recirculation (EGR) system

Refer to illustration 3.13

General description

1 The EGR system is designed to reintroduce small amounts of exhaust gas into the combustion cycle, thus reducing the generation of nitrous oxide emissions. The amount of exhaust gas reintroduced and the timing of the cycle is controlled by various factors such as engine speed, altitude, manifold vacuum, exhaust system backpressure, coolant temperature and throttle angle.

2 All EGR valves are vacuum actuated and the vacuum diagram for your particular vehicle is shown on the *Emissions Control Information label* in the engine compartment.

3 The electronic EGR valve used in EEC-IV systems controls EGR flow with an EGR valve position (EVP) sensor attached to the top of the valve. The valve is operated by a vacuum signal from the dual EGR solenoid valves or the electronic vacuum regulator which actuates the valve diaphragm. As supply vacuum overcomes the spring load, the diaphragm is actuated, lifting the pintle off the seat and allowing exhaust gas to recirculate. The amount of flow is proportional to the pintle position. The EVP sensor sends an electrical signal indicating its position to the ECA.

Checking

Note: *Aside from the following check and maintenance steps, the electronic EGR valve cannot be diagnosed or serviced by the home mechanic. Additional checks must be done by a dealer service department.*

4 Make sure the vacuum hoses are in good condition and hooked up correctly.
5 Clean the inlet and outlet ports with a wire brush or scraper. Do not sandblast the valve or clean it with gasoline or solvents as they will damage the valve.
6 To perform a leakage test, connect a vacuum pump to the EGR valve.
7 Apply 5-to-6 in-Hg of vacuum to the valve.
8 Trap the vacuum — it should not drop more than 1 in-Hg in 30 seconds.
9 If the specified conditions are not met, the EGR valve, O-ring or EVP must be replaced.

Component replacement

10 Detach the cable from the negative terminal of the battery.
11 Unplug the electrical connector from the EGR valve position sensor.
12 Unscrew the threaded fitting that attaches the EGR pipe to the EGR valve.

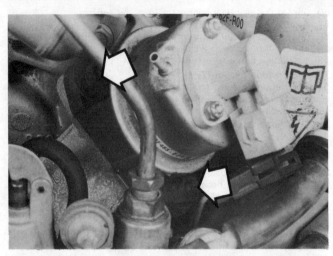

3.13   To remove the EGR valve, unplug the connector to the valve position sensor, disconnect the threaded fitting between the EGR pipe and the valve and remove the valve mounting bolts

13 Remove the two mounting bolts **(see illustration)** and detach the valve.
14 Remove the old gasket.
15 If you're replacing the EGR valve but not the position sensor, remove the sensor from the old valve and install it on the new valve.
16 Installation is the reverse of removal.

***

4   Managed air thermactor system (2.8L V6)

Refer to illustrations 4.3, 4.47 and 4.48

General description

1   The thermactor (air injection) exhaust emission control system reduces carbon monoxide and hydrocarbon content in the exhaust gases by injecting fresh air into the hot exhaust gases leaving the ex-

haust ports. When fresh air is mixed with hot exhaust gases, oxidation is increased, reducing the concentration of hydrocarbons and carbon monoxide and converting them into harmless carbon dioxide and water.
2   Vehicles with a 2.8L V6 utilize a ''managed air'' thermactor system, which diverts thermactor air either upstream to the exhaust manifold check valve or downstream to the rear section check valve and dual bed catalyst. An extended idle air bypass system in carburetor equipped vehicles also vents thermactor air to the atmosphere during extended idling.
3   An air control valve is used to direct the air upstream or downstream. An air bypass valve is used to dump air to the atmosphere. On the 2.8L V6, the two valves are combined into a single air bypass/control valve **(see illustration)**.

Checking

Extended idle air bypass system
4   The normally closed Idle Tracking Switch (ITS) opens when the throttle returns to idle, signalling the EEC-IV module to de-energize the normally closed solenoid. When this occurs, vacuum is removed from the normally closed bypass valve and causes the bypass valve to dump secondary thermactor air to the atmosphere.
5   With the engine warmed up and the transmission in Neutral, momentarily increase engine speed, then allow it to return to idle. If, after 2-1/2 minutes, the thermactor bypass valve dumps secondary air through the vents, the system is okay. If it doesn't, check the routing and condition of the hoses. If the hoses are okay, check the bypass valve function. If the bypass valve is okay, check battery voltage to the ITS and continuity through the (normally closed) ITS while manually cycling the switch. If the ITS is okay, verify that the solenoid functions properly (that it actually opens and closes). If the solenoid is okay, check the vacuum signal to the solenoid. If the vacuum signal is okay, the problem is with the ECA. Further checking of the system must be performed by a dealer service department.

Air supply pump
6   Check and adjust the drivebelt tension (refer to Chapter 1).
7   Disconnect the air supply hose at the air bypass valve inlet.
8   The pump is operating satisfactorily if air flow is felt at the pump outlet with the engine running at idle, increasing as the engine speed is increased.
9   If the air pump doesn't pass the above tests, replace it with a new or rebuilt unit.

4.3   Typical managed air thermactor system with combined bypass/control valve — electronically controlled

Air bypass valve

10 With the engine running at idle, disconnect the hose from the valve outlet.

11 Remove the vacuum hose from the port and remove or bypass any restrictors or delay valves in the vacuum hose.

12 Verify that vacuum is present in the vacuum hose by putting your finger over the end.

13 Reconnect the vacuum hose to the port.

14 With the engine running at 1500 rpm, the air pump supply air should be felt or heard at the air bypass valve outlet.

15 With the engine running at 1500 rpm, disconnect the vacuum hose. Air at the valve outlet should be decreased or shut off and air pump supply air should be felt or heard at the silencer ports.

16 Reconnect all hoses.

17 If the normally closed air bypass valve doesn't successfully pass the above tests, check the air pump (refer to Steps 4 and 5).

18 If the air pump is operating satisfactorily, replace the air bypass valve with a new one.

Air supply control valve

19 With the engine running at 1500 rpm, disconnect the hose at the air supply control valve inlet and verify that air is flowing through the hose.

20 Reconnect the hose to the valve inlet.

21 Disconnect the hoses at the vacuum port and at outlets A and B **(see illustration 4.3)**.

22 With the engine running at 1500 rpm, air flow should be felt at outlet B with little or no air flow at outlet A.

23 With the engine running at 1500 rpm, connect a line from any manifold vacuum fitting to the vacuum port.

24 Air flow should be present at outlet A with little or no air flow at outlet B.

25 Reconnect all hoses.

26 If all conditions above are not met, replace the air control valve with a new one.

Combination air bypass/air control valve

27 Disconnect the hoses from outlets A and B **(see illustration 4.3)**.

28 Disconnect the vacuum hose at port D and plug the hose.

29 With the engine running at 1500 rpm, verify that air flows from the bypass vents.

30 Unplug and reconnect the vacuum hose at port D, then disconnect and plug the hose attached to port S.

31 Verify that vacuum is present in the hose to port D by momentarily disconnecting it.

32 Reconnect the vacuum hose to port D.

33 With the engine running at 1500 rpm, verify that air is flowing out of outlet B with no air flow present at outlet A.

34 Attach a length of hose to port S.

35 With the engine running at 1500 rpm, apply vacuum to the hose and verify that air is flowing out of outlet A.

36 Reconnect all hoses. Be sure to unplug the hose to Port S before reconnecting it.

37 If all conditions above are not met, replace the combination valve with a new one.

Check valve

38 Disconnect the hoses from both ends of the check valve.

39 Blow through both ends of the check valve, verifying that air flows in one direction only.

40 If air flows in both directions or not at all, replace the check valve with a new one.

41 When reconnecting the valve, make sure it is installed in the proper direction.

Thermactor system noise test

42 The thermactor system is not completely noiseless. Under normal conditions, noise rises in pitch as the engine speed increases. To determine if noise is the fault of the air injection system, detach the drivebelt (after verifying that the belt tension is correct) and operate the engine. If the noise disappears, proceed with the following diagnosis. **Caution:** *The pump must accumulate 500 miles (vehicle miles) before the following check is valid.*

43 If the belt noise is excessive:

a) Check for a loose belt and tighten as necessary (refer to Chapter 1).

b) Check for a seized pump and replace it if necessary.

c) Check for a loose pulley. Tighten the mounting bolts as required.

d) Check for loose, broken or missing mounting brackets or bolts.

Tighten or replace as necessary.

44 If there is excessive mechanical noise:

a) Check for an overtightened mounting bolt.

b) Check for an overtightened drivebelt (refer to Chapter 1).

c) Check for excessive flash on the air pump adjusting arm boss and remove as necessary.

d) Check for a distorted adjusting arm and, if necessary, replace the arm.

45 If there is excessive thermactor system noise (whirring or hissing sounds):

a) Check for a leak in the hoses (use a soap and water solution to find the leaks) and replace the hose(s) as necessary.

b) Check for a loose, pinched or kinked hose and reassemble, straighten or replace the hose and/or clamps as required.

c) Check for a hose touching other engine parts and adjust or re-route the hose to prevent further contact.

d) Check for an inoperative bypass valve (refer to Step 10) and replace if necessary.

e) Check for an inoperative check valve (refer to Step 38) and replace if necessary.

f) Check for loose pump or pulley mounting fasteners and tighten as necessary.

g) Check for a restricted or bent pump outlet fitting. Inspect the fitting and remove any casting flash blocking the air passageway. Replace bent fittings.

h) Check for air dumping through the bypass valve (only at idle). On many vehicles, the thermactor system has been designed to dump air at idle to prevent overheating the catalytic converter. This condition is normal. Determine that the noise persists at higher speeds before proceeding.

i) Check for air dumping through the bypass valve (the decel and idle dump). On many vehicles, the thermactor air is dumped into the air cleaner or the remote silencer. Make sure that the hoses are connected properly and not cracked.

46 If there is excessive pump noise, make sure the pump has had sufficient break-in time (at least 500 miles). Check for a worn or damaged pump and replace as necessary.

Component replacement

47 To replace the air bypass valve, air supply control valve, check valve, combination air bypass/air control valve or the silencer, label and disconnect the hoses leading to them, **(see illustration)**, replace

4.47 When replacing a combination bypass/control valve assembly, be sure to label the hoses correctly to ensure that they are properly reinstalled

1 Vacuum line to control solenoid
2 Combination air bypass and air control valve hose
3 Vacuum line to control solenoid
4 Hose and check valve for catalytic converter (check valve not visible in photo)
5 Hose and check valve for exhaust manifolds

the faulty component and reattach the hoses to the proper ports. Make sure the hoses are in good condition. If not, replace them with new ones.

48 To replace the air supply pump, first loosen the appropriate engine drivebelts (refer to Chapter 1), then remove the faulty pump from the mounting bracket (see illustration). Label all wires and hoses as they're removed to facilitate installation of the new unit.

49 After the new pump is installed, adjust the drivebelts to the specified tension (refer to Chapter 1).

5 Fuel evaporative emissions control system

Refer to illustrations 5.2a, 5.2b, 5.2c, 5.4 and 5.16

General description

1   This system is designed to prevent hydrocarbons from being released into the atmosphere by trapping and storing fuel vapor from the fuel tank, the carburetor or the fuel injection system.

2   The serviceable parts of the system include a charcoal filled canister and the connecting lines between the fuel tank, fuel tank filler cap and the carburetor or fuel injection system (see illustrations).

3   Vapor trapped in the gas tank is vented through a valve in the top of the tank. The vapor leaves the valve through a single line and is routed to a carbon canister located between the left front wheel well and the front bumper, where it's stored until the next time the engine is started.

4   The canister outlet is connected to an electrically actuated canister purge solenoid (see illustration) that is, in turn, connected to the air cleaner housing. The canister purge solenoid valve is normally closed. When the engine is started, the solenoid is energized by a signal from the ECA and allows intake vacuum to open the line between the canister and the air cleaner housing, which draws vapor stored in the canister through the air cleaner and into the engine where it's burned.

5   The thermal vent valve is a temperature actuated off/on valve in the carburetor-to-canister vent line and is closed when the engine compartment is cold. This prevents fuel tank vapor (generated when the engine heats up before the engine compartment does) from being vented through the carburetor float bowl and forces it instead into the carbon canister. This effect can occur, for example, when sunlight

4.48   To remove the air pump, loosen the hose clamp and detach the hose, remove the lower bolt (arrow) and remove the belt, then remove the upper bolt (arrow) and remove the pump

strikes a vehicle that has been sitting out all night and begins to warm the fuel tank. With the thermal vent valve closed, the vapor cannot enter the carburetor float bowl vent valve, but is routed instead to the carbon canister. As the engine compartment warms up during normal engine operation, the thermal vent valve opens. When the engine is again turned off, the thermal vent valve (now open because underhood temperature is above 120°F) allows fuel vapor generated in the carburetor float bowl to pass through the valve and be stored in the carbon canister. As the thermal vent valve cools, it closes and the cycle begins again.

VIEW Z

FRONT OF ENGINE

TO PURGE NIPPLE IN CARBURETOR SPACER

TO FUEL TANK

RH FENDER APRON

CARBON CANISTER

TO PURGE NIPPLE IN CARBURETOR SPACER

VIEW Z

5.2a   Typical evaporative emission system for the 2.8L V6

FUEL TANK VAPOR HOSE

CARBON CANISTER

5.2b Typical evaporative emission system for the 2.3L four

HOSE AND TUBE MUST MAINTAIN CONTINUOUS DOWNHILL SLOPE FROM THROTTLE BODY

FRONT OF ENGINE

RH FENDER APRON

NOTE: HOSE MUST BE ROUTED BEHIND ALTERNATOR

PURGE SOLENOID

HOSE & VALVE ASSY

FUEL TANK VAPOR HOSE

HOSE ASSY

5.2c Typical evaporative emission system for the 3.0L V6

CANISTER ASSY

PCV HOSE

FRONT OF VEHICLE

Checking

Charcoal canister

6   There are no moving parts and nothing to wear in the canister. Check for loose, missing, cracked or broken fittings and inspect the canister for cracks and other damage. If the canister is damaged, replace it (refer to Step 15).

Canister purge valve

7   Clearly label all vacuum hoses and ports, then detach the hoses from the valve.

8   Remove the valve.

9   Apply vacuum to port B **(see illustration 5.4)**. The valve should be closed (no air flows through it). If air does flow, the valve is open. Replace it with a new one.

10   After applying and maintaining 16 in-Hg vacuum to port A, apply vacuum to port B again. Air should pass through (the valve should open). If no air flows, the valve is closed. Replace it. **Caution:** *Never apply vacuum to port C. Doing so may dislodge the internal diaphragm and the valve will be permanently damaged.*

Carburetor fuel bowl solenoid vent valve

11   Remove the valve (refer to Step 19).

12   Apply 9-to-14 volts to the valve electrical connector terminals with jumper wires. The valve should close, preventing air from passing through. If the valve doesn't close, replace it.

Carburetor fuel bowl thermal vent valve

Note: *You'll need an oven and an accurate pyrometer or thermometer to test the fuel bowl thermal vent valve.*

5.4   A typical canister purge solenoid (A) and carburetor fuel bowl thermal vent valve (B) on a 2.8L V6 — consult your VECI label to determine the approximate location of these components on your vehicle

13 Remove the valve (refer to Step 19).
14 The vent should be fully closed at 90°F and below and open at 120°F and above. If it isn't, replace it.

Component replacement

Charcoal canister

15 Locate the canister on the right side of the engine compartment.
16 Remove the single mounting bolt **(see illustration)** above the canister.
17 Lower the canister, detach the hose from the purge valve, or purge solenoid valve, and remove the canister.
18 Installation is the reverse of removal.

All other components

19 Referring to the appropriate vacuum hose and vacuum valve schematics in this Section and on the VECI label of your vehicle, locate the component to be replaced.
20 Label the hoses and fittings, then detach the hoses and remove the component.
21 Installation is the reverse of removal.

6   Positive Crankcase Ventilation (PCV) system

Refer to illustrations 6.1 and 6.2

General description

1   The Positive Crankcase Ventilation (PCV) system **(see illustration)**

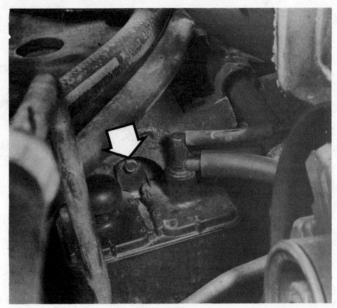

5.16   To remove the charcoal canister, clearly label then detach the vacuum hoses and remove the mounting bolt (arrow)

6.1   Typical Positive Crankcase Ventilation (PCV) system

cycles crankcase vapors back through the engine where they are burned. The PCV valve regulates the amount of ventilating air and blow-by gas to the intake manifold and prevents backfire from traveling into the crankcase.
2   The PCV system consists of a replaceable PCV valve **(see illustration)**, a crankcase ventilation filter (integral with the oil filler cap on some vehicles, separate on others) and the connecting hoses.
3   The air source for the crankcase ventilation system is in the air cleaner. Air passes through the PCV filter (in the rocker arm cover or the oil filler cap) and through a hose connected to the air cleaner housing. On vehicles with a PCV filter integrated into the oil filler cap, the cap is sealed at the opening to prevent the entrance of outside air. From the oil filler cap, or separate PCV filter in the rocker arm cover, the air flows into the rocker arm chamber and the crankcase, from which it circulates up into another section of the rocker arm chamber and finally enters a spring loaded regulator valve (PCV valve) that controls the amount of flow as operating conditions vary. The vapors are routed to the intake manifold through the crankcase vent hose tube and fittings. This process goes on continuously while the engine is running.

Checking

4   Checking procedures for the PCV system components are included in Chapter 1.

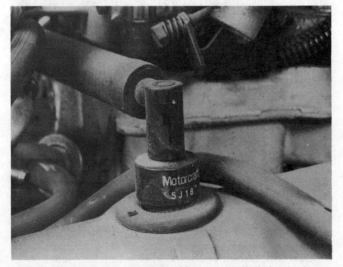

6.2   Typical PCV valve (2.8L V6 shown) installation in the rocker arm cover

Component replacement

5   Component replacement involves simply installing a new valve or hose in place of the one removed during the checking procedure.

---

7   Inlet air temperature control system (2.8L V6)

Refer to illustrations 7.17, 7.22 and 7.23

General description

1   The inlet air temperature control system provides heated intake air during warmup, then maintains the inlet air temperature within a 70°F to 105°F operating range by mixing warm and cool air. This allows leaner fuel/air mixture settings for the carburetor, which reduces emissions and improves driveability.
2   Two fresh air inlets — one warm and one cold — are used. The balance between the two is controlled by intake manifold vacuum. A vacuum motor, which operates a heat duct valve in the air cleaner, is controlled by an Inlet Air Solenoid (IAS) valve, located behind the vacuum reservoir on the left side of the engine compartment, which is under the control of the ECA. The ECA, in turn, monitors the temperature of the intake air with the Air Charge Temperature (ACT) sensor.
3   When the underhood temperature is cold, warm air radiating off the exhaust manifold is routed by a shroud which fits over the manifold up through a hot air inlet tube and into the air cleaner **(see illustration in Chapter 4)**. This provides warm air for the carburetor, resulting in better driveability and faster warmup. As the underhood temperature rises, a heat duct valve is gradually closed by the vacuum motor and the air cleaner draws air through a cold air duct instead. The result is a consistent intake air temperature.

Checking

Note: *Make sure that the engine is cold before beginning this test.*

4   Always check the vacuum source, the IAS valve and the integrity of all vacuum hoses between the source, the IAS valve and the vacuum motor before beginning the following test. Do not proceed until they're okay.
5   Apply the parking brake and block the wheels.
6   Detach, but do not remove, the air cleaner housing and element (see Chapter 4).
7   Turn the air cleaner housing upside down so the vacuum motor door is visible. The door should be open. If it isn't, it may be binding or sticking. Make sure that it's not rusted in an open or closed position by attempting to move it by hand. If it's rusted, it can usually be freed by cleaning and oiling the hinge. If it fails to work properly after servicing, replace it.
8   If the vacuum motor door is okay but the motor still fails to operate correctly, check carefully for a leak in the hose leading to it. Check the vacuum source to and from the bimetal sensor and the time delay valve as well. If no leak is found, replace the vacuum motor (refer to Step 16).
9   Start the engine. If the duct door has moved or moves to the "heat on" (closed to fresh air) position, go to Step 13.
10   If the door stays in the "heat off" (closed to warm air) position, place a finger over the bimetal sensor bleed. The duct door must move rapidly to the "heat on" position. If the door doesn't move to the "heat on" position, stop the engine and replace the vacuum motor (refer to Step 16). Repeat this Step with the new vacuum motor.
11   With the engine off, cool the bimetal sensor and the Cold Weather Modulator (CWM) by spraying them with cold water (wait for 20 seconds after the liquid contacts the sensor and CWM).
12   Restart the engine. The duct door should move to the "heat on" position. If the door doesn't move or moves only partially, replace the TVS.
13   Start and run the engine briefly (less than 15 seconds). The duct door should move to the "heat on" position.
14   Shut off the engine and watch the duct door. It should stay in the "heat on" position for at least two minutes.
15   If it doesn't stay in the "heat on" position for at least two minutes, replace the IAS (refer to Step 23) and repeat this Step after cooling the CWM and bimetal again.

Component replacement

Vacuum motor
16   Detach the air cleaner housing assembly (see Chapter 4).

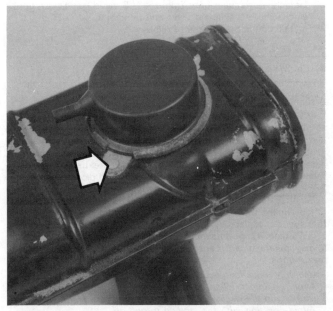

7.17   To remove the vacuum motor, drill out the retaining rivet (arrow), remove the strap and remove the motor — use a sheet metal screw to attach the retaining strap when installing a new motor

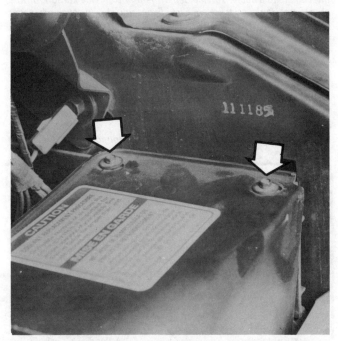

7.22   To remove the vacuum reservoir, which is located on the left side of the engine compartment, remove these two screws (arrows) and lift the reservoir out of the way

---

17   Locate the vacuum motor **(see illustration)**.
18   Detach the vacuum hose and drill out the retaining strap rivet.
19   Remove the motor.
20   Installation is the reverse of removal. Use a sheet metal screw of the appropriate diameter to reattach the strap.

Inlet air solenoid (IAS) valve
21   Detach the cable from the negative terminal of the battery.
22   Remove the two mounting screws from the vacuum reservoir **(see illustration)** and remove the reservoir.

23 Detach the vacuum hose from the IAS valve (see illustration).
24 Unclip the IAS solenoid valve and remove it.
25 Installation is the reverse of removal.

8   Catalytic converter

Refer to illustration 8.1

General description

1   The catalytic converter (see illustration) is designed to reduce hydrocarbon, carbon monoxide and nitrogen oxide pollutants in the exhaust. The converter "oxidizes" these components (speeds up the heat producing chemical reaction between the exhaust gas constituents) and converts them to water and carbon dioxide.
2   The converter, which closely resembles a muffler, is located in the exhaust system immediately behind the short elbow shaped section of pipe below the exhaust manifold (you'll need to raise the vehicle to inspect or replace it).
3   **Warning:** *If large amounts of unburned gasoline enter the converter, it may overheat and cause a fire. Always observe the following precautions:*

 Use only unleaded gasoline
 Avoid prolonged idling
 Do not run the engine with a nearly empty fuel tank
 Avoid coasting with the ignition turned off

Checking

Note: *An infrared sensor is required to check the actual operation of the catalytic converter. Such a device is prohibitively expensive. Take the vehicle to a dealer service department or a service station for this procedure. However, there are a few things you should check whenever the vehicle is raised for any reason.*

4   Check the converter for dents (maximum 3/4-inch deep) and other damage which could affect its performance.
5   Inspect the heat insulator plates above and below the catalytic converter for damage.

Component replacement

Warning: *Don't attempt to remove the catalytic converter until the complete exhaust system is cool.*
Note: *The catalytic converter cannot be unbolted from the exhaust*

7.23   To remove the Idle Air Solenoid (IAS) valve, detach the vacuum hose and unclip the valve

system. It must be cut off with a torch. But a replacement converter can be bolted onto the existing system. See Chapter 4 for exploded drawings of the exhaust system.

6   Raise the vehicle and support it securely on jackstands. Apply penetrating oil to the clamp bolts and allow it to soak in.
7   Release the hose clamp and detach the hose from the thermactor pipe inlet.
8   Remove the flange bolts from the flange between the elbow and exhaust pipe at the front and rear ends of the center section of the exhaust system. Remove the old gaskets if they are stuck to the pipes.
9   Remove the catalytic converter and center section of the exhaust as an assembly.
10 Installation is the reverse of removal. Be sure to use new exhaust pipe gaskets at the flanges at both ends.
11 It's always a good idea to inspect and, if necessary, replace the rubber exhaust pipe hangers while the vehicle is raised (refer to Chapter 4).
12 Start the engine and check carefully for exhaust leaks.

8.1   Typical catalytic converter with a three-way catalyst (reduction of NOx) and conventional oxidation catalyst (reduction of HC and CO)

Chapter 7 Part A   Manual transmission

Contents

Specifications

Torque specifications

	Ft-lbs
Shift lever bolt	6 to 9
Driveshaft U-bolt	8 to 15
Clutch housing-to-engine bolt	28 to 38
Transmission insulator bolt	60 to 80
Transmission insulator stud nut	71 to 94
Transmission-to-bellhousing bolt	30 to 40
Starter-to-clutch housing bolt	15 to 20

1   General information

This portion of Chapter 7 deals with the manual transmission. Part B covers the automatic transmission. The manual transmission installed in these vehicles is a 5-speed unit manufactured by Mazda.

Due to the complexity of the transmissions and the special tools and expertise required to perform an overhaul, it is not advised that this job be undertaken by the home mechanic. Therefore, the procedures in this Chapter are limited to routine adjustments and removal and installation procedures.

Depending on the expense involved in having a faulty transmission overhauled, it may be an advantage to consider replacing the unit with either a new or rebuilt one. Your local dealer or transmission shop should be able to supply you with information concerning cost, availability and exchange policy. Regardless of how you decide to remedy a transmission problem, however, you can still save considerable expense by removing and installing the unit yourself.

2   Transmission mount — check and replacement

Refer to illustrations 2.2 and 2.3

1   Insert a large screwdriver or pry bar into the space between the transmission extension housing and the crossmember and pry up.

2.2 Pry on the transmission mount with a bar or large screwdriver to check for excessive looseness

2   The transmission should not spread excessively away from the insulator **(see illustration)**.
3   To replace, remove the two nuts attaching the insulator to the crossmember and the two bolts attaching the insulator to the transmission **(see illustration)**.
4   Raise the transmission with a jack and remove the insulator, noting which holes are used in the crossmember for proper alignment during installation.
5   Installation is the reverse of the removal procedure.

---

3   Manual transmission — removal and installation

Refer to illustrations 3.8, 3.13, 3.14 and 3.15
Removal

1   Disconnect the negative cable at the battery. Place the cable out of the way so it cannot accidentally come in contact with the negative terminal of the battery, as this would once again allow power into the electrical system of the vehicle.
2   Place the gearshift selector in Neutral.
3   Remove the four shift boot-to-floor bolts and lift the boot assembly up.
4   Remove the shift lever assembly (Section 6).

2.3   Transmission mount insulator installation details

5   Raise the vehicle and support it securely on jackstands.
6   Remove the starter (Chapter 5).
7   Disconnect the hydraulic line from the clutch slave cylinder by removing the clip and releasing the fitting.
8   Disconnect the speedometer and electrical connections from the transmission **(see illustration)**.
9   Remove the driveshaft (Chapter 8).
10   Remove the transmission insulator-to-crossmember nuts and loosen the front insulator-to-crossmember bracket nuts and bolts.
11   Support the transmission with a jack or dolly (use chains or nylon straps to secure it to the jack).
12   Support the engine with another jack or a jackstand, using a block of wood to protect the oil pan.
13   Remove the crossmember **(see illustration)**.
14   Remove the clutch housing-to-engine bolts and carefully move the transmission to the rear until the input shaft is clear of the clutch components and the transmission can be lowered from the vehicle **(see illustration)**.

Installation

15   If the clutch slave cylinder release bearing was removed, install it over the transmission input shaft with the tabs aligned with the slots in the clutch housing **(see illustration)**. Install the bolts and tighten them to the specified torque.
16   Raise the transmission into position and move it forward, making sure the input shaft engages in the pilot bearing in the flywheel and the clutch housing fits over the pilot dowel pins on the engine.
17   Install the clutch housing-to-engine bolts. Tighten the bolts to the specified torque.
18   Install the crossmember with the bolts finger-tight.
19   Lower the transmission until the insulator studs protrude through the crossmember and install the nuts. Tighten the insulator and crossmember nuts and bolts to the specified torque and remove the jack.

3.8   Speedometer and electrical connections on the transmission

3.13   Transmission crossmember and insulator details

3.14 The transmission can be lowered once the input shaft is clear of the clutch components. Note the jackstand supporting the engine and the safety chain around the transmission

WOOD BLOCK AND SAFETY STAND

RELEASE BEARING

CLUTCH HOUSING

SLAVE CYLINDER

3.15 Clutch slave cylinder and release bearing installation details

20 Connect the speedometer and the electrical connections to the transmission. Connect the clutch hydraulic line.
21 Install the starter (Chapter 5).
22 Install the shift lever assembly.
23 Push the shift boot down into place and install the bolts.
24 Connect the negative battery cable.
25 Bleed the clutch hydraulic system as described in Chapter 8.

---

4 Speedometer pinion gear and seal — removal and installation

---

Refer to illustrations 4.3 and 4.4

1 Remove the bolt on the speedometer cable retaining bracket and remove the bracket and bolt as an assembly.
2 Pull the pinion gear assembly straight out of the transmission extension housing.
3 Use a small screwdriver to remove the retaining clip from the pinion gear and slide the gear off the cable (**see illustration**).
4 To replace the O-ring, use a screwdriver to remove the O-ring from the retaining groove (**see illustration**).

4.3 Pry the retaining clip off the pinion gear so the gear can be removed from the cable

4.4 Use a small screwdriver to pry the O-ring out of its groove

6.3 Shift lever assembly details

6.2 Use a socket and extension to remove the shift boot
retaining bolts

5   Lubricate the new O-ring and slide it onto the pinion shaft until
it seats in the retaining groove.
6   Install the new gear and secure with the retaining clip.
7   Install the pinion gear assembly and secure it with the retaining
bracket and bolt.

5   Extension housing oil seal — replacement

1   Raise the vehicle and support it securely on jackstands.
2   Remove the driveshaft (Chapter 8). Scribe marks on the driveshaft
and yoke and the rear axle companion flange to assure proper positioning of the driveshaft during assembly.
3   Remove the oil seal from the end of the extension housing with
a seal removing tool or a special Ford tool T71P-7657-A. If there is
access, a thin blade screwdriver or chisel may also be used to remove
the seal and the extension housing bushing, which is behind the seal.
4   Before installing the new seal inspect the sealing surface of the

universal joint yoke for scoring. If scoring is found, replace the yoke.
5   Inspect the counterbore of the housing for burrs. Remove burrs
with emery cloth or medium grit wet-and-dry sandpaper.
6   Install the new extension housing bushing and oil seal after coating
the inside diameter of the seal with silicone sealant and the end of the
rubber boot portion with grease.

6   Transmission shift lever assembly — removal and installation

Refer to illustrations 6.2 and 6.3
1   Turn the shift knob ball counterclockwise to remove it from the
lever.
2   Remove the shift boot bolts and pull the boot up the shift lever
(see illustration).
3   Remove the four shift lever assembly-to-transmission shift rail adap-
tor bolts and lift the assembly from the transmission **(see illustration)**.
4   Prior to installation, lubricate the shift lever contact surfaces with
multi-purpose grease.
5   Lower the shift assembly into the transmission. Coat the threads
of the retaining bolts with thread sealant and install them. Tighten the
bolts to the specified torque.
6   Install the shift boot and knob ball.

Chapter 7 Part B   Automatic transmission

Contents

Specifications

General

Transmission type	A4LD
Fluid type...................................	See Chapter 1

Torque specifications   Ft-lbs

Transmission band locknut	35 to 45
Torque converter-to-driveplate nut	12 to 16
Transmission-to-engine bolt and nut	28 to 38
Crossmember through-bolt	71 to 94
Insulator nut	60 to 80
Starter bolt	15 to 20

1   General information

Due to the complexity of the automatic transmission covered in this manual and to the specialized equipment necessary to perform most service operations, this Chapter addresses only those procedures concerning routine maintenance and adjustment. Except for removal and installation of the transmission assembly, major repair operations should be undertaken by a professional mechanic with the proper facilities.

These models are equipped with the A4LD 4-speed automatic overdrive transmission. The A4LD automatic is the first Ford Motor Company production automatic transmission to use electronic controls integrated into the on-board EEC-IV system. These controls operate a piston/plate clutch in the torque converter that eliminates converter slip when applied.

Ford specifies a different grade transmission fluid than other manufacturers, and this must be used when refilling or adding fluid. The fluid specification for your vehicle can be found embossed on the transmission fluid dipstick or on the certification label on the left front door post. Additional information concerning automatic transmission fluid level checking can be found in Chapter 1.

2 General diagnosis

Automatic transmission malfunctions may be caused by four general conditions: poor engine performance, improper adjustments, hydraulic malfunctions and mechanical malfunctions. Diagnosis of these problems should always begin with the easily checked items such as fluid level and condition, band adjustment and shift linkage adjustment. Perform a road test to determine if the problem has been corrected or if more diagnosis is necessary. If the problem persists after the preliminary tests and corrections are completed, additional diagnosis should be undertaken by a dealer or repair shop.

3.3   Use an open end wrench to remove the two torque
converter cover bolts

3 Automatic transmission — removal and installation

Refer to illustrations 3.3, 3.5, 3.6, 3.8, 3.9, 3.19 and 3.22

Removal

1   Disconnect the negative cable at the battery. Place the cable out of the way so it cannot accidentally come in contact with the negative terminal of the battery, as this would once again allow power into the electrical system of the vehicle.
2   Raise the vehicle and support it securely on jackstands.
3   Drain the transmission fluid (Chapter 1).
4   Remove the torque converter cover (**see illustration**).
5   Mark one of the torque converter studs and the driveplate with white paint so they can be installed in the same position (**see illustration**).
6   Use a suitable large socket and bar on the crankshaft bolt at the front of the engine to lock the engine from turning over and then remove the four torque converter-to-driveplate nuts (**see illustration**). Turn the crankshaft bolt for access to each nut on the torque converter. On 4-cylinder engines, make sure not to turn the engine in a counterclockwise direction (viewed from the front).
7   Remove the driveshaft (Chapter 8).
8   Disconnect the speedometer cable (**see illustration**).
9   Disconnect the electrical connectors from the transmission (**see illustration**).
10 Disconnect the vacuum hose from the modulator.
11 Remove the starter (Chapter 5).
12 Remove the transmission fluid filler tube.
13 Support the transmission with a jack and raise the transmission slightly. A safety chain should also be used around the transmission to ensure that it stays securely on the jack.
14 Unbolt the shift cable bracket from the transmission.
15 Remove the insulator-to-transmission nuts.
16 Remove the crossmember-to-frame through-bolts.
17 Lower the transmission slightly — only enough to gain access to the oil cooler fluid lines — and disconnect and plug the lines at the transmission. Be prepared to catch some spilling fluid as this is done.
18 Inside the passenger compartment, remove the engine cover and remove the top two transmission bellhousing-to-engine stud nuts. On some models the ignition coil is mounted on these studs as well.
19 Use a socket on a long extension and ratchet to remove the remaining transmission bellhousing-to-engine bolts (**see illustration**).
20 Disconnect the exhaust system bolts at the manifolds and lower the system to provide clearance for removal of the transmission.
21 Move the transmission to the rear to disengage it from the engine

3.5   Mark the torque converter stud and driveplate with
white paint so they can be reinstalled in the same position

3.6   With the engine locked from turning, use a socket
and extension to remove the torque converter nuts

3.8 Two types of speedometer connections are used; the plug-in electrical type and the gear type retained by a bolt

3.9 Various connections at the transmission

3.19 Transmission-to-engine bolts — note the use of studs at the upper portion of the engine

Left — V6 engines   *Right — Four-cylinder engine*

block dowel pins and make sure the torque converter is detached from the driveplate. Lower the transmission from the vehicle.

Installation

22 Prior to installation, make sure the torque converter hub is securely engaged in the pump. This can be checked by measuring the distance between the outer surface of the hub and the transmission flange to make sure this dimension is 7/16 to 9/16-inch **(see illustration)**.

23 Raise the transmission into position, making sure to keep it level so the torque converter does not slide forward. Connect the transmission cooler lines.

24 Turn the torque converter to line up the drive studs with the holes in the driveplate. The white paint mark on the driveplate and the stud made during Step 5 must be lined up.

25 Move the transmission carefully forward until the dowel pins are engaged and the torque converter is engaged.

26 Install the transmission housing-to-engine bolts and nuts. Tighten the bolts and nuts to the specified torque.

27 Install the torque converter-to-driveplate nuts. Tighten the nuts to the specified torque.

3.22 Dimension A should be between 7/16 and 9/16-inch for the torque converter hub to be properly seated in the pump

28 Install the transmission mount crossmember and through-bolts. Tighten the bolts and nuts to the specified torque.
29 Lower the transmission until the insulator studs extend through the crossmember and install the nuts. Tighten the nuts to the specified torque.
30 Install the fluid filler tube.
31 Install the starter.
32 Connect the vacuum modulator hose.
33 Connect the shift linkage and cables.
34 Plug in the transmission electrical connectors.
35 Install the torque converter cover.
36 Connect the driveshaft.
37 Connect the speedometer.
38 Adjust the shift linkage (Section 6).
39 Lower the vehicle.
40 Fill the transmission (Chapter 1), run the vehicle and check for fluid leaks.

4 Automatic transmission selector lever assembly — removal and installation

Refer to illustration 4.2

1   Under the vehicle, remove the retaining clip and disconnect the shift cable from the selector lever.
2   Inside the passenger compartment, grasp the floor carpet center retainer securely and pull up sharply to remove it from the base of the lever assembly **(see illustration)**.

4.2 Transmission shift selector details

3   Remove the four retaining bolts and lift the selector lever assembly from the vehicle.
4   If it is necessary to remove the selector handle and button, grasp the handle securely with the shifter in Drive and pull straight up. If the handle does not come off easily, tap from below with a rubber mallet. To install, place the handle/button in position, making sure the handle chrome ring is lined up with the selector handle groove. Strike the center of handle with a rubber mallet until it is seated.
5   To install, place the selector assembly in position and install the bolts. Tighten the bolts securely.
6   Place the carpet retainer in position and press down evenly until it snaps in place.
7   Under the vehicle, connect the shift cable to the selector lever.
8   Adjust the linkage (Section 6).

5 Neutral start switch — removal and installation

Refer to illustration 5.4

1   Jack up the vehicle and support it securely on jackstands to gain access to the neutral start switch, located on the side of the transmission **(see illustration 3.9)**.
2   Disconnect the ground cable at the battery.
3   Disconnect the electrical connector from the neutral start switch.
4   Use tool T74P-77247-A to remove the switch **(see illustration)**.
Caution : *Use of other tools could crush or puncture the walls of the switch.*

5.4 **The neutral start switch can be unscrewed after unplugging it — the switch is very fragile so a special socket is recommended for installation**

5   Install the switch and tighten securely.
6   Install the electrical connector and lower the vehicle.
7   Connect the negative battery cable.
8   Check that the engine starts only when the selector is in the Neutral and Park positions.

6 Automatic transmission shift linkage — adjustment

Refer to illustrations 6.3a and 6.3b

1   Raise the vehicle and support it securely on jackstands.
2   In the passenger compartment, place the shift lever in the D (Over-drive) position.
3   Under the vehicle, loosen the adjustment screw on the shift cable end and disconnect the manual lever ballstud **(see illustrations)**.
4   Place the manual lever on the transmission in the D (Overdrive) position by moving it all the way to the rear and then moving it three detents forward. Hold the shift lever against the rear stop.
5   Connect the cable end fitting to the manual shift lever and tighten the adjustment screw securely.
6   After adjustment, check for proper Park engagement; the control lever must move to the right when engaged in the Park detent.
7   Lower the vehicle and check the control lever in all detent positions with the engine running to ensure the correct detent/transmission action, readjusting as necessary.

7 Overdrive band — adjustment

Refer to illustration 7.2

1   Clean all dirt from the front (overdrive) band adjusting screw area located on the left side of the transmission. Remove and discard the locknut.
2   Install a new locknut on the adjusting screw. Using tool T71P-

**PAWL POSITION FOR AUTOMATIC TRANSMISSION
MANUAL LINKAGE ADJUSTMENT**

6.3a Shift linkage adjustment details

6.3b The shifter pawl must be against the D (overdrive)
position during adjustment

77370-A or a torque wrench and socket as an equivalent, tighten the adjusting screw until the tool handle clicks **(see illustration)**. The tool is preset and breaks loose when the torque reaches 10 ft-lbs.
3   Back off the adjusting screw exactly two turns.
4   Hold the adjusting screw to keep it from turning and tighten the locknut.

8   Intermediate band — adjustment

Refer to illustration 8.3

1   Clean all dirt from the band adjusting screw area located on the left side of the transmission to the rear of the overdrive band screw (see Section 7). Remove and discard the locknut.

2   Install a new locknut on the adjusting screw.
3   Tighten the adjusting screw using tool T71P-77370-A which is a preset torque wrench that releases when the torque reaches 10 ft-lbs, or a torque wrench and socket as an equivalent **(see illustration)**.
4   Back off the adjusting screw exactly two turns.
5   Hold the adjusting screw to keep it from turning and tighten the locknut.

9   Extension housing oil seal — replacement

Refer to illustrations 9.3 and 9.7

1   Raise the vehicle and support it securely on jackstands.
2   Remove the driveshaft (Chapter 8). Scribe marks on the driveshaft

7.2   Adjustment of the overdrive band requires a torque wrench or a special preset torque tool (shown)

8.3   Intermediate band adjustment

9.3 Be very careful when prying out the extension seal so
that the sealing surface is not damaged

9.7 A punch and hammer can be used to tap the new
extension seal evenly into the bore. A large socket or
length of pipe of the proper diameter can also be used

and yoke and the rear axle companion flange to assure proper positioning of the driveshaft during assembly.
3   Remove the oil seal from the end of the extension housing with
a seal removing tool. If there is access, a thin blade screwdriver or chisel
may also be used to remove the seal (see illustration).
4   Before installing the new seal inspect the sealing surface of the
universal joint yoke for scoring. If scoring is found, replace the yoke.

5   Inspect the counterbore of the housing for burrs. Remove any burrs
with emery cloth or medium grit wet-and-dry sandpaper.
6   Coat the inside diameter of the seal with multi-purpose grease.
7   Install the new seal into the extension housing (see illustration).
8   The remainder of the installation is the reverse of the removal
procedures.

Chapter 8 Clutch and drivetrain

Contents

Specifications

Clutch
Slave cylinder pushrod travel . . . . 0.295 in

Torque specifications   Ft-lbs
Pressure plate-to-flywheel bolts . . . . 15 to 24
Clutch housing-to-engine bolts . . . . 28 to 38
Clutch housing-to-transmission nuts . . . . 30 to 40
Clutch master cylinder nuts . . . . 15 to 20
Clutch slave cylinder bolts . . . . 13 to 19

Driveshaft
Torque specifications   Ft-lbs
Universal joint strap nuts . . . . 8 to 15

Rear axle
Torque specifications   Ft-lbs
Differential cover bolts . . . . 15 to 20
Pinion shaft lock bolt . . . . 15 to 30
Brake backing plate/bearing retainer nuts (Dana model 30) . . . 25 to 35
Rear lower control arm-to-rear axle housing . . . . 100 to 129
Rear upper control arm-to-rear axle housing . . . . 100 to 145

1   General information

The information in this Chapter deals with the components from the rear of the engine to the rear wheels, except for the transmission, which is dealt with in the previous Chapter. For the purposes of this Chapter, these components are grouped into three categories; clutch, driveshaft and rear axle. Separate Sections within this Chapter offer general descriptions and checking procedures for each of these three groups.

As nearly all the procedures covered in this Chapter involve working under the vehicle, make sure it is firmly supported on sturdy jackstands or on a hoist where the vehicle can be easily raised and lowered.

2   Clutch — description and check

Refer to illustration 2.1

1   All models equipped with a manual transmission feature a single dry plate, diaphragm spring-type clutch (**see illustration**). The actuation is through a hydraulic system.

2   When the clutch pedal is depressed, hydraulic fluid (under pressure from the clutch master cylinder) flows into the slave cylinder. The slave cylinder is connected to the release bearing which is constantly in contact with the pressure plate diaphragm spring release fingers. The slave cylinder pushes the release bearing against the pressure plate release fingers, disengaging the clutch plate.

3   The hydraulic system locates the clutch pedal and provides clutch adjustment automatically, so no adjustment of the linkage or pedal is required.

4   Terminology can be a problem regarding the clutch components because common names have in some cases changed from that used by the manufacturer. For example, the driven plate is also called the clutch plate or disc, the clutch release bearing is sometimes called a throwout bearing, the slave cylinder is sometimes called the operating cylinder.

5   Other than to replace components with obvious damage, some preliminary checks should be performed to diagnose a clutch system failure.

   a) The first check should be of the fluid level in the clutch master cylinder (see Fluid level checks in Chapter 1). If the fluid level is low, add fluid as necessary and re-test. If the master cylinder runs dry, or if any of the hydraulic components are serviced, bleed the hydraulic system as described in Section 8.

   b) To check "clutch spin down time", run the engine at normal idle speed with the transmission in Neutral (clutch pedal up — engaged). Disengage the clutch (pedal down), wait nine seconds and shift the transmission into Reverse. No grinding noise should be heard. A grinding noise would indicate component failure in the pressure plate assembly or the clutch disc.

   c) To check for complete clutch release, run the engine (with the brake on to prevent movement) and hold the clutch pedal approximately 1/2-inch from the floor mat. Shift the transmission between 1st gear and Reverse several times. If the shift is not smooth, component failure is indicated.

   d) Visually inspect the clutch pedal bushing at the top of the clutch pedal to make sure there is no sticking or excessive wear.

3   Clutch components — removal, inspection and installation

Refer to illustrations 3.7, 3.12, 3.14 and 3.16

Warning: *Dust produced by clutch wear and deposited on clutch components contains asbestos, which is hazardous to your health. DO NOT blow it out with compressed air and DO NOT inhale it. DO NOT use gasoline or petroleum-based solvents to remove the dust. Brake system cleaner should be used to flush the dust into a drain pan. After the clutch components are wiped clean with a rag, dispose of the contaminated rags and cleaner in a covered container.*

Removal

1   Access to the clutch components is normally accomplished by removing the transmission, leaving the engine in the vehicle. If, of course, the engine is being removed for major overhaul, then the opportunity should always be taken to check the clutch for wear and replace worn components as necessary. The following procedures will assume that the engine will stay in place.

2   Disconnect the hydraulic line from the slave cylinder (see Section 6).

3   Referring to Chapter 7 Part A, remove the transmission from the vehicle. Support the engine while the transmission is out. Preferably, an engine hoist from above should be used. However, if a jack is used underneath the engine, make sure a piece of wood is used between the jack and oil pan to spread the load. **Caution:** *The pickup for the*

CLUTCH HOUSING, DISC AND PRESSURE PLATE
INSTALLATION-2.8L GASOLINE ENGINE

PILOT BEARING

CLUTCH DISC

CLUTCH PLATE
AND COVER

RELEASE
BEARING
AND HUB

CLUTCH
HOUSING

FLAT WASHER

BOLT

CLUTCH SLAVE
CYLINDER
ASSEMBLY

RETAINER
CLIP

COVER
PLATE

FLYWHEEL

BOLT

PART OF
TRANSMISSION

2.1   Exploded view of the clutch components

oil pump is very close to the bottom of the oil pan. If the pan is bent or distorted in any way, engine oil starvation could occur.

4 Remove the clutch housing-to engine bolts. Remove the housing. It may have to be gently pried off the alignment dowels with a screwdriver or pry bar.

5 The slave cylinder and release bearing can remain attached to the housing for the time being.

6 To support the clutch disc during removal, install a clutch alignment tool through the middle of the clutch.

3.7 After removal of the transmission, this will be the view of the clutch components. Before removing the pressure plate (1), mark its relationship to the flywheel (2) so it can be reinstalled in the same position

7 Carefully inspect the flywheel and pressure plate for indexing marks. These can be an X, an O, or a white-painted letter. If these cannot be found, scribe marks yourself so that the pressure plate and the flywheel will be in the same alignment upon installation (**see illustration**).

8 Turning each bolt only one turn at a time, slowly loosen the pressure plate-to-flywheel bolts. Work in a diagonal pattern, again, loosening each bolt a little at a time until all spring pressure is relieved. Then grasp the pressure plate firmly and completely remove the bolts, followed by the pressure plate and clutch disc.

Inspection

9 Ordinarily, when a problem occurs in the clutch, it can be attributed to wear of the clutch driven plate assembly (clutch disc). However, all components should be inspected at this time.

10 Inspect the flywheel for cracks, heat checking, grooves or other signs of obvious defects. If the imperfections are slight, a machine shop can machine the surface flat and smooth, which is highly recommended regardless of the surface appearance. Refer to Chapter 2 for the flywheel removal and installation procedure.

11 Inspect the pilot bearing as outlined in Section 4.

12 Inspect the facing on the clutch disc. There should be at least 1/16-inch of lining above the rivet heads. Check for loose rivets, distortion, cracks, broken springs and any other obvious damage (**see illustration**). As mentioned above, ordinarily the disc is replaced as a matter of course, so if in doubt about the quality, replace it with a new one.

13 Check the release bearing for roughness or binding. If bearing operation is anything but smooth, replace it (see Section 7).

14 Check the flatness of the pressure plate with a straightedge. Look for signs of overheating, cracks, deep grooves and ridges. The inner end of the diaphragm spring fingers should not show any signs of uneven wear. Replace the pressure plate with a new one if its condition is in doubt (**see illustration**).

Installation

15 Before installation, carefully wipe clean the flywheel and pressure plate machined surfaces. It is important that no oil or grease is on these

3.12 The clutch disc

1 Lining — this will wear down in use
2 Markings — ''Flywheel side'' or similar
3 Rivets — these secure the

lining and will damage the flywheel or pressure plate if allowed to contact the surfaces

3.14 Replace the pressure plate if any of these conditions are noted

3.16   Use a clutch alignment tool to hold the clutch disc in place while installing the pressure plate and also center the disc when tightening the bolts. This particular tool, made of plastic, is available at most auto parts stores and isn't very expensive

surfaces or the facing of the clutch disc. Handle these parts only with clean hands.

16   Position the clutch disc and pressure plate against the flywheel with the clutch disc held in place with a clutch alignment tool (see illustration). Make sure the disc is installed properly (most replacement discs will be marked ''flywheel side'' or similar. If not marked, install the disc with the damper springs toward the transmission).

17   Tighten the pressure plate-to-flywheel bolts only finger tight, working around the pressure plate.

18   Center the clutch disc by inserting the alignment tool through the splined hub and into the pilot bearing in the flywheel, if not already done. Tighten the pressure plate-to-flywheel bolts a little at a time, working in a criss-cross pattern to prevent distorting the cover. After all of the bolts are snug, tighten them to the specified torque. Remove the alignment tool.

19   Install the transmission and all components removed previously, tightening all fasteners to the specified torque.

4   Pilot bearing — inspection and replacement

Refer to illustrations 4.1, 4.5 and 4.9

1   The clutch pilot bearing is a needle roller type bearing which is pressed into the rear of the crankshaft (see illustration). It is pregreased at the factory and does not require additional lubrication. Its primary purpose is to support the front of the transmission input shaft. The pilot bearing should be inspected whenever the clutch components are removed from the engine. Due to its inaccessibility, if you are in doubt as to its condition, replace it with a new one. **Note:** *If the engine has been removed from the vehicle, disregard the following steps which do not apply.*

4.1   The pilot bearing incorporates an O-ring seal which cannot be replaced separately. If there is any evidence that the seal has been leaking, or if the bearing is dry, replace it

4.5   One method of removing the pilot bearing is with the use of an internal puller connected to a slide hammer

removed from the engine. Due to its inaccessibility, if you are in doubt as to its condition, replace it with a new one. **Note:** *If the engine has been removed from the vehicle, disregard the following steps which do not apply.*

2   Remove the transmission (refer to Chapter 7 Part A)

3   Remove the clutch components (Section 3).

4   Inspect for any excessive wear, scoring, lack of grease, dryness or obvious damage. If any of these conditions are noted, the bearing should be replaced. A flashlight will be helpful to direct light into the recess.

5   Removal can be accomplished with a special puller and slide hammer (see illustration), but an alternative method also works very well.

6   Find a solid steel bar which is slightly smaller in diameter than the bearing. Alternatives to a solid bar would be a wood dowel or a socket with a bolt fixed in place to make it solid.

7   Check the bar for fit — it should just slip into the bearing with very little clearance.

8   Pack the bearing and the area behind it (in the crankshaft recess) with heavy grease. Pack it tightly to eliminate as much air as possible.

9   Insert the bar into the bearing bore and strike the bar sharply with a hammer which will force the grease to the backside of the bearing and push it out (see illustration). Remove the bearing and clean all grease from the crankshaft recess.

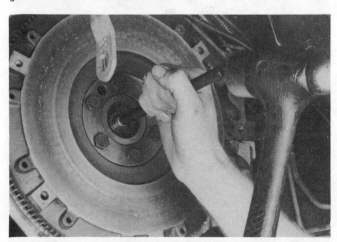

4.9   By packing the opening behind the bearing with grease, a tight fitting rod will then force the grease against the backside of the bearing when hit with a hammer, pushing it out of the bore

10 To install the new bearing, lightly lubricate the outside surface with lithium-based grease, then drive it into the recess with a soft-face hammer.

11 Install the clutch components, transmission and all other components removed previously, tightening all fasteners properly.

5   Clutch master cylinder — removal, overhaul and installation

Refer to illustration 5.4

Note: *Before beginning this procedure, contact local parts stores or dealers concerning the purchase of a rebuild kit or a new master cylinder. Availability and cost of the necessary parts may dictate whether the cylinder is rebuilt or replaced with a new one. If it is decided to rebuild the cylinder, inspect the inside bore as described in Step 7 before purchasing parts.*

Removal

1   Disconnect the cable from the negative battery terminal.

2   Under the dashboard, disconnect the pushrod from the top of the clutch pedal. It is held in place with a retainer bushing and must be pried off with a screwdriver.

3   Disconnect the hydraulic line at the clutch slave cylinder (see Section 6) then free the hydraulic line from the clips on the underbody siderail. Have rags handy as some fluid will be lost as the line is removed. **Caution:** *Do not allow brake fluid to come into contact with paint as it will damage the finish.*

4   Remove the two bolts which secure the master cylinder to the engine firewall (**see illustration**).

5   Slide the clutch fluid reservoir off its mounting slots and remove the cylinder, line and reservoir from the vehicle, again being careful not to spill any fluid.

Overhaul

6   It is not necessary to disconnect the fluid reservoir hose from the master cylinder unless the cylinder is being replaced.

7   Disassemble the cylinder and inspect the bore of the master cylinder for deep scratches, scoring, pitting or ridges. The surface must be smooth to the touch. If the bore is not perfectly smooth, the master

cylinder must be replaced with a new or factory rebuilt unit.

8   If you elect to rebuild the cylinder, follow the instructions included with the rebuild kit and be sure to install all of the parts that are supplied.

9   Before reassembly, lubricate the inside bore of the cylinder and the seals with plenty of fresh brake fluid (DOT 3).

Installation

10 Guide the master cylinder into its hole in the firewall, install the two mounting bolts and tighten them to the specified torque. Position the reservoir in its mounting slots.

11 Connect the hydraulic line to the slave cylinder, then secure the hydraulic line to the routing clips.

12 Inside the vehicle, connect the pushrod to the clutch pedal and install the retainer bushing.

13 Fill the clutch master cylinder reservoir with brake fluid conforming to DOT 3 specifications and bleed the clutch system as outlined in Section 8.

14 Reconnect the negative battery cable.

6   Clutch slave cylinder — removal, overhaul and installation

Refer to illustrations 6.3a, 6.3b, 6.5 and 6.6

Warning: *Dust produced by clutch wear and deposited on clutch components may contain asbestos, which is hazardous to your health. DO NOT blow it out with compressed air and DO NOT inhale any of it. DO NOT use gasoline or petroleum-based solvents to remove the dust. Brake system cleaner should be used to flush the dust into a drain pan. After the clutch components are wiped clean with a rag, dispose of the contaminated rags and cleaner in a covered container.*

Note: *Before beginning this procedure, contact local parts stores or dealers concerning the purchase of a rebuild kit or a new slave cylinder. Availability and cost of the necessary parts may dictate whether the cylinder is rebuilt or relaced with a new one. If it is decided to rebuild the cylinder, inspect the bore of the cylinder before purchasing parts.*

Removal

1   Disconnect the cable from the negative battery terminal.

2   Raise the vehicle and support it securely on jackstands.

5.4 Clutch master cylinder, slave cylinder and associated components

CLUTCH SLAVE
CYLINDER ASSEMBLY

RETAINER
CLIP

6.3a To disconnect the hydraulic line from the clutch
slave cylinder on 1986 and 1987 vehicles, simply pull out
the retainer clip and separate the line from the cylinder

REMOVAL

DISCONNECT TOOL
T88T-70522-A

6.3b To disconnect the hydraulic line from the slave
cylinder on 1988 vehicles, use the tool shown (or an
equivalent substitute) to push the white plastic collar back
while pulling on the line

3   Disconnect the hydraulic line at the slave cylinder. On 1986 and
1987 models, remove the retainer clip from the hydraulic fitting and
slide the line from the slave cylinder (see illustration). On 1988 models,
slide the white plastic sleeve toward the slave cylinder while lightly
pulling on the hydraulic line (see illustration). Have a small can or some
rags handy to catch the spilling fluid.
4   Remove the transmission as described in Chapter 7 Part A.
5   On 1986 and 1987 models, remove the four nuts that retain the
clutch housing to the transmission. Separate the two and remove the
slave cylinder from the clutch housing (see illustration).
6   On 1988 models, remove the two slave cylinder bolts and pull the
cylinder off of the transmission input shaft (see illustration).
7   Separate the release bearing from the slave cylinder as described
in Section 7.

Overhaul

8   Remove the piston from the slave cylinder body, drain the fluid
and inspect the bore for scratches, scoring, ridges or pitting. If any
imperfections are found, the slave cylinder must be replaced.

9   If it is decided to rebuild the cylinder, follow the instructions included in the rebuild kit and be sure to install all of the parts that are
supplied.
10 Before reassembly, lubricate the piston, cylinder and seals with
plenty of clean brake fluid (DOT 3).

Installation

11 Install the release bearing to the slave cylinder (Section 7).
12 On 1986 and 1987 models, place the slave cylinder in the clutch
housing and assemble the housing to the transmission, tightening the
nuts to the specified torque.
13 On 1988 models, slide the cylinder over the transmission input
shaft and install the two bolts, tightening them to the specified torque.
14 Install the transmission.
15 Connect the hydraulic line to the slave cylinder, fill the fluid reservoir with brake fluid conforming to DOT 3 specifications and bleed the
clutch system as outlined in Section 8.
16 Reconnect the negative battery cable.

RELEASE
BEARING

CLUTCH
HOUSING

SLAVE
CYLINDER

6.5 On 1986 and 1987 vehicles the slave cylinder is
sandwiched between the clutch housing and the
transmission. Remove the four nuts (arrows) and carefully
pry the housing off

TRANSMISSION
BELL HOUSING

TRANSMISSION
INPUT SHAFT

HYDRAULIC
BLEED SCREW

HYDRAULIC
CLUTCH
LINE
COUPLING

FRONT
OF
VEHICLE

CONCENTRIC
SLAVE
CYLINDER

BOLT
(2 REQ'D)

6.6 On 1988 models, remove the two bolts and slide the
assembly from the input shaft

7 Clutch release bearing — removal, inspection and installation

Refer to illustrations 7.2 and 7.3

Warning: *Dust produced by clutch wear and deposited on clutch components may contain asbestos, which is hazardous to your health. DO NOT blow it out with compressed air and DO NOT inhale any of it. DO NOT use gasoline or petroleum-based solvents to remove the dust. Brake system cleaner should be used to flush the dust into a drain pan. After the clutch components are wiped clean with a rag, dispose of the contaminated rags and cleaner in a covered container.*

Removal

1   Remove the transmission following the procedure described in Chapter 7 Part A.
2   On 1986 and 1987 vehicles, dislodge the bearing from the bearing carrier **(see illustration)** by bending back the plastic tabs with a small screwdriver.
3   On 1988 vehicles, turn the bearing/carrier assembly until resistance is felt, then turn it slightly further which will disengage the carrier from the slave cylinder **(see illustration)**.

RELEASE
BEARING

BEARING
CARRIER

7.2   Pry back the four plastic tabs on the carrier and remove the bearing

SLAVE
CYLINDER   PRELOAD
SPRING

REMOVAL

FRONT OF VEHICLE

RELEASE BEARING/
CARRIER ASSEMBLY

TRANSMISSION
INPUT SHAFT

TAB

INSTALLATION

7.3   To remove the release bearing/carrier on 1988 models, twist the bearing until it "unlocks". To install it, just push it on until the tab on the slave cylinder engages with the carrier

Inspection

4   Inspect the bearing for cracks, wear and other damage. Hold the center of the bearing and turn the outer race while applying pressure to it. If the bearing doesn't turn smoothly or if it is noisy, replace it with a new one. It is a good idea to replace the bearing whenever a clutch job is performed, to decrease the possibility of bearing failure in the future, although Ford states that this is not absolutely necessary.
5   If it is decided to re-use the old release bearing, clean the external surfaces and inside diameter with a solvent-moistened rag. Do not immerse the bearing in solvent, as it is packed with grease from the factory (sealed for life) and to do so would ruin it.

Installation

6   Fill the groove in the inside diameter of the bearing with lithium based grease. Also apply a thin coat of this grease to the entire inner diameter.
7   The remainder of the assembly procedure is the reverse of removal. Be sure to bleed the clutch hydraulic system as described in Section 8.

8   Clutch hydraulic system — bleeding

Refer to illustration 8.4

1   The hydraulic system should be bled of all air whenever any part of the system has been removed or if the fluid level has been allowed to fall so low that air has been drawn into the master cylinder. The procedure is very similar to bleeding a brake system.
2   Fill the master cylinder with new brake fluid conforming to DOT 3 specifications. **Caution:** *Do not re-use any of the fluid coming from the system during the bleeding operation or use fluid which has been inside an open container for an extended period of time.*
3   Raise the vehicle and place it securely on jackstands to gain access to the slave cylinder bleeder screw, which is located next to the hydraulic line inlet connection.
4   Remove the dust cap (if equipped) which fits over the bleed screw. Place a box end wrench over the bleed screw and then push a length of plastic hose over the screw **(see illustration)**. Place the other end of the hose into a clear container with about two inches of brake fluid. The hose end must be in the fluid at the bottom of the container.

HOSE   BOX END
WRENCH   BLEED
SCREW

8.4   The slave cylinder bleeder screw opening is located on the left side of the transmission. Place the other end of the tube into a container of clean brake fluid. Any air will show up as bubbles in the tube or container

5   Have an assistant depress the clutch pedal and hold it. Open the bleeder valve on the slave cylinder, allowing fluid to flow through the hose. Close the bleeder valve when your assistant signals that the clutch pedal is at the bottom of its travel. Once closed, have your assistant release the pedal.
6   Continue this process until all air is evacuated from the system, indicated by a full, solid stream of fluid being ejected from the bleeder valve each time and no air bubbles in the hose or container. Keep a close watch on the fluid level inside the master cylinder; if the level drops too low, air will be sucked back into the system and the process will have to be started all over again.

9.4   Clutch pedal mounting details

9   Clutch pedal — removal and installation

Refer to illustration 9.4

1   Disconnect the cable from the negative battery terminal.
2   Disconnect the clutch master cylinder pushrod from the pedal by prying the retainer bushing off with a screwdriver.
3   Disconnect and remove the starter/clutch interlock switch (see Section 10).
4   Remove the pedal pivot pin retainer clip and slide the pedal to the left to remove it (**see illustration**). Insert a long narrow screwdriver or rod through the opposite side of the bracket to hold the brake pedal in place while the clutch pedal is removed.
5   Wipe clean all parts; however, do not use cleaning solvents on the bushings. Replace all worn parts with new ones and lightly lubricate the bushings with engine oil.
6   Installation is the reverse of removal. Check that the starter/clutch interlock switch allows the vehicle to be started only with the clutch pedal fully depressed.

10   Starter/clutch interlock switch — removal and installation

Refer to illustrations 10.2 and 10.7

1   Detach the wire harness connector from the interlock switch.
2   Remove the interlock switch-to-bracket screw and pry the end of the rod off of the clutch pedal pin (**see illustration**).
3   Position the adjuster clip approximately 1-inch from the end of the rod.
4   Install the end of the rod onto the clutch pedal pin.
5   With the clutch pedal all the way up, swing the switch down into place. Install the mounting screw and tighten it securely.
6   Push the clutch pedal to the floor which automatically adjusts the switch.
7   Confirm that the engine starts only when the clutch pedal is depressed to the floor. If it doesn't, remove the adjusting clip from the rod and position it closer to the switch (**see illustration**). Push the pedal to the floor and check the switch operation again. If the engine still doesn't crank over, or cranks over when the pedal is in the released position, replace the switch with a new one.

11   Driveshaft and universal joints — description and check

1   The driveshaft (or prop shaft as it is often called) is a tube running between the transmission and the rear end. Universal joints are located

at either end of the driveshaft and permit power to be transmitted to the rear wheels at varying angles.
2   The driveshaft features a splined yoke at the front, which slips into the rear extension of the transmission. This arrangement allows the driveshaft to slide back and forth within the transmission as the vehicle is in operation. An oil seal is used to prevent leakage of fluid at this point and to keep dirt and contaminants from entering the transmission. If leakage is evident at the front of the driveshaft, replace this oil seal referring to the procedures in Chapter 7 Part A (manual transmission) or Chapter 7 Part B (automatic transmission).
3   The driveshaft assembly requires very little service. The universal joints are lubricated for life and require replacement should a fault develop. The driveshaft must be removed from the vehicle for this procedure.
4   Since the driveshaft is a balanced unit, it is important that no undercoating, mud, etc. be allowed to stay on it. When the vehicle is raised for service it is a good idea to clean the driveshaft and inspect for any obvious damage. Also check that the small weights used to originally balance the driveshaft are in place and securely attached. Whenever the driveshaft is removed it is important that it be reinstalled in the same relative position to preserve this balance.
5   Problems with the driveshaft are usually indicated by a noise or vibration while driving the vehicle. A road test should verify if the problem is the driveshaft or another vehicle component:
a)   On an open road, free of traffic, drive the vehicle and note the engine speed (rpm — tachometer) at which the problem is most evident.

10.2   Location of the starter/clutch interlock switch

10.7   To readjust the switch, open the two halves of the clip and lock it to the rod closer to the shaft. Push the pedal to the floor once to adjust it

b) With this noted, drive the vehicle again, this time manually keeping the transmission in 1st, then 2nd, then 3rd gear ranges and running the engine up to the engine speed noted.

c) If the noise or vibration occurs at the same engine speed regardless of which gear the transmission is in, the driveshaft is not at fault because the speed of the driveshaft varies in each gear.

d) If the noise or vibration decreased or was eliminated, visually inspect the driveshaft for damage, material on the shaft which would effect balance, missing weights or damaged universal joints. Another possibility for this condition would be tires which are out of balance.

6   To check for worn universal joints:

a) On an open road, free of traffic, drive the vehicle slowly until the transmission is in high gear. Let off on the accelerator, allowing the vehicle to coast, then accelerate. A clunking or knocking noise will indicate worn universal joints.

b) Drive the vehicle at a speed of about 10 to 15 mph and then place the transmission in Neutral, allowing the vehicle to coast. Listen for abnormal driveline noises.

c) Raise the vehicle and support it securely on jackstands. With the transmission in Neutral, manually turn the driveshaft, observing the universal joints for excessive play.

12   Driveshaft — removal and installation

Refer to illustration 12.3

Removal

1   Disconnect the cable from the negative terminal of the battery.
2   Block the front tires to prevent movement and raise the vehicle. Support it securely on jackstands. Place the transmission in Neutral with the parking brake off.
3   Using white paint or a hammer and punch, place marks on the driveshaft and the differential pinion flange in line with each other (**see illustration**). This is to make sure the driveshaft is reinstalled in the same position to preserve the balance of the system.
4   Remove the rear universal joint strap bolts and the straps. Turn the driveshaft (or tires) as necessary to bring the bolts into the most accessible position.
5   Tape the bearing caps to the spider to prevent the caps from coming off during removal.
6   Lower the rear of the driveshaft and then slide the front from the transmission.
7   To prevent loss of fluid and protect against contamination while the driveshaft is out, wrap a plastic bag over the transmission housing and hold it in place with a rubber band.

12.3   Before removing the driveshaft, mark the relationship of the shaft to the differential pinion yoke. A screwdriver inserted through the joint will keep it from turning while the nuts are loosened

Installation

8   Remove the plastic bag on the transmission and wipe clean the area. Inspect the oil seal carefully. Procedures for replacement of this seal can be found in Chapter 7 Part B.
9   Slide the front of the driveshaft into the transmission.
10   Raise the rear of the driveshaft into position, checking to be sure that the marks are in perfect alignment. If not, turn the rear wheels to match the pinion flange and the driveshaft.
11   Remove the tape securing the bearing caps and install the straps and bolts. Tighten to the proper torque specification.

13   Universal joints — replacement

Refer to illustrations 13.2a, 13.2b, 13.4 and 13.9

Note: *A press or large vise will be required for this procedure. It may be advisable to take the driveshaft to a local dealer or machine shop where the universal joints can be replaced for you, normally at a reasonable charge.*

1   Remove the driveshaft as discussed in the previous Section.
2   Using small pliers, remove the snap-rings from the spider (**see illustrations**).

13.2a   Remove the snap-rings with a pair of pliers

13.2b   Exploded view of the universal joint components

13.4 To press the universal joint out of the driveshaft, set it up in a vise as shown. The small socket (at left) will push the joint and bearing cap into the large socket (at right)

13.9 If the snap-ring will not seat in its groove, strike the yoke with a brass hammer. This will relieve the tension that has set up in the yoke, and slightly spring the yoke ears. This should also be done if the joint feels tight when assembled

3   Supporting the driveshaft, place it in position on either an arbor press or on a workbench equipped with a vise. **Caution:** *Never clamp the driveshaft tube or yoke in the jaws of a vise.*
4   Place a piece of pipe (about 1-1/4 inch inside diameter) or a socket with the same inside diameter over one of the bearing caps. Position a socket which is of slightly smaller diameter than the cap on the opposite bearing cap (**see illustration**) and use the vise or press to force the cap out (inside the pipe or large socket), stopping just before it comes completely out of the yoke. Use the vise or large pliers to work the cap the rest of the way out.
5   Transfer the sockets to the other side and press the opposite bearing cap out in the same manner.
6   Pack the new universal joint bearings with grease. Ordinarily, specific instructions for lubrication will be included with the universal joint servicing kit and should be followed carefully.
7   Position the spider in the yoke and partially install one bearing cap into the yoke.
8   Start the spider into the bearing cap and then partially install the other cap. Align the spider and press the bearing caps into position, being careful not to damage the dust seals.
9   Install the snap-rings. If difficulty is encountered in seating the snap rings, strike the driveshaft yoke sharply with a hammer. This will spring the yoke ears slightly and allow the snap ring groove to move into position (**see illustration**).
10 Follow the same procedures to replace the rear universal joint, noting that only one-half of the spider needs to be pressed out, since the other two ends are held to the pinion flange with straps and bolts.
11 Install the driveshaft and all components previously removed.

14   Rear axle — description and check

1   There are three types of rear axles available on the vehicles covered by this manual — the Ford 7.5 inch ring gear, the Dana Model 30, or as an option, a limited-slip version of the Ford 7.5 inch rear axle. This rear end, called the Traction-Lok Limited Slip differential, incorporates two sets of multi-disc clutches to control differential action.
2   Information regarding the rear axle can be found on the Axle Identification Tag, which is located under the differential cover-to-carrier bolt in the 2 o'clock position.
3   Many times a fault is suspected in the rear axle area when, in fact, the problem lies elsewhere. For this reason, a thorough check should be performed before assuming a rear axle problem.
4   The following noises are those commonly associated with rear axle diagnosis procedures:
   a) Road noise is often mistaken for mechanical faults. Driving the vehicle on different surfaces will allow you to determine whether the road surface is the cause of the noise. Road noise will remain the same if the vehicle is under power or coasting.
   b) Tire noise is sometimes mistaken for mechanical problems. Tires which are worn or low on pressure are particularly susceptible

to emitting vibrations and noises. Tire noise will remain about the same during varying driving situations, where rear axle noise will change during coasting, acceleration, etc.
   c) Engine and transmission noise can be deceiving because it will travel along the driveline. To isolate engine and transmission noises, make a note of the engine speed at which the noise is most pronounced. Stop the vehicle and place the transmission in Neutral and run the engine to the same speed. If the noise is the same, the rear axle is not at fault.
5   Overhaul and general repair of the rear axle components is beyond the scope of the home mechanic due to the many special tools and critical measurements required for the many parts to operate properly. Thus, the procedures listed here will involve seal replacements to stop oil leakage, axle and bearing replacement and removal of the entire unit for repair or replacement.

15   Axleshaft — removal and installation

Refer to illustrations 15.3a, 15.3b, 15.4, 15.5, 15.9, and 15.10
1   Raise the rear of the vehicle, support it securely and remove the wheel and brake drum (refer to Chapter 9).

Ford 7.5 Inch rear end

2   Unscrew and remove the cover from the differential carrier and allow the oil to drain into a container.
3   Unscrew and remove the lock bolt from the differential pinion shaft. Slide the notched end of the pinion shaft out of the differential case as far as it will go (**see illustrations**).
4   Push the outer (flanged) end of the axleshaft in and remove the C-ring from the inner end of the shaft (**see illustration**).
5   Withdraw the axleshaft, taking care not to damage the oil seal in the end of the axle housing as the splined end of the axleshaft passes through it (**see illustration**).
6   Installation is the reverse of removal. Tighten the lock bolt to the specified torque.
7   Refer to Chapter 1 for the proper cover installation procedure.
8   Refill the axle with the correct quantity and grade of lubricant (Chapter 1).

Dana Model 30 rear end

9   Remove the four brake backing plate/bearing retainer nuts, working through the hole in the axle flange (**see illustration**). These nuts must be replaced with new ones upon reassembly.
10 Attach a slide hammer and axleshaft puller adapter to the axle flange and remove the axleshaft from the housing (**see illustration**).
11 Installation is the reverse of the removal procedure. Be sure to lubricate the bearing with gear lubricant, install new backing plate/bearing retainer nuts and tighten them to the specified torque.

15.3a   Use a large screwdriver placed between the rear axle case and a ring gear bolt to keep the differential case from turning when removing the pinion shaft lock bolt

15.3b   Rotate the differential case 180° and slide the pinion shaft out of the case until the stepped part of the shaft contacts the ring gear

15.4   Push in on the axle flange and remove the C-lock from the inner end of the axleshaft

15.5   Pull the axle out of the housing, supporting it with one hand to prevent damage to the seal

15.9   Access to the four bearing retainer nuts is through the hole in the axle flange

15.10   A slide hammer and axle flange adapter will be necessary to remove the axle/bearing assembly from the housing

16.2   If a seal remover tool isn't available, a pry bar or even the end of the axle can be used to pop the seal out of its bore

16.3   A large socket or a piece of pipe (as shown here) can be used to install the seal. The diameter of the tool should be just slightly smaller than the outside diameter of the seal

16   Axleshaft oil seal — replacement

Refer to illustrations 16.2 and 16.3

1   Remove the axleshaft as described in the preceding Section.

Ford 7.5 Inch rear end

2   Pry out the old oil seal from the end of the axle housing, using a large screwdriver or the inner end of the axleshaft itself as a lever (**see illustration**).
3   Using a large socket or section of pipe as a seal driver (**see illustration**), tap the seal into position so that the lips are facing in and the metal face is visible from the end of the axle husing. When correctly installed, the face of the oil seal should be flush with the end of the axle housing. Lubricate the lips of the seal with gear oil.
4   Installation of the axleshaft is described in the preceding Section.

Dana Model 30 rear end

5   The axleshaft oil seal/bearing/retainer are pressed onto the axleshaft and require special tools and a hydraulic press to replace them. For service regarding these components, take the axleshaft to an automotive machine shop.

17   Axleshaft bearing — replacement

Refer to illustrations 17.2 and 17.4

Ford 7.5 Inch rear end

1   Remove the axleshaft (refer to Section 15) and the oil seal (refer to Section 16).
2   A bearing puller will be required or a tool which will engage behind the bearing will have to be fabricated (**see illustration**).
3   Attach a slide hammer and pull the bearing from the axle housing.
4   Clean out the bearing recess and drive in the new bearing using a properly sized bearing driver (**see illustration**).
5   Discard the old oil seal and install a new one (Section 16), then install the axleshaft.

Dana Model 30 rear end

6   Remove the axleshaft as descsribed in Section 15. The axleshaft bearing, oil seal and retainer are pressed onto the axleshaft and require special tools and a hydraulic press to replace them. For service regarding these procedures, take the axleshaft to an automotive machine shop.

17.2   To remove the axle bearing, insert a bearing removal tool attached to a slide hammer through the center of the bearing, pull the tool up against the bearing and use the slide hammer to yank the bearing from the axle housing

17.4   A correctly-sized bearing driver must be used to drive the bearing into the housing

18.5   Disconnect the rear brake hose from the hydraulic line at the frame bracket. Use a backup wrench on the fitting of the hose to prevent twisting the line

18.8   Unbolt the rear lower control arms from the axle housing

18   Rear axle assembly — removal and installation

Refer to illustrations 18.5, 18.8, 18.9 and 18.10

Removal

1   Loosen the rear wheel lug nuts, raise the rear of the vehicle and support it securely on jackstands positioned under the frame. Remove the wheels.
2   Support the rear axle assembly with a floor jack placed under the differential.
3   Disconnect the two rear parking brake cables from the equalizer and push the cable casings through the crossmember (see Chapter 9).
4   Remove the driveshaft following the procedure described in Section 12.
5   Disconnect the rear brake hose from the hydraulic line at the frame **(see illustration)**. Plug the hydraulic line and the flexible hose to prevent excessive fluid loss and contamination.
6   Remove the lower mounting bolts from the shock absorbers.
7   Remove the coil springs (see Chapter 10).
8   Unbolt the lower control arms from the rear axle housing **(see illustration)**.
9   Remove the upper control arm-to-rear axle bolt and separate the control arm from the axle housing **(see illustration)**.
10   Scribe a line on the upper control arm bushing marking the position of the cam adjuster in the bushing **(see illustration)**.
11   Slowly lower the axle assembly from the vehicle.

18.9   Unbolt the rear upper control arm from the axle housing

18.10   Mark the position of the cam adjuster in the bushing

UPPER CONTROL ARM

CAM ADJUSTER

SCRIBE MARK ON CAM ADJUSTER AND BUSHING

BUSHING

Installation

12 Raise the axle into position and fit the upper control arm over the bushing, checking to be sure that the cam adjuster is still in alignment. Install the bolt and nut, tightening them snugly. Do not fully tighten the nut at this time.

13 Connect the lower control arms to the axle housing and install the bolts. Do not tighten these bolts to the specified torque at this time.

14 Install the coil springs (Chapter 10).

15 Raise the axle far enough to allow the shock absorber lower mounting bolts to be installed. Again, don't fully tighten these bolts yet.

16 Connect the brake hose to the hydraulic line on the frame and tighten the fitting securely. Make sure the hose isn't kinked when in the installed position.

17 Install the wheels.

18 Lower the vehicle and tighten the lug nuts to the specified torque. Jounce the rear of the vehicle a couple of times, allowing the suspension to come to rest at normal ride height. Slide under the vehicle and tighten the upper control arm-to-axle housing bolt nut, the lower control arm-to-axle housing mounting bolt nuts and the shock absorber lower mounting bolt nuts to the specified torque values.

19 Reconnect the parking brake cables.

20 Bleed the brakes as described in Chapter 9.

Chapter 9   Brakes

Contents

Specifications

General
Brake fluid type . . . .   See Chapter 1

Disc brakes
Disc minimum thickness . . . .   Stamped on inside hub surface of disc
Disc runout limit . . . .   0.003 in
Minimum brake pad thickness . . . .   See Chapter 1

Drum brakes
Drum maximum diameter . . . .   Cast into the brake drum
Minimum brake lining thickness . . . .   See Chapter 1

Torque specifications

	Ft-lbs
Master cylinder-to-booster nuts	13 to 25
Power brake booster nuts	13 to 25
Brake backing plate-to-axle housing	25 to 35
Wheel cylinder bolts	9 to 13

---

1   General information

Description

All models are equipped with disc type front and drum type rear brakes which are hydraulically operated and vacuum assisted.

The front brakes feature a single piston, floating caliper design. The rear drum brakes are single anchor type with a single two piston wheel cylinder.

The front disc brakes automatically compensate for pad wear during usage. The rear drum brakes also feature automatic adjustment.

Front brake pads tend to wear at a faster rate than rear brake shoes. Consequently, it's important to inspect the brake pads frequently to make sure they haven't worn to the point where the disc itself is scored or damaged.

All models are equipped with a cable actuated parking brake which operates the rear brakes.

The hydraulic system is a dual line type with a dual master cylinder and separate systems for the front and rear brakes. In the event of brake line or seal failure, half the brake system will still operate. On 1986 models, the master cylinder also incorporates two pressure control valves that reduce the pressure to the rear brakes in order to limit rear wheel lockup during hard braking. On 1987 and 1988 vehicles, a remote combination valve is used which performs the same function. This valve also allows full pressure to the rear brakes if the front system pressure is greatly reduced.

Precautions

Use only DOT 3 brake fluid.

The brake pads and linings may contain asbestos fibers, which are hazardous to your health if inhaled. When working on brake system components, carefully clean all parts with denatured alcohol or brake cleaner. Don't allow the fine dust to become airborne.

Safety should be paramount when working on brake system components. Don't use parts or fasteners that aren't in perfect condition and be sure that all clearances and torque specifications are adhered to. If you're at all unsure about a certain procedure, seek professional advice. When finished working on the brakes, test them carefully under controlled conditions before driving the vehicle in traffic. If a problem is suspected in the brake system, don't drive the vehicle until the fault is corrected.

2 Disc brake pads — replacement

Refer to illustrations 2.4a through 2.4m

Warning: *Disc brake pads must be replaced on both front wheels at the same time — never replace the pads on only one wheel. Also, the dust created by the brake system may contain asbestos, which is harm-* ful to your health. Never blow it out with compressed air and don't inhale any of it. An approved filtering mask should be worn when working on the brakes. Do not, under any circumstances, use petroleum-based solvents to clean brake parts. Use brake cleaner or denatured alcohol only! When servicing the disc brakes, use only high quality, nationally recognized brand name pads.

1   Remove about two-thirds of the fluid from the master cylinder reservoir.

2   Loosen the wheel lug nuts, raise the vehicle and support it securely on jackstands. Remove the front wheels.

3   Check the brake disc carefully as outlined in Section 4. If machining is necessary, follow the procedure in Section 4 to remove the disc.

4   Follow the accompanying photos, beginning with illustration 2.4a, for the actual pad replacement procedure. Be sure to stay in order and read the information in the caption under each illustration.

5   Once the new pads are in place and the caliper pins have been installed, install the wheels and lower the vehicle to the ground. **Note:** *If the brake hose was disconnected from the caliper for any reason, the brake system must be bled as described in Section 9.*

6   Fill the master cylinder reservoir with new brake fluid and slowly pump the brakes a few times to seat the pads against the rotor.

7   Check the fluid level in the master cylinder reservoir(s) one more time and then road test the vehicle carefully before driving it in traffic.

2.4a   Using a large C-clamp, push the piston back into the caliper bore just enough to allow the caliper to easily slide off the rotor

2.4b   Squeeze the end of the lower caliper pin with a pair of pliers and knock the pin into the groove as far as possible, . . .

2.4c   . . . then use a hammer and punch to drive the pin out completely. Proceed to remove the upper caliper pin in the same manner

2.4d   Slide the caliper off the brake disc

2.4e   Push the outer pad towards the piston to dislodge the torque buttons (A), then slide the pad out of the caliper

2.4f   Set the caliper on top of the upper control arm in such a way that it won't fall off. DO NOT let it hang by the brake hose

2.4g   Using a screwdriver engaged behind the anti-rattle spring, pry the lower end of the inner pad out of the spindle flank

2.4h   Install a new anti-rattle clip on the bottom of the inner brake pad

2.4i   Place the lower end of the inner pad into its slot on the spindle then push the top of the pad into position against the brake disc

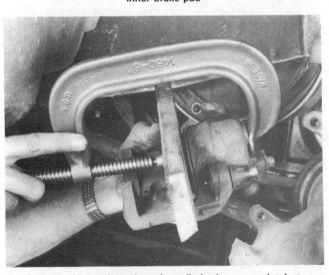

2.4j   Push the piston into the cylinder bore completely to provide room for the new pads — use a block of wood and a C-clamp, but don't use excessive force or damage to the plastic piston will result

2.4k   Push the outer pad into position on the caliper ears,
making sure the torque buttons seat fully into the
retention notches

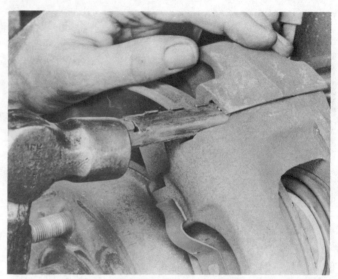

2.4l   Place the caliper and outer pad assembly over the
disc and inner pad, then drive the caliper pins into
their grooves

2.4m   When both pins have been installed, check to be
sure that the pin tabs on each side of the spindle flank
are exposed

3.2   Removing the brake hose fitting bolt (be sure to use
new sealing washers on each side of the fitting to prevent
fluid leaks)

3   Caliper — removal, overhaul and installation

Refer to illustrations 3.2, 3.4, 3.5, 3.6, 3.13, 3.15, 3.16a and 3.16b
Note: *Some brake calipers on these vehicles feature cast iron caliper housings and plastic pistons (one per caliper). If an overhaul is indicated (usually because of fluid leakage) explore all options before beginning the job. New and factory-rebuilt calipers are available on an exchange basis, which makes this job quite easy. If it is decided to rebuild the calipers, make sure that a rebuild kit is available before proceeding.*

Removal

1   Raise the vehicle and support it securely on jackstands. Remove the wheel.
2   Disconnect the brake hose fitting from the back of the caliper by removing the bolt (**see illustration**). Have a rag handy to catch fluid spills and wrap a plastic bag around the end of the hose to prevent fluid loss and contamination. Discard the inlet fitting washers; use new ones during reassembly. **Note:** *If the caliper will not be completely removed from the vehicle — as for a pad inspection or disc removal — leave the hose connected and place the caliper on top of the upper*

control arm in such a way that it won't fall off. This will save the trouble of bleeding the brake system.
3   Refer to the first few Steps in Section 2 to separate the caliper from the spindle.

Overhaul

4   Place a block of wood in the center of the caliper and then force the piston out of its bore by directing compressed air into the inlet opening (**see illustration**). Use care when doing this, as the piston could be ejected with some force.
5   Pry the dust boot out of the caliper — be careful not to gouge the bore (**see illustration**).
6   Using a wood or plastic tool, remove the rubber piston seal from the caliper bore (**see illustration**). *Do not use a metal tool, as the bore can be easily damaged.*
7   Carefully inspect the piston and the bore for score marks, nicks, cracks, corrosion and damage of any kind. If any of the above are found, the caliper should be replaced with a new or rebuilt unit.
8   Remove the bleeder valve and rubber cap.
9   Inspect the guide pins for corrosion and damage. Replace them

3.4   With the caliper padded to catch the piston, use compressed air to force the piston out of its bore. Make sure your hands or fingers are not between the piston and caliper

3.5   Carefully pry the dust boot out of the caliper

3.6   The piston seal should be removed with a plastic or wooden tool to avoid damage to the bore and seal groove. A pencil will do the job

3.13   Push the new seal into the piston groove with your fingers, then check to see that it isn't twisted or kinked

with new ones if necessary.

10   Use clean brake fluid or denatured alcohol to clean all the parts. **Warning:** *Do not, under any circumstances, use petroleum-based solvents to clean brake parts.* Allow all parts to dry, preferably using compressed air to blow out all passages. Make sure the compressed air is filtered, as a harmful lubricant residue will be present in unfiltered systems.

11   Check the fit of the piston in the bore by sliding it into the caliper. The piston should move easily.

12   Install the rubber cap over the bleeder valve and thread the valve into the caliper. Tighten it securely.

13   Lubricate the new piston seal with silicone grease or clean brake fluid. Position the seal in the caliper bore groove, making sure that the seal does not twist **(see illustration)**.

14   Using silicone grease or clean brake fluid, lubricate the piston and the caliper bore.

15   Push the piston into the caliper by hand as far as possible. Using a C-clamp and a block of wood, push the piston all the way to the bottom of the bore. Work slowly, keeping an eye on the side of the piston, making sure it enters the bore perfectly straight, with no resistance **(see illustration)**.

3.15   Use a C-clamp and a block of wood to bottom the piston in the caliper bore. Make sure it goes in perfectly straight, or the sides of the piston may be damaged, rendering it useless

3.16a   Position the dust boot in the caliper and stretch the inner diameter of the seal over the piston. Make sure the bead on the boot seats in the piston groove

3.16b   Using a hammer and punch, lightly tap the dust boot into its recess

4.3   Check the disc surface for deep grooves and score marks (be sure to inspect both sides)

4.4   Use a dial indicator to check disc runout — if the reading exceeds the maximum allowable runout limit, the rotor will have to be machined or replaced

4.5a   The minimum thickness limit can be found cast into the inside of the disc

4.5b   Use a micrometer to measure disc thickness at several points around the rotor

16 Install the dust boot in its bore with the open side of the casing face down. Stretch the inner part of the boot over the piston and drive the seal into place **(see illustrations)**.
17 Refer to Section 2 for the caliper installation procedure.

Installation

18 Install the inlet fitting bolt (with **new** washers) and tighten it securely.
19 Pump the brake pedal a few times to bring the pads into contact with the rotor.
20 Bleed the brakes as described in Section 9. This is not necessary if the inlet fitting was left connected to the caliper.
21 Install the wheel and lower the vehicle. Test the brake operation carefully before placing the vehicle into normal service.

---

4 Brake disc — inspection, removal and installation

Refer to illustrations 4.3, 4.4, 4.5a and 4.5b

Inspection

1 Loosen the wheel lug nuts, raise the vehicle and support it securely on jackstands. Remove the wheel.
2 Remove the caliper and inner brake pad (refer to Section 2).
3 Visually inspect the disc surface for score marks and other damage. Light scratches and shallow grooves are normal after use and may not be detrimental to brake operation. Deep score marks — over 0.015-inch (0.38 mm) — require disc removal and refinishing by an automotive machine shop. Be sure to check both sides of the disc **(see illustration)**.
4 To check disc runout, attach a dial indicator to the brake caliper and locate the stem about 1/2-inch from the outer edge of the disc and just touching the disc surface **(see illustration)**. Set the indicator to zero and turn the disc. The indicator reading should not exceed the specified limit. If it does, the disc should be resurfaced by an automotive machine shop. **Note:** *Professionals recommend resurfacing of brake discs regardless of the dial indicator reading (to produce a smooth, flat surface that will eliminate brake pedal pulsations and other undesireable symptoms related to questionable discs). At the very least, if you elect not to have the discs resurfaced, deglaze the brake pad surface with medium-grit emery cloth (use a swirling motion to ensure a non-directional finish).*
5 The disc must never be machined to a thickness under the specified minimum allowable thickness, which is cast into the inside of the disc itself **(see illustration)**. The disc thickness can be checked with a micrometer **(see illustration)**.

Removal and installation

6 Refer to Section 2 and remove the brake caliper. **Warning:** *Don't allow the caliper to hang by the brake hose and don't disconnect the hose from the caliper.*
7 Refer to Chapter 1, ''Front wheel bearing check, repack and adjustment'' for the remainder of the rotor removal and installation procedure.

---

5 Rear brake shoes — replacement

Refer to illustrations 5.4, 5.5a through 5.5x and 5.8

Warning: *The brake shoes must be replaced on both rear wheels at the same time — never replace the shoes on only one wheel. Also, brake system dust contains asbestos, which is harmful to your health. Never blow it out with compressed air and don't inhale any of it. Do not, under any circumstances, use petroleum-based solvents to clean brake parts. Use brake cleaner or denatured alcohol only. Whenever the brake shoes are replaced, the return and hold-down springs should also be replaced. Due to the continous heating/cooling cycle that the springs are subjected to, they lose their tension over a period of time and may allow the shoes to drag on the drum and wear at a much faster rate than normal. When replacing the rear brake shoes, use only high quality, nationally recognized brand-name parts.*

1 Remove about two-thirds of the brake fluid from the master cylinder reservoir.
2 Loosen the wheel lug nuts, block the front wheels and raise the rear of the vehicle. Support it on jackstands. Remove the rear wheels from the vehicle.

5.4 Remove glaze from the drum surface with medium-grit emery cloth

3 Remove the brake drums from the axle flanges. If the drums won't come off, make sure the parking brake is completely released. If it still won't come off, remove the rubber plug in the backing plate and back off the adjuster screw, retracting the brake shoes from the drum **(see illustration 5.8)**.
4 Check the drum for cracks, score marks, deep grooves and signs of overheating of the shoe contact surface. If the drums have blue spots, indicating overheated areas, they should be replaced. Also, look for grease or brake fluid on the shoe contact surface. Grease and brake fluid can be removed with denatured alcohol or brake cleaner, but the brake shoes must be replaced if they are contaminated. Surface glazing, which is a glossy, highly polished finish, can be removed with medium-grit emery cloth **(see illustration)**. **Note:** *Professionals recommend resurfacing the drums whenever a brake job is done. Resurfacing will eliminate the possibility of out-of-round drums. If the drums are worn so much that they can't be resurfaced without exceeding the maximum allowable diameter (stamped into the drum), then new ones will be required.*
5 Follow the accompanying photos (illustrations 5.5a through 5.5x) for the actual shoe replacement procedure. Be sure to stay in order and read the information in the caption under each illustration.

5.5a Rear drum brake components — left side shown

5.5b Before removing any internal drum brake components, wash them off with brake cleaner and allow them to dry — position a drain pan under the brake to catch the residue — DO NOT USE COMPRESSED AIR TO BLOW THE BRAKE DUST FROM THE PARTS!

5.5c Pull outward on the adjuster lever and turn the star wheel to retract the brake shoes

5.5d Pull back on the self-adjuster cable and push the adjusting lever toward the rear, unhooking it from the secondary brake shoe

5.5e Remove the primary and secondary shoe return springs. The spring removal tool shown here can be purchased at most auto parts stores and greatly simplifies this step

5.5f Remove the self-adjuster cable and anchor pin plate from the anchor pin

5.5g Remove the secondary shoe retractor spring and cable guide from the secondary shoe

5.5h   Remove the primary shoe hold down spring and pin . . .

5.5i   . . . then lift the primary shoe and adjusting screw from the backing plate

5.5j   Remove the parking brake link

5.5k   Remove the secondary shoe hold down spring and pin, lift the shoe from the backing plate. Pry the parking brake lever retaining clip off of the pivot pin . . .

5.5l   . . . then separate the lever from the secondary shoe. Be careful not to lose the spring washer

5.5m   Lubricate the brake shoe contact areas (arrows) with high temperature grease

5.5n   Attach the new shoe to the parking brake lever, install the spring washer and retaining clip on the pivot pin then crimp the clip closed with a pair of pliers

5.5o   Install the secondary shoe and hold down spring to the backing plate, then position the end of the parking brake link into the notch in the shoe (arrow)

5.5p   Lubricate the adjusting screw with high temperature multi-purpose grease

5.5q   Place the primary shoe against the backing plate then install the hold down spring. Make sure the parking brake strut and wheel cylinder pushrods engage in the brake shoe slots

5.5r   Install the anchor pin plate . . .

5.5s   . . . and the self-adjuster cable

5.5t   Hook the end of the secondary shoe retractor spring through the cable guide and into the hole in the shoe, then stretch the spring over the anchor pin

5.5u   Install the primary shoe retractor spring. The tool shown here is available at most auto parts stores and makes this step much easier and safer

5.5v   Hook the adjuster lever spring into the hole at the bottom of the primary shoe

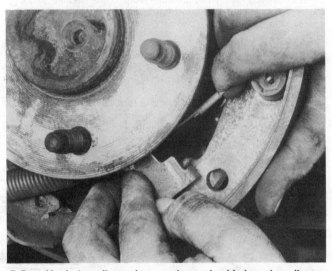

5.5w   Hook the adjuster lever spring and cable into the adjuster lever and pull the cable down and to the rear, inserting the hook on the lever into the hole in the secondary shoe

5.5x   Wiggle the brake assembly to ensure that the shoes are centered on the backing plate

5.8   Using a screwdriver or brake adjuster tool, turn the adjuster wheel in the direction shown until the shoes drag on the brake drum. Then, insert a small screwdriver through the backing plate to move the adjusting lever away from the adjuster wheel and turn the wheel in the opposite direction until the drum turns freely

6   Once the new shoes are in place, install the drums to the axle flanges.

7   Remove the rubber plug from the brake backing plate.

8   Insert a narrow screwdriver or brake adjusting tool through the adjustment hole and turn the star wheel until the brakes drag slightly as the drum is turned **(see illustration)**.

9   Turn the star wheel in the opposite direction until the drum turns freely. Keep the adjuster lever from contacting the star wheel or it won't turn. This can be done by pushing on it with a narrow screwdriver.

10 Repeat the adjustment on the opposite wheel.

11 Install the plugs in the backing plate access holes.

12 Install the wheels and lower the vehicle. Tighten the lug nuts to the specified torque.

13 Top up the master cylinder with brake fluid and pump the pedal several times. Lower the vehicle and make a series of quick, harsh stops in forward and reverse to allow the brakes to further adjust themselves. Confirm proper brake operation before placing the vehicle in normal traffic service.

---

6   Wheel cylinder — removal, overhaul and installation

Refer to illustrations 6.4 and 6.7

Note: *If an overhaul is indicated (usually because of fluid leakage) explore all options before beginning the job. New wheel cylinders are available, which makes this job quite easy. If it is decided to rebuild the wheel cylinder, make sure that a rebuild kit is available before proceeding.*

Removal

1   Raise the rear of the vehicle and support it securely on jackstands.

2   Remove the brake shoe assembly (Section 5).

3   Carefully clean all dirt and foreign material from around the wheel cylinder.

4   Disconnect the brake fluid inlet line **(see illustration)**. Do not pull the brake line away from the wheel cylinder.

5   Remove the two bolts that retain the wheel cylinder to the brake backing plate.

6.4   Completely loosen the inlet tube fitting then remove the two mounting bolts

6   Remove the wheel cylinder from the brake backing plate and place it on a clean workbench. Immediately plug the brake line to prevent fluid loss and contamination.

Overhaul

7   Remove the bleeder valve, seals, pistons, boots and spring assembly from the cylinder body **(see illustration)**.

8   Clean the wheel cylinder with brake fluid, denatured alcohol or brake system cleaner. **Warning:** *Do not, under any circumstances, use petroleum based solvents to clean brake parts.*

9   Use compressed air to remove excess fluid from the wheel cylinder and to blow out the passages.

10 Check the cylinder bore for corrosion and scoring. Crocus cloth may be used to remove light corrosion and stains, but the cylinder must be replaced with a new one if the defects cannot be removed easily, or if the bore is scored.

6.7   Exploded view of the wheel cylinder

11 Lubricate the new seals with brake fluid.

12 Assemble the brake cylinder, making sure the boots are properly seated.

Installation

13 Place the wheel cylinder in position against the backing plate and install the bolts, tightening them to the specified torque.

14 Connect the brake line and install the brake shoe assembly.

15 Bleed the brakes following the procedure described in Section 9.

---

7   Master cylinder — removal, overhaul and installation

Note: *Before deciding to overhaul the master cylinder, investigate the availability and cost of a new or factory rebuilt unit and also the availability of a rebuild kit.*

Removal

Refer to illustration 7.2

1   Place rags under the brake line fittings and prepare caps or plastic bags to cover the ends of the lines once they are disconnected. **Caution:**

7.2   Unscrew the brake line fittings from the master cylinder — a flare nut wrench is recommended

7.7   Use a Phillips head screwdriver to push the primary piston into the cylinder, then remove the snap-ring

7.8   Remove the primary piston assembly from the cylinder

7.9   Tap the master cylinder against a block of wood to eject the secondary piston assembly

7.10   If it is necessary to remove the fluid reservoir (to replace leaking seals or a broken reservoir), gently pry it off with a screwdriver or pry bar

7.14   Coat the secondary piston with clean brake fluid and install it into the master cylinder — spring end first

Brake fluid will damage paint. Cover all body parts and be careful not to spill fluid during this procedure.

2   Loosen the tube nuts at the ends of the brake lines where they enter the master cylinder. To prevent rounding off the flats on these nuts, a flare-nut wrench, which wraps around the nut, should be used **(see illustration)**.

3   Pull the brake lines away from the master cylinder slightly and plug the ends to prevent contamination.

4   Disconnect the brake warning lamp electrical connector, remove the two master cylinder mounting nuts and remove the master cylinder from the vehicle.

5   Remove the reservoir cap, then discard any fluid remaining in the reservoir.

Overhaul

Refer to illustrations 7.7, 7.8, 7.9, 7.10, 7.14 and 7.19

6   Mount the master cylinder in a vise with the vise jaws clamping on the mounting flange.

7   Remove the primary piston snap ring by depressing the piston and extracting the ring with a pair of snap ring pliers **(see illustration)**.

8   Remove the primary piston assembly from the cylinder bore **(see illustration)**.

9   Remove the secondary piston assembly from the cylinder bore. It may be necessary to remove the master cylinder from the vise and invert it, carefully tapping it against a block of wood to expel the piston **(see illustration)**.

10   If fluid has been leaking past the reservoir grommets, pry the reservoir from the cylinder body with a screwdriver **(see illustration)**. Remove the grommets.

11   Inspect the cylinder bore for corrosion and damage. If any corrosion

or damage is found, replace the master cylinder body with a new one, as abrasives cannot be used on the bore.

12   Lubricate the new reservoir grommets with silicone lubricant and press them into the master cylinder body. Make sure they're properly seated.

13   Lay the reservoir on a hard surface and press the master cylinder body onto the reservoir, using a rocking motion.

14   Lubricate the cylinder bore and primary and secondary piston assemblies with clean brake fluid. Install the secondary piston assembly into the cylinder **(see illustration)**.

PLUGS

REAR BRAKE OUTLET PORT

7.19   When bench bleeding the master cylinder, start with the rear brake outlet port

15 Install the primary piston assembly in the cylinder bore, depress it and install the snap ring.
16 Inspect the reservoir cap and diaphragm for cracks and deformation. Replace any damaged parts with new ones and attach the diaphragm to the cover.
17 **Note:** *Whenever the master cylinder is removed, the complete hydraulic system must be bled. The time required to bleed the system can be reduced if the master cylinder is filled with fluid and bench bled (refer to Steps 18 through 22) before the master cylinder is installed on the vehicle.*
18 Insert threaded plugs of the correct size into the cylinder outlet holes and fill the reservoirs with brake fluid. The master cylinder should be supported in such a manner that brake fluid will not spill during the bench bleeding procedure.
19 Loosen one plug at a time, starting with the rear outlet port first, and push the piston assembly into the bore to force air from the master cylinder **(see illustration)**. To prevent air from being drawn back into the cylinder, the appropriate plug must be replaced before allowing the piston to return to its original position.
20 Stroke the piston three or four times for each outlet to ensure that all air has been expelled.
21 Since high pressure is not involved in the bench bleeding procedure, an alternative to the removal and replacement of the plugs with each stroke of the piston assembly is available. Before pushing in on the piston assembly, remove one of the plugs completely. Before releasing the piston, however, instead of replacing the plug, simply put your finger tightly over the hole to keep air from being drawn back into the master cylinder. Wait several seconds for the brake fluid to be drawn from the reservoir to the piston bore, then repeat the procedure. When you push down on the piston it will force your finger off the hole, allowing the air inside to be expelled. When only brake fluid is being ejected from the hole, replace the plug and go on to the other port.
22 Refill the master cylinder reservoirs and install the diaphragm and cover assembly.

Installation

23 Carefully install the master cylinder by reversing the removal steps, then bleed the brakes (refer to Section 9).

8   Brake hoses and lines — inspection and replacement

Refer to illustration 8.3

Inspection

1 About every six months, with the vehicle raised and supported securely on jackstands, the rubber hoses which connect the steel brake lines with the front and rear brake assemblies should be inspected for cracks, chafing of the outer cover, leaks, blisters and other damage. These are important and vulnerable parts of the brake system and inspection should be complete. A light and mirror will be helpful for a thorough check. If a hose exhibits any of the above conditions, replace it with a new one.

8.3   To disconnect a brake hose from the brake line fitting, place a backup wrench on the hose fitting (A) and loosen the tube nut (B) with a flare nut wrench. Remove the U-clip (C) to detach the hose from the frame bracket

Flexible hose replacement

2 Clean all dirt away from the ends of the hose.
3 Disconnect the brake line from the hose fitting using a back-up wrench on the fitting **(see illustration)**. Be careful not to bend the frame bracket or line. If necessary, soak the connections with penetrating oil.
4 Unbolt the hose bracket from the strut assembly.
5 Remove the U-clip from the female fitting at the bracket **(see illustration 8.3)** and remove the hose from the bracket.
6 Disconnect the hose from the caliper, discarding the copper washers on either side of the fitting block.
7 Using new copper washers, attach the new brake hose to the caliper.
8 Pass the female fitting through the frame bracket. With the least amount of twist in the hose, install the fitting in this position (use the paint stripe on the hose to help determine twist). **Note:** *The weight of the vehicle should be on the suspension, so the vehicle should not be raised while positioning the hose.*
9 Install the U-clip in the female fitting at the frame bracket.
10 Attach the brake line to the hose fitting using a back-up wrench on the fitting.
11 Mount the brake hose bracket to the strut assembly.
12 Carefully check to make sure the suspension or steering components don't make contact with the hose. Have an assistant push on the vehicle and also turn the steering wheel from lock-to-lock during inspection.
13 Bleed the brake system as described in Section 9.

Rigid brake line replacement

14 When replacing brake lines, be sure to use the correct parts. Don't use copper tubing for any brake system components. Purchase steel brake lines from a dealer or auto parts store.
15 Prefabricated brake line, with the tube ends already flared and fittings installed, is available at auto parts stores and dealers. These lines are also bent to the proper shapes.
16 If prefabricated lines aren't available, obtain the recommended steel tubing and fittings to match the line to be replaced. Determine the correct length by measuring the old brake line (a piece of string can usually be used for this) and cut the new tubing to length, allowing about 1/2-inch extra for flaring the ends.
17 Install the fitting over the cut tubing and flare the ends of the line with a flaring tool.
18 If necessary, carefully bend the line to the proper shape. A tube bender is recommended for this. **Warning:** *Do not crimp or damage the line.*
19 When installing the new line, make sure it's securely supported in the brackets and has plenty of clearance between moving or hot components.
20 After installation, check the master cylinder fluid level and add fluid as necessary. Bleed the brake system as outlined in the next Section and test the brakes carefully before driving the vehicle in traffic.

9 Brake hydraulic system — bleeding

Refer to illustration 9.8

Warning: *Wear eye protection when bleeding the brake system. If the fluid comes in contact with your eyes, immediately rinse them with water and seek medical attention.*

1   Bleeding the hydraulic system is necessary to remove any air that manages to find its way into the system as a result of removal and installation of a hose, line, caliper, wheel cylinder or master cylinder. Use only the specified fluid in this system or extensive damage could result. It will probably be necessary to bleed the system at all four brakes if air has entered the system due to low fluid level, or if the brake lines have been disconnected at the master cylinder.

2   If a brake line was disconnected only at one wheel, then only that caliper (or wheel cylinder) must be bled.

3   If a brake line is disconnected at a fitting located between the master cylinder and any of the brakes, that part of the system served by the disconnected line must be bled.

4   Remove any residual vacuum from the power brake booster by applying the brake several times with the engine off.

5   Remove the master cylinder reservoir cap and fill the reservoir with brake fluid. Reinstall the cover. **Note:** *Check the fluid level often during the bleeding operation and add fluid as necessary to prevent the level from falling low enough to allow air bubbles into the master cylinder.*

6   Have an assistant on hand, as well as a supply of new brake fluid, an empty clear plastic container, a length of 3/16-inch clear plastic or vinyl tubing to fit over the bleeder screw and a wrench to open and close the bleeder screw.

7   Beginning at the right rear wheel, loosen the bleeder screw slightly, then tighten it to a point where it's snug but can still be loosened quickly and easily.

8   Place one end of the tubing over the bleeder screw and submerge the other end in brake fluid in the container **(see illustration)**.

9   Have an assistant pump the brakes a few times to get pressure in the system, then hold the pedal down.

10   While the pedal is held down, open the bleeder screw until brake fluid begins to flow. Watch for air bubbles to exit the submerged end of the tube. When the fluid flow slows after a couple of seconds, tighten the screw and have your assistant release the pedal.

11   Repeat Steps 9 and 10 until no more air is seen leaving the tube, then tighten the bleeder screw and proceed to the left rear wheel, the right front wheel and the left front wheel, in that order, and perform the same procedure. Be sure to check the fluid in the master cylinder

9.8   When bleeding the brakes, a hose is connected to the bleeder valve at the caliper or wheel cylinder and then submerged in brake fluid. Air will be seen as bubbles in the tube and container. All air must be expelled before moving to the next wheel

reservoir frequently.

12   Never use old brake fluid. It contains moisture which will deteriorate the brake system components.

13   Refill the master cylinder with fluid at the end of the operation.

14   Check the operation of the brakes. The pedal should feel solid when depressed, with no sponginess. If necessary, repeat the entire process.

Warning: *Do not operate the vehicle if you are in doubt about the effectiveness of the brake system.*

10 Parking brake cables — replacement

Refer to illustrations 10.2a, 10.2b, 10.3, 10.4, 10.6, 10.9 and 10.12

Note: *The parking brake system is self-adjusting.*

Front cable

1   Raise the vehicle and support it securely on jackstands. Make sure the parking brake handle is in the released position.

2   Firmly grasp the front cable near the equalizer and pull it toward the rear. Clamp a pair of locking pliers on the cable right where the cable casing fastens to the frame **(see illustrations)**.

10.2a   Parking brake cable routing details

10.2b From underneath the vehicle, pull the front parking brake cable to the rear and clamp a pair of locking pliers on it, right where it exits the cable casing at the frame crossmember

10.3 Insert a drill bit or nail through the pawl lock-out hole to release the tension on the front parking brake cable

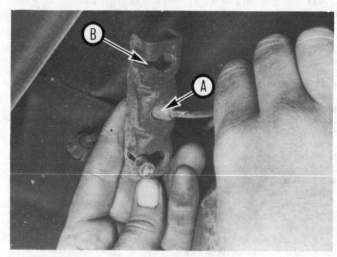

10.4 Disconnect the front cable (A) from the equalizer (B)

3   Remove the parking brake handle boot cover and insert a steel pin (a nail or drill bit will work) into the pawl lock-out pin hole from the inboard side (larger hole) at a slightly upward and forward angle. Push the pin in as far as it will go then maneuver it downward and to the rear to move the adjuster pawl out of the way. The pin should now pass through the outer hole **(see illustration)**.

4   Disconnect the front cable from the equalizer **(see illustration)** and remove the locking pliers.

5   Depress the tangs that retain the cable casing to the frame cross-member **(see illustration 10.2b)** and push the cable and casing through the frame. Repeat this procedure to the front end of the casing at the parking brake handle reinforcement bracket.

6   Remove the cable anchor pin from the control assembly and guide the cable from the adjuster mechanism **(see illustration)**.

7   To install the new cable, reverse the removal procedure. Make sure that all of the cables are connected to the equalizer before the steel pin is removed from the parking brake handle.

Rear cable(s)

8   Perform Steps 1 and 2 of the front cable replacement procedure.

9   Unhook the rear cable from the equalizer, compress the retainer tangs and push the cable and casing through the frame crossmember **(see illustration)**.

10.6 Remove the cable anchor pin from the adjuster wheel, then free the cable from the adjuster mechanism

10.9 Unhook the rear cable(s) from the equalizer, squeeze the tangs on the retainers and push the cable and casing through the crossmember

10.12   Depress the retention tangs to free the cable and casing from the brake backing plate

10 Pull the cable and casing through the guide brackets near the shock absorber upper mount.

11 Remove the brake drum and brake shoe assembly following the procedure described in Section 5.

12 Lift the cable out of the slot in the parking brake lever, then depress the tangs on the cable casing retainer in the backing plate **(see illustration)**.

13 Installation is the reverse of the removal procedure.

---

11   Parking brake handle — removal and installation

Refer to illustration 11.3

1   Refer to Section 10, Steps 1 through 3 for the adjusting mechanism tension release procedure.

2   Remove the front cable anchor pin from the adjusting mechanism and guide the cable from the adjuster **(see illustration 10.6)**.

3   Remove the two mounting bolts and remove the parking brake handle **(see illustration)**.

4   Do not remove the lock-out pin from the hole in the handle until the handle is installed and all of the parking brake cables are connected.

5   Installation is the reverse of the removal procedure.

12.2   Remove the brake booster pushrod retaining clip (arrow) and slide the rod and brake light switch off of the pedal pin

11.3   Parking brake handle installation details

---

12   Brake pedal — removal and installation

Refer to illustrations 12.2, 12.4a and 12.4b

Removal

1   Disconnect the cable from the negative battery terminal.

2   Working under the dash, unplug the connector from the brake light switch. Remove the brake booster pushrod retaining clip and slide the pushrod and switch off of the pedal pin **(see illustration)**.

3   On vehicles equipped with manual transmissions, disconnect the clutch master cylinder pushrod from the pedal (refer to Chapter 8 if necessary).

4   Remove the right-side retainer from the pedal pivot shaft **(see illustrations)**. Support the brake pedal and slide the shaft out to the left. On manual transmission vehicles, the pivot shaft is connected to the clutch pedal, so the clutch pedal must be removed as well.

12.4a   Brake pedal mounting details — automatic transmission

12.4b   Brake pedal mounting details — manual transmission

13.6   The following under-dash components must be removed to allow power brake booster removal:

1 Brake light switch connector   3 Pushrod
2 Pushrod retaining clip   4 Booster mounting nuts

5   Inspect the bushings for wear, replacing them as necessary. Lubricate the bushings and pivot shaft with a light coat of engine oil prior to installation.

Installation

6   Place the pedal into position and install the pivot shaft and retainer.
7   Attach the brake booster pushrod and brake light switch and install the retaining clip. On manual transmission vehicles install the clutch master cylinder pushrod.
8   Connect the wire harness to the brake light switch and pump the brake pedal several times to ensure proper operation. Reconnect the battery.

13   Power brake booster — removal, installation and adjustment

Refer to illustrations 13.6 and 13.11

1   The power brake booster unit requires no special maintenance apart from periodic inspection of the vacuum hose and the case.
2   Dismantling of the brake booster requires special tools and is not ordinarily done by the home mechanic. If a problem develops, install a new or factory rebuilt unit.

Removal

3   Remove the master cylinder (refer to Section 7 in this Chapter).
4   Disconnect the vacuum hose where it attaches to the power brake booster.
5   Working in the passenger compartment under the steering column, unplug the wiring connector from the brake light switch, then remove the pushrod retaining clip and nylon washer from the brake pedal pin. Slide the pushrod off the pin.
6   Remove the nuts attaching the brake booster to the firewall **(see illustration)**.
7   Carefully detach the booster from the firewall and lift it out of the engine compartment.

Installation

8   Place the booster into position on the firewall and tighten the mounting nuts. Connect the pushrod and brake light switch to the brake pedal. Install the retaining clip in the brake pedal pin.
9   Install the master cylinder and vacuum hose. Refer to Section 7

13.11   To adjust the booster master cylinder pushrod, fabricate a gauge block of the dimensions shown. Place it against the master cylinder mounting surface of the booster and adjust the end of the pushrod so it just touches the slot in the gauge block

for the master cylinder bleeding procedure.
10 Carefully check the operation of the brakes before driving the vehicle in traffic.

Adjustment

11 Some boosters feature an adjustable pushrod. They are matched to the booster at the factory and most likely will not require adjustment,

but if a misadjusted pushrod is suspected, a gauge can be fabricated out of heavy gauge sheet metal using the accompanying template **(see illustration)**.

12 Some common symptoms caused by a misadjusted pushrod include dragging brakes (if the pushrod is too long) or excessive brake pedal travel accompanied by a groaning sound from the brake booster (if the pushrod is too short).

13 To check the pushrod length, unbolt the master cylinder from the booster and position it to one side. It isn't necessary to disconnect the hydraulic lines, but be careful not to bend them.

14 Place the pushrod gauge against the master cylinder mounting surface of the booster **(see illustration 13.11)**. The pushrod should just touch the inner edge of the slot in the gauge. If it doesn't, adjust it by holding the knurled portion of the pushrod with a pair of pliers and turning the end with a wrench.

15 When the adjustment is complete, reinstall the master cylinder and check for proper brake operation before driving the vehicle in traffic.

14 Brake light switch — removal and installation

Removal

1 Locate the switch near the top of the brake pedal and disconnect the wiring harness **(see illustration 12.2)**.

2 Remove the pushrod retaining clip and nylon washer from the brake pedal pin and slide the pushrod off far enough for the outer hole of the switch to clear the pin. Now pull up on the switch to remove it.

Installation

3 Position the switch so it straddles the pushrod and the slot on the inner side of the switch rests on the pedal pin. Slide the pushrod and switch back onto the pin, then install the nylon washer and retaining clip.

4 Reconnect the wiring harness.

5 Check the brake lights for proper operation.

Chapter 10 Suspension and steering systems

Contents

Specifications

Torque specifications
Front suspension   Ft-lbs

Upper control arm-to-adjusting arm nuts	70 to 100
Crossmember-to-frame rail bolts	
Front	135 to 145
Center and rear	145 to 155
Lower control arm pivot bolts	
1986, 1987	187 to 260
1988	100 to 140
Lower balljoint-to-spindle nut*	80 to 120
Upper balljoint-to-spindle pinch bolt and nut	27 to 37

Rear suspension

Upper control arm-to-right frame bracket nut and bolt	100 to 145
Upper control arm-to-left frame bracket nut	60 to 100
Upper control arm-to-axle housing nut and bolt	100 to 145
Lower control arm-to-axle housing nut and bolt	100 to 145
Lower control arm-to-frame bracket nut and bolt	100 to 145

Steering system

Tie-rod end-to-spindle arm nuts*	52 to 74
Steering gear mounting bolts	65 to 90
Intermediate shaft-to-steering gear pinion shaft bolt........	30 to 42
Intermediate shaft-to-steering column shaft nut and bolt	30 to 42
Steering wheel hub bolt	23 to 33

* Tighten to the minimum specified torque, then align the next castellation in the nut with the cotter pin hole.

1 General information

Refer to illustrations 1.1 and 1.2

Warning: *Whenever any of the suspension or steering fasteners are loosened or removed they must be inspected and if necessary, replaced with new ones of the same part number or of original equipment quality and design. Torque specifications must be followed for proper reassembly and component retention. Never attempt to heat, straighten or weld any suspension or steering component. Instead, replace any bent or damaged part with a new one.*

The front suspension is independent, allowing each wheel to compensate for road surface changes without appreciably affecting the other. Each wheel is connected to the frame by a spindle, balljoints and upper and lower control arms. Each side uses a coil spring mounted between the lower control arm and the frame. Shock absorbers are positioned in the center of the coil spring, with the upper end fastened to the chassis and the lower end bolted to the lower control arm. Body side roll is controlled by a stabilizer bar.

The rear suspension is comprised of the axle, two coil springs, shock absorbers, two lower control arms and one upper control arm.

The steering system consists of the steering wheel, steering column, an articulated intermediate shaft, the steering gear (either power or manual), power steering pump and the tie rods, which connect the steering gear to the spindle.

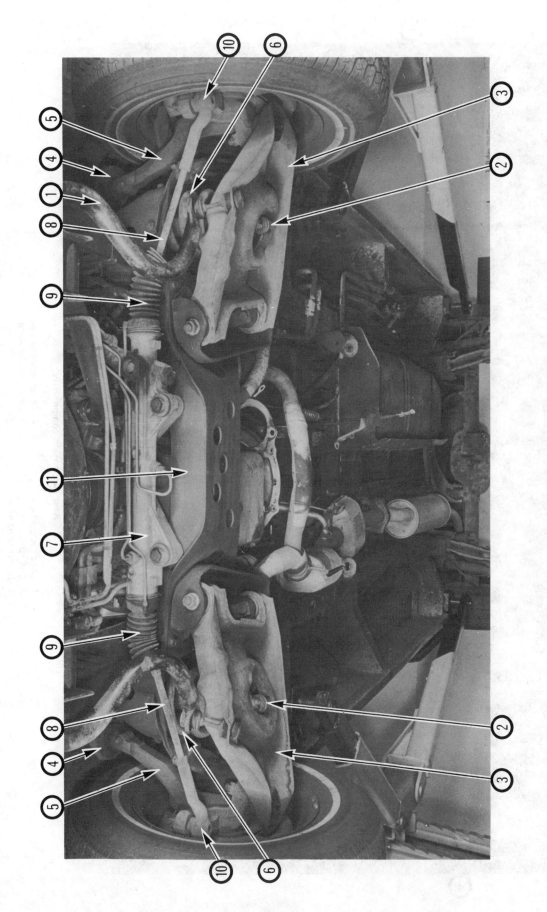

1.1 Front suspension and steering components

1 Stabilizer bar
2 Shock absorber
3 Lower control arm
4 Upper control arm

5 Spindle
6 Coil spring
7 Steering gear

8 Tie-rod
9 Steering gear boot
10 Tie-rod end
11 Front crossmember

234

1.2 Rear suspension components

1 Shock absorber
2 Coil spring
3 Lower control arm

4 Upper control arm
5 Rear axle housing

2.3 A pair of locking pliers clamped to the stabilizer bar link will prevent it from turning while loosening the nut

2.4 The stabilizer bar is held to the frame with two brackets like this. The rubber bushings should be replaced if they are hard, cracked or otherwise deformed

2 Front stabilizer bar — removal and installation

Refer to illustrations 2.3 and 2.4

Removal

1 Raise the vehicle and support it securely on jackstands. Apply the parking brake.
2 Remove the air deflector (see Chapter 11).
3 Remove the stabilizer bar-to-lower control arm nuts and bolts, noting how the links, washers and bushings are positioned. Clamp a pair of locking pliers to the stabilizer bar link to prevent it from turning **(see illustration)**.
4 Remove the stabilizer bar bracket bolts and detach the bar from the vehicle **(see illustration)**.
5 Pull the brackets off the stabilizer bar and inspect the bushings for cracks, hardening and other signs of deterioration. If the bushings are damaged, replace them with new ones.

Installation

6 Position the stabilizer bar bushings on the bar with the slits facing the front of the vehicle.
7 Push the brackets over the bushings and raise the bar up to the frame. Install the bracket bolts but don't tighten them completely at this time.
8 Install the stabilizer bar-to-lower control arm nuts and rubber bushings and tighten them securely.
9 Tighten the bracket bolts.

3.2 If the shock absorber upper mounting nut is rusted tight, it will probably be necessary to hold the stem from turning with a pair of locking pliers

3 Front shock absorbers — removal and installation

Refer to illustrations 3.2 and 3.3

Removal

1 Loosen the wheel lug nuts, raise the vehicle and support it securely on jackstands. Apply the parking brake. Remove the wheel.
2 Remove the upper shock absorber stem nut. Use an open end wrench to keep the stem from turning. If the nut won't loosen because of rust, squirt some penetrating oil on the stem threads and allow it to soak in for awhile. It may be necessary to keep the stem from turning with a pair of locking pliers, since the flats provided for a wrench are quite small **(see illustration)**.
3 Remove the two lower shock mount bolts **(see illustration)** and pull the shock absorber out through the bottom of the lower control arm. Remove the washers and the rubber grommets from the top of the shock absorber.

3.3 The lower end of the shock absorber is bolted to the lower control arm

5.3a   To separate the upper control arm from the spindle, support the lower control arm with a jack, remove the pinch bolt . . .

5.3b   . . . then carefully pry the ball stud out of the spindle

Installation

4   Extend the new shock absorber as far as possible. Position a new washer and rubber grommet on the stem and guide the shock up through the coil spring and into the upper mount.

5   Install the upper rubber grommet and washer and wiggle the stem back-and-forth to ensure that the grommets are centered in the mount. Tighten the stem nut securely.

6   Install the lower mounting bolts and tighten them securely.

4   Balljoints — replacement

If a problem develops with an upper or lower balljoint, the entire upper or lower control arm must be replaced, as the balljoints are not serviceable separately. Refer to Section 5 or 6 for the upper or lower control arm removal and installation procedure.

5   Upper control arm — removal and installation

Refer to illustrations 5.3a, 5.3b, 5.4a and 5.4b

Removal

1   Loosen the wheel lug nuts, raise the front of the vehicle and support it securely on jackstands. Apply the parking brake. Remove the wheel.

2   Support the lower control arm with a jack and raise it until the upper control arm no longer contacts the rebound bumper. The support point must be as close to the balljoint as possible to give maximum leverage on the lower control arm.

3   Remove the upper balljoint stud-to-spindle pinch bolt, then carefully pry the upper control arm from the spindle (see illustrations). Note: *DO NOT use a ''pickle fork'' type balljoint separator — it may damage the balljoint seals.*

4   Remove the control arm-to-adjusting arm nuts, recording the posi-

5.4a   Upper control arm, mounting brackets and crossmember installation details

SHIMS

COWL DRAIN BRACKET

BOLT

BOLT

RETAINER

SCREW AND WASHER ASSEMBLY

ADJUSTING ARM

WASHER

UPPER CONTROL ARM

UPPER BALL JOINT AND BOOT SEAL

MOUNTING BRACKETS

NO.1 CROSSMEMBER ASSEMBLY

FLAT PLATE

NUT AND WASHER ASSEMBLY

NUT AND WASHER ASSEMBLY

INBOARD VIEW

ADJUSTING ARM

UPPER CONTROL ARM

FRONT MOUNTING BRACKET

REAR MOUNTING BRACKET

5.4b The control arm is fastened to the adjusting arm with two nuts. Be sure to reinstall the alignment shims in the same positions

tion of any alignment shims. They must be reinstalled in the same location to maintain wheel alignment **(see illustrations)**.

5   Detach the control arm from the adjusting arm. **Note:** *The adjusting arm bushings are not serviceable. If they are damaged or worn out, the adjusting arm and mounting brackets must be replaced as an assembly.*

6   To remove the adjusting arm and mounting bracket assembly, position another jack under the crossmember and remove the mounting bracket-to-frame bolts and nuts **(see illustration 5.4a)**. DO NOT remove the jack that is supporting the lower control arm!

Installation

7   If the adjusting arm and mounting bracket assembly was removed, position it on the frame rail and install the bolts, tightening them to the specified torque.

8   Position the control arm on the adjusting arm and install the nuts loosely. Install any alignment shims that were removed. Tighten the nuts to the specified torque.

9   Insert the balljoint stud into the spindle, install the pinch bolt and tighten the nut to the specified torque.

10 Install the wheel and lug nuts and lower the vehicle. Tighten the lug nuts to the specified torque.

11 Drive the vehicle to an alignment shop to have the front end alignment checked and, if necessary, adjusted.

6 Lower control arm — removal and installation

Refer to illustration 6.5

Removal

1   Loosen the wheel lug nuts, raise the vehicle and support it securely on jackstands. Apply the parking brake. Remove the wheel.

2   Remove the shock absorber (refer to Section 3).

3   Disconnect the stabilizer bar from the lower control arm (Section 2).

4   Remove the coil spring as described in Section 8.

5   Remove the cotter pin and back off the lower control arm balljoint stud nut two turns. Using a two-jaw puller, break the balljoint loose from the spindle and remove the nut **(see illustration)**.

6   Remove the control arm from the vehicle. **Note:** *The control arm bushings are not serviceable. If the bushings are worn out, the entire control arm must be replaced.*

Installation

7   Insert the balljoint stud into the spindle, tighten the nut to the specified torque and install a new cotter pin. If necessary, tighten the nut slightly to align a slot in the nut with the hole in the balljoint stud.

8   Install the coil spring (Section 8) and the lower control arm pivot bolts and nuts, but don't completely tighten them at this time.

9   Install the shock absorber.

10 Connect the stabilizer bar to the lower control arm.

11 Install the wheel and lug nuts, lower the vehicle and tighten the

lug nuts to the specified torque.

12 With the vehicle at normal ride height, tighten the lower control arm pivot bolt nuts to the specified torque.

13 Drive the vehicle to an alignment shop to have the front end alignment checked and, if necessary, adjusted.

7 Spindle — removal and installation

Removal

1   Loosen the wheel lug nuts, raise the vehicle and support it securely on jackstands placed under the frame. Apply the parking brake. Remove the wheel.

2   Remove the brake caliper and place it on top of the upper control arm (see Chapter 9 if necessary).

3   Remove the brake disc and hub assembly (see ''Wheel bearings'' in Chapter 1).

4   Remove the splash shield from the spindle.

5   Separate the tie-rod end from the spindle arm (see Section 17).

6   Position a floor jack under the lower control arm and raise it slightly to take the spring pressure off the suspension stop. The jack must remain in this position throughout the entire procedure.

7   Remove the cotter pins from the lower balljoint studs and back off the nut two turns.

8   Break the balljoint loose from the spindle with a two-jaw puller **(see illustration 6.5)** or an equivalent balljoint separator. **Note:** *A pickle fork type balljoint separator may damage the balljoint seals.*

9   Remove the upper control arm-to-spindle pinch bolt and separate the control arm from the spindle **(see illustration 5.3b)**.

10 Remove the nut from the lower balljoint stud, separate the lower control arm from the spindle and remove the spindle from the vehicle.

Installation

11 Place the spindle between the upper and lower control arms and insert the balljoint studs into the knuckle, beginning with the lower balljoint. Install the bolt and nut and tighten them to the specified torque. Install a new cotter pin, tightening the nut slightly to align a slot in the nut with the hole in the balljoint stud, if necessary.

12 Install the splash shield.

13 Connect the tie-rod end to the spindle arm and tighten the nut to the specified torque. Be sure to use a new cotter pin.

14 Install the brake disc and adjust the wheel bearings following the procedure outlined in Chapter 1.

15 Install the brake caliper.

16 Install the wheel and lug nuts. Lower the vehicle to the ground and tighten the nuts to the specified torque.

6.5 A two-jaw puller can be used to disconnect the lower balljoint from the spindle. Notice that the nut hasn't been completely removed — this is to prevent the two components from separating violently

8.4   Support the inner edge of the lower control arm with a jack and loop a length of chain through the spring and around the control arm, bolting the ends together. Remove the pivot bolts and carefully lower the jack

8.8   Once the coil spring is fully extended, it can be guided out from between the spring pocket and lower control arm

8.11   Insert a long punch through the frame bracket and into the lower control arm bushing to help align the hole

9.2   Removing the shock absorber lower mounting bolt

8   Front coil spring — removal and installation

Refer to illustrations 8.4, 8.8 and 8.11
Removal
1   Loosen the wheel lug nuts, raise the vehicle and support it securely on jackstands placed under the frame. Apply the parking brake. Remove the wheel.
2   Remove the shock absorber (Section 3).
3   Disconnect the stabilizer bar from the lower control arm (Section 2).
4   Position a jack under the inner edge of the lower control arm **(see illustration)**. Make sure the jack is centered from front to rear.
5   Loop a length of safety chain up through the control arm and coil spring and bolt the ends of the chain together. Make sure there's enough slack in the chain so it won't inhibit spring extension when the control arm is lowered **(see illustration 8.4)**.
6   Raise the jack slightly to relieve spring pressure from the control arm pivot bolts and remove the nuts and bolts.
7   Slowly lower the jack until the coil spring is fully extended.
8   Unbolt the safety chain and maneuver the coil spring out **(see illustration)**. Do not apply downward pressure on the lower control arm as it may damage the balljoint. If the upper coil spring insulator is not on the top of the spring, reach up in the spring pocket and retrieve it.

Installation
9   Place the insulators on the top and bottom of the coil spring (the top of the spring is flat on the end, with a gripper notch near the end of the spring coil).
10   Install the top of the spring into the spring pocket and the bottom in the lower control arm. The end of the lower spring coil must be seated in the lowest recessed portion of the spring seat.
11   Place the jack under the lower control arm, install the safety chain and slowly raise the control arm into place. When the bolt holes are aligned, install the bolts with the bolt heads towards the center of the control arm. It may be necessary to insert a punch through the mounting bracket and into the control arm bushing to align the holes **(see illustration)**. Do not completely tighten the nuts at this time.
12   Install the shock absorber (Section 3).
13   Attach the stabilizer bar to the lower control arm (Section 2).
14   Install the wheel and lug nuts. Lower the vehicle and tighten the lug nuts to the specified torque.
15   Reach under the vehicle and tighten the lower control arm pivot bolt nuts to the specified torque.
16   Drive the vehicle to an alignment shop to have the front end alignment checked and, if necessary, adjusted.

10.5a Rear coil spring and lower control arm installation details

10.5b Remove the nut on the underside of the lower control arm to free the bottom of the spring. This should only be done when the coil spring is fully extended.

10.6 Reach through the coil spring with a wrench to remove the spring upper retainer bolt

9 Rear shock absorbers — removal and installation

Refer to illustration 9.2

1 Raise the rear of the vehicle and support it securely on jackstands. Block the front wheels to keep the vehicle from rolling.
2 Remove the shock absorber lower mounting bolt and nut **(see illustration)**.
3 Remove the shock absorber upper mounting bolt and slide the shock absorber off the bolt that protrudes through the frame.
4 Installation is the reverse of the removal procedure.

10 Rear coil spring — removal and installation

Refer to illustrations 10.5a, 10.5b and 10.6

Removal

1 Raise the rear of the vehicle and support it securely on jackstands

placed under the frame rails. Block the front wheels.
2 Place a jack under the rear axle housing and raise it slightly to take the weight off the shock absorber.
3 Unbolt the lower end of the shock absorber from the rear axle.
4 Slowly lower the jack until the springs are fully extended.
5 Remove the coil spring lower retainer nut from underneath the control arm **(see illustrations)**.
6 Remove the coil spring upper retainer bolt **(see illustration)**.
7 Remove the coil spring, retainers and insulators. Inspect the insulators for cracks and general wear, replacing them if necessary.

Installation

8 Place the lower insulator on the frame and the upper insulator on top of the spring (the top of the spring is the end with the smaller diameter, tapered coils that are painted white).
9 Place the spring between the control arm and the frame. Install the upper retainer and bolt, tightening it securely.
10 Install the lower retainer and tighten the nut securely.
11 Connect the shock absorber to its lower mounting bracket, lower the vehicle and tighten the mounting bolt securely.

11   Rear suspension control arms — removal and installation

Refer to illustration 11.5

Upper control arm

Removal

1   Raise the rear of the vehicle and support it securely on jackstands placed beneath the frame rails. Block the front wheels.
2   Position a jack under the differential and raise it slightly.
3   Remove the shock absorber lower mounting bolts and nuts.
4   Slowly lower the jack until the springs are no longer compressed. Keep an eye on the brake hose — if the axle is lowered too far it could be damaged.
5   Remove the upper control arm-to-rear axle bolt and nut **(see illustration)**. Separate the control arm from the axle and mark the position of the cam adjuster in the axle bushing.

11.5   **Remove the upper control arm mounting bolts and nuts in the sequence shown**

6   Remove the control arm-to-right side frame bracket bolt and nut **(see illustration 11.5)**.
7   Remove the control arm-to-left side frame bracket nut, washer and outer bushing **(see illustration 11.5)**.
8   Remove the control arm from the vehicle. **Note:** *The pressed-in bushing on the right side of the control arm is replaceable, but special tools are necessary to remove and install it. If the bushing is worn out, take the control arm to a dealer service department or automotive machine shop.*

Installation

9   Insert the control arm stud (with inner washer and bushing) into the left side frame bracket. Install the outer bushing and washer then install the nut finger-tight.
10   Push the right side of the arm into the right side frame bracket and install the bolt and nut, but don't tighten it to the specified torque yet.
11   Check to be sure that the cam adjuster in the axle bushing is still in alignment with the previously applied mark.
12   Connect the arm to the rear axle and install the bolt and nut, but don't tighten it fully yet.
13   Raise the axle to normal ride height and connect the lower end of the shock absorber to the mounting brackets. Tighten the mounting bolts securely.
14   Tighten all of the upper control arm bolts to the specified torque.

Lower control arm

Removal

15   Raise the rear of the vehicle and support it securely on jackstands placed under the frame rails. Block the front wheels.
16   Place a jack under the rear axle housing and raise it slightly to take the load off the shock absorbers. Unbolt the shock absorber from the rear axle.
17   Slowly lower the jack until the coil spring is no longer compressed. Keep an eye on the brake hose — it could be damaged if the axle is lowered too far. Remove the lower spring retainer nut from the underside of the control arm **(see illustration 10.5b)**.
18   Remove the lower control arm-to-axle housing bolt and nut, noting the direction in which it was installed **(see illustration 10.5a)**.
19   Remove the lower control arm-to-frame bolt and nut **(see illustra-

tion 10.5a)**. Remove the control arm from the vehicle.
Note: *The pressed-in bushings at either end of the control arm are replaceable, but special tools are necessary to remove and install them. If the bushings are worn out, take the control arm to a dealer service department or automotive machine shop.*

Installation

20   Position the forward end of the control arm in the frame bracket and install the bolt and nut. The bolt head must be facing toward the inside of the vehicle. Do not fully tighten it at this time.
21   Swing the trailing end of the control arm up into the rear axle bracket and install the bolt and nut, but don't fully tighten them yet. The bolt head must be on the inboard side of the axle bracket.
22   Place the spring insulator on the lower control arm, raise the rear axle until it touches the coil spring and install the spring lower retainer. Tighten the nut securely.
23   Connect the shock absorber to the rear axle housing and install the bolt loosely.
24   Lower the vehicle to the ground and tighten the control arm mounting bolts to the specified torque. Tighten the shock absorber bolts securely.

12   Steering wheel — removal and installation

Refer to illustrations 12.2a, 12.2b, 12.3 and 12.4

1   Disconnect the cable from the negative terminal of the battery.
2   Remove the two horn pad screws and pull the horn pad from the steering wheel. Disconnect the horn electrical connector **(see illustrations)**.
3   Remove the steering wheel retaining bolt, then mark the relationship of the steering shaft to the hub (if marks don't already exist or don't line up) to simplify installation and ensure steering wheel

12.2a   **Remove the horn pad retaining screws . . .**

12.2b   **. . . then pull the horn pad off the platic tabs and disconnect the horn electrical connector**

12.3 Before removing the steering wheel, check to see if any alignment marks exist (arrows) — if not, use a sharp scribe or white paint to index the steering wheel hub to the steering shaft

12.4 Remove the wheel from the shaft with a puller — DO NOT beat on the shaft!

alignment **(see illustration)**.

4   Use a puller to disconnect the steering wheel from the shaft **(see illustration)**.

5   To install the wheel, align the mark on the steering wheel hub with the mark on the shaft and slip the wheel onto the shaft. Install the hub bolt and tighten it to the specified torque.

6   Connect the horn electrical connector and install the horn pad.

7   Connect the negative battery cable.

13 Intermediate shaft — removal and installation

Refer to illustrations 13.2a and 13.2b

1   Turn the front wheels to the straight ahead position.

2   Using white paint, place alignment marks on the upper universal joint, the steering shaft, the lower universal joint and the steering gear input shaft **(see illustrations)**.

3   Remove the upper and lower universal joint pinch bolts.

4   Pry the intermediate shaft out of the steering shaft universal joint with a large screwdriver, then pull the shaft from the steering gearbox.

5   Installation is the reverse of the removal procedure. Be sure to align the marks and tighten the pinch bolts to the specified torque.

14 Steering gear — removal and installation

Refer to illustrations 14.2 and 14.5

Note: *This procedure applies to both power and manual steering gear assemblies. When working on a vehicle equipped with a manual steering gear, simply ignore any references made to the power steering system.*

Removal

1   Raise the front of the vehicle and support it securely on jackstands. Apply the parking brake.

2   Place a drain pan under the steering gear (power steering only). Remove the power steering pressure and return lines and cap the ends to prevent excessive fluid loss and contamination **(see illustration)**.

3   Mark the relationship of the lower intermediate shaft universal joint to the steering gear input shaft **(see illustration 13.2b)**. Remove the lower intermediate shaft pinch bolt.

4   Separate the tie-rod ends from the spindle arms (see Section 17).

13.2a Place matchmarks (arrow) on the intermediate shaft-to-steering shaft joint

13.2b Also place alignment marks from the lower universal joint to the steering gear input shaft

RETURN HOSE
ASSEMBLY

PRESSURE HOSE
ASSEMBLY

14.2 Disconnect the power steering pressure and return lines from the steering gear and plug the lines to prevent contaminants from entering

5   Support the steering gear and remove the steering gear-to-frame mounting bolts **(see illustration)**. Lower the unit, separate the intermediate shaft from the steering gear input shaft and remove the steering gear from the vehicle.

Installation

6   Raise the steering gear into position and connect the intermediate shaft, aligning the marks.
7   Install the mounting bolts and washers and tighten them to the specified torque.
8   Connect the tie-rod ends to the spindle arms (Section 17)
9   Install the lower intermediate shaft pinch bolt and tighten it to the specified torque.
10   Connect the power steering pressure and return hoses to the steering gear and fill the power steering pump reservoir with the recommended fluid (Chapter 1).
11   Lower the vehicle and bleed the steering system as outlined in Section 16.

14.5   Location of the steering gear mounting bolts (arrows)

---

15   Power steering pump — removal and installation

Refer to illustrations 15.3a, 15.3b, 15.4, 15.5, 15.8a and 15.8b

Removal

1   Disconnect the cable from the negative terminal of the battery.
2   Place a drain pan under the power steering pump. Remove the

drivebelt (Chapter 1).
3   Using a special power steering pump pulley remover or a two-jaw puller, remove the pulley from the pump **(see illustrations)**.
4   Remove the pressure and return hoses from the backside of the pump and allow the fluid to drain **(see illustration)**. Plug the hoses to

15.3a   This special tool, designed for removing power steering pulleys is available at tool stores and some auto parts stores

15.3b   A two jaw puller can also be used to remove the pulley, but only if it is compact enough to work in the confines of the engine compartment

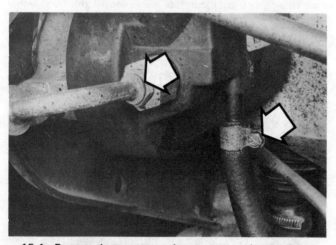

15.4   Remove the power steering pressure and return lines (arrows); use a back-up wrench on the pressure fitting — the return hose is retained by a hose clamp

15.5   Remove the three power steering pump mounting bolts and remove the pump from the mounting bracket

15.8a This special tool, designed for installing the power steering pulley is available at tool stores and some auto parts stores

15.8b A long bolt with the same thread pitch as the internal threads of the power steering pump shaft, nut, washer and a socket that is the same diameter as the pulley hub can be used to install the pulley on the shaft

prevent contaminants from entering.

5   Remove the pump mounting bolts (see illustration) and lift the pump from the vehicle, taking care not to spill fluid on the painted surfaces.

Installation

6   Position the pump in the mounting bracket and install the bolts. Tighten the bolts securely.

7   Connect the hoses to the pump. Tighten the fittings securely.

8   Press the pulley onto the pump shaft using a special pulley installer tool (see illustration). An alternative tool can be fabricated from a long bolt, nut, washer and a socket of the same diameter as the pulley hub (see illustration). Push the pulley onto the shaft until the front of the hub is flush with the end of the shaft, but no further.

9   Install the drivebelt.

10   Fill the power steering reservoir with the recommended fluid and bleed the system following the procedure described in the next Section.

16 Power steering system — bleeding

1   Following any operation in which the power steering fluid lines have been disconnected, the power steering system must be bled to remove all air and obtain proper steering performance.

2   With the front wheels in the straight ahead position, check the power steering fluid level and, if low, add fluid until it reaches the Cold mark on the dipstick.

3   Start the engine and allow it to run at fast idle. Recheck the fluid

level and add more if necessary to reach the Cold mark on the dipstick.

4   Bleed the system by turning the wheels from side-to-side, without hitting the stops. This will work the air out of the system. Keep the reservoir full of fluid as this is done.

5   When the air is worked out of the system, return the wheels to the straight ahead position and leave the vehicle running for several more minutes before shutting it off.

6   Road test the vehicle to be sure the steering system is functioning normally and noise free.

7   Recheck the fluid level to be sure it is up to the Hot mark on the dipstick while the engine is at normal operating temperature. Add fluid if necessary (see Chapter 1).

17 Tie-rod ends — removal and installation

Refer to illustrations 17.2a, 17.2b and 17.4

Removal

1   Loosen the wheel lug nuts. Raise the front of the vehicle, support it securely, block the rear wheels and set the parking brake. Remove the front wheel.

2   Hold the tie-rod with a pair of locking pliers and loosen the jam nut enough to mark the position of the tie-rod end in relation to the threads (see illustrations).

17.2a Hold the tie-rod with a pair of locking pliers and loosen the jam nut

17.2b Use white paint to mark the position of the tie-rod end on the tie-rod

3   Remove the cotter pin and loosen the nut on the tie-rod end stud.
4   Disconnect the tie-rod from the steering knuckle arm with a puller **(see illustration)**. Remove the nut and separate the tie-rod.
5   Unscrew the tie-rod end from the tie-rod.

Installation

6   Thread the tie-rod end on to the marked position and insert the tie-rod stud into the steering knuckle arm. Tighten the jam nut securely.
7   Install the castellated nut on the stud and tighten it to the specified torque. Install a new cotter pin.
8   Install the wheel and lug nuts. Lower the vehicle and tighten the lug nuts to the specified torque.
9   Have the alignment checked by a dealer service department or an alignment shop.

18   Steering gear boots — replacement

Refer to illustrations 18.3a and 18.3b

1   Loosen the lug nuts, raise the vehicle and support it securely on jackstands. Remove the wheel.
2   Refer to Section 17 and remove the tie-rod end and jam nut.
3   Remove the steering gear boot clamps and slide the boot off **(see illustrations)**.
4   Before installing the new boot, wrap the threads and serrations on the end of the steering rod with a layer of tape so the small end of the new boot isn't damaged.
5   Slide the new boot into position on the steering gear until it seats in the groove in the steering rod and install new clamps.
6   Remove the tape and install the tie-rod end (Section 17).
7   Install the wheel and lug nuts. Lower the vehicle and tighten the lug nuts to the specified torque.

19   Wheels and tires — general information

Refer to illustration 19.1

All vehicles covered by this manual are equipped with metric-sized fiberglass or steel belted radial tires **(see illustration)**. Use of other size or type of tires may affect the ride and handling of the vehicle. Don't mix different types of tires, such as radials and bias belted, on the same vehicle as handling may be seriously affected. It's recommended that tires replaced in pairs on the same axle, but if only one tire is being

17.4   Use a two-jaw puller to detach the tie-rod end from the spindle arm. Notice that the nut has been loosened, but not removed. This will prevent the components from separating violently

replaced, be sure it's the same size, structure and tread design as the other.
Because tire pressure has a substantial effect on handling and wear, the pressure on all tires should be checked at least once a month or before any extended trips (see Chapter 1).
Wheels must be replaced if they are bent, dented, leak air, have elongated bolt holes, are heavily rusted, out of vertical symmetry or if the lug nuts won't stay tight. Wheel repairs that use welding or peening are not recommended.
Tire and wheel balance is important in the overall handling, braking and performance of the vehicle. Unbalanced wheels can adversely affect handling and ride characteristics as well as tire life. Whenever a tire is installed on a wheel, the tire and wheel should be balanced by a shop with the proper equipment.

18.3a   Remove the outer boot clamp with a pair of pliers

18.3b   Loosen the inner boot clamp screw and slide the boot off the rack housing

METRIC TIRE SIZES

P 185 / 80 R 13

TIRE TYPE
P · PASSENGER
T · TEMPORARY
C · COMMERCIAL

SECTION WIDTH
(MILLIMETERS)
185
195
205
ETC

ASPECT RATIO
(SECTION HEIGHT)
(SECTION WIDTH)
70
75
80

CONSTRUCTION TYPE
R · RADIAL
B · BIAS · BELTED
D · DIAGONAL (BIAS)

RIM DIAMETER
(INCHES)
13
14
15

19.1 Metric tire size code

A Section width
B Section height

20.1 Front end alignment details

A minus B = C (degrees camber)
D = caster (measured in degrees)
E minus F = toe-in (measured in inches)
G = toe-in (expressed in degrees)

20 Front end alignment — general information

Refer to illustration 20.1

A front end alignment refers to the adjustments made to the front wheels so they are in proper angular relationship to the suspension and the ground. Front wheels that are out of proper alignment not only affect steering control, but also increase tire wear. The front end adjustments normally required are camber, caster and toe-in **(see illustration)**.

Getting the proper front wheel alignment is a very exacting process, one in which complicated and expensive machines are necessary to perform the job properly. Because of this, you should have a technician with the proper equipment perform these tasks. We will, however, use this space to give you a basic idea of what is involved with front end alignment so you can better understand the process and deal intelligently with the shop that does the work.

Toe-in is the turning in of the front wheels. The purpose of a toe specification is to ensure parallel rolling of the front wheels. In a vehicle with zero toe-in, the distance between the front edges of the wheels will be the same as the distance between the rear edges of the wheels. The actual amount of toe-in is normally only a fraction of an inch. Toe-in adjustment is controlled by the tie-rod end position on the inner tie-rod. Incorrect toe-in will cause the tires to wear improperly by making them scrub against the road surface.

Camber is the tilting of the front wheels from the vertical when viewed from the front of the vehicle. When the wheels tilt out at the top, the camber is said to be positive (+). When the wheels tilt in at

the top the camber is negative (–). The amount of tilt is measured in degrees from the vertical and this measurement is called the camber angle. This angle affects the amount of tire tread which contacts the road and compensates for changes in the suspension geometry when the vehicle is cornering or travelling over an undulating surface.

Caster is the tilting of the front steering axis from the vertical. A tilt toward the rear is positive caster and a tilt toward the front is negative caster.

Caster is adjusted by moving shims from one end of the upper control arm mount to the other.

Chapter 11 Body

Contents

Specifications

Torque specifications

	Ft-lbs
Front door hinge bolt	13 to 20
Front seat belt D ring bolt........................	22 to 32
Front seat belt retractor assembly bolt	22 to 32
Seat belt anchor bolts	22 to 32
Liftgate hinge bolt	13 to 20
Dual rear door hinge bolt	13 to 20

---

1 General information

The vehicles covered in this manual have a separate frame and body. The body is metal with the exception of the rear liftgate, which is constructed of fiberglass.

As with other parts of the vehicle, proper maintenance of body components plays an important part in retention of the vehicle's market value. It is far less costly to handle small problems before they grow into larger ones. Information in this Chapter will tell you all you need to know to keep seals sealing, body panels aligned and general appearance up to par.

Major body components which are particularly vulnerable in accidents are removable. These include the hood, grille and doors. It is often cheaper and less time consuming to replace an entire panel than it is to attempt a restoration of the old one. However, this must be decided on a case-by-case basis.

2 Maintenance — body and frame

1   The condition of your vehicle's body is very important, because it is on this that the second hand value will mainly depend. It is much more difficult to repair a neglected or damaged body than it is to repair mechanical components. The hidden areas of the body, such as the fender wells, the frame, and the engine compartment, are equally important, although they obviously do not require as frequent attention as the rest of the body.

2   Once a year, or every 12,000 miles, it's a good idea to have the underside of the body and the frame steam cleaned. All traces of dirt and oil will be removed and the underside can then be inspected carefully for rust, damaged brake lines, frayed electrical wiring, damaged cables and other problems. The front suspension components should be greased after completion of this job.

3   At the same time, clean the engine and the engine compartment

using either a steam cleaner or a water soluble degreaser.

4   The fender wells should be given particular attention, as under-coating can peel away and stones and dirt thrown up by the tires can cause the paint to chip and flake, allowing rust to set in. If rust is found, clean down to the bare metal and apply an anti-rust paint.

5   The body should be washed as needed. Wet the vehicle thoroughly to soften the dirt, then wash it down with a soft sponge and plenty of clean soapy water. If the surplus dirt is not washed off very carefully, it will in time wear down the paint.

6   Spots of tar or asphalt coating thrown up from the road should be removed with a cloth soaked in solvent.

7   Once every six months, give the body and chrome trim a thorough waxing. If a chrome cleaner is used to remove rust from any of the vehicle's plated parts, remember that the cleaner also removes part of the chrome, so use it sparingly.

3   Maintenance — upholstery and carpets

1   Every three months remove the carpets or mats and clean the in-terior of the vehicle (more frequently if necessary). Vacuum the upholstery and carpets to remove loose dirt and dust.

2   If the upholstery is soiled, apply upholstery cleaner with a damp sponge and wipe it off with a clean, dry cloth.

4   Body repair — minor damage

See color photo sequence ''Repair of minor scratches''

1   If the scratch is superficial and does not penetrate to the metal of the body, repair is very simple. Lightly rub the scratched area with a fine rubbing compound to remove loose paint and built up wax. Rinse the area with clean water.

2   Apply touch-up paint to the scratch, using a small brush. Continue to apply thin layers of paint until the surface of the paint in the scratch is level with the surrounding paint. Allow the new paint at least two weeks to harden, then blend it into the surrounding paint by rubbing with a very fine rubbing compound. Finally, apply a coat of wax to the scratch area.

3   If the scratch has penetrated the paint and exposed the metal of the body, causing the metal to rust, a different repair technique is re-quired. Remove all loose rust from the bottom of the scratch with a pocket knife, then apply rust inhibiting paint to prevent the formation of rust in the future. Using a rubber or nylon applicator, coat the scratched area with glaze-type filler. If required, the filler can be mixed with thinner to provide a very thin paste, which is ideal for filling narrow scratches. Before the glaze filler in the scratch hardens, wrap a piece of smooth cotton cloth around the tip of a finger. Dip the cloth in thin-ner and then quickly wipe it along the surface of the scratch. This will ensure that the surface of the filler is slightly hollow. The scratch can now be painted over as described earlier in this section.

Repair of dents

4   When repairing dents, the first job is to pull the dent out until the affected area is as close as possible to its original shape. There is no point in trying to restore the original shape completely as the metal in the damaged area will have stretched on impact and cannot be restored to its original contours. It is better to bring the level of the dent up to a point which is about 1/8-inch below the level of the sur-rounding metal. In cases where the dent is very shallow, it is not worth trying to pull it out at all.

5   If the back side of the dent is accessible, it can be hammered out gently from behind using a soft-face hammer. While doing this, hold a block of wood firmly against the opposite side of the metal to ab-sorb the hammer blows and prevent the metal from being stretched.

6   If the dent is in a section of the body which has double layers, or some other factor makes it inaccessible from behind, a different technique is required. Drill several small holes through the metal inside the damaged area, particularly in the deeper sections. Screw long, self tapping screws into the holes just enough for them to get a good grip in the metal. Now the dent can be pulled out by pulling on the pro-truding heads of the screws with locking pliers.

7   The next stage of repair is the removal of paint from the damaged area and from an inch or so of the surrounding metal. This is easily done with a wire brush or sanding disk in a drill motor, although it can be done just as effectively by hand with sandpaper. To complete the preparation for filling, score the surface of the bare metal with a screw-driver or the tang of a file or drill small holes in the affected area. This will provide a good grip for the filler material. To complete the repair, see the Section on filling and painting.

Repair of rust holes or gashes

8   Remove all paint from the affected area and from an inch or so of the surrounding metal using a sanding disk or wire brush mounted in a drill motor. If these are not available, a few sheets of sandpaper will do the job just as effectively.

9   With the paint removed, you will be able to determine the severity of the corrosion and decide whether to replace the whole panel, if pos-sible, or repair the affected area. New body panels are not as expensive as most people think and it is often quicker to install a new panel than to repair large areas of rust.

10   Remove all trim pieces from the affected area except those which will act as a guide to the original shape of the damaged body, such as headlight shells, etc. Using metal snips or a hacksaw blade, remove all loose metal and any other metal that is badly affected by rust. Ham-mer the edges of the hole inward to create a slight depression for the filler material.

11   Wire brush the affected area to remove the powdery rust from the surface of the metal. If the back of the rusted area is accessible, treat it with rust-inhibiting paint.

12   Before filling is done, block the hole in some way. This can be done with sheet metal riveted or screwed into place, or by stuffing the hole with wire mesh.

13   Once the hole is blocked off, the affected area can be filled and painted. See the following sub-section on filling and painting.

Filling and painting

14   Many types of body fillers are available, but generally speaking, body repair kits which contain filler paste and a tube of resin hardener are best for this type of repair work. A wide, flexible plastic or nylon applicator will be necessary for imparting a smooth and contoured finish to the surface of the filler material. Mix up a small amount of filler on a clean piece of wood or cardboard (use the hardener sparingly). Follow the manufacturer's instructions on the package, otherwise the filler will set incorrectly.

15   Using the applicator, apply the filler paste to the prepared area. Draw the applicator across the surface of the filler to achieve the desired contour and to level the filler surface. As soon as a contour that ap-proximates the original one is achieved, stop working the paste. If you continue, the paste will begin to stick to the applicator. Continue to add thin layers of paste at 20-minute intervals until the level of the filler is just above the surrounding metal.

16   Once the filler has hardened, the excess can be removed with a body file. From then on, progressively finer grades of sandpaper should be used, starting with a 180-grit paper and finishing with 600-grit wet-or-dry paper. Always wrap the sandpaper around a flat rubber or wooden block, otherwise the surface of the filler will not be completely flat. During the sanding of the filler surface, the wet-or-dry paper should be periodically rinsed in water. This will ensure that a very smooth finish is produced in the final stage.

17   At this point, the repair area should be surrounded by a ring of bare metal, which in turn should be encircled by the finely feathered edge of good paint. Rinse the repair area with clean water until all of the dust produced by the sanding operation is gone.

18   Spray the entire area with a light coat of primer. This will reveal any imperfections in the surface of the filler. Repair the imperfections with fresh filler paste or glaze filler and once more smooth the surface with sandpaper. Repeat this spray-and-repair procedure until you are satisfied that the surface of the filler and the feathered edge of the paint are perfect. Rinse the area with clean water and allow it to dry completely.

19   The repair area is now ready for painting. Spray painting must be carried out in a warm, dry, windless and dust free atmosphere. These conditions can be created if you have access to a large indoor work area, but if you are forced to work in the open, you will have to pick the day very carefully. If you are working indoors, dousing the floor in the work area with water will help settle the dust which would other-wise be in the air. If the repair area is confined to one body panel, mask off the surrounding panels. This will help minimize the effects of a slight

mismatch in paint color. Trim pieces such as chrome strips, door handles, etc., will also need to be masked off or removed. Use masking tape and several thicknesses of newspaper for the masking operations.

20   Before spraying, shake the paint can thoroughly, then spray a test area until the spray painting technique is mastered. Cover the repair area with a thick coat of primer. The thickness should be built up using several thin layers of primer rather than one thick one. Using 600-grit wet-or-dry sandpaper, rub down the surface of the primer until it is very smooth. While doing this, the work area should be thoroughly rinsed with water and the wet-or-dry sandpaper periodically rinsed as well. Allow the primer to dry before spraying additional coats.

21   Spray on the top coat, again building up the thickness by using several thin layers of paint. Begin spraying in the center of the repair area and then, using a circular motion, work out until the whole repair area and about two inches of the surrounding original paint is covered. Remove all masking material 10 to 15 minutes after spraying on the final coat of paint. Allow the new paint at least two weeks to harden, then use a very fine rubbing compound to blend the edges of the new paint into the existing paint. Finally, apply a coat of wax.

5   Body and frame repair — major damage

1   Major damage must be repaired by an auto body/frame repair shop with the necessary welding and hydraulic straightening equipment.
2   If the damage has been serious, it is vital that the frame be checked for proper alignment or the vehicle's handling characteristics may be adversely affected. Other problems, such as excessive tire wear and wear in the driveline and steering may occur.
3   Due to the fact that many of the major body components (hood, doors, etc.) are separate and replaceable units, any seriously damaged components should be replaced rather than repaired. Sometimes these components can be found in a wrecking yard that specializes in used vehicle components, often at considerable savings over the cost of new parts.

6   Maintenance — hinges and locks

Every 3000 miles or three months, the door and hood hinges should be lubricated with a few drops of oil. Lubricate the locks with graphite spray. The door striker plates should also be given a thin coat of white lithium-base grease to reduce wear and ensure free movement.

7   Windshield and fixed glass — replacement

Replacement of the windshield and fixed glass requires the use of special fast-setting adhesive/caulk materials and some specialized tools. It is recommended that these operations should be left to a dealer or a shop specializing in glass work.

8.1   Mark around the hood bolts with white paint before removal so the hood can be reinstalled in the same position

8   Hood — removal and installation

Refer to illustration 8.1

1   Mark the position of the retaining bolts with a sharp scribe or white paint **(see illustration)**.
2   Use rags or pads to protect the cowling and windshield area from the rear of the hood.
3   Disconnect the release cable and the engine compartment light from the hood.
4   With an assistant supporting its weight, remove the bolts and lift the hood from the vehicle.
5   Installation is the reverse of removal.

9   Hood release latch and cable — removal and installation

Refer to illustrations 9.1, 9.3a, 9.3b and 9.4

Latch

1   Mark its position with white paint or by scribing with a pencil, disconnect the cable, remove the two retaining bolts and lift the latch from the vehicle **(see illustration)**.
2   Installation is the reverse of removal.

Cable

3   In the engine compartment, disconnect the cable at the latch and retaining clips **(see illustrations)**.

9.1   Hood latch details

9.3a   After unbolting the latch, remove the screw and disengage the cable

9.3b Disconnect the latch cable clips in the engine compartment

9.4 Remove the trim panel for access to the cable release handle bolts

4   In the passenger compartment, remove the retaining screw, pull back the trim panel and remove the two cable release lever retaining bolts **(see illustration)**.

5   Connect a thin piece of wire or string to the end of the cable in the engine compartment and then pull the cable through into the engine compartment. Attach the wire or string to the new latch cable assembly and pull it through into the engine compartment.

6   Connect the cable to the latch and clips in the engine compartment and install the release lever and trim panel in the passenger compartment.

10   Cowl ventilator grille — removal and installation

Refer to illustration 10.2

1   Remove the windshield wiper arms (Chapter 12).

2   Remove the retaining screws and lift the grille from the vehicle **(see illustration)**.

3   Installation is the reverse of removal.

10.2 With the screws removed, the cowl vent grille can be lifted from the opening

11   Engine cover — removal and installation

Refer to illustration 11.1

1   Release the four engine cover retaining latches (two on each side) **(see illustration)**.

2   Rotate the engine cover down and rearward to remove it. On floor-shift models it may be necessary to shift the lever out of the Park position for additional clearance (set the parking brake and block the wheels to prevent the vehicle from rolling).

3   To install, place the cover in position, making sure the rubber gaskets are aligned to make a good seal, and then secure it by pushing the latches forward.

12   Front fender — removal and installation

Refer to illustration 12.2

1   Remove the grille (Section 13) and headlight(s) (Chapter 11).

2   Remove the retaining bolts and clips which secure the fender along

ENGINE COVER

COVER RELEASE (TWO EACH SIDE)

11.1 Engine cover latch details

12.2   Front fender details

BODY SIDE ASSEMBLY

FRONT FENDER ASSEMBLY

BODY SIDE ASSEMBLY

FLAT WASHER

NUT AND RETAINER

SCREW AND WASHER ASSEMBLY

SCREW AND WASHER

FRONT BUMPER MOUNTING BRACKET

the inside of the engine compartment, at the door and along the bottom **(see illustration)**.

3   Carefully lift the fender away. On the passenger side, disconnect the antenna cable.

4   Installation is the reverse of removal.

13   Radiator grille — removal and installation

Refer to illustrations 13.2 and 13.4

1   Remove the six retaining screws along the top edge of the grille.

2   Press down on the bumper cover for access and remove the two lower grille screws **(see illustration)**.

3   Loosen the headlight bezel screws and pull the tops of the bezels forward to provide clearance for grille removal.

4   Hold the bezels out of the way, grasp the grille securely and lift it from the vehicle **(see illustration)**.

5   Installation is the reverse of removal.

14   Front air deflector — removal and installation

Refer to illustration 14.1

1   Remove the torx-head screws retaining the air deflector to the bumper **(see illustration)**.

2   Use a large screwdriver or pry bar to pry the retaining clips loose and disengage the air deflector from the bumper.

3   To install, place the air deflector in position, press the clips in place and install the screws.

15   Bumpers — removal and installation

Refer to illustrations 15.1, 15.3a and 15.3b

Front bumper

1   Remove the retaining screws and clips and remove the bumper

13.2   Push down on the bumper cover for access to the two lower grille screws

13.4   Hold the headlight bezel out of the way while lifting the grille out

cover (see illustration).

2   Remove the bumper end bracket assemblies and lower the bumper from the vehicle.

3   Installation is the reverse of removal.

Rear bumper

4   Remove the retaining bolts and push pins and lower the bumper from the vehicle (see illustrations).

5   Installation is the reverse of removal.

16   Side window — removal and installation

Refer to illustration 16.6

1   Remove the window trim moulding.

2   Remove the window assembly retaining nuts.

3   With an assistant supporting the window from the outside of the vehicle, push the assembly out and remove it from the vehicle.

4   Prior to installation, clean the old sealer from around the window assembly and opening.

14.1   Use a torx head tool to remove the air deflector screws

15.1   Front bumper cover details

15.3a   Rear bumper details

15.3b   Dual rear door model rear bumper details

FIXED WINDOW

SLIDING WINDOW

16.6 Side window installation details

5   Apply a 1/4-inch bead of butyl sealer around the window assembly opening.
6   Place the window assembly in place and install the retaining nuts **(see illustration)**. Tighten the nuts securely.

17 Door trim panel — removal and installation

Refer to illustrations 17.1, 17.2, 17.3, 17.6 and 17.12

Front door

1   Remove the screws and pry the finish panel out of the door **(see illustration)**
2   On manual window regulator models, remove the screw and lift off the crank. On power regulator models, pry off the control switch assembly and unplug it **(see illustration)**.
3   Insert a screwdriver between the door panel and the door and, working around the outer circumference, disengage the clips **(see illustration)**.
4   Once the clips are disengaged, pull the door panel out at the bottom and lift straight up to remove it from the door.
5   To install, lower the top of the panel into position in the door, line up the clips and press them into place, working around the panel until they are all seated.

Sliding door

6   Remove the retaining nuts and screws and pry off the garnish moulding **(see illustration)**.
7   Remove the retaining screws, insert a screwdriver between the

17.1 Front door trim panel details

17.2   Use a screwdriver to pry out the power window switch

17.3   Use a large screwdriver to disengage the door panel retainers

SLIDING DOOR WINDOW GARNISH MOULDING RETAINER

SLIDING DOOR WINDOW GARNISH MOULDING

NUT

VIEW A

PUSH PIN

SLIDING DOOR TRIM PANEL ASSEMBLY

HIGH-SERIES

TAPE

SLIDING DOOR TRIM PANEL ASSEMBLY

SLIDING DOOR WINDOW GARNISH MOULDING

PUSH PIN

VIEW A

17.6   Side door trim panel details

MID-SERIES

This photo sequence illustrates the repair of a dent and damaged paintwork. The procedure for the repair of a hole is similar. Refer to the text for more complete instructions

After removing any adjacent body trim, hammer the dent out. The damaged area should then be made slightly concave

Use coarse sandpaper or a sanding disc on a drill motor to remove all paint from the damaged area. Feather the sanded area into the edges of the surrounding paint, using progressively finer grades of sandpaper

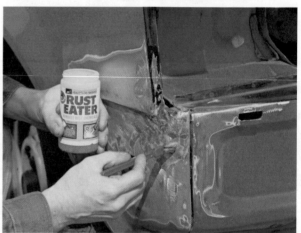

The damaged area should be treated with rust remover prior to application of the body filler. In the case of a rust hole, all rusted sheet metal should be cut away

Carefully follow manufacturer's instructions when mixing the body filler so as to have the longest possible working time during application. Rust holes should be covered with fiberglass screen held in place with dabs of body filler prior to repair

Apply the filler with a flexible applicator in thin layers at 20 minute intervals. Use an applicator such as a wood spatula for confined areas. The filler should protrude slightly above the surrounding area

Shape the filler with a surform-type plane. Then, use water and progressively finer grades of sandpaper and a sanding block to wet-sand the area until it is smooth. Feather the edges of the repair area into the surrounding paint.

Use spray or brush applied primer to cover the entire repair area so that slight imperfections in the surface will be filled in. Prime at least one inch into the area surrounding the repair. Be careful of over-spray when using spray-type primer

Wet-sand the primer with fine (approximately 400 grade) sandpaper until the area is smooth to the touch and blended into the surrounding paint. Use filler paste on minor imperfections

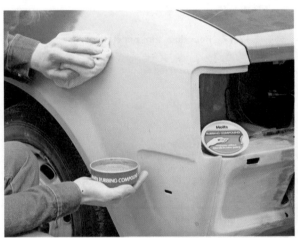

After the filler paste has dried, use rubbing compound to ensure that the surface of the primer is smooth. Prior to painting, the surface should be wiped down with a tack rag or lint-free cloth soaked in lacquer thinner

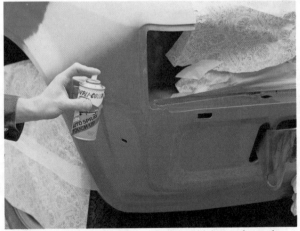

Choose a dry, warm, breeze-free area in which to paint and make sure that adjacent areas are protected from over-spray. Shake the spray paint can thoroughly and apply the top coat to the repair area, building it up by applying several coats, working from the center

After allowing at least two weeks for the paint to harden, use fine rubbing compound to blend the area into the original paint. Wax can now be applied

17.12   Rear door trim panel details

18.3   Front door retaining bolt locations

door panel and the door and, working around the outer circumference, disengage the clips.
8   Lift the trim panel off.
9   Installation is the reverse of removal.

Rear door

10   Remove the window moulding.
11   Remove the door trim retaining screws.
12   Lift the trim panel off (**see illustration**).
13   Installation is the reverse of removal.

---

18   Front door — removal and installation

Refer to illustration 18.3

1   Remove the door trim panel (Section 17) and unplug any electrical connectors.
2   Carefully scribe around the hinges and bolts with a sharp awl or paint. This will locate the present door alignment and help during installation.
3   With an assistant supporting its weight, remove the retaining bolts (**see illustration**) and lift the door off the hinges. **Caution:** *The door is quite heavy, so support it fully during removal.*
4   To install, place the door in position and install the bolts. Align

the door using the marks made on removal and tighten the bolts to the specified torque.

---

19   Sliding door — removal, installation and adjustment

Refer to illustrations 19.1, 19.2a, 19.2b, 19.5, 19.6 and 19.7

Removal and installation

1   Remove the body side filler assembly from the sliding door track (**see illustration**).
2   With an assistant supporting the door weight, remove the bolts from the upper bracket and lower guide (**see illustrations**).
3   Support the door and guide it rearward and out of the track.
4   Installation is the reverse of removal.

Adjustment

Fore-and-aft

5   Fore-and-aft adjustment of the sliding door is accomplished by loosening the three center hinge-to-door bolts and adjusting the hinge assembly as necessary to secure the proper door fit (**see illustration**). After adjustment, tighten the bolts securely.

19.1   Use a Phillips head screwdriver to remove the sliding door filler retaining screw (arrow)

19.2a   Mark the locations of the bolts and bracket with a scribe or pencil and then remove the bolts from the upper bracket . . .

19.2b   . . . and the lower guide

19.5 The sliding door can be adjusted fore-and-aft after loosening the three door hinge assembly bolts

19.6 Front upper edge adjustment to the sliding door is made at the upper guide roller after loosening the two nuts

19.7 Adjust the lower front edge of the sliding door after loosening the adjusting nut

Front upper

6   Loosen the two body side door bracket-to-upper guide roller assembly nuts and move the roller in or out as required to obtain flush fit of the door **(see illustration)**. Tighten the nuts securely after adjustment.

Front lower

7   Adjust the lower front edge of the sliding door by loosening the adjusting nut on the lower guide assembly and then moving the door in or out until a flush fit is obtained **(see illustration)**. Tighten the adjusting nut securely.

Striker

8   The rear latch striker can be adjusted in or out to properly position the rear edge of the door for correct fit as described in Section 22.

20 Rear door — removal and installation

Refer to illustrations 20.1 and 20.2

Liftgate

1   With an assistant supporting its weight, disconnect the liftgate support struts after pushing off the clips with a screwdriver **(see illustration)**.

20.1 Use a screwdriver to pry off the liftgate support strut clips

20.2 Liftgate hinge details

2   Remove the hinge screw and washer assemblies and lift off the liftgate **(see illustration)**.
3   Installation is the reverse of removal.
4   The liftgate can be adjusted by loosening the hinge nut and washer which runs through the interior header. These nuts are accessible after removing the overhead trim panel across the rear opening. To move the liftgate in or out, spacer plates can be used (or removed) between the hinge assembly and the body **(see illustration 20.2)**.

Dual door

5   The procedure for these doors is essentially the same as for the front doors (see Section 18).

21   Front door window regulator — removal and installation

Refer to illustrations 21.3a and 21.3b
1   Remove the door trim panel (Section 17).
2   Remove the front door window glass (Section 22).
3   Use a suitable punch and hammer to drive out the heads of the rivets retaining the regulator to the door. Drill out the remainder of the rivets with a 1/4-inch drill bit, taking care not to enlarge the holes **(see illustrations)**. On power regulators, unplug the connector. Remove the regulator from the vehicle.
4   Lift the regulator from the door.
5   To install, place the regulator in position on the door and install the new rivets. If rivets are not available, use 1/4-inch bolts with nuts to retain the regulator.
6   The remainder of installation is the reverse of removal.

22   Front door window glass — removal and installation

Refer to illustration 22.3
1   Disconnect the negative cable at the battery.
2   Remove the door trim panel and watershield.
3   With the glass in the full up position, remove the rear glass run from the door **(see illustration)**.
4   Lower the glass to provide access to the glass bracket and retaining rivets.
5   Use a suitable punch and hammer to drive out the heads of the rivets retaining the glass to the bracket. Drill out the remainder of the rivets with a 1/4-inch drill bit, taking care not to enlarge the holes.
6   Lift the glass from the bracket.
7   To install, lower the glass into position.
8   Align the glass and bracket retaining holes and install the rivets.
9   Raise the glass to the full up position.
10   Install the rear rear glass run and retainer.
11   Install the watershield and door trim panel.

21.3a   Typical manual window regulator installation details

21.3b   Power window regulator details

22.3 Front door window glass details

23.1 Western-type exterior mirror details

23.4 Conventional-type mirror details

---

23 Exterior mirror — removal and installation

Refer to illustrations 23.1 and 23.4

Western-type mirror

1   Remove the four screws attaching the mirror and lift the mirror off the vehicle **(see illustration)**.
2   Installation is the reverse of removal.

Conventional mirror

3   With the window lowered, remove the door trim panel (Section 17).
4   Remove the two retaining nuts and lift the mirror from the vehicle **(see illustration)**.
5   Installation is the reverse of removal.

---

24 Lower instrument trim panel — removal and installation

Refer to illustrations 24.1 and 24.6

1   Remove the two screws located in the glove compartment **(see illustration)**.

24.1 Lower instrument trim panel component layout

2   Remove the screw located under the lower right of the lower panel-to-cowl side bracket.
3   Pry off the fuse panel cover.
4   Remove the vertical screw located on the right side of the steering column.
5   Unplug the wiring connector.
6   Pull the lower panel sharply rearward to unsnap it from the two retaining pins and lower from the instrument panel **(see illustration)**.
7   Installation is the reverse of removal.

25 Seats — removal and installation

Refer to illustrations 25.1, 25.3a and 25.3b

Front seats

1   Remove the retaining bolts, disconnect any electrical or other connectors and lift the seat from the vehicle **(see illustration)**.
2   Installation is the reverse of removal. Tighten the retaining bolts to the specified torque.

Rear seats

3   Lift the seat latch handle (one for bucket seats, two for bench seats) to the rear, which will cause the seat to move rearward **(see illustrations)**.

24.6 Pull the panel off the retaining pins (arrows) and lower it from the dash

25.1 Typical front seat details

25.3a Rear quick release bucket seat details

REAR FLOOR RETAINER

FRONT FLOOR RETAINER

VIEW A

J-ROD HOOK

REAR BENCH SEAT ASSEMBLY

POSITIVE STOP

J-ROD HOOK

VIEW A

25.3b Bench-type seat rear quick release details

BODY LOCK PILLAR TAPE

BOLT

VIEW B
VIEW C

NOTE:
ENSURE THAT WEBBING IS NOT TWISTED BETWEEN ANCHOR PLATE AND RETRACTOR AND IS INSERTED IN THE LOOP

FRONT SEAT BELT ASSEMBLY

BOLT

FRONT SEAT BELT ASSEMBLY

FRONT SEAT SHOULDER STRAP LOOP

BOLT

FRONT SEAT BELT PLUG

VIEW A

BOLT

FRONT SEAT BELT ASSEMBLY

NOTE:
ANCHOR PLATE TO BE ALIGNED WITH FLOORPAN BEAD AS SHOWN
VIEW A

FRONT SEAT BELT ASSEMBLY

FRONT SEAT SHOULDER STRAP COVER (BASE BELTS ONLY)

BOLT

SCREW

FRONT SEAT

VIEW B

FRONT SEAT BELT ASSEMBLY

VIEW C

26.3 Front seat belt details

26.12 Rear bench seat belt details

4   Lift the latch J-rod hook end out of the locking hole(s) in the attaching plate.
5   Push the seat rearward and lift it from the vehicle.
6   To install, lower the seat into position with the front and rear retainers in the floor openings at the rear edge.
7   Engage the J-rod hook end into the slot at the front floor attaching plate and then rotate the latch handle(s) forward, moving the seat forward, engaging it with the floor attachments and continue pushing until the seat is locked in place. The handle must be rotated all the way forward so that it contacts the positive stop on the front attachment.

26 Seat belts — check and replacement

Refer to illustrations 26.3 and 26.12

Check

1   Inspect the seat belt system for frayed belts, binding of the retractor mechanism and loose bolts. Replace any worn or damaged components with new ones.

Replacement

Front seat belts

2   Remove the D ring cover or trim panel and retractor assembly bolt.
3   Lift up on the carpet and remove the floor anchor bolt **(see illustration)**.
4   Remove the D ring bolt and remove the belt from the vehicle.
5   To install, place the belt in position and install the D ring bolt. Tighten the bolt to the specified torque.
6   Feed the belt into the slotted shoulder strap loop, making sure not to twist it.
7   Install the D ring cover or trim panel.
8   Feed the anchor and tongue through the slot in the trim panel and install the floor anchor bolt. Tighten the bolt to the specified torque.

Rear bucket seat belts

9   Remove the plug fom the buckle boot and snap open the cover for access to the retaining bolt.
10 Remove the retaining bolts and lift off the belt assemblies.
11 Installation is the reverse of removal.

Bench seat belts

12 Remove the belt assembly-to-seat structure bolts **(see illustration)**.
13 Remove the belts by pulling the belt and anchor plates through the grommet in the seat cushion.
14 Installation is the reverse of removal.

Chapter 12 Chassis electrical system

Contents

Specifications

Bulb application

	Number
Brake/tail lights	1157
Rear license plate light	194
Front parking/turn signal light	1157
Headlights	HP6054
Back-up light	1156
Heater indicator light	1445
Courtesy light	912
Dome lamp	211-2
Fuel computer	194
Cargo lamp	211-2

1 General information

The electrical system is a 12-volt, negative ground type. Power for the lights and all electrical accessories is supplied by a lead/acid-type battery which is charged by the alternator.

This Chapter covers repair and service procedures for the various electrical components not associated with the engine. Information on the battery, alternator, distributor and starter motor can be found in Chapter 5.

When working on electrical system components, disconnect the negative battery cable from the battery to prevent electrical shorts and/or fires.

2 Electrical troubleshooting — general information

A typical electrical circuit consists of an electrical component, any switches, relays, motors, etc. related to that component and the wiring and connectors that connect the component to both the battery and the chassis. To aid in locating a problem in any electrical circuit, wiring diagrams are included at the end of this book.

Before tackling any troublesome electrical circuit, first study the appropriate diagrams to get a complete understanding of what makes up that individual circuit. Trouble spots, for instance, can often be narrowed down by noting if other components related to that circuit are operating properly or not. If several components or circuits fail at one time, chances are the problem lies in the fuse or ground connection, as several circuits are often routed through the same fuse and ground connections.

Electrical problems often stem from simple causes, such as loose or corroded connections, a blown fuse or a melted fusible link. Always visually inspect the condition of the fuse, wires and connections in a problem circuit before troubleshooting it.

If testing instruments are going to be utilized, use the diagrams to plan ahead of time where you will make the necessary connections in order to accurately pinpoint the trouble spot.

The basic tools needed for electrical troubleshooting include a circuit tester or voltmeter (a 12-volt bulb with a set of test leads can also be used), a continuity tester, which includes a bulb, battery and set of test leads, and a jumper wire, preferably with a circuit breaker incorporated, which can be used to bypass electrical components.

Voltage checks should be performed if a circuit is not functioning properly. Connect one lead of a circuit tester to either the negative battery terminal or a known good ground. Connect the other lead to a connector in the circuit being tested, preferably nearest to the battery or fuse. If the bulb of the tester lights up, voltage is present, which means that the part of the circuit between the connector and the battery is problem free. Continue checking the rest of the circuit in the same fashion. When you reach a point at which no voltage is present, the problem lies between that point and the last test point with voltage. Most of the time the problem can be traced to a loose connection. **Note:** *Keep in mind that some circuits receive voltage only when the ignition key is in the Accessory or Run position.*

One method of finding shorts in a circuit is to remove the fuse and connect a test light or voltmeter in its place to the fuse terminals. There should be no voltage present in the circuit. Move the wiring harness from side-to-side while watching the test light. If the bulb goes on, there is a short to ground somewhere in that area, probably where the insulation has rubbed through. The same test can be performed on each component in the circuit, even a switch.

Perform a ground test to check whether a component is properly grounded. Disconnect the battery and connect one lead of a self-powered test light, known as a "continuity tester," to a known good ground. Connect the other lead to the wire or ground connection being tested. If the bulb goes on, the ground is good. If the bulb does not go on, the ground is not good.

A continuity check determines if there are any breaks in a circuit — if it is conducting electricity properly. With the circuit off (no power in the circuit), a self-powered continuity tester can be used to check the circuit. Connect the test leads to both ends of the circuit (or to the "power" end and a good ground), and if the test light comes on the circuit is passing current properly. If the light doesn't come on, there is a break somewhere in the circuit. The same procedure can be used to test a switch, by connecting the continuity tester to the power in and power out sides of the switch. With the switch turned on, the test light should come on.

When diagnosing for possible open circuits, it is often difficult to locate them by sight because oxidation or terminal misalignment are hidden by the connectors. Merely wiggling a connector on a sensor or in the wiring harness may correct the open circuit condition. Remember this if an open circuit is indicated when troubleshooting a circuit. Intermittent problems may also be caused by oxidized or loose connections.

Electrical troubleshooting is simple if you keep in mind that all electrical circuits are basically electricity running from the battery, through the wires, switches, relays, fuses and fusible links to each electrical component (light bulb, motor, etc.) and back to ground, from which it is passed back to the battery. Any electrical problem is an interruption in the flow of electricity to and from the battery.

3 Fuses — general information

Refer to illustrations 3.2a and 3.2b

The electrical circuits of the vehicle are protected by a combination of fuses, circuit breakers and fusible links. The fuse block is located under the dash on the driver's side.

FUSE PANEL
ACCESS COVER

3.2a The fuse block is located behind an access cover under the instrument panel to the left of the steering column

Each fuse protects one or more circuits. The protected circuit is identified on the fuse panel cover **(see illustrations)**. On these models, miniaturized fuses are installed in the fuse block. These compact fuses, with blade terminal design, allow fingertip removal and installation.

If an electrical component fails, always check the fuse first.

A blown fuse, which is nothing more than a broken element, is easily identified through the plastic body. Visually inspect the element for evidence of damage. If a continuity check is called for, the blade terminals are exposed in the fuse body.

Be sure to replace blown fuses with the correct type. Fuses of different ratings are physically interchangeable, but only fuses of the proper rating should be used. Replacing a fuse with one of a higher or lower value than specified is not recommended. Each electrical circuit needs a specific amount of protection. The amperage value of each fuse is molded into the fuse body. **Caution:** *Never bypass a fuse with pieces of metal or foil. Serious damage to the electrical system could result.*

If the replacement fuse immediately fails, do not replace it again until the cause of the problem is isolated and corrected.

3.2b The removable cover over the fuse block contains fuse and circuit information for your vehicle

REMOVE EXISTING VINYL TUBE SHIELDING
REINSTALL OVER FUSE LINK BEFORE CRIMPING
FUSE LINK TO WIRE ENDS

TAPE

TAPE OR STRAP

TYPICAL REPAIR USING THE SPECIAL #17 GA. (9.00" LONG-YELLOW) FUSE LINK REQUIRED FOR THE AIR/COND.
CIRCUITS (2) #687E AND #261A LOCATED IN THE ENGINE COMPARTMENT

FUSE LINK

TAPE OR STRAP

TYPICAL REPAIR FOR ANY IN-LINE FUSE LINK USING THE SPECIFIED GAUGE FUSE LINK FOR THE SPECIFIC CIRCUT

TAPE

TYPICAL REPAIR USING THE EYELET TERMINAL FUSE LINK OF THE SPECIFIED GAUGE FOR ATTACHMENT TO A CIRCUIT WIRE END

TAPE

(3) FUSE LINKS

TYPICAL REPAIR ATTACHING THREE LIGHT GAUGE
FUSE LINKS TO A SINGLE HEAVY GAUGE FEED WIRE

TAPE

TAPE

$

D3AZ-14488-Y BUTT CONNECTOR
FOR 10 OR 12 GA. WIRE

DOUBLED WIRE CRIMPED

#10 OR 12 GA. WIRE

LIGHT GAUGE WIRE

$

D3AZ-14488-Z BUTT CONNECTOR
FOR #14 OR 16 WIRE

$

4.1 Fusible link servicing procedures

4 Fusible links — replacement

Refer to illustration 4.1

Some circuits are protected by fusible links. These links are used in circuits which are not ordinarily fused, such as the ignition circuit. If a circuit protected by a fusible link becomes inoperative, inspect for a blown fusible link.

Although fusible links appear to be of heavier gauge than the wire they are protecting, their appearance is due to thicker insulation. All fusible links are four wire gauges *smaller* than the wire they are designed to protect. The location of the fusible links on your particular vehicle can be determined by referring to the wiring diagrams at the end of this Chapter.

Fusible links cannot be repaired. If you must replace one, make sure that the new fusible link is a duplicate of the one removed with respect to gauge, length and insulation. Original and Ford replacement fusible links have insulation that is flame proof. Do not fabricate a fusible link from ordinary wire — the insulation may not be flame proof. **Warning:** *Do not mistake a resistor wire for a fusible link. The resistor wire is generally longer and is identified by a "Resistor — don't cut or splice" warning.*

Charging system fusible link

1   To replace the fusible link in the charging system, proceed as follows:
   a) Disconnect the negative cable at the battery.
   b) Disconnect the fusible link from the wiring harness or the fusible link eyelet terminal from the battery terminal of the starter relay (on some vehicle applications, the fusible link is looped outside the wire harness) **(see illustration).**
   c) Cut the damaged fusible link and the splices from the wires to which it is attached. Disconnect the feed wire part of the wiring and cut out the damaged portion as closely as possible behind the splice in the harness. If the fusible link wire insulation is burned or opened, disconnect the feed as close as possible behind the splice in the harness. If the damaged fusible link is between two splices (the weld points in the harness), cut out the damaged portion as close as possible to the weld points.
   d) Strip the insulation back approximately 1/2-inch.
   e) Splice and solder the new fusible link to the wires from which the old link was cut. Use rosin core solder at each end of the new link to obtain a good solder joint.
   f) Wrap the splices completely with vinyl electrical tape around the soldered joint. No wires should be exposed.
   g) Securely connect the eyelet terminals (if any) to the battery stud on the starter relay.
   h) Install the repaired wiring as before, using existing clips, if provided.
   i) Connect the battery ground cable.
   j) Test the circuit for proper operation.

All other fusible links

2   To service any other blown fusible link, use the following procedure:
   a) Determine which circuit is damaged, its location and the cause of the open fusible link. If the damaged fusible link is one of three fed by a common 10 or 12 gauge feed wire, determine the specific affected circuit.
   b) Disconnect the negative cable at the battery.
   c) Cut the damaged fusible link from the wiring harness and discard it. If the fusible link is one of three circuits fed by a single wire, cut it out of the harness at each splice and discard it.
   d) Identify and procure the proper fusible link and butt connectors for attaching the fusible link to the harness.
3   To service any fusible link in a three-link group with one feed:
   a) After cutting the open link out of the harness, cut each of the remaining undamaged fusible links close to the feed wire weld.
   b) Strip approximately 1/2-inch of insulation from the detached ends of the two good fusible links. Insert two wire ends into one end of a Ford butt connector and carefully push one stripped end of the replacement fusible link into the same end of the butt connector and crimp all three firmly together. **Note:** *Be very careful when fitting the three fusible links into the butt connector — the*

internal diameter is a snug fit for three wires. Be sure to use a proper crimping tool. Pliers, side cutters, etc. will not apply the proper crimp to retain the wires.
   c) After crimping the butt connector to the three fusible links, cut the weld portion from the feed wire and strip about 1/2-inch of insulation from the cut end. Insert the stripped end into the open end of the butt connector and crimp very firmly.
   d) To attach the remaining end of the replacement fusible link, strip about 1/2-inch of insulation from the wire end of the circuit from which the blown fusible link was removed and firmly crimp a butt connector to the stripped wire. Insert the end of the replacement link into the other end of the butt connector and crimp firmly.

5 Circuit breakers — general information

Circuit breakers protect components such as power windows, power door locks and headlights. Some circuit breakers are located in the fuse box. Refer to the wiring diagrams at the end of this book for the location of the circuit breakers located elsewhere on this vehicle.

Because a circuit breaker resets itself automatically, an electrical overload in a circuit breaker protected system will cause the circuit to fail momentarily, then come back on. If the circuit does not come back on, check it immediately. Once the condition is corrected, the circuit breaker will resume its normal function.

6 Turn signal and hazard flashers — check and replacement

Refer to illustration 6.1

Turn signal flasher

1   The turn signal flasher, a small canister shaped unit located in the fuse block **(see illustration)**, flashes the turn signals.
2   When the flasher unit is functioning properly, an audible click can be heard during its operation. If the turn signals fail on one side or the other and the flasher unit does not make its characteristic clicking sound, a faulty turn signal bulb is indicated.
3   If both turn signals fail to blink, the problem many be due to a blown fuse, a faulty flasher unit, a broken switch or a loose or open connection. If a quick check of the fuse box indicates that the turn signal fuse has blown, check the wiring for a short before installing a new fuse.
4   To replace the flasher, simply pull it out of the fuse block or wiring harness.
5   Make sure that the replacement unit is identical to the original. Compare the old one to the new one before installing it.
6   Installation is the reverse of removal.

Hazard flasher

7   The hazard flasher, a small canister shaped unit located in the fuse block, flashes all four turn signals simultaneously when activated.

6.1 The turn signal flasher is located at the lower corner of the fuse panel (arrow)

7.7   With the ignition key lock cylinder in the Run position, push in on the release lever to release the cylinder

8.7   Unplug the ignition switch connector (lower arrows) and unscrew the break-off head bolts (upper arrows)

8   The hazard flasher is checked in a fashion similar to the turn signal flasher (see Steps 2 and 3).
9   To replace the hazard flasher, pull it from the back of fuse block.
10   Make sure the replacement unit is identical to the one it replaces. Compare the old one to the new one before installing it.
11   Installation is the reverse of removal.

7   Ignition key lock cylinder — replacement

Refer to illustration 7.7

1   Disconnect the negative cable at the battery. Place the cable out of the way so it cannot accidentally come in contact with the negative terminal of the battery, as this would once again allow power into the electrical system of the vehicle.
2   Remove the steering wheel (Chapter 10).
3   If your vehicle is equipped with a tilt column, remove the steering column collar.
4   Remove the four retaining screws and detach the column cover.
5   Locate the key warning buzzer electrical lead (the insulated single wire coming out of the key lock cylinder housing), trace it back to the pigtail connector near the multi-terminal connector for the ignition switch and unplug it.
6   Turn the lock key to the Run position.
7   Place a 1/8-inch punch in the hole in the casting surrounding the lock cylinder. Depress the punch while pulling out on the lock cylinder to remove it from the column housing **(see illustration)**.
8   Install the lock cylinder by turning it to the Run position and depressing the retaining pin. Insert the lock cylinder into the lock cylinder housing. Make sure the cylinder is completely seated and aligned in the interlocking washer before turning the key to the Off position. This will permit the retaining pin to extend into the hole.
9   Turn the lock to ensure that the operation is correct in all positions.
10   The remainder of installation is the reverse of removal.

8   Ignition switch — replacement

Refer to illustration 8.7

1   Disconnect the negative cable at the battery. Place the cable out of the way so it cannot accidentally come in contact with the negative terminal of the battery, as this would once again allow power into the electrical system of the vehicle.
2   Remove the steering wheel (Chapter 10).
3   On tilt column models, grasp the upper extension shroud and

remove it by squeezing it at the top and bottom and popping it free of the retaining plate.
4   Remove the screws and detach the steering column bottom cover.
5   Remove the screws and detach the panel to the right of the steering column.
6   Remove the key lock cylinder (Section 7).
7   Unplug the ignition switch electrical connector and use a hammer and chisel to unscrew the break-off head bolts one turn counterclockwise **(see illustration)**.
8   Use pliers to unscrew the bolts and remove them.
9   Disengage the ignition switch from the actuator pin.
10   Make sure the actuator pin slot in the new ignition switch is in the Run Positon. **Note:** *A new replacement switch assembly will be set in the On (Run) position.*
11   Place the new switch in position and install the break-off head bolts. Tighten each bolt until the head breaks off.
12   Plug the electrical connector into the switch.
13   Install the steering column shroud and any other panels which were removed.
14   Install the ignition key lock cylinder.
15   Install the steering wheel.
16   Connect the battery negative cable.

9   Turn signal switch — removal and installation

Refer to illustrations 9.6a and 9.6b

1   Disconnect the negative cable at the battery. Place the cable out of the way so it cannot accidentally come in contact with the negative terminal of the battery, as this would once again allow power into the electrical system of the vehicle.
2   Remove the steering wheel.
3   Remove the steering column cover.
4   Remove the ignition key lock cylinder (Section 7).
5   Remove the control lever by grasping it securely and pulling it directly out of the switch.
6   Remove the two retaining screws, pull the switch out, unplug the connector and withdraw the switch assembly from the steering column **(see illustrations)**.
7   Plug in the electrical connector, place the new switch in position and install the screws. Tighten the screws securely.
8   Install the steering column cover.
9   Install the ignition key lock cylinder.
10   Install the switch lever by aligning the key on the lever with the keyway in the switch and pushing the lever in until it engages.
11   Install the steering wheel.
12   Connect the negative battery cable.

9.6a Remove the upper . . .

9.6b . . . and lower turn signal switch retaining screws (arrow)

10 Headlight switch and rheostat — removal and installation

Refer to illustrations 10.2, 10.3, 10.4, 10.5 and 10.9

Headlight switch

1 Disconnect the negative cable at the battery. Place the cable out of the way so it cannot accidentally come in contact with the negative terminal of the battery, as this would once again allow power into the electrical system of the vehicle.
2 Remove the five instrument cluster panel retaining screws, pry up on the panel and remove it **(see illustration)**.
3 Remove the three switch control pod retaining screws **(see illustration)**.
4 Disengage the clip at the corner and rotate the pod out of the instrument panel for access to the switch **(see illustration)**.

10.2 Instrument cluster panel assembly

10.3 The headlight switch control pod is retained by three screws

10.4 Disengage the clip and rotate the control pod out of the instrument panel for access to the switch

10.5   The rear of the control pod shows the electrical connectors at the back of the switches

10.9   Push the clip away from the switch with your thumb and unplug the connector

11.2a   Typical headlight door assembly

BULB ASSEMBLY

HEADLAMP DOOR ASSEMBLY

SCREW

PUSH IN NUT ASSEMBLY

CLIP

(3 REQ'D)

5   Unplug the connector, remove the retaining screws and lift the switch from the pod **(see illustration)**.
6   Installation is the reverse of removal.

Rheostat

7   Remove the fuse panel cover to gain access to the rheostat.
8   Remove the two retaining screws and lower the rheostat from the instrument panel.
9   Unplug the electrical connector and remove the rheostat from the vehicle **(see illustration)**.
10   Installation is the reverse of removal.

11   Headlights — removal and installation

Refer to illustrations 11.2a, 11.2b, 11.2c, 11.3, 11.4, 11.5 and 11.8

1   Disconnect the negative cable at the battery. Place the cable out of the way so it cannot accidentally come in contact with the negative terminal of the battery, as this would once again allow power into the electrical system of the vehicle.
2   Remove the headlight door retaining screws and clips **(see illustrations)**.

11.2b   A torx-head screwdriver is required to remove the headlight door screws

11.2c   On some models the lower retaining screw is hidden by the bumper cover

11.3   Push down on the bumper cover and lift out the headlight door

11.4   Use a Phillips screwdriver to remove the retaining ring screws — do not disturb the adjusting screws

3   Grasp the headlight door securely, push down on the bumper cover and remove the door **(see illustration)**.
4   Remove the headlight retaining ring screws **(see illustration)**, taking care not to disturb the adjustment screws **(see illustration 12.1)**.
5   Remove the retaining ring and pull the headlight out sufficiently to allow the connector to be unplugged **(see illustration)**.
6   Remove the headlight.
7   To install, plug the connector securely into the headlight, place the headlight in position and install the retaining ring and screws. Tighten the screws securely.
8   Place the headlight door in position, align the clips with their mounting holes and push the door firmly into place **(see illustration)**.
9   Install the headlight screws and connect the battery negative cable.

12   Headlights — adjustment

Refer to illustration 12.1

Note: *It is important that the headlights be aimed correctly. If adjusted incorrectly they could blind the driver of an oncoming vehicle and cause a serious accident or seriously reduce your ability to see the road. The headlights should be checked for proper aim every 12 months and any time a new headlight is installed or front end body work is performed. It should be emphasized that the following procedure is only an interim step which will provide temporary adjustment until the headlights can be adjusted by a properly equipped shop.*

1   Headlights have two spring loaded adjusting screws, one on the

11.5   Support the headlight and pull the connector straight off

11.8   Line up the headlight door clip with the holes and push in to seat them

12.1   Headlight assembly and adjusting screws

top controlling up-and-down movement and one on the side controlling left-and-right movement **(see illustration)**.

2   There are several methods of adjusting the headlights. The simplest method requires a blank wall 25 feet in front of the vehicle and a level floor.

3   Position masking tape vertically on the wall in reference to the vehicle centerline and the centerlines of both headlights.

4   Position a horizontal tape line in reference to the centerline of all the headlights. **Note:** *It may be easier to position the tape on the wall with the vehicle parked only a few inches away.*

5   Adjustment should be made with the vehicle sitting level, the gas tank half-full and no unusually heavy load in the vehicle.

6   Starting with the low beam adjustment, position the high intensity zone so it is two inches below the horizontal line and two inches to the right of the headlight vertical line. Adjustment is made by turning the top adjusting screw *clockwise* to raise the beam and *counterclockwise* to lower the beam. The adjusting screw on the side should be used in the same manner to move the beam left or right.

7   With the high beams on, the high intensity zone should be vertically centered with the exact center just below the horizontal line. **Note:** *It may not be possible to position the headlight aim exactly for both high and low beams. If a compromise must be made, keep in mind that the low beams are the most used and have the greatest effect on driver safety.*

8   Have the headlights adjusted by a dealer service department at the earliest opportunity.

13   Bulb replacement

Refer to illustrations 13.2, 13.4, 13.6, 13.7, 13.10, 13.13, 13.14 and 13.17

Parking, turn and front side lamps

1   Remove the headlight door assembly **(see illustrations 11.2a, 11.2b and 11.2c)**.

13.2   Pull the bulb holder out for access to the bulb

2   Hold the headlight door out of the way and pull the bulb holder out **(see illustration)**.

3   Push the bulb in and turn it counterclockwise to remove it.

Engine compartment lamp

4   Remove the lamp protective shield, grasp the bulb and pull it out of the socket **(see illustration)**. Push the new bulb securely in place.

Instrument cluster

Warning: *The manufacturer recommends that on electronic display instrument clusters, the bulbs be replace by a dealer because they are under pressure and could shatter causing personal injury.*

13.4 Engine compartment lamp details

13.6 The bulb holders are located on the back of the instrument cluster and are removed by turning them about 1/4 turn

13.7 Dome/reading lamp bulb assembly

5   Remove the instrument cluster (Section 18).
6   The instrument cluster bulbs can be replaced after rotating the holders and lifting them out (**see illustration**).

Dome lamp

7   Use a screwdriver to pry the lens cover off and replace the bulb by grasping it securely and pulling it from the lamp assembly (**see illustration**).

Map reading lamp

8   To replace the bulb in the center section, snap the lens carefully out of the lamp body and then remove the bulb (**see illustration 13.7**).
9   To replace the bulb in the movable lamp gimble, depress the legs of the bulb cover with a thin tool and remove it. Snap the bulb gently from the socket.

Cargo lamp

10 Remove the two lens screws, lift off the lens and remove the bulb by depressing it and rotating it in a counterclockwise direction (**see illustration**).

13.10 Cargo lamp blub details

13.13   Pull the tail light lens away from the body — the sealant may make this job difficult

13.14   Rotate the bulb holders counterclockwise to remove them

VIEW A

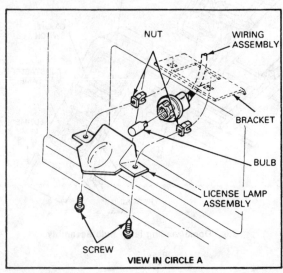

13.17   Dual rear door license plate light installation

14.1   Horn current draw check

17   On dual door models, remove the license plate assembly and pull the bulb out of the socket **(see illustration).**

---

14   Horn — check and replacement

Refer to illustrations 14.1 and 14.5

Check

1   If the horn does not sound, first make sure the mounting bolt is securely tightened. Connect one jumper wire from the horn mounting bracket bolt to the negative battery terminal and another jumper wire from the horn terminal to the positive battery terminal **(see illustration).**
2   If the horn does not sound and there is no sparking at the battery terminal, disconnect the jumper wires. Turn the adjusting screw counterclockwise between 1/4 and 3/8 turn and then use pliers to lock it from turning by squeezing the housing extrusions. If the horn does not sound when the jumper wires are reconnected, replace it with a new one.

Replacement

3   Disconnect the negative cable at the battery.
4   Unplug the horn electrical connector.
5   Remove the mounting bolt(s) and lift the horn from the vehicle **(see illustration).**
6   Installation is the reverse of removal.

Brake and tail lamp

11   Open the rear liftgate or doors.
12   Remove the four tail light lens retaining screws.
13   Grasp the inner edge of the lens and rotate it away from the body to break it loose from the sealant **(see illustration).**
14   Turn the bulb holders counterclockwise to remove them **(see illustration).**
15   Turn the bulbs counterclockwise to remove them from the holders.

License plate lamp

16   On liftgate models, remove the two screws, lift off the bulb cover and pull the bulb from the socket.

14.5 Horn installation

FRONT OF VEHICLE

HORN ASSEMBLY (HI PITCH)

FENDER APRON (RH)

HORN ASSEMBLY (LOW PITCH)

VIEW SHOWING INSTALLATION WITH DUAL HORNS

FRONT OF VEHICLE

FENDER APRON (RH)

HORN ASSEMBLY (LOW PITCH)

VIEW SHOWING STANDARD HORN

15 Radio and speakers — removal and installation

Refer to illustrations 15.3, 15.7, and 15.9

1   Disconnect the negative cable at the battery. Place the cable out of the way so it cannot accidentally come in contact with the negative terminal of the battery, as this would once again allow power into the electrical system of the vehicle.

Radio

2   Carefully pry off the finish panel.
3   Remove the retaining screws **(see illustration)**.
4   Pull the radio from the instrument panel, disconnect the antenna and electrical connectors and remove it from the vehicle.
5   Installation is the reverse of removal.

Speakers

Instrument panel mounted
6   Remove the instrument panel pad (Section 17).
7   Remove the retaining screws and lift the speaker out **(see illustration)**. Unplug the electrical connector and remove the speaker.
8   Installation is the reverse of removal.

15.3 Radio retaining screw locations (arrows)

SCREW AND WASHER

RH SIDE SHOWN

SPEAKER ASSEMBLY

SPRING NUT

WIRING ASSEMBLY

SCREW AND WASHER

LH SIDE SHOWN

SPEAKER ASSEMBLY

SPRING NUT

WIRING ASSEMBLY

15.7 Instrument panel mounted speaker assembly

Body side mounted

9   Pry the speaker grille off and remove the speaker retaining screws **(see illustration)**.

10   Disengage the speaker from the mounting plate, disconnect the wiring assembly and remove the speaker.

11   Installation is the reverse of removal.

Rear door mounted

12   On liftgate models, remove the trim panel (Chapter 11). Remove

the mounting screws, withdraw the speaker and unplug the electrical connector and remove the speaker from the vehicle.

13   Installation is the reverse of removal.

14   On dual door models, remove the four screws and detach the speaker enclosure and bracket.

15   Remove the bracket assembly, unplug the wiring connector at the enclosure and remove the speaker.

16   Installation is the reverse or removal.

15.9 Side mounted speaker assembly

16   Radio antenna — removal and installation

Refer to illustrations 16.1, 16.4 and 16.5

Antenna mast

1   Unscrew the antenna mast from the base (see illustration).
2   Installation is the reverse of removal.

Cable

3   Remove the radio and disconnect the cable.
4   Disengage the cable from the clips and retainers along the top of the heater assembly (see illustration).
5   Carefully pry off the radio antenna base cap, remove the mounting screws and pull the base and cable assembly out of the fender (see illustration).
6   Installation is the reverse of removal.

17   Instrument panel — removal and installation

Refer to illustrations 17.3 and 17.7

1   Disconnect the negative cable at the battery.
2   Remove the instrument cluster retaining screws and tap up at the corners to disengage the cluster from the control pods.

16.1   Unscrew the antenna mast with a box end wrench

16.4   Disconnect the radio cable at the heater assembly clips

16.5   Radio antenna cable and base mounting details

SCREW AND WASHER (3 REQ'D)

INSTRUMENT CLUSTER PANEL ASSEMBLY

UPPER PANEL ASSEMBLY

SCREW AND WASHER

UPPER PANEL ASSEMBLY

SCREW

SCREW (2 REQ'D)

U-NUT

INSTRUMENT PANEL ASSEMBLY

INSTRUMENT PANEL ASSEMBLY

U-NUT

LOWER INSTRUMENT PANEL ASSEMBLY

LOWER INSTRUMENT PANEL ASSEMBLY

SCREW AND WASHER

PANEL AND REGISTER ASSEMBLY

SCREW AND WASHER

PANEL ASSEMBLY

SCREW AND WASHER

17.3 Instrument panel cluster and upper panel

VEHICLE IDENTIFICATION PLATE

RIVET

U-NUT

U-NUT

SCREW AND WASHER

VIEW C

NUT

SCREW AND WASHER

I/P LOWER CENTER BRACE

INSTRUMENT PANEL ASSEMBLY

SCREW AND WASHER

VIEW B

VIEW A

INSTRUMENT PANEL ASSEMBLY

SCREW AND WASHER W611102-S2

INSTRUMENT PANEL ASSEMBLY

I/P LOWER CENTER BRACE

VIEW A

INSTRUMENT PANEL ASSEMBLY

SCREW AND WASHER

BRACKET COVER

SCREW AND WASHER

BRACKET (LH)

LEFT HAND SIDE VIEW IN CIRCLE B

INSTRUMENT PANEL ASSEMBLY

BRACKET (RH)

SCREW AND WASHER

RIGHT HAND SIDE VIEW IN CIRCLE C

17.7 Instrument panel details

3 Remove the upper panel retaining screws (see illustration).
4 Remove the retaining screws and remove the cluster panel.
5 Lift the upper instrument panel out of the dash.
6 Remove the lower instrument panel trim panel (Chapter 11).
7 Remove the two left side and one right side instrument panel cowl side attachment screws (see illustration).
8 Remove the lower center instrument panel brace screws.
9 Remove the steering column-to-instrument panel bolts.
10 Disconnect the wiring connectors and lift the instrument panel from the vehicle.
11 To install, place the panel in position on the cowl side brackets and align the centering stud into the cowl top. Line up the panel darts in the grooves on the cowl side brackets.
12 Connect the wiring connectors.
13 Install the steering column-to-instrument panel bolts.
14 Install the cowl top and side attachment screws.
15 Install the lower center brace screws.
16 Install the center brace-to-dash screws.
17 Install the upper instrument panel and cluster panel.
18 Install the lower instrument trim panel.

18 Instrument cluster — removal and installation

Refer to illustration 18.6
1 Disconnect the negative cable at the battery.
2 Remove the instrument cluster panel assembly (Section 17).
3 Remove the instrument cluster retaining screws.
4 On conventional clusters, reach behind the cluster and disconnect the speedometer cable.
5 Pull the cluster out and unplug the electrical connectors.
6 Lift the cluster from the instrument panel (see illustration).
7 Installation is the reverse of removal. On conventional clusters, apply speedometer cable lubricant to the drive hole of the speedometer.

18.6 Instrument cluster mounting

19 Speedometer cable — replacement

Refer to illustration 19.2
1 Disconnect the negative cable at the battery.
2 Disconnect the speedometer cable at the transmission (see illustration).
3 Detach the cable from the fasteners in the engine compartment and pull it up to provide enough slack to allow disconnection from the speedometer.

19.2 Speedometer cable installation

4　Remove the instrument cluster screws and disconnect the speedometer cable from the back of the cluster.
5　Remove the cable from the vehicle.
6　Installation is the reverse of removal.

20　Power door lock switch and actuator motor — removal and installation

Refer to illustration 20.2

Switch

1　Disconnect the negative cable from the battery and then carefully pry the switch trim bezel off with a thin screwdriver.
2　Remove the wiring connector retaining nuts from the back of the bezel and then pry the switch off the bezel (see illustration).
3　Installation is the reverse of removal.

Door lock

4　Disconnect the negative cable at the battery.
5　Remove the door trim panel (Chapter 11).
6　Detach the actuator motor link from the door latch.
7　Use a drill with a suitable size drill bit to drill out the actuator motor retaining rivet.
8　Unplug the electrical connector and lift the motor and bracket from the door.
9　To install, plug in the electrical connector, place the actuator motor in position and install a new rivet. The rivet must be installed securely or the motor and bracket will move during operation, causing rattles and binding.

20.2　Power door lock switch details

10　Connect the actuator motor link to the door latch.
11　Connect the battery cable and check the actuator for proper operation.
12　Install the door trim panel.

21　Windshield wiper arm — removal and installation

Refer to illustrations 21.1 and 21.2

1　Use a screwdriver to pry the windshield wiper arm release lever out (see illustration).
2　Disconnect the washer fluid hose by pushing it off with a small screwdriver (see illustration).

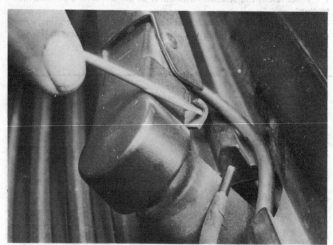

21.1　Lift the release lever out with a small screwdriver

21.2　Push the washer hose off with a screwdriver

22.4　Detach the wiper actuating arm clip by prying up with a small screwdriver

22.5　Wiper motor retaining nuts (arrows)

23.3 Use pliers to pull the motor assembly out of the reservoir

3   Lift the wiper arm off and remove it from the vehicle.
4   Installation is the reverse of removal.

---

22 Windshield wiper motor — removal and installation

Refer to illustrations 22.4 and 22.5

1   Disconnect the negative cable at the battery.
2   Remove the wiper arms (Section 21).
3   Remove the cowl ventilator grille (Chapter 11).
4   Remove the clip from the wiper motor and disconnect the wiper actuating arms **(see illustration).**
5   Unplug the electrical connector, remove the retaining nuts and lower the wiper motor into the engine compartment **(see illustration).**
6   Installation is the reverse of removal.

---

23 Windshield washer motor, seal and pump — removal and installation

Refer to illustrations 23.3 and 23.5

1   Remove and drain the washer reservoir (Chapter 3).
2   Use a small screwdriver and pry out the retaining ring.

23.5 The pump must be lubricated as shown before installation

3   Use pliers to grip the wall around the electrical terminal and pull the motor, seal and impeller assembly from the reservoir **(see illustration).**
4   Clean all foreign material from the pump chamber before installing the pump assembly into the reservoir.
5   Lubricate the outside diameter of the seal with a powdered graphite to prevent the seal from sticking to the reservoir **(see illustration).**
6   Align the small projection on the motor end with the slot in the reservoir and assemble so the seal seats against the bottom of the motor cavity.
7   Use a 1-inch (12 point preferably) socket to hand press the retaining ring securely against the motor. **Caution:** *Do not operate the pump until the reservoir has been filled with fluid.*
8   Replace the reservoir. Plug in the electrical connector and insert the hose.
9   Fill the reservoir.
10   Check for leaks.

COLOR ABBREVIATIONS

BL	Blue	N	Natural
BK	Black	O	Orange
BR	Brown	PK	Pink
DB	Dark Blue	P	Purple
DG	Dark Green	R	Red
GR	Green	T	Tan
GY	Gray	W	White
LB	Light Blue	Y	Yellow
LG	Light Green		

Wiring diagram color codes. If more than one color is indicated on the diagram — such as BL/O — this means the wire is blue with an orange stripe

Electric fuel pump wiring schematic

Speed control system wiring schematic

Circuit Number	Circuit Description	Gage	Primary Color	Secondary Color
511A	Brake Switch (Load Side) to Clutch Switch	18	Light Green	
511	Stoplamp Switch to Turn Signal Switch	18	Light Green	
511B	Clutch Switch to Amplifier Disable	18	Light Green	
57B	Sensor Ground	20	Black	
150	Sensor Signal to Amplifier	20	Dark Green	White
57	Amplifier Ground	18	Black	Black
151	Amplifier Control Line	20	Light Blue	Purple
296	Ignition Switch (Accy) to Amplifier	18	White	Light Green
149	Servo Feedback Pot – 10 Amplifier	20	Brown	Red
148	Servo Feedback Pot Position to Amplifier	20	Yellow	Light Green
147	Servo Feedback Pot – 10 Amplifier	20	Purple	

'18 Yellow/Light Green (some models)

Circuit Number	Circuit Description	Gage	Primary Color	Secondary Color
146	Servo Vent Solenoid Control	20	White	Pink
145	Servo Vacuum Solenoid Control	20	Gray	Black
144	Servo Solenoid Feed	20	Orange	Yellow
296A	Steering Column Connector to Brush Assembly	18	White	Purple
57A	Steering Column Ground	18	Black	
10	Stoplamp Switch Feed	18	Light Green	Red
6	Steering Column Connector to Horn	16*	Yellow	Light Green
460	Battery to Horn Relay	16	Yellow	Light Blue
1	Horn Relay to Horn	16	Dark Blue	

Wiring schematic for alternators with integral regulator

Wiring schematic for the interior warning system — standard instrumention on left and electronic instrumentation on right

Illuminated entry schematic

Typical engine electrical wiring harness — 2.3 L engine shown

CONTROL PANEL

HEADLAMP SWITCH

WINDSHIELD WIPER AND WASHER SWITCH

WARNING CHIMES

WIRING ASSEMBLY

WIRING ASSEMBLY

CLUSTER ASSEMBLY

VIEWS C AND D

HEATER BLOWER SWITCH

HEATER OR A/C CONTROL

CONTROL ILLUMINATION

UPPER INSTRUMENT PANEL ASSEMBLY WIRING SHIELD

TO RADIO RECEIVER

WIRING ASSEMBLY

WIRING ASSEMBLY

WIRING ASSEMBLY

LOWER INSTRUMENT PANEL

SCREW

VIEW B

VIEW A

DAY/NIGHT ILLUMINATION RELAY

TO HEATED REAR WINDOW (WITH OR WITHOUT CLOCK)

TO AUXILIARY AIR CONDITIONER AND/OR AUXILIARY HEATER

STEERING COLUMN HORN WIRING

VIEW E

VIEW F

FUSE PANEL

STRAP

WIRING ASSEMBLY

STEERING COLUMN HORN WIRING

VIEW SHOWING HORN WIRING CONNECTOR INSTALLATION
VIEW F

UPPER INSTRUMENT PANEL ASSEMBLY

RELAY ASSEMBLY

BRACKET

WIRING ASSEMBLY

DAY/NIGHT ILLUMINATION RELAY

LOWER INSTRUMENT PANEL ASSEMBLY

VIEW E

HEATER AND/OR A/C CONTROL

HEATER BLOWER SWITCH

MODE SWITCH

WATER VALVE SWITCH

WIRING ASSEMBLY

UPPER INSTRUMENT PANEL ASSEMBLY

CONTROL ILLUMINATION

VIEW SHOWING WIRING FOR OPTIONAL (BMB) FRONT AIR CONDITIONING (WITHOUT AUXILIARY HEATER) (WIRING INSTALLATION SAME AS HEATER EXCEPT AS SHOWN)
VIEW D

HEATER BLOWER SWITCH

HEATER AND/OR A/C CONTROL

WIRING ASSEMBLY

MODE SWITCH

CONTROL ILLUMINATION

VIEW SHOWING WIRING FOR STANDARD PRODUCTION HEATER (WITHOUT AUXILIARY HEATER)
VIEW C

WIRING ASSEMBLY

SCREW (2 REQ'D)

VIEW A

WIRING ASSEMBLY

TO ELECTRONIC INSTRUMENT CLUSTER KEYBOARD ASSEMBLY

VIEW B

Wiring harness for the electronic instrument panel

Wiring harness for the standard, mechanical instrument panel

Wiring diagram for the electronic stereo sound system

Wiring diagram for the premium sound system

Heater/air conditioning wiring schematic

Auxiliary heater/air conditioning wiring schematic

A/C FUNCTION SWITCH CONTINUITY PATH	
DEFROST	181 TO 249 AND 348
MIX	181 TO 249 AND 348
HEAT	181 TO 249 AND 348
OFF	181
VENT	181 TO 249
NORM	181 TO 249 AND 348
MAX	181 TO 249 AND 348

Rear window defrost electrical schematic

Power door lock wiring schematic

Index

HAYNES AUTOMOTIVE MANUALS

THE BOOK

NOTE: New manuals are added to this list on a periodic basis. If you do not see a listing for your vehicle, consult your local Haynes dealer for the latest product information.

ALFA ROMEO
531 **Alfa Romeo** Sedan & Coupe '73 thru '80

AMC
Jeep CJ — see JEEP (412)
694 **Mid-size models**, Concord, Hornet, Gremlin & Spirit '70 thru '83
*934 **(Renault) Alliance & Encore** all models '83 thru '85

AUDI
162 **100** all models '69 thru '77
615 **4000** all models '80 thru '87
428 **5000** all models '77 thru '83
*1117 **5000** all models '84 thru '86
207 **Fox** all models '73 thru '79

AUSTIN
049 **Healey 100/6 & 3000** Roadster '56 thru '68
Healey Sprite — see MG Midget Roadster (265)

BLMC
260 **1100, 1300 & Austin America** '62 thru '74
527 **Mini** all models '59 thru '69
*646 **Mini** all models '69 thru '87

BMW
276 **320i** all 4 cyl models '75 thru '83
*632 **528i & 530i** all models '75 thru '80
240 **1500 thru 2002** all models except Turbo '59 thru '77
348 **2500, 2800, 3.0 & Bavaria** all models '69 thru '76

BUICK
Century (Front wheel drive) — see GENERAL MOTORS A-Cars (829)
*627 **Mid-size** all rear-drive **Regal & Century** models with V6, V8 and Turbo '74 thru '87
Skyhawk — see GENERAL MOTORS J-Cars (766)
552 **Skylark** all X-car models '80 thru '85

CADILLAC
Cimarron — see GENERAL MOTORS J-Cars (766)

CAPRI
296 **2000 MK I** Coupe all models '71 thru '75
283 **2300 MK II** Coupe all models '74 thru '78
205 **2600 & 2800** V6 Coupe all models '71 thru '75
375 **2800 Mk II** V6 Coupe all models '75 thru '78
Mercury (in-line engines) — see FORD Mustang (654)
Mercury (V6 & V8 engines) — see FORD Mustang (558)

CHEVROLET
554 **Camaro** V8 all models '70 thru '81
*866 **Camaro** all models '82 thru '87
Cavalier — see GENERAL MOTORS J-Cars (766)
Celebrity — see GENERAL MOTORS A-Cars (829)
*625 **Chevelle, Malibu & El Camino** all V6 & V8 models '69 thru '86
449 **Chevette & Pontiac T1000** all models '76 thru '87
550 **Citation** all models '80 thru '85
274 **Corvette** all V8 models '68 thru '82
*1336 **Corvette** all models '84 thru '87

*704 **Full-size Sedans** Caprice, Impala, Biscayne, Bel Air & Wagons, all V6 & V8 models '69 thru '86
319 **Luv Pick-up** all 2WD & 4WD models '72 thru '82
*626 **Monte Carlo** all V6, V8 & Turbo models '70 thru '86
241 **Nova** all V8 models '69 thru '79
420 **Pick-ups — Chevrolet & GMC**, all V8 & in-line 6 cyl 2WD & 4WD models '67 thru '87
*831 **S-10 & GMC S-15 Pick-ups** all models '82 thru '87
*345 **Vans — Chevrolet & GMC**, V8 & in-line 6 cyl models '68 thru '85
208 **Vega** all models except Cosworth '70 thru '77

CHRYSLER
*1337 **Chrysler & Plymouth Mid-size** front wheel drive '82 thru '86
K-Cars — see DODGE Aries/Plymouth Reliant (723)
Laser — see DODGE Daytona & Chrysler Laser (1140)

DATSUN
402 **200SX** all models '77 thru '79
*647 **200SX** all models '80 thru '83
228 **B-210** all models '73 thru '78
525 **210** all models '79 thru '82
206 **240Z, 260Z & 280Z** Coupe & 2+2 '70 thru '78
563 **280ZX** Coupe & 2+2 '79 thru '83
300ZX — see NISSAN (1137)
679 **310** all models '78 thru '82
123 **510 & PL521 Pick-up** '68 thru '73
430 **510** all models '78 thru '81
372 **610** all models '72 thru '76
277 **620 Series Pick-up** all models '73 thru '79
235 **710** all models '73 thru '77
*771 **720 Series Pick-up** all models (including 4WD) '80 thru '85
*376 **810/Maxima** all gasoline models '77 thru '84
124 **1200** all models '70 thru '73
368 **F10** all models '76 thru '79
Pulsar — see NISSAN (876)
Sentra — see NISSAN (982)
Stanza — see NISSAN (981)

DODGE
*723 **Aries & Plymouth Reliant** all models '81 thru '86
*1231 **Caravan & Plymouth Voyager** Mini-Vans all models '84 thru '86
699 **Challenger & Plymouth Sapporo** all models '78 thru '83
236 **Colt** all models '71 thru '77
419 **Colt (rear wheel drive)** all models '77 thru '80
*610 **Colt & Plymouth Champ (front wheel drive)** all models '78 thru '87
*556 **D50 & Plymouth Arrow Pick-ups** '79 thru '86
234 **Dart & Plymouth Valiant** all 6 cyl models '67 thru '76
*1140 **Daytona & Chrysler Laser** all models '84 thru '86
*545 **Omni & Plymouth Horizon** all models '78 thru '84
*912 **Pick-ups** all full-size models '74 thru '86
*349 **Vans — Dodge & Plymouth** V8 & 6 cyl models '71 thru '86

FIAT
080 **124 Sedan & Wagon** all ohv & dohc models '66 thru '75
094 **124 Sport Coupe & Spider** '68 thru '78
087 **128** all models '72 thru '79
310 **131 & Brava** all models '75 thru '81
038 **850 Sedan, Coupe & Spider** '64 thru '74
479 **Strada** all models '79 thru '82
*273 **X1/9** all models '74 thru '80

FORD
788 **Bronco and Pick-ups** '73 thru '79
*880 **Bronco and Pick-ups** '80 thru '86
295 **Cortina MK III** 1600 & 2000 ohc '70 thru '76
268 **Courier Pick-up** all models '72 thru '82
*789 **Escort & Mercury Lynx** all models '81 thru '87
560 **Fairmont & Mercury Zephyr** all in-line & V8 models '78 thru '83
334 **Fiesta** all models '77 thru '80
359 **Granada & Mercury Monarch** all in-line, 6 cyl & V8 models '75 thru '80
*754 **Ford & Mercury Full-size,** FORD: LTD ('75 thru '82); Custom 500; Country Squire; Crown Victoria, MERCURY: Marquis ('75 thru '82); Gran Marquis; Colony Park, all V8 models '75 thru '84
773 **Ford & Mercury Mid-size** FORD: Torino; Gran Torino; Elite; Ranchero; LTD II; LTD ('83 thru '84); Thunderbird ('75 thru '82), MERCURY: Montego; Comet; Marquis ('83 thru '86); Cougar ('75 thru '82); LINCOLN: Versailles, all 4 cyl, in-line 6 cyl, V6 & V8 models '75 thru '80
*654 **Mustang & Mercury Capri** all in-line models & Turbo '79 thru '87
*558 **Mustang & Mercury Capri** all V6 & V8 models '79 thru '87
*1418 **Tempo & Mercury Topaz** all gasoline models '84 thru '87
357 **Mustang V8** all models '65 thru '73
231 **Mustang II** all 4 cyl, V6 & V8 models '74 thru '78
204 **Pinto** all models '70 thru '74
649 **Pinto & Mercury Bobcat** all models '75 thru '80
*1026 **Ranger & Bronco II** all gasoline models '83 thru '86
*344 **Vans** all V8 Econoline models '69 thru '86

GENERAL MOTORS
*829 **A-Cars** — Chevrolet Celebrity, Buick Century, Pontiac 6000 & Oldsmobile Cutlass Ciera all models '82 thru '87
*766 **J-Cars** — Chevrolet Cavalier, Pontiac J-2000, Oldsmobile Firenza, Buick Skyhawk & Cadillac Cimarron all models '82 thru '87

GMC
Vans & Pick-ups — see CHEVROLET (420, 831, 345)

HONDA
138 **360, 600 & Z Coupe** all models '67 thru '75
351 **Accord CVCC** all models '76 thru '83
*1221 **Accord** all models '84 thru '85
160 **Civic 1200** all models '73 thru '79

(continued on next page)

Haynes Publications Inc., P.O. Box 978, Newbury Park, CA 91320 ● (818) 889-5400 ● (805) 498-6703

HAYNES AUTOMOTIVE MANUALS (continued from previous page)

(continued from previous page)

NOTE: New manuals are added to this list on a periodic basis. If you do not see a listing for your vehicle, consult your local Haynes dealer for the latest product information.

HONDA (continued)
- **633** Civic 1300 & 1500 CVCC all models '80 thru '83
- **297** Civic 1500 CVCC all models '75 thru '79
- *1227 Civic all models except 16-valve CRX & 4 WD Wagon '84 thru '86
- *601 Prelude CVCC all models '79 thru '82

JAGUAR
- **098** MK I & II, 240 & 340 Sedans '55 thru '69
- *242 XJ6 all 6 cyl models '68 thru '86
- *478 XJ12 & XJS all 12 cyl models '72 thru '85
- **140** XK-E 3.8 & 4.2 all 6 cyl models '61 thru '72

JEEP
- **412** CJ all models '49 thru '86

LADA
- *413 1200, 1300. 1500 & 1600 all models including Riva '74 thru '86

LANCIA
- **533** Lancia Beta Sedan, Coupe & HPE all models '76 thru '80

LAND ROVER
- **314** Series II, IIA, & III all 4 cyl gasoline models '58 thru '86
- **529** Diesel all models '58 thru '80

MAZDA
- **648** 626 Sedan & Coupe (rear wheel drive) all models '79 thru '82
- *1082 626 (front wheel drive) all gas models '83 thru '87
- *267 B1600, B1800 & B2000 Pick-ups '72 thru '84
- **370** GLC Hatchback (rear wheel drive) all models '77 thru '83
- **757** GLC (front wheel drive) all models '81 thru '85
- **109** RX2 all models '71 thru '75
- **096** RX3 all models '72 thru '76
- **460** RX-7 all models '79 thru '85

MERCEDES-BENZ
- **346** 230, 250 & 280 Sedan, Coupe & Roadster all 6 cyl sohc models '68 thru '72
- **983** 280 123 Series all gasoline models '77 thru '81
- **698** 350 & 450 Sedan, Coupe & Roadster all models '71 thru '80
- **697** Diesel 123 Series 200D, 220D, 240D, 240TD, 300D, 300CD, 300TD, 4- & 5-cyl incl. Turbo '76 thru '85

MERCURY
- **Bobcat** — *see FORD Pinto & Bobcat (649)*
- **Capri in-line** — *see FORD Mustang & Mercury Capri (654)*
- **Capri V6 & V8** — *see FORD Mustang & Mercury Capri (558)*
- **Full-size** — *see FORD Full-size (754)*
- **Mid-size** — *see FORD Mid-size (773)*
- **Lynx** — *see FORD Escort & Lynx (789)*
- **Monarch** — *see FORD Granada & Monarch (359)*
- **Zephyr** — *see FORD Fairmont & Zephyr (560)*

MG
- **475** MGA all models '56 thru '62
- **111** MGB Roadster & GT Coupe all models '62 thru '80
- **265** MG Midget & Austin Healey Sprite Roadster '58 thru '80

MITSUBISHI
- **Pick-up** — *see Dodge D-50 (556)*

MORRIS
- **074** (Austin) Marina 1.8 all models '71 thru '75

- **024** Minor 1000 sedan & wagon '56 thru '71

NISSAN
- *1137 300ZX all models '84 thru '86
- *876 Pulsar all models '83 thru '86
- *982 Sentra all models '82 thru '86
- *981 Stanza all models '82 thru '86

OLDSMOBILE
- *658 Cutlass all standard gasoline V6 & V8 models '74 thru '87
- **Cutlass Ciera** — *see GENERAL MOTORS A-Cars (829)*
- **Firenza** — *see GENERAL MOTORS J-Cars (766)*
- **Omega** — *see PONTIAC Phoenix & Omega (551)*

OPEL
- **157** (Buick) Manta Coupe 1900 all models '70 thru '74

PEUGEOT
- **161** 504 all gasoline models '68 thru '79
- **663** 504 all diesel models '74 thru '83

PLYMOUTH
- **425** Arrow all models '76 thru '80
- **Arrow Pick-up** — *see DODGE D50 & Arrow Pickups (556)*
- **Champ** — *see DODGE Colt & Champ (610)*
- **Horizon** — *see DODGE Omni & Horizon (545)*
- **Reliant** — *see DODGE Aries & Reliant (723)*
- **Sapporo** — *see DODGE Challenger & Sapporo (699)*
- **Valiant & Barracuda** — *see DODGE Dart (234)*
- **Vans** — *see DODGE & Plymouth Vans (349)*
- **Voyager** — *see DODGE Caravan & Voyager (1231)*

PONTIAC
- **T1000** — *see CHEVROLET Chevette (449)*
- **J-2000** — *see GENERAL MOTORS J-Cars (766)*
- **6000** — *see GENERAL MOTORS A-Cars (829)*
- *1232 Fiero all models '84 thru '87
- **555** Firebird all V8 models except Turbo '70 thru '81
- *867 Firebird all models '82 thru '87
- **551** Phoenix & Oldsmobile Omega all X-car models '80 thru '84

PORSCHE
- *264 911 all Coupe & Targa models except Turbo '65 thru '85
- **239** 914 all 4 cyl models '69 thru '76
- **397** 924 all models including Turbo '76 thru '82
- *1027 944 all models including Turbo '83 thru '86

RENAULT
- **141** 5 Le Car all models '76 thru '83
- **079** 8 & 10 all models with 58.4 cu in engines '62 thru '72
- **097** 12 Saloon & Estate all models 1289 cc engines '70 thru '80
- **768** 15 & 17 all models '73 thru '79
- **081** 16 all models 89.7 cu in & 95.5 cu in engines '65 thru '72
- **598** 18i & Sportwagon all models '81 thru '86
- **Alliance & Encore** — *see AMC (934)*
- **984** Fuego all models '82 thru '85

ROVER
- **085** 3500 & 3500S Sedan 215 cu in engines '68 thru '76
- *365 3500 SDI V8 all models '76 thru '84

SAAB
- **198** 95 & 96 V4 all models '66 thru '75
- **247** 99 all models including Turbo '69 thru '80
- *980 900 all models including Turbo '79 thru '85

SUBARU
- **237** 1100, 1300, 1400 & 1600 all models '71 thru '79
- *681 1600 & 1800 2WD & 4WD all models '80 thru '86

TOYOTA
- **150** Carina Sedan all models '71 thru '74
- **229** Celica ST, GT & liftback all models '71 thru '78
- **437** Celica all models '78 thru '81
- *935 Celica all models except front wheel drive and Supra '82 thru '85
- **680** Celica Supra all models '79 thru '81
- **1139** Celica Supra all models '82 thru '86
- **201** Corolla 1100, 1200 & 1600 all models '67 thru '74
- **361** Corolla all models '75 thru '79
- *961 Corolla all models (rear wheel drive) '80 thru '82
- *1025 Corolla all models (front wheel drive) 1984
- *636 Corolla Tercel all models '80 thru '82
- **230** Corona & MK II all 4 cyl sohc models '69 thru '74
- **360** Corona all models '74 thru '82
- *532 Cressida all models '78 thru '82
- **313** Land Cruiser all models '68 thru '82
- **200** MK II all 6 cyl models '72 thru '76
- *1339 MR2 all models '85 thru '87
- **304** Pick-up all models '69 thru '78
- *656 Pick-up all models '79 thru '85
- **787** Starlet all models '81 thru '84

TRIUMPH
- **112** GT6 & Vitesse all models '62 thru '74
- **113** Spitfire all models '62 thru '81
- **028** TR2, 3, 3A, 4 & 4A Roadsters '52 thru '67
- **031** TR250 & TR6 Roadsters '67 thru '76
- **322** TR7 all models '75 thru '81

VW
- **091** 411 & 412 all 103 cu in models '68 thru '73
- **036** Bug 1200 all models '54 thru '66
- **039** Bug 1300 & 1500 '65 thru '70
- **159** Bug 1600 all basic, sport & super (curved windshield) models '70 thru '74
- **110** Bug 1600 Super all models (flat windshield) '70 thru '72
- **238** Dasher all gasoline models '74 thru '81
- *884 Rabbit, Jetta, Scirocco, & Pick-up all gasoline models '74 thru '84 & Convertible '80 thru '85
- **451** Rabbit, Jetta & Pick-up all diesel models '77 thru '84
- **082** Transporter 1600 all models '68 thru '79
- **226** Transporter 1700, 1800 & 2000 all models '72 thru '79
- **084** Type 3 1500 & 1600 all models '63 thru '73
- *1029 Vanagon all air-cooled models '80 thru '83

VOLVO
- **203** 120, 130 Series & 1800 Sports '61 thru '73
- **129** 140 Series all models '66 thru '74
- **244** 164 all models '68 thru '75
- *270 240 Series all models '74 thru '86
- **400** 260 Series all models '75 thru '82

ABCDE FGHIJ KLMNO PORST

Over 100 Haynes motorcycle manuals also available

---

* Listings shown with an asterisk (*) indicate model coverage as of this printing. These titles will be periodically updated to include later model years — consult your Haynes dealer for more information.

Haynes Publications Inc., P.O. Box 978, Newbury Park, CA 91320 • (818) 889–5400 • (805) 498–6703